JOHN 11–21

WISDOM COMMENTARY

Volume 44B

John 11–21

Mary L. Coloe, PBVM

Mary Ann Beavis
Volume Editor

Barbara E. Reid, OP
General Editor

A Michael Glazier Book

LITURGICAL PRESS
Collegeville, Minnesota

www.litpress.org

A Michael Glazier Book published by Liturgical Press

1   2   3   4   5   6   7   8   9

Library of Congress Cataloging-in-Publication Data

Names: Coloe, Mary L., 1949– author. | Beavis, Mary Ann, editor. | Reid, Barbara E., editor.

Title: John / Mary L. Coloe, PBVM ; Mary Ann Beavis, volume editor ; Barbara E. Reid, OP, general editor.

Description: Collegeville, Minnesota : Liturgical Press, [2021] | Series: Wisdom commentary ; volume 44A-44B | "A Michael Glazier book." | Includes bibliographical references and index. | Contents: John 1-10 — John 11-21. | Summary: "This commentary on the Gospel of John provides a feminist interpretation of Scripture in serious, scholarly engagement with the whole text, not only those texts that explicitly mention women. It addresses not only issues of gender but also those of power, authority, ethnicity, racism, and classism"— Provided by publisher.

Identifiers: LCCN 2021003113 (print) | LCCN 2021003114 (ebook) | ISBN 9780814681688 (hardcover) | ISBN 9780814688144 (hardcover) | ISBN 9780814681930 (epub) | ISBN 9780814681930 (mobi) | ISBN 9780814681930 (pdf) | ISBN 9780814688397 (epub) | ISBN 9780814688397 (mobi) | ISBN 9780814688397 (pdf)

Subjects: LCSH: Bible. John—Commentaries. | Bible. John—Feminist criticism.

Classification: LCC BS2615.53 .C65 2021 (print) | LCC BS2615.53 (ebook) | DDC 226.5/07—dc23

LC record available at https://lccn.loc.gov/2021003113

LC ebook record available at https://lccn.loc.gov/2021003114

With gratitude for the Wisdom people
who have been my
teachers, mentors, and friends.

ὑμᾶς δὲ εἴρηκα φίλους

Sandra M. Schneiders, IHM; Francis J. Moloney, SDB;
Dorothy A. Lee; and Brendan Byrne, SJ

Contents

List of Abbreviations   ix

Author's Introduction   xiii

John 11:1-54   Sophia Is Justified by Her Works:
   The Raising of Lazarus   313

John 11:55–12:50   Sophia's Testing Begins   333

John 13–17   Sophia's Banquet: Overview   353

John 13:1-38   Sophia's Gifts   359

John 14:1-31   Sophia's Household   381

John 15:1-17   Sophia's Friends   401

John 15:18–16:4a   Sophia's Friends to Be Tested by
   the Synagogue   431

John 16:4b-33   Sophia's Friends to Be Tested by the World   443

John 17:1-26   Sophia's Prayer for Her Friends   457

John 18:1–19:42   Sophia's Hour Arrives   473

John 20:1-31   Sophia's Radiance   507

John 21:1-25   Sophia Has Built Her House—
   The Gospel Continues   537

Afterword   551

Works Cited   553

Index of Scripture References and Other Ancient Writings   571

Index of Modern Authors and Subjects   585

Abbreviations

AB	Anchor Bible
ABD	*Anchor Bible Dictionary.* Edited by David Noel Freedman. 6 vols. New York: Doubleday, 1992
ABR	*Australian Biblical Review*
ABRL	Anchor Bible Reference Library
AGJU	Arbeitum zur Geschichte des antiken Judentums und des Urchristentums
AJEC	Ancient Judaism and Early Christianity
AnBib	Analecta Biblica
ATANT	Abhandlungen zur Theologie des Alten und Neuen Testaments
BDAG	Bauer, Walter, William F. Arndt, F. Wilbur Gringrich, and Frederick W. Danker. *Greek-English Lexicon of the New Testament and Other Early Christian Literature.* 3rd ed. Chicago: University of Chicago Press, 2000.
BETL	Bibliotheca Ephemeridum Theologicarum Lovaniensium
Bib	*Biblica*
BibInt	Biblical Interpretation Series
BibSem	The Biblical Seminar
BMSEC	Baylor–Mohr Siebeck Studies in Early Christianity
BN	*Biblische Notizen*

BNTC	Black's New Testament Commentary
BSac	*Bibliotheca Sacra*
BTB	*Biblical Theology Bulletin*
BZAW	Beihefte zur Zeitschrift für die alttestamentliche Wissenschaft
BZNW	Beihefte zur Zeitschrift für die neutestamentliche Wissenschaft
CahRB	Cahiers de la Revue biblique
CBET	Contributions to Biblical Exegesis and Theology
CBQ	*Catholic Biblical Quarterly*
CNT	Commentaire du Nouveau Testament
CTR	*Criswell Theological Review*
DSD	*Dead Sea Discoveries*
EJL	Early Judaism and Its Literature
ETL	*Ephemerides Theologicae Lovanienses*
ExpTim	*Expository Times*
FCNTECW	Feminist Companion to the New Testament and Early Christian Writings
HBT	*Horizons in Biblical Theology*
HTCNT	Herder's Theological Commentary on the New Testament
HTR	*Harvard Theological Review*
HUCA	*Hebrew Union College Annual*
HUT	Hermeneutische Untersuchungen zur Theologie
IBT	Interpreting Biblical Texts
Int	*Interpretation*
JBL	*Journal of Biblical Literature*
JBQ	*Jewish Bible Quarterly*
JECH	*Journal of Early Christian History*
JSJ	*Journal for the Study of Judaism in the Persian, Hellenistic, and Roman Periods*
JSNT	*Journal for the Study of the New Testament*

JSOTSup	Journal for the Study of the Old Testament Supplement Series
JTS	*Journal of Theological Studies*
LASBF	*Liber Annus Studii Biblici Franciscani*
LCL	Loeb Classical Library
LG	Lumen Gentium
LNTS	Library of New Testament Studies
LXX	Septuagint
MilS	*Milltown Studies*
MT	Masoretic Text
NBf	*New Blackfriars*
NCBC	New Cambridge Bible Commentary
NIDB	*New Interpreter's Dictionary of the Bible.* Edited by Katharine Doob Sakenfeld. 5 vols. Nashville, TN: Abingdon, 2006–2009.
NovT	*Novum Testamentum*
NovTSup	Supplements to Novum Testamentum
NRTh	*La nouvelle revue théologique*
NT	New Testament
NTL	New Testament Library
NTS	*New Testament Studies*
NTSI	The New Testament and the Scriptures of Israel
OT	Old Testament
OTS	Old Testament Studies
QD	Quaestiones Disputatae
RB	*Revue biblique*
RBS	Resources for Biblical Study
RSR	*Recherches de science religieuse*
SA	Studiea Anselmina
SANT	Studien zum Alten und Neuen Testaments
SBFA	Studium Biblicum Franciscanum Analecta

SBLDS	Society of Biblical Literature Dissertation Series
SBLMS	Society of Biblical Literature Monograph Series
SBLRBS	Society of Biblical Literature Resources for Biblical Studies
SemeiaSt	Semeia Studies
SNTSMS	Society for New Testament Studies Monograph Series
SNTW	Studies of the New Testament and Its World
SP	Sacra Pagina Series
STRev	*Sewanee Theological Review*
TDNT	*Theological Dictionary of the New Testament.* Edited by Gerhard Kitteland and Gerhard Friedrich. Translated by Geoffrey W. Bromiley. 10 vols. Grand Rapids, MI: Eerdmans, 1964-76.
TS	*Theological Studies*
WBC	Word Bible Commentary
WCS	Wisdom Commentary Series
WO	*Die Welt des Orients*
WUNT	Wissenschaftliche Untersuchungen zum Neuen Testament
ZNW	*Zeitschrift für die neutestamentliche Wissenschaft und die Kunde der älteren Kirche*

Author's Introduction

We begin with a brief reminder of some of the key themes highlighted in the first volume on John 1–10. The Gospel is a narrative where there is a plot announced in the prologue: that believers will become children of God (1:12) and that there is a force of evil at work to frustrate this goal and keep humanity under the power of "the ruler of this world" (12:31; 14:30; 16:11). Within the narrative the primary character is Jesus, and belief in him draws one into a kinship relationship with God and leads one to "eternity life" (3:15). In the prologue Jesus is introduced as the *Logos* who tabernacles with us (1:14). In the narrative Jesus in his words and deeds acts as divine Wisdom (Gk. *Sophia*) and the primary symbol shifts from tabernacle to temple. Jesus/Sophia speaks to Nicodemus about being born again into the kindom[1] of God (3:3) and so gains eternity life now. At Cana and in Samaria Jesus acts as the messianic bridegroom offering temple waters of life-giving and healing as Samaria and Judea are united and God's sanctuary dwells with them (4:40; cf. Ezek 37:26-27).

Then, across the major Jewish festivals of Sabbath (chap. 5), Passover (chap. 6), Tabernacles (7:1–10:21), and Dedication (10:22-39), Jesus/Sophia appropriates the major symbols and rituals of these feasts. The festivals are not replaced; rather, in Jesus/Sophia they experience their fullness in the presence of the "I am" whom they celebrate. Through this public ministry primarily in Jerusalem, some come to believe in him, but

---

1. See excursus on ἡ βασιλεία τοῦ θεοῦ: The Kindom of God in Mary L. Coloe, *John 1–10*, WCS 44A (Collegeville, MN: Liturgical Press, 2021), 105.

there are others who cannot accept that the authority behind his words and deeds is God, whom Jesus calls "Father." Even some of his disciples turn from him (6:66) and mount opposition to him (8:31). These former disciples, by choosing not to accept Jesus, align themselves now with children of the devil (8:44). The satanic power of evil works through some of his listeners who attempt to stone him (8:59).

While most of the characters, both believers and nonbelievers, are ethnically Jews, Jesus's opponents are usually named "the Jews" as if the other characters are not Jews. I have argued that this labelling of the opponents as "the Jews" is a deliberate rhetorical ploy to establish a distinction between the Jesus believers and the Torah-followers at the end of the first century CE, following the destruction of the temple in 70 CE by Rome.[2] This act brought about the destruction of the central rituals within Second Temple Judaism and propelled Judaism to recast its identity focused on the law and its teaching.

In the final decades of the first century two groups were emerging from a shared faith, shared traditions, shared Scripture, and shared worship of the God of the ancestors. One group was shaping its identity on the person of Jesus, while the other group was shaping its identity around the law. Over the course of two to three centuries these groups would more clearly separate and become known as Christianity and Rabbinic Judaism. The Gospel of John is written at the start of this process, where most believers are Jews, and yet the rhetoric of the Gospel establishes that "the Jews" are "Other" and that the law is their law and no longer "ours."

---

2. See the discussion of "the Jews" as a character in the author's introduction, the essay by Ruth Sheridan at the end of chap. 2, and the excursus on the Feasts of the Jews at chap. 5 in Coloe, *John 1–10*, lxxi–lxxii, 76–81, 137–39.

John 11:1-54

Sophia Is Justified by Her Works:[1]
The Raising of Lazarus

For God created us for incorruption [ἀφθαρσίᾳ],
and made us in the image of his own eternity [ἀϊδιότητος]. (Wis 2:23)

But the souls of the righteous are in the hand of God,
and no torment will ever touch them.
In the eyes of the foolish they seemed to have died,
and their departure was thought to be a disaster,
and their going from us to be their destruction;
but they are at peace.
For though in the sight of others they were punished,
their hope is full of immortality [ἀθανασίας]. (Wis 3:1-4)

Within the Fourth Gospel, chapters 11 and 12 are pivotal. On the one hand, they bring the Book of Signs (1:19–12:50) to a conclusion with the raising of Lazarus and the ensuing consequences; on the other, they foreshadow events that will occur in the Book of Glory: foot anointing/footwashing followed by death and resurrection (13:1–20:31).

---

1. Matt 11:19.

While Lazarus never speaks, his presence pervades both chapters (11:1, 2, 5, 11, 14, 43; 12:1, 2, 9, 10, 17). In Lazarus's silence, it is the words and actions of Martha and Mary that carry the theological message of chapter 11, and Mary's action of anointing the feet of Jesus (12:1-7) anticipates Jesus's kneeling and washing the feet of his disciples in chapter 13. These two chapters bring Jesus's public ministry to a close and instigate the culmination of his mission with the decision of the Jewish leadership to put him to death (11:53). Jesus recognizes that the time for his glorification has arrived when he states, "The hour has come" (12:23). He then withdraws into the company of his disciples to prepare them for his coming departure (chaps. 13–17).

TRANSLATION MATTERS

Throughout this commentary I have translated the term οἱ Ἰουδαῖοι as "the Jews," in quotation marks to highlight that this term has more a symbolic meaning than a historical reference. Throughout most of the Gospel these characters are portrayed in opposition to Jesus. In John 11, οἱ Ἰουδαῖοι do not have that characteristic stance. These Jews are there consoling the family, and then many come to faith in Jesus (11:45), and in John 12 many go out to greet Jesus (12:13). Scenes such as this remind the reader that all the participants in the narrative are Jews and it is incorrect to label all Jews as Jesus's opponents, even if the narrative rhetoric tries to establish a distinction between the followers of Moses and the followers of Jesus. This distinction was a concern late in the first century for the Johannine community. For more on this issue, see the discussion in the author's introduction in Mary L. Coloe, *John 1–10*, WCS 44A (Collegeville, MN: Liturgical Press, 2021), lxxi–lxxii. In chapter 11 οἱ Ἰουδαῖοι accurately describes those from the district of Judea and so they could be called Judeans; I will continue to translate the term as the Jews, but omit the quotation marks.

Structurally, chapter 11 begins with an introduction of the characters, the place and the critical issue of Lazarus's death (vv. 1-6), followed by the decisions of Jesus and the disciples to move back into Judean territory (vv. 7-17) from across the Jordan (10:40).[2] The core theological issue is clarified in verses 17-37, where Martha and Mary express the same belief, that Lazarus died because of Jesus's absence (v. 21, 32). Feminists readily see their actions and dialogue with Jesus as the focus of this chapter,

---

2. There are many suggested structures for this dramatic episode. I am guided by the repetition of words, indicated by italics, to break the long narrative into smaller segments. I also consider vv. 17-20, 30-31, and 33-35 as narrative "fillings" moving the narrative forward.

in contrast to many scholars who place the focus on Jesus and Lazarus with "the two women left vaguely in the background."[3] Jesus corrects the false equation of death with his absence. A similar false equation is then voiced by the Jews gathered around Mary (v. 37). Although Jesus had said to Martha that believers will never die (v. 25), the lingering doubt of Mary, Martha, and the Jews can only be changed through Jesus's actions in calling Lazarus back into a life that they can recognize (vv. 38-44). Then follow the reactions. The drama of Lazarus's restoration to life in Bethany leads many of the Jews to faith (v. 45) but also to the decision by the Jewish leadership to put Jesus to death because they fear reprisals from Rome (vv. 46-53). The narrator brings the episode to a conclusion with Jesus's movement away toward the wilderness (v. 54).

The passage can be shown schematically:

Introduction (vv. 1-6)

The decision and proverb (vv. 7-16)

Jesus's absence means death—Martha, Mary, the Jews (vv. 17-37)

Jesus/Sophia demonstrates eternity life (vv. 38-44)

Reactions (vv. 45-54)[4]

Theological Background

Ideas about life after death developed in late Second Temple Judaism, so late that there are no textual indications in the Hebrew Scriptures, only in the Greek Septuagint. And here there are two different approaches. One belief considers that after this mortal life, the individual remains in death until the end-of-time final victory of God. At that time, God will raise the dead to life in order to judge whether they are righteous or evil. Those judged as righteous will live on with God, while the evil ones will be banished. There is no clear sense of what happens to the evil ones, except that they will not participate in God's blessing. This perspective can be found in the books of Maccabees and Daniel (2 Macc 7:9, 14; Dan 12:2-3). Bodily resurrection is therefore a necessary part of

3. Satoko Yamaguchi, *Mary and Martha: Women in the World of Jesus* (Maryknoll, NY: Orbis Books, 2002), 113.

4. While Bibles include vv. 55-57 in chap. 11, the statement "Now the Passover of the Jews was near" (v. 55) indicates a new section, as the same statement marked the beginning of the Jewish festivals across chaps. 5 to 10 (e.g., 6:4; 7:2; cf. 5:1; 10:22).

the afterlife, to enable God's justice to be demonstrated in condemnation or blessing.[5] This schema is termed "resurrection eschatology" by Sandra Schneiders[6] and is the schema we find in the writings of Paul and the Synoptic Gospels, illustrated especially in Matthew 25:31-46.

But this is not the only possible afterlife scenario. In the last century of the biblical period, perhaps as late as 50 CE,[7] an Alexandrian Jew, writing within the wisdom tradition, presented an alternative understanding, not only of the afterlife, but of this life as well.[8] When considering human existence, the author of Wisdom presents an interpretation of the two creation accounts in Genesis 1–3. Because human beings are made in the image of God (Wis 2:23) they can participate in God's immortality.[9] God's own incorruptible Spirit (Wis 12:1) maintains life and is God's gift to the righteous (Wis 8:21), allowing them to enjoy life forever "in the hand of God" (Wis 3:1). Life, properly understood, is more than mere existence; it is communion with God enjoyed by the just (Wis 4:10-14), and physical death neither destroys nor interrupts this. In fact, for the righteous physical demise is not really death, for they only "seem to die" (Wis 3:2). Thus, Wisdom (*Sophia*) brings eschatological life into the present for those who choose her path. In this theology, eternity life, the life of God, is possible for the righteous *now*.[10]

5. For detailed discussion of the afterlife envisaged in Daniel and the books of the Maccabees, see Marie-Emile Boismard, *Our Victory over Death: Resurrection?*, trans. Madeleine Beaumont (Collegeville, MN: Liturgical Press, 1999), chaps. 1 and 2.

6. Sandra M. Schneiders, "The Johannine Resurrection Narrative: An Exegetical Study of John 20 as a Synthesis of Johannine Spirituality" (DST [unpublished], Pontificia Universitas Gregoriana, 1975), 76. Boismard also distinguishes two different eschatological understandings that he calls "a resurrection current" and "an immortality current." See Boismard, *Our Victory over Death*, viii.

7. John Collins (*Jewish Wisdom in the Hellenistic Age* [Edinburgh: T&T Clark, 1997], 179) suggests that the book of Wisdom was written in Alexandria between 30 BCE and 70 CE. David Winston (*The Wisdom of Solomon*, AB 43 [New York: Doubleday, 1979], 23) places it in Alexandria during the reign of Caligula (37–41 CE).

8. I have summarized the development of the concept of an afterlife and the different theologies about this in an essay: Mary L. Coloe, " 'The End Is Where We Start From': Afterlife in the Fourth Gospel," in *Lebendige Hoffnung—Ewiger Tod?! Jenseitsvorstellungen im Hellenismus, Judentum und Christentum (Living Hope—Eternal Death?! Conceptions of the Afterlife in Hellenism, Judaism and Christianity)*, ed. Manfred Lang and Michael Labhan (Leipzig: Evangelische Verlagsanstalt, 2007), 177–99.

9. Winston, *The Wisdom of Solomon*, 29–30.

10. See also the comments in chap. 3 on the discussion between Jesus and Nicodemus where "eternity life" is first mentioned and described as the quality of divine life in eternity.

The book of Wisdom does not make explicit whether the just pass from death immediately into heavenly existence with God, or whether there is some intermediate state. While the statement is made that their souls live on in a place of peace (Wis 3:23), in the hand of God (Wis 3:1), it is not clear that this is "heaven" as this expression may simply mean protected by God (cf. Deut 33:3).[11] What is clear is that there is continuous life, that the person is not reduced to nonexistence. So while there may be some time in Sheol for the just and the wicked, these souls are not mere shades without life; they remain alive awaiting the time when, for the righteous, they will "abide with him in love" (Wis 3:9).

There are two major issues in the book of Wisdom that distinguish its theology from that of Daniel and Maccabees. The first is what is meant by the term "life." In the book of Wisdom life is a participation already in the eternity life that is the Divine prerogative and a gift of Sophia. "I considered these things inwardly, and pondered in my heart, that in kinship with wisdom there is immortality [ἀθανασία]" (Wis 8:17). According to the book of Wisdom, the righteous already have the gift of God's own "immortal [ἄφθαρτόν] spirit" (Wis 12:1) enabling them to "live forever [εἰς τὸν αἰῶνα ζῶσιν]" (Wis 5:15).

This quality of life is a gift for those who embrace Sophia and are drawn into kinship with her, and for Sophia's kin physical death will not destroy or even interrupt life. Physical death will be a transition for the immortal soul/spirit. In physical death there is the separation of spirit and body, but the spirit continues to participate in life or, in the case of the wicked, to remain in their state of deadness. The second issue is that this theology does not seem to require bodily resurrection, for the inner spirit/soul lives on. Bodily resurrection on the last day may happen but is not essential in this schema.[12] In this schema there is no need for a final judgment as judgment is already made in the choices operating in a person's lifetime. The end time will be a manifestation and confirmation of these choices. With no final judgment, and the spirit continuing to live on beyond the grave, there is no need of resurrection, understood

---

11. Boismard, *Our Victory over Death*, 72.

12. Sandra Schneiders comments, "Bodily resurrection is compatible with, perhaps even implicit in, but not explicitly affirmed in sapiential eschatology. It *could* easily become explicit, however, if the right pressures were brought to bear up it, e.g., by the Easter experience of the first followers of Jesus." Sandra M. Schneiders, *Jesus Risen in Our Midst: Essays on the Resurrection of Jesus in the Fourth Gospel* (Collegeville, MN: Litrugical Press, 2013), 75.

as the reuniting of body and spirit. While there is no necessity for resurrection, this eschatological framework does not rule out the possibility of resurrection. We therefore find in the book of Wisdom a type of realized eschatology where end-time realities impinge on life in this world.

Jesus/Sophia Offers the Gift of Eternity Life

From the prologue onward, the Gospel of John has presented Jesus in the light of Israel's wisdom traditions.[13] The Word, like Wisdom/Sophia, preexists with God (Sir 1:1; Prov 8:23; John 1:1), is an active agent in creation (Prov 8:27-31; John 1:3), and has come to dwell in Israel (Sir 24:8-12; Bar 3:36–4:1; John 1:11a). The Word, like Sophia, has known both rejection and acceptance (1 En 42:1-2; John 1:11b). In the gospel narrative, Jesus acts as Sophia who gathers disciples and invites them to dwell with her (Sir 51:23; John 1:35-51), offering them nourishment (Sir 24:19-22; Prov 9:1-6; John 6), friendship (Wis 7:27; John 15:15), and salvation (Wis 9:18; John 3:16). Sophia lives with God and is loved by God (Prov 8:30-31; Wis 8:3; John 5:20; 10:17); she is an initiate in the knowledge of God and an associate in God's works (Wis 8:4; John 8:29, 38, 42, 55).[14] I conclude this very brief overview with the words of Michael Willett: "Wisdom strides through the Gospel in the person of Jesus of Nazareth. He is Wisdom incarnate, God reaching out to humanity to the fullest extent, as a human being."[15]

In this Gospel Jesus/Sophia offers a gift of eternity life (ζωὴν αἰώνιον)[16] in the present. Of the seventeen times the expression "eternity life" is used, only twice does it appear directed toward the future (4:14; 12:25).[17]

---

13. For more detail, see Coloe, *John 1–10*, 2–5.

14. The narrative will later show that Jesus, like Sophia, will call disciples "children" (Prov 2:1; Sir 2:1; 4:10-11; Wis 2:13; John 13:13) and "friends" (Wis 7:27; John 15:15).

15. Michael E. Willett, *Wisdom Christology in the Fourth Gospel* (San Francisco: Mellen Research University Press, 1992), 127.

16. See Coloe, *John 1–10*, xlviii, n. 9 for an explanation of why I translate ζωὴν αἰώνιον as "eternity life." The expressions ζωὴν αἰώνιον (3:15, 16) and βασιλεία [τοῦ] θεοῦ (3:3, 5) are both found in the Fourth Gospel and in the OT are found only in the book of Wisdom (5:15; 10:10). Jörg Frey comments, "From Jn 3,15 onwards, the Gospel uses the term ζωὴ αἰώνιος instead of βασιλεία τοῦ θεοῦ, and the development in Jn 3 shows that 'to have eternal life' is introduced as a substitute for the phrase 'to see' or 'to enter' God's kingdom." Jörg Frey, "Eschatology in the Johannine Circle," in *Theology and Christology in the Fourth Gospel: Essays by the Members of the SNTS Johannine Writings Seminar*, ed. Gilbert Van Belle, Jan G. van der Watt, and P. Maritz (Leuven: Peeters, 2005), 73.

17. In 4:14 the emphasis is on the future gift of water while 12:25, which uses the present tense, is in the center of two indefinite conditions expressed in the subjunc-

Thus the Johannine use of the term "eternity life" places this life in the present, which is consistent with the offer of Sophia in the book of Wisdom described above (Wis 5:15; 8:13). The identification of Jesus and Sophia lies at the heart of the central theological issue raised by Martha, Mary, and the Jews. With this background to Jewish concepts of life after death, and the particular Wisdom Christology of the Fourth Gospel, we are now in a position to read the text.

Introduction (11:1-6)

The opening verses introduce the place, the characters, and the episode to follow. These verses show a number of textual difficulties. The mention of Mary's anointing Jesus, which has not yet happened, indicates that at some stage in the Gospel's production the anointing, found now in chapter 12, had preceded this episode or that this verse has been added by a later editor,[18] or the evangelist presumes that the audience knew this anointing story from the tradition. Also, there are serious textual difficulties as a number of manuscripts show evidence that Martha's name has been added to the narrative.

Mary, Martha, and Mary Magdalene: One Woman or Three?

In a recent article in the *Harvard Theological Review*,[19] I raised the question of whether Martha was present in the earliest text of John 11–12. I examined over one hundred of the oldest extant Greek and Old Latin manuscripts as well as many patristic quotations. The starting point for my study is the instability around Martha in

---

tive and so this verse also carries the subjunctive sense "if anyone." Eleven times the expression is used with a verb in the present (3:36; 4:36; 5:24, 39; 6:27, 47, 54, 68; 10:28; 12:50; 17:3) and on four occasions with the subjunctive (3:14, 16; 6:40; 17:2), which has no time significance since it describes a possibility or a probability; William D. Mounce, *Basics of Biblical Greek: Grammar* (Grand Rapids: Zondervan, 1993), 282–83.

18. See Andrew T. Lincoln, *The Gospel according to Saint John*, BNTC (London: Continuum, 2005), 318; Raymond E. Brown, *The Gospel according to John*, 2 vols., AB 29–29A (New York: Doubleday, 1966, 1970), 1:423.

19. Elizabeth Schrader, "Was Martha of Bethany Added to the Fourth Gospel in the Second Century?," *HTR* 110 (2017): 360–92.

John 11:1-6

[11:1]Now a certain man was ill, Lazarus of Bethany, the village of Mary and her sister Martha. [2]Mary was the one who anointed the Lord with perfume and wiped his feet with her hair; her brother Lazarus was ill. [3]So the sisters sent a message to Jesus, "Lord, he whom you love is ill." [4]But when Jesus heard it, he said, "This illness does not lead to death; rather it is for God's glory, so that the Son of God may be glorified through it." [5]Accordingly, though Jesus loved Martha and her sister and Lazarus, [6]after having heard that Lazarus was ill, he stayed two days longer in the place where he was.

our most ancient witness of the Lazarus story, P[66].[20]

In 𝔓[66]'s version of John 11:1, the name Μαρια, "Maria," has been changed to the name Μαρθα, "Martha," by replacing the Greek *iota* in Maria with a *theta*; in 𝔓[66]'s version of John 11:3, one woman's name has been crossed out and changed to αἱ ἀδελφαὶ ("the sisters"). In fact, there is instability around Martha's presence for five entire verses in 𝔓[66]. By using actual readings from 𝔓[66] and just two other crucial witnesses of the Fourth Gospel, I offer a tentative reconstruction of what the earliest text of John 11:1-5 may have been:

[1]There was a certain sick man, Lazarus of Bethany, the village of Mary his sister.
[2]Now this was the Mary who anointed the Lord with ointment and wiped his feet with her hair, whose brother Lazarus was sick.
[3]Therefore Mary sent to him, saying, "Lord, behold, the one you love is sick."
[4]But when Jesus heard he said to her, "The sickness is not unto death, but for the glory of God, so that the Son may be glorified through it."

20. New Testament papyri written in Greek use a standardized identification system that includes a capital or gothic "𝔓" for "papyrus," followed by the number assigned to that manuscript. 𝔓[66] is part of the Bodmer Papyri and contains portions of the Gospel of John from around 200 CE. It is part of a collection found near Dishna, Egypt, that was purchased in the 1950s by Martin Bodmer. Its calligraphy style suggests it may have been produced by a professional scribe or possibly in a scriptorium. Alex Ramos, "Bodmer Papyri," in *The Lexham Bible Dictionary*, ed. John D. Barry et al. (Bellingham, WA: Lexham Press, 2016).

⁵Now Jesus loved Lazarus and his sister.

By examining the Fourth Gospel's greater text transmission in manuscripts and patristic quotations, my study demonstrates that Martha's presence shows significant textual instability throughout the Lazarus episode; there are traces of her absence in 18 percent of the Greek manuscripts and 30 percent of the *Vetus Latina* (Old Latin) manuscripts, as well as in some patristic quotations from Tertullian, Origen, Ambrose, Chrysostom, and Cyril of Alexandria. Thus, I conclude that this Lukan figure may not have been present in a predecessor text form of the Fourth Gospel that circulated in the second century.

Many well-known redaction critics (such as Marie-Émile Boismard, Robert Fortna, and John P. Meier[21]) have already hypothesized that Martha was not present in an earlier form of this gospel story; they have all suggested that Martha was added at a later stage by the evangelist. By contrast, due to discrepancies in the text transmission, my study suggests that Martha was more likely to have been added by later editors or scribes familiar with the Gospel of Luke 10:38-42.

A second consideration in my study is the possibility that the word Magdalene was a type of "nickname" combining the Aramaic word *migdal* (tower) and the Greek name *Eleni* ("Helen"), resulting in the name "Towering Helen." This is in contrast to the notion that Mary came from a supposed village called Magdala. Expressing a similar view, Mary Ann Beavis writes, "The city at the site of present-day Mejdel/Migdal was consistently called Tarichea by Josephus, never Magdala. . . . Luke's observation that Mary was 'the one called Magdalene' (8:2) suggests that μαγδαληνή was a nickname or title from the Aramaic *magdala* ('Mary the Tower' or 'Mary the Great'), like 'Simon called Peter' (Matt 10:2; Acts 10:32; 11:13; cf. John 1:42), 'Simon called the Zealot' (Luke 6:15), or 'Joseph called Barsabbas' (Acts 1:23), not a reference to her place of origin."[22]

In conclusion, I argue that without Martha present in the Fourth Gospel, Mary of

21. Marie-Émile Boismard, "Papyrus Bodmer II. Supplément de Jean," *RB* 70 (1962): 124–25; Robert T. Fortna, *The Fourth Gospel and Its Predecessor: From Narrative Source to Present Gospel* (Philadelphia: Fortress, 1989), 98, 101; John P. Meier, *A Marginal Jew: Rethinking the Historical Jesus*, vol. 2: *Mentor, Message, and Miracles*, ABRL (New York: Doubleday, 1994), 831.
22. Mary Ann Beavis, "Reconsidering Mary of Bethany," *CBQ* 74 (2012): 286, 287.

Bethany is far more likely to be Mary called Magdalene, due to strong parallelisms between the two "resurrection" narratives of Lazarus (John 11) and Jesus (John 20). Thus the addition of Martha may be an early and successful attempt to split one very prominent Johannine figure, Mary, into three different women: Mary of Bethany, Mary Magdalene, and Martha. Such an editorial change would have had profound exegetical consequences, not the least of which would be a major diminishment of Mary Magdalene's role in the Fourth Gospel. Instead of *one* woman speaking the crucial christological confession (John 11:27), anointing Jesus (John 12:3), standing at the cross (John 19:25), and being the first person to witness the risen Jesus (John 20:11-17), these pivotal moments in the narrative have now been divided among *three* women. If all of these actions belonged to Mary Magdalene alone in the earliest circulating version of the Fourth Gospel, the consequent implications of her leadership and authority may have been too problematic to be accepted into the canonical version. Thus the editorial interpolation of Martha may be an early and deliberate editorial diffusion of Mary Magdalene's prominence in the Fourth Gospel.

Elizabeth Schrader

Elizabeth Schrader proposes that the original account focused on Mary and Lazarus, and the text suggests that she, not Lazarus, is the most significant character, as the village of Bethany is described as that "of Mary [and Martha]" while Lazarus is simply "from/of Bethany."[23] The introduction speaks twice of Jesus's love for Lazarus (vv. 3, 5) and his sisters (v. 5). In response to the message, Jesus reinterprets the meaning of Lazarus's illness, that it will demonstrate the glory of God and that it will also lead to the glorification of the Son.[24] This cryptic comment prophetically indicates what will happen to Lazarus and also that this episode

23. If Schrader is correct in her hypothesis, it increases the status of Mary within the tradition but at the same time displaces Martha who appears only in John 11 and possibly in Luke 10:38-42, if the Mary and Martha in this short Lukan passage are the sisters of Lazarus of Bethany. This issue will be discussed further in the passion narrative. In this analysis of chap. 11, I will follow the text of the NRSV and refer to both Mary and Martha.

24. In examining the episode of the man born blind (John 9) I noted that the grammatical use of ἵνα need not mean purpose but simply a result. Daniel B. Wallace (*Greek Grammar Beyond the Basics: An Exegetical Syntax of the New Testament* [Grand Rapids: Zondervan, 1996], 473) writes that ἵνα followed by the subjunctive "indicates a consequence of the verbal action that is not intended." As a consequence of Lazarus's death Jesus may be glorified.

will lead to the "lifting up" of Jesus in his passion (11:50-53), when he will be glorified (17:5, 22, 24). For this glorification to happen, Lazarus must be dead rather than simply ill, and so Jesus delays his departure.

The Decision and Proverb (11:7-16)

When Jesus makes the decision to go to Bethany, about two miles from Jerusalem, his disciples object, reminding him of the recent opposition he faced (10:31, 39). Jesus/Sophia provides a typical "wisdom" response in the form of a parable about night and day similar to his earlier teaching (9:4-5).[25] The parable is introduced by a retort question, expressing a degree of frustration at the disciples' lack of understanding.[26] Rudolph Bultmann considers the question "is in characteristic Semitic style for the introduction of a parabolic saying."[27] The parable is expanded by the evangelist and given a deeper meaning because of Jesus's identity as "the light of the world" (8:12). Those (like Lazarus) who see the light of the world are not in darkness.[28] The contrast between light and darkness leads into the situation of Lazarus where Jesus speaks in images of sleep and awakening. The disciples are meant to follow the logic of the parable and understand that Jesus is the life. As Jesus/Sophia's friend, Lazarus is not walking in the darkness of death. This is what the disciples should believe, but the response by Thomas, speaking only of death, indicates their lack of comprehension. Jesus/Sophia is going to Bethany "so that you may believe" (v. 14).

Jesus's Absence Means Death—Martha, Mary, the Jews (11:17-37)

Following the narrative comment providing information about Jesus's arrival, the length of time since Lazarus's death, and the characters, Martha expresses the critical faith issue. Lazarus is dead, but Jesus's presence might have prevented this. This view is also held by Mary (v. 32) and the

---

25. Raymond F. Collins, *These Things Have Been Written: Studies on the Fourth Gospel*, Louvain Theological and Pastoral Monographs 2 (Louvain: Peeters, 1990), 146–49.

26. "Speakers use retort questions in natural discourse as a sarcastic response mechanism to make a point about a previous utterance. For example: (Speaker 1) Can I borrow your computer? (Speaker 2, Retort question) Is the Pope Catholic?" Douglas Estes, *The Questions of Jesus in John: Logic, Rhetoric and Persuasive Discourse*, BIS 115 (Leiden: Brill, 2013), 140–41.

27. Rudolph Bultmann, *The Gospel of John: A Commentary*, trans. George R. Beasley Murray et al. (Oxford: Blackwell, 1971), 399 n. 1.

28. See comments in Coloe, *John 1–10*, 26–27 and in chap. 3 on the symbolism of light and darkness in this Gospel.

⁷Then after this he said to the disciples, "Let us go to Judea again." ⁸The disciples said to him, "Rabbi, the Jews were just now trying to stone you, and are you going there again?" ⁹Jesus answered, "Are there not twelve hours of daylight? Those who walk during the day do not stumble, because they see the light of this world. ¹⁰But those who walk at night stumble, because the light is not in them." ¹¹After saying this, he told them, "Our friend Lazarus has fallen asleep, but I am going there to awaken him." ¹²The disciples said to him, "Lord, if he has fallen asleep, he will be all right." ¹³Jesus, however, had been speaking about his death, but they thought that he was referring merely to sleep. ¹⁴Then Jesus told them plainly, "Lazarus is dead. ¹⁵For your sake I am glad I was not there, so that you may believe. But let us go to him." ¹⁶Thomas, who was called the Twin, said to his fellow disciples, "Let us also go, that we may die with him."

¹⁷When Jesus arrived, he found that Lazarus had already been in the tomb four days. ¹⁸Now Bethany was near Jerusalem, some two miles away, ¹⁹and many of the Jews had come to Martha and Mary to console them about their brother. ²⁰When Martha heard that Jesus was coming, she went and met him, while Mary stayed at home. ²¹Martha said to Jesus, "Lord, if you had been here, my brother would not have died. ²²But even now I know that God will give you whatever you ask of him." ²³Jesus

Jews consoling Mary (v. 32, 36). Jesus responds with words of promise, "Your brother will rise again" (v. 23), which Martha understands in the conventional way of "resurrection on the last day" (v. 24). But this is not the eschatology of divine Sophia. Those who are friends of Sophia have already been gifted with "eternity life," and physical death does not annul this. Lazarus still lives! Jesus responds to Martha by identifying himself here and now ("I *am*") as "the resurrection and the life" (v. 25). He then clarifies two situations. First, those who believe, even though they pass through death (like Lazarus), continue to live (ζήσεται). And second, those who are alive and believe shall never die.

Jesus's statement, "Those who believe in me, even though they die, will live," is a generalized conditional statement expressed in the subjunctive mood (ἀποθάνῃ, "they die"), which then uses the future form of the verb ζήσεται, "will live." But ζήσεται is not referring to something that may happen in the future—"there is no future subjunctive."²⁹ The

29. Mounce, *Basics of Biblical Greek*, 282. "Because the aorist subjunctive is built on the unaugmented aorist tense stem, a first aorist subjunctive may look like a future (e.g., ἀγαπήσω). But remember, there is no future subjunctive."

said to her, "Your brother will rise again." [24]Martha said to him, "I know that he will rise again in the resurrection on the last day." [25]Jesus said to her, "I am the resurrection and the life. Those who believe in me, even though they die, will live, [26]and everyone who lives and believes in me will never die. Do you believe this?" [27]She said to him, "Yes, Lord, I believe that you are the Messiah, the Son of God, the one coming into the world."

[28]When she had said this, she went back and called her sister Mary, and told her privately, "The Teacher is here and is calling for you." [29]And when she heard it, she got up quickly and went to him. [30]Now Jesus had not yet come to the village, but was still at the place where Martha had met him. [31]The Jews who were with her in the house, consoling her, saw Mary get up quickly and go out. They followed her because they thought that she was going to the tomb to weep there. [32]When Mary came where Jesus was and saw him, she knelt at his feet and said to him, "Lord, if you had been here, my brother would not have died." [33]When Jesus saw her weeping, and the Jews who came with her also weeping, he was greatly disturbed in spirit and deeply moved. [34]He said, "Where have you laid him?" They said to him, "Lord, come and see." [35]Jesus began to weep. [36]So the Jews said, "See how he loved him!" [37]But some of them said, "Could not he who opened the eyes of the blind man have kept this man from dying?"

verb "will live," while looking as if Jesus speaks about a future event, needs to be understood as governed by the subjunctive and thus reflects "a condition the fulfillment of which is realized in the *present time*."[30] Thus, the statement may be translated: "Those who believe in me, even if they die, yet live." From Jesus/Sophia's perspective, Lazarus lives on, in the eternity life of God. He then asks Martha, "Do you believe this?"

Martha's words are deceptively hopeful, but rather than respond to Jesus's question with a simple "yes," which would indicate her understanding of Jesus and his words, she replies with three titles showing that she *has come* to believe in Jesus as the Christ, the Son of God, and the one coming into the world.[31] Two of these titles have been used previously and are not necessarily affirming Jesus as the "resurrection

30. Wallace, *Greek Grammar Beyond the Basics*, 470.

31. Francis J. Moloney, "Can Everyone Be Wrong? A Reading of John 11:1–12:8," *NTS* 49 (2003): 518. Moloney points out that Martha's use of the perfect πεπίστευκα describes a faith that preceded this moment. "Martha has always believed that Jesus is 'the Christ, the son of God, he who is coming into the world' (v. 27). *She is replying in categories that may sound Johannine (see 20.31) but do not respond to the question Jesus asked her*" (514, emphasis original).

and the life" and as divine Sophia able to bestow the gift of eternity life in the present. Martha is bound within her own preconceptions and traditional Jewish theology.

A second narrative comment (vv. 30-31) shifts the scene from Martha to Mary, who also conveys a limited understanding as she "falls [ἔπεσεν] at his feet" (v. 32) and repeats the words of Martha, equating life only with the physical presence of Jesus: "Lord, if you had been here, my brother would not have died" (v. 32).

The faith displayed by both Martha and Mary is much disputed. Martha's words identifying Jesus as the Christ, the Son of God (11:27), are the same words used later to express the goal of Johannine faith at the conclusion of the Gospel (20:31). Because of this Elisabeth Schüssler Fiorenza considers that "Martha represents the full apostolic faith of the Johannine community, just as Peter did for the Matthean community."[32] Similarly, Sandra Schneiders writes, "Martha demonstrates true and perfect Johannine belief in the word of Jesus."[33] Adele Reinhartz praises Martha's faith even prior to "the empirical evidence that his assertions are true."[34] On this point of Martha's faith I disagree. I think that her response to Jesus does not yet extend to belief in eternity life now, which is what Jesus's words call her to. Later, at the tomb, her lack of faith is expressed in her concern about the "stench" if the stone is removed (11:39). Only the cross and resurrection will reveal the full meaning of "the Christ and Son of God."

While Francis Moloney sees Mary's action of kneeling/falling at Jesus's feet as a gesture of faith,[35] I consider her posture an expression of petition, not Johannine faith, at this point. The verb ἔπεσεν is from πίπτω, which is literally "to fall down" but is also "a sign of devotion or humility, before high-ranking persons or divine beings, especially when one approaches with a petition."[36] Mary's faith will be demonstrated in the following chapter when, with prophetic insight, she anoints Jesus's feet.

32. See Elisabeth Schüssler Fiorenza, *In Memory of Her: A Feminist Theological Reconstruction of Christian Origins* (New York: Crossroad, 1983), 329. See also Margaret Daly-Denton, *John: An Earth Bible Commentary; Supposing Him to Be the Gardener*, Earth Bible Commentary (London: Bloomsbury T&T Clark, 2017), 147.

33. Sandra M. Schneiders, *Written That You May Believe: Encountering Jesus in the Fourth Gospel*, rev. and exp. ed. (New York: Crossroad, 2003), 179.

34. Adele Reinhartz, "From Narrative to History: The Resurrection of Mary and Martha," in *A Feminist Companion to the Hebrew Bible in the New Testament*, ed. Athalya Brenner (Sheffield: Sheffield Academic, 1996), 217.

35. Moloney, "Can Everyone Be Wrong?," 515–16.

36. BDAG, 815–16.

The lack of comprehension shown by Martha and Mary deeply moves Jesus, and his inner turmoil is described in a third narrative comment (vv. 33-35)—"he was greatly disturbed [ἐνεβριμήσατο] in spirit and deeply moved [ἐτάραξεν]." Jesus's reactions indicate his immense distress and frustration that even now, as his ministry draws to a close, his two much-loved friends still fail to understand him.[37] "Jesus is angered and deeply disturbed even to the point of tears by the universal lack of faith."[38] When Jesus is invited to see the tomb of Lazarus he expresses further emotions: "Jesus began to weep [ἐδάκρυσεν]" (v. 35). This is a different emotional response from his earlier reactions to Mary (κλαίοντας, v. 33) and his later reaction to the Jews (ἐμβριμώμενος, v. 38). This emotion is interpreted by the onlookers as grief in the face of his love for Lazarus: "See how he loved him" (v. 36). But the Jews have misunderstood his tears. His weeping (δακρύω) is not the same as the mourning (κλαίω) of Martha and the Jews. Moloney recalls Jesus's initial reaction when told of Lazarus's illness:

> Jesus is not weeping over the loss of his friend. . . . This is not a sickness unto death; it is for the glory of God and the means by which the Son of God will be glorified (v. 4). Jesus, the resurrection and the life, is angered, deeply moved, and he weeps, as all his attempts to lead his disciples, Martha and Mary into a true understanding of life and death meet failure.[39]

I offer a further interpretation of Jesus's tears. From Jesus's perspective, his friend Lazarus is now embraced by eternity life with God; the human experience of death is, for Jesus, the return to his Father (13:1, 3; 14:12; 16:17, 28; 17:11). In fact, Jesus never uses the word "death" or "die" to speak of what awaits him and instead speaks of being "lifted up/exalted" or "the hour" or "return."[40] From this perspective, how could Jesus feel

37. Jesus's distress at this point is not grief. The verb ἐμβριμάομαι means "to have an intense, strong feeling of concern, often with the implication of indignation" (Johannes P. Louw and Eugene A. Nida, eds., *Greek-English Lexicon of the New Testament: Based on Semantic Domains*, 2 vols., 2nd ed. [New York: United Bible Societies, 1996], 1:293). For a detailed discussion of ἐμβριμάομαι, see Stephen Voorwinde, *Jesus' Emotions in the Fourth Gospel*, LNTS 284 (London: T&T Clark, 2005), 169–77.

38. Moloney, "Can Everyone Be Wrong?," 518.

39. Ibid., 519. Brendan Byrne suggests that Jesus's tears at this point express the conflict and personal cost faced by Jesus. In raising Lazarus to life, Jesus sets in motion "forces leading to death for himself." Brendan Byrne, *Lazarus: A Contemporary Reading of John 11:1-46* (Homebush: St. Paul, 1991), 73.

40. The closest Jesus comes to speaking of his death is in the image of the good shepherd who "lays down his life" (10:16, 17, 28) or the wheat grain that must die in order to bear fruit (12:24).

sadness for Lazarus—except a sadness for what he is about to do so that his disciples and friends might believe? Lazarus is to be called away from eternity life with God and back into mortal human life. This may bring joy and faith to his sisters and friends in Bethany but great loss for Lazarus.

The Word of Jesus Brings Resurrection (11:38-44)

In response to the comment by the Jews—"Could not he who opened the eyes of the blind man have kept this man from dying?"—Jesus approaches the tomb once again angered and "greatly disturbed" (ἐμβριμώμενος) by their lack of faith. Martha, in spite of Jesus's earlier words, cannot see beyond death and the corruption expected after four days in the tomb. In Jewish tradition, physical corruption identifies when the soul has definitely left the body.[41] Knowing what is about to occur, Jesus challenges her to believe so that she will perceive, with the eyes of faith, the glory of God, as Jesus had earlier told his disciples, "This illness . . . is for God's glory" (11:4). Jesus then prays for all in the crowd gathered at the tomb, his disciples, Martha, Mary, and the Jews, that they may believe. His prayer is not for power to raise Lazarus, since he knows that the Father has already given him the power "to give life" (5:21). Calling Lazarus forth demonstrates the truth of Jesus's words that "whoever believes in me, even if they die, yet lives" (11:25). As the embodiment of Sophia, Jesus calls his friend Lazarus by name, and as Sophia's friend Lazarus already enjoys immortality (ἀθανασίαν): "because of her I shall have immortality" (Wis 8:13) and eternity life (Wis 5:15; εἰς τὸν αἰῶνα ζῶσιν). Alive and able to hear the voice of Jesus, Lazarus responds and leaves the tomb. Jesus's final command is to release him from the unnecessary trappings of death.

Reactions (11:45-54)

There is no expression of faith on the part of Martha or Mary, but among the Jews there is a division, with many believing while others go

---

41. John Lightfoot quotes Genesis Rabba 100 [64a], "The very height of mourning is not till the third day. For three days the spirit wanders about the sepulcher, expecting if it may return into the body. But when it sees that the form or aspect of the face is changed, then it hovers no more, but leaves the body to itself" (*A Commentary on the New Testament from the Talmud and Hebraica*, 4 vols. [Peabody, MA: Hendrickson, 1979], 3:367). See also H. Strack and P. Billerbeck, *Kommentar zum Neuen Testament aus Talmud und Midrasch*, 6 vols. (Munich: C. H. Beck, 1922–1961), 2:544–45.

John 11:38-54

[38]Then Jesus, again greatly disturbed, came to the tomb. It was a cave, and a stone was lying against it. [39]Jesus said, "Take away the stone." Martha, the sister of the dead man, said to him, "Lord, already there is a stench because he has been dead four days." [40]Jesus said to her, "Did I not tell you that if you believed, you would see the glory of God?" [41]So they took away the stone. And Jesus looked upward and said, "Father, I thank you for having heard me. [42]I knew that you always hear me, but I have said this for the sake of the crowd standing here, so that they may believe that you sent me." [43]When he had said this, he cried with a loud voice, "Lazarus, come out!" [44]The dead man came out, his hands and feet bound with strips of cloth, and his face wrapped in a cloth. Jesus said to them, "Unbind him, and let him go."

[45]Many of the Jews therefore, who had come with Mary and had seen what Jesus did, believed in him. [46]But some of them went to the Pharisees

to the Pharisees, who, unlike the Sadducees, believe in a resurrection of the body on the last day. Rather than prompting faith in Jesus, the raising of Lazarus brings the Sadducees and Pharisees together in the Council of the Sanhedrin (v. 47).[42] Fearing the destruction by the Romans—of their temple, their "holy place," and their nation—leads to the ironic judgment by Caiaphas the high priest that one man must die for the nation (v. 50). In an attempt to preserve *their* temple, the council condemns Jesus, the temple of God (2:21), to death (v. 53). The narrator's comment then transforms Caiaphas's words from a death warrant to a prophecy of life, for although Jesus is about to die, the Lazarus story witnesses that life continues beyond death, and through his death Jesus passes into the eternity life beyond death, when he can gather into one "the dispersed children of God" (v. 52). This statement recalls the promise of the prologue that those who believe will be given the power to become the children of God (1:12). It is also the gift of Sophia enabling the righteous to be "numbered among

42. Following a review of many sources, Lester Grabbe ("Sanhedrin, Sanhedriyyot, or Mere Invention?," *JSJ* 39 [2008]: 1–19) concludes that after the demise of the monarchy, the leader of the Jewish community was the high priest, assisted by other leading priests and nonpriestly nobility, including notable Pharisees. This group is thought to have totaled seventy-one based on the tradition that Moses was assisted by seventy judges (Num 11:16). For a thorough investigation of the power of the Sanhedrin and its ability to pronounce the death sentence during Roman rule, see George R. Dekle Sr., *The Case against Christ: A Critique of the Prosecution of Jesus* (Newcastle upon Tyne: Cambridge Scholars, 2011), esp. chap. 3.

and told them what he had done. ⁴⁷So the chief priests and the Pharisees called a meeting of the council, and said, "What are we to do? This man is performing many signs. ⁴⁸If we let him go on like this, everyone will believe in him, and the Romans will come and destroy both our holy place and our nation." ⁴⁹But one of them, Caiaphas, who was high priest that year, said to them, "You know nothing at all! ⁵⁰You do not understand that it is better for you to have one man die for the people than to have the whole nation destroyed." ⁵¹He did not say this on his own, but being high priest that year he prophesied that Jesus was about to die for the nation, ⁵²and not for the nation only, but to gather into one the dispersed children of God. ⁵³So from that day on they planned to put him to death.

⁵⁴Jesus therefore no longer walked about openly among the Jews, but went from there to a town called Ephraim in the region near the wilderness; and he remained there with the disciples.

the children of God" (Wis 5:5).[43] There is a hint given here that the attempt to kill Jesus/Sophia will be procreative, bearing children of God.

Jesus reacts by withdrawing from public, and this withdrawal is ascribed by the narrator to the threat to him by the Jewish leadership.[44]

Unbind Her and Let Her Go[45]

The words spoken to Lazarus are words many women long to hear addressed to themselves. Across the globe women are bound: in poverty, in sex-slavery, in lack of education, in hygiene, in lack of any voice within family or vote in society. Women are bound in arranged marriages, forced to endure genital mutilation, domestic violence, sexual harassment, and a "glass (read concrete) ceiling" on professional advancement. *Gender Equality and Female*

43. This place in the book of Wisdom is the only occurrence of the phrase "children of God" in the OT.

44. Rudolph Schnackenburg (*The Gospel according to St John*, trans. K. Smyth et al., HTCNT, 3 vols. [London: Burns & Oates, 1968–1982], 2:351) identifies Ephraim (v. 54) as the modern-day village Et-Taiyibe, twenty kilometers northeast of Jerusalem, and notes that it appears on the Madaba map as "Ephron or Ephraim, where the Lord came from."

45. See also the excursus "Women and the Eucharist" at John 6 in Coloe, *John 1–10*, 188–90.

Empowerment stand as goal 5 in the United Nations Sustainable Goals.[46] Freeing of bonds is the first step, to be followed by "let her go"—the freedom to live as a fully gifted human being made in the image of God.

The World Council of Churches expresses the commitments of many Christian churches toward justice and equality for women under the heading "Just Community of Women and Men."[47] Unfortunately the Roman Catholic Church is not a member of this council. On the eve of the 1995 Beijing Women's Conference then-Pope John Paul II stated:

> Women's dignity has often been unacknowledged and their prerogatives misrepresented; they have often been relegated to the margins of society and even reduced to servitude. This has prevented women from truly being themselves and it has resulted in a spiritual impoverishment of human-ity. . . . As far as personal rights are concerned, there is an urgent need to achieve real equality in every area. . . . [T]his is a matter of justice but also of necessity.[48]

Following such a strong unequivocal statement it could be expected that action would follow, but nothing has. Within the Catholic Church it seems that women receive a second-rate baptism not fully incorporating them into the risen Christ with his threefold office of prophetic, royal, and priestly functions (LG 31). Women are still bound by man-made laws preventing their service as eucharistic celebrants. Not only do these laws bind women, but they also bind God, as God is not to give the vocation of ministerial priesthood to a woman; this service is reserved for men only. It is similar to the issue confronting Peter in Acts when he tried to teach God that some animals were unclean and not to be eaten (Acts 10:14). So while Lazarus is released, his sisters are still bound.

46. United Nations Sustainable Development Goals, https://www.un.org/sustainabledevelopment/gender-equality/.

47. World Council of Churches, "Just Community of Women and Men," https://www.oikoumene.org/en/what-we-do/women-and-men.

48. "Letter of Pope John Paul II to Women," 3–4. http://www.vatican.va/content/john-paul-ii/en/letters/1995/documents/hf_jp-ii_let_29061995_women.html.

John 11:55–12:50

Sophia's Testing Begins

Let us lie in wait for the righteous man,
because he is inconvenient to us and opposes our actions;
he reproaches us for sins against the law,
and accuses us of sins against our training.
He professes to have knowledge of God,
and calls himself a child of the Lord. . . .
He calls the last end of the righteous happy,
and boasts that God is his father.
Let us see if his words are true. (Wis 2:12-13, 16b-17)

The third and final Passover in John's Gospel follows the narration of Lazarus's raising, and the threat of death looms large, not only for Jesus, but also for Lazarus. Using the time indicator "the next day" (12:12), the approaching Passover could be divided into two major sections. The first section, 11:55–12:11,[1] narrates Jesus's anointing in the midst of plots by the Jewish leaders to arrest Jesus (11:55) in order to "put him to death" (11:53) and also to execute Lazarus (12:10). The second section (12:12-43) begins on "the next day" with Jesus's entry into

---

1. I consider that 11:55 marks the start of a new section as the statement "Now the Passover of the Jews was near" is almost a formulaic introduction for the festivals; e.g., 2:13; 6:4; 7:2.

Jerusalem followed by various responses. This section describes Jesus's self-awareness that his hour has come (12:23) and what this will mean for himself (12:27-29), for the "ruler of this world" (v. 31), and for "all people" (v. 32). The final verses (12:44-50) form an epilogue to Jesus's public ministry. These verses summarize Jesus's teaching in terms of his mission from the Father.[2]

Section 1: 11:55–12:11 Plot against Jesus; anointing; plot against Lazarus

Section 2: 12:12-43 Entry into Jerusalem and responses

Epilogue: 12:44-50

The momentum of the narrative slows down after this chapter. From chapters 13 to 17 the narrative describes a meal and Jesus interacting with his disciples, primarily through a discourse.

Section 1: Plots of Death and Mary's Anointing (11:55–12:11)

This passage marks the beginning of the final Passover in the Fourth Gospel (cf. 2:13; 6:4), which was one of the three major pilgrim festivals in Judaism. To enter fully into the celebration many Jews would come early to undertake a ritual cleansing so that they would then only need a simplified footwashing before entering the temple. The pilgrims are on the lookout for Jesus, and there is no hint that this is any more than curiosity. The leadership are also on the lookout, but their motive is to arrest him and then carry out the words of Caiaphas, "it is better for you to have one man die for the people than to have the whole nation destroyed" (11:50). The crowd and the leaders are searching not only for Jesus but also for Lazarus, whose return to life has encouraged faith in Jesus. As the embodiment of Sophia, the introduction describes the plots against him. "Let us lie in wait for the righteous man" (Wis 2:12).

Mary's Prophetic and Priestly Anointing

The Gospel has established that the woman who anointed Jesus was Mary, the sister of Lazarus (11:2). Some consider that this Mary was also known as Mary Magdalene, either naming a characteristic of Mary, such as

2. On the use of "father" as a Johannine image, see my comments in the author's introduction and also the essay by Dorothy Lee, "The Iconic Father," following the analysis of John 5 in Mary L. Coloe, *John 1–10*, WCS 44A (Collegeville, MN: Liturgical Press, 2021), lxxv–lxxvi, 156.

John 11:55–12:11

⁵⁵Now the Passover of the Jews was near, and many went up from the country to Jerusalem before the Passover to purify themselves. ⁵⁶They were looking for Jesus and were asking one another as they stood in the temple, "What do you think? Surely he will not come to the festival, will he?" ⁵⁷Now the chief priests and the Pharisees had given orders that anyone who knew where Jesus was should let them know, so that they might arrest him.

¹²:¹Six days before the Passover Jesus came to Bethany, the home of Lazarus, whom he had raised from the dead. ²There they gave a dinner for him. Martha served, and Lazarus was one of those at the table with him. ³Mary took a pound of costly perfume made of pure nard, anointed Jesus'

her height or status, thus "towering" Mary, or referring to a village called Magdala where she lived but came to Bethany due to Lazarus's illness.[3]

In the midst of plots and the threat of death, the narrative presents the scene of Jesus's anointing by Mary, the sister of Lazarus of Bethany (11:1). All the Gospels have a narrative about a woman washing/anointing Jesus's feet/head. Luke places this episode earlier in Jesus's ministry (Luke 7:36-50) while Mark and Matthew link it to his passion (Mark 14:3-9; Matt 26:6-13).[4] Etienne Trocmé has argued for an archetypal passion narrative that could have come into existence as early as ten years after the death of Jesus and could then form the basis of pre-Gospel passion sources within various Christian communities.[5] With many other

3. See Mary Ann Beavis, "Reconsidering Mary of Bethany," *CBQ* 74 (2012): 281–97 and the excursus "Mary, Martha, and Mary Magdalene: One Woman or Three?" by Elizabeth Schrader in chap. 11, pp. 319–22. See the discussion about the "Marys" in Mary Ann Beavis and Ally Kateusz, eds., *Rediscovering the Marys: Maria, Mariamne, Miriam*, Scriptural Traces: Critical Perspectives on the Reception and Influence of the Bible 22 (London: T&T Clark, 2020).

4. I agree with the position of Robert Holst, who makes a strong case for there being one anointing incident that has made its way into the Gospels in three different, independent forms: Mark/Matthew, John, and Luke; see Robert Holst, "The One Anointing of Jesus: Another Application of the Form-Critical Method," *JBL* 95 (1976): 435–46. See also the comments by Kathleen E. Corley (*Private Women, Public Meals: Social Conflict in the Synoptic Tradition* [Peabody, MA: Hendrickson, 1993]): "It is more than likely that behind this and other accounts in the Gospels (Matt 26:6-13; Mark 14:3-9; Luke 7:36-50; John 12:1-8) lies one original chreia, which has been variously elaborated or expanded by the individual writers" (122). Also Marianne Sawicki, *Seeing the Lord: Resurrection and Early Christian Practices* (Minneapolis: Fortress, 1994), 149–154.

5. Etienne Trocmé, *The Passion as Liturgy: A Study in the Origin of the Passion Narratives in the Four Gospels* (London: SCM, 1983), 54. "The archetype of the Passion narratives was based on a selection of facts known from various sources and chosen

feet, and wiped them with her hair. The house was filled with the fragrance of the perfume. ⁴But Judas Iscariot, one of his disciples (the one who was about to betray him), said, ⁵"Why was this perfume not sold for three hundred denarii and the money given to the poor?" ⁶(He said this not because he cared about the poor, but because he was a thief; he kept the common purse and used to steal what was put into it.) ⁷Jesus said, "Leave her alone. She bought it so that she might keep it for the day of my burial. ⁸You always have the poor with you, but you do not always have me."

⁹When the great crowd of the Jews learned that he was there, they came not only because of Jesus but also to see Lazarus, whom he had raised from the dead. ¹⁰So the chief priests planned to put Lazarus to death as well, ¹¹since it was on account of him that many of the Jews were deserting and were believing in Jesus.

commentators, I would agree that even Mark, the first Gospel, appears to draw on a preexisting passion tradition, and perhaps even a passion narrative, that included an anointing.⁶ Once the event became linked to the passion, perhaps in a pre-Gospel passion source, Mark and John redacted it to conform to their own particular interests. Mark makes this a messianic anointing of Jesus's head and links this anointing with the hasty burial of Jesus where there is no ritual anointing of his body.

John has the anointing of Jesus's feet, possibly reflecting the original event. The words of Jesus interpret Mary's actions linking it to his future death, which only Mary foresees with prophetic insight. When Jesus arrived in Bethany to be greeted by Martha, Mary remained in the house with other Jews who were consoling her (11:31). When Jesus raised Lazarus, many of these believed in him (11:45), but some went and reported him to the Pharisees. It is possible that Mary knew from this that Jesus was under threat. With insight and prescience she anoints Jesus's feet with a lavish amount of costly perfume.

Footwashing was a normal way of welcoming a guest into a household by offering a basin of water and towel. The guest would slip off their

---

for reasons yet undecided. It was a continuous and reasonably coherent narrative arranged in an order dictated by the logic of narration and by its *Sitz im Leben* and the practical use it was put to." This pre-Gospel narrative included the anointing (p. 74). On a possible early dating for this archetype based on Jewish liturgical Haggadah models, see pp. 81–85.

6. On the existence of a pre-Gospel passion tradition and a passion narrative, see Raymond E. Brown, *The Death of the Messiah: From Gethsemane to the Grave*, ABRL, 2 vols. (New York: Doubleday, 1994), 1:83–84, 92.

sandals, wash and dry their own feet, then enter the home. Washing was also a ritual performed prior to entering the temple. At the entrance to the temple were many ritual baths (*mikvot*) where women and men who had come as pilgrims to Jerusalem could cleanse themselves by full submersion. Once this had been carried out, they were considered purified and only needed to wash their feet each time they entered the temple. With insight about the threat Jesus is under, and now with complete faith in his identity as the tabernacling presence of God able to raise her brother to life, Mary prepares Jesus for his final return to God's heavenly temple.[7]

The Fourth Gospel has four significant differences from the accounts of Mark and Matthew. These four features raise Mary's status to that of prophet and priest, like Moses.

1. A time frame is given—six days before the Passover.
2. The woman is named as Mary, sister to Martha and Lazarus from John 11.[8]
3. The fragrance of the perfume fills the house.
4. Judas is named and described as the one to criticize her action.

There are echoes in Mary's anointing of Jesus with the building and anointing of the tabernacle in the Sinai wilderness. Moses experienced the glory of God for six days (Exod 24:15-16). Then God gave him the paradigm of the tabernacle, including instructions about the anointing oil (Exod 25:8-9). The tabernacle was then made modelling God's work of creation.[9] Instructions for the making of the tabernacle included that it was to be made from an "offering to the Lord; let whoever is of a generous heart bring the Lord's offering" (Exod 35:5).[10] When the tabernacle was finished, Moses was commanded to "take the anointing oil, and anoint the tabernacle" (Exod 40:9). When all this is done, "the glory of

---

7. More will be said about the customs and cultic significance of footwashing at John 13.

8. In the accounts of Mark, Matthew, and Luke, the anointing woman is not named.

9. The expression "The Lord said to Moses" occurs seven times, marking six stages of making the tabernacle (25:1; 30:11, 17, 22, 34; 31:1), and the seventh occasion is an instruction about the Sabbath (31:12). See also the work of Shimon Bakon, "Creation, Tabernacle and Sabbath," *JBQ* 25 (1997): 79–85; Eric E. Elnes, "Creation and Tabernacle: The Priestly Writer's 'Environmentalism,'" *HBT* 16 (1994): 144–55. The concluding statement, "so Moses finished the work" (Exod 40:33), echoes the words of Genesis, "And on the seventh day God finished the work" (Gen 2:2).

10. Judas's complaint functions to highlight the generosity of Mary.

the LORD filled the tabernacle" (Exod 40:33-34). A similar expression is used when the Jerusalem temple is built by Solomon: "the glory of the LORD filled the house of the LORD" (1 Kgs 8:10-11).

Echoes of the building of the tabernacle and temple pervade the episode in John 12:1-11. For six days there was a presence of the glory cloud of YHWH on Sinai prior to the revelation of the tabernacle's model. As "the hour" approaches, God's glory, tabernacled in the flesh of Jesus (1:14), will be present with the disciples for only six days, leading up to the full manifestation of his glory on the cross. Just as Moses took specially prepared oil and, acting as a priest, anointed the tabernacle, Mary anoints Jesus, whose flesh is the tabernacle of God's presence (1:14).

In the account of the building of the tabernacle, the description of the spices emphasizes their purity and abundance (Exod 30:23). John 12 similarly emphasizes the purity of the perfume and its expense (12:3, 5), which highlight Mary's generous heart. Finally, the expression unique to the Fourth Gospel, "the house was filled with the fragrance of the perfume" (12:3), recalls the description of God's glory filling the tabernacle (Exod 40:35) and later the temple in Chronicles where "the house of the LORD was filled with the cloud of glory" (2 Chr 5:13).

Following Judas's complaint about the expense of the perfume used by Mary, Jesus rebuffs his criticism by pointing to Mary's prescience, "Let her be. She kept [τηρήσῃ] it for the day of my burial." Not only has Mary anointed the tabernacle of Jesus's body, as Moses once anointed the wilderness tabernacle, but she has shown prophetic foresight in recognizing what no other disciple has realized: that Jesus is about to return to his Father's house, through death. In John, unlike Mark, there is no suggestion that Mary is carrying out a ritual anointing of Jesus's body prior to burial. Only his feet are anointed since footwashing was necessary before entering the temple precincts.[11] What Mary does for Jesus he will do for his disciples[12] to prepare them for his death and to help them understand its meaning. In death, Jesus is returning to his Father's house (the temple; cf. 2:16), the heavenly dwelling of God, so in preparation for his entering into the presence of God, Mary prophetically washes his feet with perfume. From the previous experience of her

---

11. Philo commented, "One should not enter with unwashed feet on the pavement of the Temple of God" (QE Sup 2.1.2).

12. As Elisabeth Schüssler Fiorenza (*In Memory of Her: A Feminist Theological Reconstruction of Christian Origins* [New York: Crossroad, 1983], 331) notes, "She anticipates Jesus' command to wash the feet of each other as a sign for the agape praxis of true discipleship."

brother Lazarus, Mary knows that death is not an end and a grave is not a final destination. Her anointing is not for Jesus's entry into a tomb but that he may tread in the heavenly temple of his Father's presence. Finally, Jesus's identity has been recognized by one of his friends, along with the cost such friendship will demand.

Satoko Yamaguchi proposes that this anointing story was remembered and passed on in women's circles, pointing to the imperative words of Jesus, "Let her be" (12:7). "In a group-oriented society, . . . it is often particularly difficult for a woman to do something that might invite displeasure or cause trouble in the group. . . . 'Let her be' is the strongest liberating support a woman could wish to receive in such a milieu."[13]

Section 2: Entry into Jerusalem and Responses (12:12-43)

The day following Mary's anointing brings the first part of John's Gospel, known as the Book of Signs, to its conclusion, with the announcement by Jesus that "the hour has come for the Son of Man to be glorified" (12:23). Some sign occurs in this episode to prompt this statement by Jesus. Up until this point, references to "the hour" have been in terms of its "not yet" status, but now this changes. The day begins with Jesus's entry into Jerusalem, which triggers many and varied responses. The account is interrupted regularly with interpretive comments by the narrator, which leads to a brief conclusion to the first part of the Gospel (vv. 44-50). The narrative has the following shape:

A. The entry into Jerusalem: the crowd and Jesus's response (vv. 12-14)
    (narrator's explanation, vv. 15-18)

B. Various responses: the Pharisees, the Greeks, Jesus, the Father, the crowd (vv. 19-32)
    (narrator's explanation, v. 33)

C. Concluding reactions: the crowd and Jesus's response (vv. 34-36)
    (narrator's explanation, vv. 37-43)

A. The Entry into Jerusalem (vv. 12-18)

The Johannine account of Jesus's entry into Jerusalem is noticeably different from the Synoptic accounts. In the Synoptics, Jesus initiates

---

13. Satoko Yamaguchi, *Mary and Martha: Women in the World of Jesus* (Maryknoll, NY: Orbis Books, 2002), 124.

John 12:12-18

¹²The next day the great crowd that had come to the festival heard that Jesus was coming to Jerusalem. ¹³So they took branches of palm trees and went out to meet him, shouting,

"Hosanna!
Blessed is the one who comes in
        the name of the Lord—
    the King of Israel!"
¹⁴Jesus found a young donkey and
    sat on it; as it is written:
¹⁵"Do not be afraid, daughter of
    Zion.

Look, your king is coming,
    sitting on a donkey's colt!"
¹⁶His disciples did not understand these things at first; but when Jesus was glorified, then they remembered that these things had been written of him and had been done to him. ¹⁷So the crowd that had been with him when he called Lazarus out of the tomb and raised him from the dead continued to testify. ¹⁸It was also because they heard that he had performed this sign that the crowd went to meet him.

the event by sending disciples to procure a donkey for him to ride into Jerusalem (Mark 11:1; Matt 21:2; Luke 19:30). The crowd then responds to Jesus's actions by spreading cloaks on the road, waving branches, and shouting acclamations. This sequence is reversed in John. The crowd, motivated by the raising of Lazarus (v. 9), takes branches and goes out to meet Jesus (v. 12). In response to the crowds, Jesus finds a young donkey and sits on it. The narrator then offers two explanations about this event: the first, in terms of what is written in the Scriptures (v. 15), which, according to the narrator, the disciples did not understand or remember until after Jesus was glorified (v. 16); second, the crowd has acted as they did because of the sign of Lazarus (vv. 17-18).

The key to the meaning of this event lies in the Scripture citations given by the crowd (Ps 118:2), then adding "the King of Israel," followed by the narrator, "Do not be afraid, daughter of Zion; Look, your king is coming, sitting on a donkey's colt!" (v. 15).[14] This citation, drawing on both Zephaniah and Zechariah, repeats the title "King" from the crowd's acclamations.

14. In this ancient text, unlike some modern narratives, I am assuming the narrator speaks reliably on behalf of the author. The narrator's explanatory comments therefore offer the reader a clue to interpreting the events. "What the narrator communicates directly to the reader through commentary is a reliable representation of the overall point of view of the omniscient author." See Francis J. Moloney, "Who Is the Reader?," *ABR* 40 (1992): 23.

On the lips of the crowd, the title "King" expresses Jewish nationalist hopes such as at the time of David or the Maccabees;[15] the palm branches (τὰ βαΐα) they wave are the same type of branch used to hail Simon the Maccabee when he arrived triumphantly in Jerusalem following his victory over the "yoke of the Gentiles" (1 Macc 13:41). While waving the branches the crowd cites Psalm 118:26, "Blessed be he who comes in the name of the Lord" (John 12:13) adding on "the King of Israel." Jesus's response is to find a young donkey and sit on it. While Jesus provides no interpretation of his actions, the narrator states that this action is "as it is written" (v. 14), and when interpreted through this citation combining both Zephaniah (3:16) and Zechariah (9:9), Jesus's symbolic action corrects the crowd's limited nationalistic perceptions.[16] The citation from Zephaniah, "Do not be afraid, daughter of Zion" (John 12:15),[17] is part of an oracle looking to the future coming of a king and the gathering of the nations to Jerusalem. "For my decision is to gather nations" (Zeph 3:8), then the speech of all (πάντας) the people will be changed "that all of them may call on the name of the LORD and serve him with one accord"

15. According to Bruce G. Schuchard (*Scripture within Scripture: The Interrelationship of Form and Function in the Explicit Old Testament Citations in the Gospel of John*, SBLDS 133 [Atlanta: Scholars Press, 1992], 77), "The palm was for the Jews a symbol which, at least from the time of the Maccabees, stood for the nation and functioned as an expression of their hope for an imminent national liberation (see 1 Macc 13.51; 2 Macc 10.7; cf. T. Naph. 5.4; Rev 7.9)." This allusion gives added meaning to the crowd's hailing Jesus as "King."

16. Note the use of the adversative conjunction δέ, "*But* Jesus found a young donkey and sat upon it" (v. 14). For further details about these two citations and references to alternative interpretations, see Mary L. Coloe, "Gentiles in the Gospel of John: Narrative Possibilities—John 12:12-43," in *Attitudes to Gentiles in Ancient Judaism and Early Christianity*, ed. David C. Sim and James S. McLaren, LNTS 499 (London: T&T Clark, 2013), 209–23.

17. In Zephaniah the citation reads, "Do not fear, O Zion," (3:16) with "Daughter Zion" named in 3:14. Zion is a term found in the Writings and Prophets as a poetic way of naming Jerusalem and, at times, specifically the temple. In these books Zion is often personified as a female figure: daughter, mother, bride, widow. By association with Jerusalem and the prophetic judgment on Israel's infidelity, Zion is also portrayed as an adulteress and whore. Such personification is termed "gendered space." Christl Maier has studied the construction of personified Zion across periods of Israel's history, offering reasons why a personification is chosen according to Israel's historical situation. See Christl M. Maier, *Daughter Zion, Mother Zion: Gender, Space, and the Sacred in Ancient Israel* (Minneapolis: Fortress, 2008).

(Zeph 3:9). Jesus is entering Jerusalem not as King of Israel but as God incarnate, who has come to gather all the nations.[18]

Daughter of Zion

The phrase θυγάτηρ Σιών (Heb: בת־ציון), "Daughter of Zion," expresses tender intimacy between parent and daughter, but it also captures the vulnerability of women during times of war and oppression. In the book of Lamentations 1, Daughter Zion personifies Jerusalem who has suffered destruction and desolation. The defilement of the temple is imaged as a rape of Daughter Zion—who has been struck down; from being princess she is now a vassal, and all revile her nakedness. Such stark imagery expresses the horror of war and the very particular fear and brutality experienced by women. Lamentations continues the outrage by changing Daughter Zion from innocent victim to the one responsible. "Blame for the destruction of Jerusalem . . . is laid squarely upon Woman Zion. 'The Lord has made her suffer for the multitude of her transgressions' (Lam 1:5c)."[19] In other words, "She asked for it"!

Because Daughter Zion has experienced the depths of distress, at the prospect of salvation she cries aloud in greatest joy, according to Zephaniah (3:14) and Zechariah (9:9). But the real-life experience of women in Japan, Bosnia, Syria, Africa, Afghanistan, and El Salvador suggests such personal reversal from lament to rejoicing is poetic imagination. The trauma never leaves.

The second part of the Scripture citation, "Look, your king is coming, sitting on a donkey's colt," continues the universalist outlook of Zephaniah by adding a citation from Zechariah 9:9: "Lo, your king comes to you; [triumphant and victorious is he, humble and riding on a donkey,[20]]

---

18. Raymond E. Brown, *The Gospel according to John*, 2 vols., AB 29–29A (New York: Doubleday, 1966, 1970), 1:462. In the later prophetic literature, as part of Israel's eschatological hopes, many nations were to be gathered to Jerusalem to worship the God of Israel (Isa 55:5; 60:5-6; Zech 2:11; 8:21-23; 14:16; Zeph 3:9; Mic 7:12). The temple was to become "a house of prayer for all nations" (LXX: πᾶσιν τοῖς ἔθνεσιν, Isa 56:7). See Duane L. Christensen, "Nations," *ABD* 4 (1996): 1044–49.

19. Gina Hens-Piazza, *Lamentations*, WCS 30 (Collegeville, MN: Liturgical Press, 2017), xl.

20. The Gospel omits the phrase from Zechariah 9:9: "triumphant and victorious is he, humble and riding on a donkey."

on a colt, the foal of a donkey."[21] By omitting part of the citation, the Gospel refrains from interpreting the action as a gesture of humility. Once again, the context in Zechariah is most significant, for this king will "command peace to the nations; his dominion shall be from sea to sea, and from the River to the ends of the earth" (Zech 9:10). While the crowd acclaimed Jesus with the title, "King of *Israel*," the particular Johannine rendition of this scene emphasizes that Jesus's actions correct this title. Jesus comes into Jerusalem for the eschatological gathering of *all* the nations, not simply the children of Israel.

B. Various Responses (vv. 19-33)

The crowd's acclamations and Jesus's corrective responses cause various reactions. The Pharisees, who do not know the narrative comments, ironically state, "Look, the world has gone after him" (v. 19). In confirmation of these words, some Greeks approach Philip wanting to see Jesus (v. 22). Given the context, these Greeks are Gentiles and their presence is a sign that the oracles about the eschatological gathering of the nations to Jerusalem are now being fulfilled.[22] In response to this sign, Jesus declares, "The hour has come for the Son of Man [ὁ υἱὸς τοῦ ἀνθρώπου] to be glorified" (v. 23).[23]

His response is followed by a heavenly voice (v. 28), which some in the crowd think is simply thunder while others think it is an angel (v. 29). Jesus then explains the significance of the voice and its promise to "glorify" God's name. "Now is the judgment of this world; now the ruler of this world will be cast out. And I, when I am lifted up from the earth,

---

21. See Schuchard, *Scripture within Scripture*, 73–84. Maarten Menken, *Old Testament Quotations in the Fourth Gospel: Studies in Textual Form*, Contributions to Biblical Exegesis and Theology 15 (Kampen: Kok Pharos, 1996), 88–95. Both also consider the description in 1 Kings 1 where Solomon sits on David's own mule as the sign that he is David's heir. On the combination of Zeph 3:16 and Zech 9:9, see also Ruth Sheridan, *Retelling Scripture: 'The Jews' and the Scriptural Citations in John 1:19–12:15*, BibInt 110 (Leiden: Brill, 2012), 219–29.

22. From this time on, the Gospel will introduce Scripture with the formula, "This was to fulfill" (12:38, 39; 13:18; 15:25; 19:24, 28, 36, 37). Up until this point the introductory formula has been "as is written" (1:23; 2:17; 6:31; 6:45; 7:38-39; 10:34; and 12:15). An excellent study of these verses is Sheridan, *Retelling Scripture*.

23. For a discussion of this apocalyptic title, see the excursus "The Son of Man—ὁ υἱὸς τοῦ ἀνθρώπου," in Mary L. Coloe, *John 1–10*, WCS 44A (Collegeville, MN: Liturgical Press, 2021), 50.

¹⁹The Pharisees then said to one another, "You see, you can do nothing. Look, the world has gone after him!" ²⁰Now among those who went up to worship at the festival were some Greeks. ²¹They came to Philip, who was from Bethsaida in Galilee, and said to him, "Sir, we wish to see Jesus." ²²Philip went and told Andrew; then Andrew and Philip went and told Jesus. ²³Jesus answered them, "The hour has come for the Son of Man to be glorified. ²⁴Very truly, I tell you, unless a grain of wheat falls into the earth and dies, it remains just a single grain; but if it dies, it bears much fruit. ²⁵Those who love their life lose it, and those who hate their life in this world will keep it for eternal life. ²⁶Whoever serves me must follow me, and where I am, there will my servant be also. Whoever serves me, the Father will honor.

²⁷"Now my soul is troubled. And what should I say—'Father, save me from this hour'? No, it is for this reason that I have come to this hour. ²⁸Father, glorify your name." Then a voice came from heaven, "I have glorified it, and I will glorify it again." ²⁹The crowd standing there heard it and said that it was thunder. Others said, "An angel has spoken to him." ³⁰Jesus answered, "This voice has come for your sake, not for mine. ³¹Now is the judgment of this world; now the ruler of this world will be driven out. ³²And I, when I am lifted up from the earth, will draw all people to myself." ³³He said this to indicate the kind of death he was to die.

will draw all [πάντας] people to myself" (vv. 31-32).²⁴ The narrator then concludes this dense theological exchange with his explanation, "He said this to show what kind of death he was to die" (v. 33).

The perspective in this section continues the shift from the limited, nationalist hopes of the crowd to a cosmological judgment that the "ruler of this world" will now be vanquished, and linked to this "now" is the declaration that the hour, spoken of throughout the Gospel,²⁵ has arrived. The shift in perspective to a cosmological victory is triggered by the arrival of "some Greeks." Their arrival on the scene brings the first

24. There is disagreement in the manuscript tradition as to whether the terms should be πάντα (all things) or πάντας (all people). 𝔓⁶⁶ and א are strong witnesses to πάντα, and the cosmic dimension of Jesus's mission has just been announced, making "all things" a credible reading; but it is also possible that the final sigma was added by a copyist who found πάντα ambiguous. See the comments in Bruce M. Metzger, *A Textual Commentary on the Greek New Testament: A Companion Volume to the United Bible Societies' Greek New Testament*, 4th rev. ed. (London: United Bible Societies, 1994), 202.

25. John 2:4; 4:21, 23; 5:25, 28; 7:30; 8:20.

part of the Gospel, the Book of Signs, to its conclusion and announces the movement into the Book of Glory. The arrival of these Gentiles is so portentous that it draws into the narrative for the first time the heavenly voice of the Father.[26]

With the coming of the Greeks/Gentiles, Jesus's immediate response is to recognize that his "hour" has arrived, the human-one is to be glorified (12:23).[27] That this hour involves his death is made clear in the brief parable of the seed that must die in order to bear fruit (12:24). The parable accepts the belief that seeds "die" when planted since their form is lost, but this "death" then leads to a flourishing of life.[28] The grain is the active agent in this transformation, for it "falls" and "dies" and then "bears." While the words "grain" and "fruit" have masculine grammatical gender, the action of germination and bearing fruit is more readily imaged in the womb-nurturing and then the opening and life-producing labor of a woman.[29] The germination and life-bearing action of Jesus/Sophia will be the hour of his exaltation (12:32) and glorification, as the divine voice testifies (12:28), and this will bring about the defeat of "the ruler of this world" (12:31).

The coming of the Greeks, representative of "the world," as noted by the Pharisees, sets into motion the ultimate cosmic victory of God. The cosmic dimension of the coming struggle is indicated by the breaking into this world of the Father's voice (12:28). What appears to be a struggle

26. There is no heavenly voice at the description of Jesus's baptism, as in the Synoptics, nor does this Gospel have an account of the transfiguration, which also features a heavenly voice in the Synoptics.

27. With the exception of 5:27 and 9:35, the title ὁ υἱὸς τοῦ ἀνθρώπου has always been used with the cross in view (3:13, 14; 6:27, 53, 62; 8:28), and even 5:27 and 9:35 are linked to the cross through the themes of judgment and revelation. See Francis J. Moloney, *The Johannine Son of Man*, Biblioteca di Scienze Religiose 14, 2nd rev. ed. (Rome: LAS, 1978), 213. See also his recent work on this title "Son of Man" and its relation to Jesus's death in Francis J. Moloney, "The Johannine Son of Man Revisited," in *Theology and Christology in the Fourth Gospel*, ed. Gilbert Van Belle, Jan G. van der Watt, and P. J. Maritz, BETL 184 (Leuven: Peeters, 2005), 202.

28. Margaret Daly-Denton, *John: An Earth Bible Commentary; Supposing Him to Be the Gardener*, Earth Bible Commentary (London: Bloomsbury T&T Clark, 2017), 162.

29. More will be said of this image of birth when discussing John 16:21-22 and 19:34. A recent study of feminine imagery in depicting Jesus both in the New Testament and early church is Sally Douglas, *Early Church Understandings of Jesus as the Female Divine: The Scandal of the Scandal of Particularity*, LNTS 557 (London: Bloomsbury T&T Clark, 2016).

between Jesus and the Jewish authorities is in fact the final eschatological struggle between God and Satanic powers.[30]

Jewish thinking at this time considered that the world was under the dominion of a power of evil, named as Satan, the devil, Belial, and here the "ruler of this world."[31] Conventional Jewish eschatology expected that the reign of evil would one day be overcome by the power of God, through a savior figure who would engage in a final and decisive cosmic battle and whose victory would inaugurate the reign of God in peace and a full flourishing of life.[32] Jesus's announcement indicates that the time of this final battle has now arrived.

As a consequence of the defeat of the "ruler of this world" through the lifting up of Jesus in his hour, "all people/things [πάντα(ς)]" will be drawn to him (12:32). Jesus's death is not only for the people of Israel; it is for all. The coming of the Greeks/Gentiles in 12:20 proleptically testifies to the fruitfulness of the hour. The seed will fall into the ground, and when it dies it will bear much fruit. The explanatory comment by the narrator brings this section to closure by signaling that the term "lifted up" indicates, with artistic irony, that the hour is both the crucifixion and the exaltation of Jesus.[33]

---

30. Adele Reinhartz (*The Word in the World: The Cosmological Tale in the Fourth Gospel*, SBLMS 45 [Atlanta: Scholars Press, 1992], esp. 2–6) speaks of this aspect of the narrative as "the cosmological tale," to distinguish it from the "historical tale" of Jesus in the early part of the first century and the "ecclesial tale" of the Johannine community in the later part of the first century.

31. On Jewish understanding of the cosmic power of evil in the first century, see Loren T. Stuckenbruck, " 'Protect them from the Evil One' (John 17:15): Light from the Dead Sea Scrolls," in *John, Qumran, and the Dead Sea Scrolls: Sixty Years of Discovery and Debate*, ed. Mary L. Coloe and Tom Thatcher, EJL 32 (Atlanta: SBL, 2011), esp. 145–59. John A. Dennis (*Jesus' Death and the Gathering of True Israel: The Johannine Appropriation of Restoration Theology in the Light of John 11:47-52*, WUNT 2:217 [Tübingen: Mohr Siebeck, 2006], 208) comments, "In good apocalyptic fashion then in John 12:31 the narrator 'pulls back the curtains' to allow the reader to peer into the cosmic struggle that will take place at the cross event."

32. The theme of a cosmic battle is a common occurrence in apocalyptic literature. A helpful discussion of this theme in relation to John's Gospel can be found in Judith Kovacs, " 'Now Shall the Ruler of This World Be Driven Out': Jesus' Death as Cosmic Battle in John 12:20-36," *JBL* 114 (1995): 227–47.

33. Space does not permit further development of the major Johannine theme of "lifting up" to mean both death and exaltation, and the associated theme of glorification. Kovacs (ibid., 246) argues that these themes are part of the Johannine portrayal of Jesus's enthronement as King through the defeat of the "the ruler of this world." She writes, "For the evangelist, the glorification of 12:23 involves more than Jesus'

C. Concluding Reactions (vv. 34-43)

The passage so far has depicted two contrasting responses to Jesus. In the first section, the crowd fails to understand Jesus's messianic identity and role. They are limited by their nationalistic hopes. By contrast, the second section depicts some Greeks who come wishing to see Jesus. The third section opens with a typical misunderstanding by the crowd (12:34). They understand Jesus's statement of being lifted up from the earth as something akin to an ascension. This puzzles them. The comment from the crowd that the Christ, the Messiah, is to remain forever reveals that, with the raising of Lazarus, they had believed that the Messianic age had arrived. The resurrection of the dead had become part of Jewish thinking by the first century, at least for some. In Jewish writing contemporary with the New Testament we find evidence of a first-century theology linking the resurrection of the dead with the coming of the Messiah, such as: "And it shall come to pass after these things, when the time of the advent of the Messiah is fulfilled, that He shall return in glory. Then all who have fallen asleep in hope of Him shall rise again" (2 Bar. 30:1-2).[34] But in these Jewish perceptions of the Messiah there was no thought that this Messiah would then return to the heavens. The resurrection of Lazarus has led some to consider that Jesus might be the Messiah, but if Jesus is to be lifted up from the earth, i.e., return to the heavens, then that would disqualify him from being the Messiah since they *"have heard* from the law that the Christ remains forever" (12:34).[35]

---

return to the 'glory he had before' (John 17:5); the cross is not merely the metaphorical jumping off point for Jesus' reascent to his heavenly Father. It is the locus of a cosmic battle, in which Jesus achieves a decisive victory over Satan."

34. 2 Baruch is a compilation of independent writings belonging to various dates between 50 and 90 CE. For a detailed discussion of this complex text in its multiple versions, see Robert Henry Charles, "2 Bar 1:1–87:1," in *Pseudepigrapha of the Old Testament* (Bellingham, WA: Logos Research Systems, 2004), 470.

35. The understanding that the Messiah would remain forever likely draws on Psalm 89, which speaks of God's anointed one, David (v. 20), and promises that "his line shall continue forever" (LXX 88:29: εἰς τὸν αἰῶνα; cf. 88:4 Ἔως τοῦ αἰῶνος; 88:37 Τὸ σπέρμα αὐτοῦ εἰς τὸν αἰῶνα μενεῖ). Donald Juel (*Messianic Exegesis: Christological Interpretation of the Old Testament in Early Christianity* [Philadelphia: Fortress, 1988], 107–8) discusses this verse in light of first-century Jewish and early Christian exegesis. See also Jocelyn McWhirter, "Messianic Exegesis in the Fourth Gospel," in *Reading the Gospel of John's Christology as Jewish Messianism: Royal, Prophetic, and Divine Messiahs*, ed. Benjamin Reynolds and Gabriele Boccaccini, AJEC 106 (Leiden: Brill, 2018), 133–34.

[34]The crowd answered him, "We have heard from the law that the Messiah remains forever. How can you say that the Son of Man must be lifted up? Who is this Son of Man?" [35]Jesus said to them, "The light is with you for a little longer. Walk while you have the light, so that the darkness may not overtake you. If you walk in the darkness, you do not know where you are going. [36]While you have the light, believe in the light, so that you may become children of light."

After Jesus had said this, he departed and hid from them. [37]Although he had performed so many signs in their presence, they did not believe in him. [38]This was to fulfill the word spoken by the prophet Isaiah:

"Lord, who has believed our
message,
and to whom has the arm
of the Lord been
revealed?"

[39]And so they could not believe, because Isaiah also said,

Jesus then sums up the struggle depicted in this passage between himself and the crowd. From the opening scene, when they hail him as the King of Israel, their understanding has been limited by nationalistic hopes. Neither his actions nor his words have been able to change their perception. Using the image of "walking in the light" or "walking in the darkness," Jesus makes a final appeal to them to believe and so to become children of the light.[36]

Jesus's words are followed by the narrator's comments (12:37-41), which sum up the theological insight that this passage has revealed and pass a commentary on the entire public ministry of Jesus. The narrator cites two passages from Isaiah (53:1 and 6:10) that continue the contrast between belief and unbelief, blindness and sight. These narrative comments reflect the perplexity of the Johannine community as they try to make sense of the fact that Jesus, and the later gospel message, was unacceptable to many within Judaism, while the community's post-

---

36. The images of walking in darkness and walking in the light may be an allusion to Isa 50:10 where these same phrases occur at the close of the Third Servant Song. This possibility is strengthened by the fact that following Jesus's words the narrator cites Isa 53:1, which is part of the Fourth Servant Song. For more on the influence of the Servant Songs on John 12:20, see H. B. Kossen, "Who Were the Greeks of John XII.20?," in *Studies in John: Presented to Dr. J. N. Sevenster on the Occasion of His Seventieth Birthday,* ed. J. N. Sevenster, NovTSup 24 (Leiden: Brill, 1970), 103–4, and Johannes Beutler, "Greeks Come to See Jesus (John 12:20f.)," *Bib* 71 (1990): 341–42. See comments in the introduction and in chap. 3 on the symbolism of light and darkness in this Gospel.

40"He has blinded their eyes
and hardened their heart,
so that they might not look with
their eyes,
and understand with their heart
and turn—
and I would heal them."
41Isaiah said this because he saw his glory and spoke about him. 42Nevertheless many, even of the authorities, believed in him. But because of the Pharisees they did not confess it, for fear that they would be put out of the synagogue; 43for they loved human glory more than the glory that comes from God.

Easter mission to Gentiles was successful. How could this be possible? The narrator's answer is that this was to fulfill the Scriptures (12:38a).

The first citation in 12:38 is an exact citation of Isaiah 53:1 (LXX), part of the Fourth Servant Song which begins, "Behold my servant shall prosper; he shall be lifted up and glorified [ὑψωθήσεται καὶ δοξασθήσεται]" (Isa 52:13; author's translation). This one verse has in close proximity two themes found in John 12:19-33, namely, exaltation and glorification. The Song continues with the rejection of the servant (Isa 53:3) and his death and burial (Isa 53:8-9), and yet the servant will see his offspring, and from the anguish of his soul (τῆς ψυχῆς αὐτοῦ, Isa 53:11) he will see the light (φῶς), and his suffering will benefit many (πολλοῖς, Isa 53:11; πολλῶν, Isa 53:12). These words and themes are echoed in John 12. Like the servant, Jesus is rejected (12:37); his soul (ἡ ψυχή μου) is troubled (12:27); he speaks of himself as the light (τὸ φῶς, v. 35); and in his lifting up in death he will draw all (πάντα) to himself (v. 31). The citation of Isaiah 53:1 and the correspondence between the fates of the servant and Jesus identify that Jesus fulfills the role of the servant for all the nations (Isa 52:15),[37] the servant who is chosen and endowed with God's spirit (Isa 42:1).

37. The original MT of Isa 52:15 reads, "*That* [אשר] which has not been told them they shall see and *that* [אשר] which they have not heard they shall understand." The Septuagint version reads "*those who* have not yet come to knowledge of the Servant will see, and *those who* have not yet heard (about him) will hear." The Septuagint reading, in conjunction with the use of ἔθνη (Isa 52:15a), indicates the servant's broader mission to the Gentiles, which is consistent with the mission indicated in earlier Servant Songs. The term ἔθνη is used to speak of Gentiles, as distinct from the λαός, the people of God. See Georg Bertram, "ἔθνος, ἐθνικός," *TDNT* 2 (1964): 364–69. As John 12 depicts Gentiles approaching Jesus (vv. 20-21), the evangelist correctly claims that the words of Isaiah have been fulfilled (12:38).

Added to the citation from the Fourth Servant Song in John 12:38 is a second citation from Isaiah offering the narrator's judgment on why Israel could not believe. While the citation obviously draws on Isaiah 6:10, the Johannine text does not agree exactly with either the LXX or MT. A question then follows. Is the evangelist citing here from memory in a free manner or is he deliberately altering the text for his own purpose? Along with most scholars, I think that the evangelist is deliberately redacting Isaiah.[38]

> Make the heart of this people fat,
>   and their ears heavy,
>   and shut their eyes;
> lest they see with their eyes,
>   *and hear with their ears,*
> and understand with their hearts,
>   and turn and be healed. (Isa 6:10; author's translation)

> He has blinded their eyes
>   and hardened their heart,
> so that they might not look with their eyes,
>   and understand with their heart and turn—
>   and I would heal them. (John 12:40)

In leaving out the reference to hearing with their ears, the Gospel emphasizes the importance of correct sight, or seeing the signs and recognizing the glory of God now revealed in Jesus. By redacting the Isaian passage in this way, the evangelist has scriptural confirmation that "the Jews" in the Gospel narrative have been blinded and are therefore unable to perceive the signs correctly. The Scriptures of Israel thus confirm that, in some way, the rejection of Jesus by many of his own and the successful mission to the Gentiles is part of the mysterious plan of God. Unlike Paul, the Fourth Evangelist does not offer further explanation of this divine action and how it might be resolved in the future, but he does offer a glimmer of hope in the final comment by the narrator: "Nevertheless many, even of the authorities, believed in him" (v. 42). The added comment that they feared to confess this lest they be put out of the synagogue (v. 42) is a further indication that this passage is the evangelist's theological reflection on the later community's experience.

---

38. See Menken, *Old Testament Quotations*, 121, as well as 100 n.7 on pesher exegesis and 106 n. 26. See also Schuchard, *Scripture within Scripture*, 98–106; Catrin H. Williams, "Isaiah in John's Gospel," in *Isaiah in the New Testament*, ed. Steve Moyise and Maarten J. J. Menken, NTSI (London: T&T Clark, 2005), 109–15.

Writing toward the end of the first century the evangelist is dealing with two historical periods: the time of Jesus, where there is little evidence that he was involved in a Gentile mission, and the later time of the early Christian community, which quite obviously had been involved in such a mission since the time of Paul. The evangelist has negotiated this by turning to the ancient prophecies that in the final days Gentiles would be included within Israel's worshiping community. The Scripture citations, drawing on Zephaniah and Zechariah, evoke the eschatological theme of the gathering of the nations, and this is confirmed by the arrival of some Greeks. This leads to Jesus's recognition that his "hour" has come. This hour will be both his death and his glorification, and through the events of this hour the eschatological promises will be realized. The final citations from Isaiah comment on why Jesus (and the Gospel) was not received within Judaism and yet was received in the post-Easter mission to the Gentiles. The Fourth Gospel therefore remains within the parameters demanded by the life and ministry of the historical Jesus, while at the same time it proleptically speaks of the future fruitfulness (v. 25) of the Gentile mission in the time of the later community.

Epilogue (12:44-50)

These verses bring to conclusion the public ministry of Jesus and emphasize his authorization to teach as he has done. With echoes of the prologue Jesus refers to himself as the one sent by God, one who makes God visible in human form and thus can make God known (1:14, 18). His mission was to bring light into the world's darkness (1:4, 5) and to lead those who believe in him out of darkness into the light. In this lies salvation, to be released from the power of darkness (8:12; 12:35).[39] The word spoken by Jesus has the authority of a commandment by the Father, and while this commandment is for eternity life, it will also act as a judge on the last day for those rejecting Jesus and his word; for the

---

39. Craig Koester writes: "Although light and darkness may signify many things, the Gospel creates a literary framework that focuses their meaning without completely delimiting it. . . . Since light manifests the power and presence of God... the darkness refers to powers that oppose God: sin and evil" (*Symbolism in the Fourth Gospel: Meaning, Mystery, Community* [Minneapolis: Fortress, 1995], 124, 125). On the symbolism of "light" and "darkness" see Coloe, *John 1–10*, 26–27.

John 12:44-50

⁴⁴Then Jesus cried aloud: "Whoever believes in me believes not in me but in him who sent me. ⁴⁵And whoever sees me sees him who sent me. ⁴⁶I have come as light into the world, so that everyone who believes in me should not remain in the darkness. ⁴⁷I do not judge anyone who hears my words and does not keep them, for I came not to judge the world, but to save the world. ⁴⁸The one who rejects me and does not receive my word has a judge; on the last day the word that I have spoken will serve as judge, ⁴⁹for I have not spoken on my own, but the Father who sent me has himself given me a commandment about what to say and what to speak. ⁵⁰And I know that his commandment is eternal life. What I speak, therefore, I speak just as the Father has told me."

word of Jesus is, in fact, the word of the Father who sent him.[40] As the embodiment of Sophia, Jesus's testing will now begin.

> He calls the last end of the righteous happy,
> and boasts that God is his father.
> Let us see if his words are true. (Wis 2:16b-17)

When Jesus cries out (ἔκραξεν, v. 44), he voices the cry of Woman Wisdom who cried aloud in the public streets (κηρύσσεται, Prov 1:21; κηρύξεις, Prov 8:1). Sophia was given a command to "make your dwelling in Jacob, and in Israel receive your inheritance" (Sir 24:8), but according to the book of Enoch, she was rejected. "Wisdom/*Sophia* went out in order to dwell among the sons of men, but did not find a dwelling. Wisdom returned to her place, and took her seat in the midst of the Angels" (1 En. 42:1-2).[41] Jesus/Sophia has come to his own and has not been received (John 1:11). Now, like Wisdom, he begins his return to the One who sent him. But first, he must offer final teaching to his disciples and prepare them for his departure.

40. Peder Borgen ("The Use of Tradition in John 12:44-50," *NTS* 26 [1979]: 18–35) explores the strong sense of agency in these verses and sees some similarity with the depiction of Moses in Sirach 45:5 which reads, "He allowed him [Moses] to hear his voice, and led him into the dark cloud and gave him the commandments face to face, the law of life and knowledge, so that he might teach Jacob the covenant and Israel his decree" (32).

41. John Ashton, "The Transformation of Wisdom: A Study of the Prologue of John's Gospel," *NTS* 32 (1986): 168–69.

John 13–17

Sophia's Banquet: Overview

[My Beloved] brought me to the banqueting house,
and his intention toward me was love. (Song 2:4)

Now before the festival of the Passover, Jesus knew that his hour had come
to depart from this world and go to the Father. Having loved his own who
were in the world, he loved them to the end. (John 13:1)

These words (13:1) announce a major shift from the public ministry of Jesus, known as the Book of Signs (chaps. 2–12), to his final days, known as the Book of Glory (chaps. 13–20 [21]). Passover is approaching, the third Passover according to Johannine chronology (2:13; 6:3); Jesus's hour, referred to frequently in the narrative, has arrived,[1] and the depths of Jesus's love of his own is made clear. God's love for the world (3:16), the Father's love of his Son (15:9; 17:23), and Jesus's love of his friends (15:9) emphasize that love is a leitmotif of this Gospel and will be given heightened focus in these final chapters.[2] Before offering a

---

1. John 2:4; 7:30; 8:20; 12:23, 27.
2. A rich analysis of the "love" motif can be found in Francis J. Moloney, *Love in the Gospel of John: An Exegetical, Theological, and Literary Study* (Grand Rapids: Baker Academic, 2013), 394–411, here 410.

formal commentary on the text, I begin by examining the nature, genre, and composition of chapters 13–17.

Beginning in chapter 13 and concluding in chapter 17 there is one setting in time and space. Jesus presides at a meal surrounded by "his own." It is a meal of farewell and so is often likened to other farewell meals in the OT and other noncanonical Jewish literature, and compared with the Testament tradition. But it does not fit comfortably within that genre.[3] It is called "discourse," but chapter 13 is a narrative describing Jesus washing the feet of those at table with him and engaging in dialogue with Peter and Judas, while chapter 17 is a prayer. A discourse more formally begins at 14:1 and ends with chapter 16. While the theme and setting is the departure of Jesus, his teaching looks beyond his personal experience to the future experience of the disciples in his absence. The disciples are mainly silent, with only the occasional question or comment breaking into the narrative (14:5, 8, 22; 16:17, 18, 29), but their presence needs to be kept in view, in spite of their silence. These chapters provide a final interpretation of what is about to happen in Jesus's arrest and crucifixion. What does the cross mean? Where is God? The discourse chapters provide insight/foresight into the meaning of the cross and resurrection—even if this is veiled in narrative time, until the gift of the Spirit allows deeper comprehension in the light of the Scriptures and the memory of Jesus's teaching. In one sense, the discourse is best understood in retrospect. This retrospective understanding is particularly important for chapters 13 and 14. These two chapters cannot fully be understood until the "hour" is brought to completion in chapters 19 and 20.

The discourse shows some obvious signs of being developed gradually, even though the final form displays a literary unity.[4] Chapters 13 and 14 appear to come to a conclusion with the words, "Rise, let us be

3. See the sidebar on the testament tradition on p. 358.
4. Speaking of these chapters as a literary unit does not deny the complex development of the text. This development allows the author to write an initial draft or even drafts before achieving the final form of the narrative. A detailed study of the possible historical development of individual units can be found in Fernando F. Segovia, *The Farewell of the Word: The Johannine Call to Abide* (Minneapolis: Fortress, 1991), esp. 283–329. See also John Painter, "The Farewell Discourses and the History of Johannine Christianity," *NTS* 27 (1981): 525–43. Painter (526) argues for three separate strata within the discourse material written in response to different crises faced by the community: 13:31–14:31; 15:1–16:4a; 16:4b-33. Whatever the historical origins of the material, the final form shows a unified literary structure that needs to include all of chap. 13.

on our way" (14:31), which can lead seamlessly into "After Jesus had spoken these words, he went out with his disciples across the Kidron valley" (18:1). It seems that chapters 15, 16, and 17 have been added to an original two-chapter discourse (13 and 14). There are shifts and changes of themes in these three chapters giving rise to theories of at least one, if not two, further additions by the same author/evangelist; these additions were made necessary perhaps through a lack of understanding by the receiving community, so more clarification is needed, or because of a change in the historical circumstances of the Johannine community. More will be said on this at the beginning of chapter 15.

When we come to this final meal, the Johannine setting is not the same as the "Last Supper" in the Synoptic Gospels. It is not a Passover meal, for this supper takes place the night before the Passover lamb is slain. It is simply a meal. There is no mention of "the twelve" who are named in the Synoptics (Matt 26:20; Mark 14:17; Luke 22:3, 30). Instead of "the twelve," the Fourth Gospel names "his own" (13:1) and his disciples (13:5, 22, 23, 35; 15:8; 16:17, 29). In our imaginative reading it would be an inaccurate understanding of the Johannine Gospel if one limited these disciples only to men or only to "the twelve." Unfortunately Christian art has often shaped the interpretation of this final meal instead of an accurate reading of the text. The meal begins with a statement of Jesus gathering his own and naming them as ones he has loved. Included in this group of beloved ones must be Mary and Martha of Bethany since the text states that these are women whom Jesus loved (11:5), along with their brother Lazarus (11:3). In Mark's Gospel we read of a number of women present at the crucifixion, "looking on from a distance; among them were Mary Magdalene, and Mary the mother of James the younger and of Joses, and Salome. These used to follow [ἠκολούθουν] him and provided for him when he was in Galilee; and there were many other women who had come up with him to Jerusalem" (Mark 15:40-41). Discipleship could be defined by the use of the verb "to follow" (ἀκολουθέιν). While the Fourth Gospel does not name women as following Jesus, it is obvious that some have, since they are present at the cross: "standing near the cross of Jesus were his mother, and his mother's sister, Mary the wife of Clopas, and Mary Magdalene" (John 19:25). It is highly probable that these women were also at the supper, even if they are not named. Along with the silent presence of women disciples at this supper are likely other silent male disciples such as Andrew (1:40) and Nathanael (1:46-49). In all the mention of disciples in the following discourse and commentary I am presuming the participation of women.

Women at the Last Supper

Including women in this final meal is an important corrective to centuries of excluding women from the table, particularly the eucharistic table. But this is not just a woman's interpretation for ideological purposes; it is also truthful and accurate according to the Gospel narratives and first-century liturgical context of a Passover meal—a household meal.

In reading the Synoptic accounts of the Last Supper literally, there is an appearance that there were only twelve men when we read in Mark, "When it was evening, he came with the twelve" (14:17).[5] But a literal reading ignores the narrative context where this mention of twelve is included within references to *disciples*: "The Teacher asks, 'Where is my guest room where I may *eat the Passover with my disciples*?' " (Mark 14:14), followed later by, "They went to a place called Gethsemane; and he said to his disciples" (Mark 14:32).[6] Matthew, even though speaking of "the twelve" at the table, then writes, "While they were eating, Jesus took a loaf of bread, and after blessing it he broke it, gave it to the *disciples*" (Matt 26:26).

The narrative context of disciples before and after what is called the "institution narrative," as well as Matthew's inclusion of *disciples*, speaks for a visualization of this scene as Jesus with a group of his disciples, and not the Leonardo da Vinci painting. Added to this, the socio-religious context of a household Passover meal makes nonsense of any imaging of the Last Supper with Jesus surrounded by just twelve men. As a household meal, women, men, and children would have participated.

Recalling this Passover meal, as it would have occurred, and then writing into the narrative the number "twelve" is for the distinctly theological purpose of linking this meal with the original Sinai covenant with Moses and the whole people of Israel. All the Synoptic Gospels describe the cup as "the blood of the covenant," with Luke describing it as a "new" covenant (Luke 22:20). Those not familiar with the Sinai covenant ceremony may not know that as part of the ritual Moses "wrote down all

5. Similarly Matt 24:20: "When it was evening, he took his place with the twelve"; and Luke 22:14: "When the hour came, he took his place at the table, and the apostles with him." Luke equates "the apostles" with "the twelve"; see 6:13; 9:1 with 9:10; 16:1 with 17:5; 22:11, 14.

6. Similarly Luke 22:39: "He came out and went, as was his custom, to the Mount of Olives; and the disciples followed him."

the words of the Lord. He rose early in the morning, and built an altar at the foot of the mountain, and set up *twelve* pillars, corresponding to the *twelve* tribes of Israel" (Exod 24:4). Here is the meaning of *the twelve* at the Last Supper— not a literal counting of those present, but a symbolic number representing all the people to be gathered into Jesus's covenant-making action to take place through his death the next day.

Along with mistaken and literal readings of this event, there is also the false interpretation of Jesus's words and actions as an "ordination" of *the twelve* into the priesthood— this is how Holy Thursday is often and wrongly celebrated. We know that the community continued to "do this" in celebrating the Lord's Supper for at least a century when there were no priests named as such and no ritual called an ordination. In the New Testament the only priests are Jewish. The letter to the Hebrews applies the symbolism of the Jewish high priest to Jesus—but there are no Christian priests in the first century. Here we need to be aware that the term "priest" (ἱερεύς) in both Judaism and pagan religions meant an official linked to the killing of an animal in a temple.

Within the New Testament the primary description of Christian worship was the "Lord's supper" (1 Cor 11:20). This was a meal celebrated within a house, and there is no indication who presided over this meal—it may have been the owner of the house, or a travelling missionary, or an early disciple if one was present—all roles that include women.

The first time there is any mention of who led the Eucharist is in the Didache (ca. 100), and in this text the presider is called a "prophet": "But permit the prophets to offer thanksgiving as much as they desire" (Did. 10:7). "Every first fruit then of the produce of the wine-vat and of the threshing-floor, of thy oxen and of thy sheep, thou shalt take and give as the first fruit to the prophets; for they are your chief-priests" (Did. 13:3). Within the New Testament, named women held all of these roles: prophet, householder, travelling missionary, apostle.[7]

7. For more details and discussion of the historical influences that led to the subjugation of women, see Mary L. Coloe, "'A Matter of Justice and Necessity': Women's Participation in the Catholic Church," *Compass: A Journal of Topical Theology* 45 (2011): 13–18. Available at http://marycoloe.org.au/homepage/Compass%202011%20A%20Matter%20of%20Justice.pdf.

Testaments

There is a tradition of leaders giving departing words to their followers, known as a "Testament."[8] Biblical examples can be seen in Jacob's final words to and blessing of his sons (Gen 49); Moses's final words to the people of Israel in the book of Deuteronomy, especially chapter 34; and the prayer of Jesus ben Sirach (Sir 51). But while there are similarities between John 13–17 and the Jewish testament tradition, there are other quite unique features that have been described as "genre bending."[9] First, through his passion, Jesus is returning to where he once was; in fact, Jesus never speaks of his approaching death but speaks instead of his homecoming to the Father (13:1, 3; 14:12; 16:10, 17, 28; 17:11). Second, Jesus's passion is a process not of death but of glorification.[10] Third, John 13–17 exhibits clearly what has been a feature of this Gospel, namely, the blurring of time and space. Finally, Jesus's words depart from the traditional "blessing" form and are words of commission, as the disciples are sent as the Father sent Jesus (17:18). In addition to these four features discussed by Harold Attridge, a further unique aspect that sets these chapters apart from the testament tradition is the gift of "another Paraclete" (14:16) to remain with the disciples.[11]

---

8. Fernando Segovia provides a helpful summary of the "testament" or "farewell type-scene." Although the "prayer of a dying hero" is part of the farewell type-scene, Segovia did not include John 17 in this volume because of its length; also he intended to make a detailed study of the prayer in a separate volume. See Segovia, *The Farewell of the Word*, esp. chap. 1.

9. See the discussion in Harold W. Attridge, "Genre Bending in the Fourth Gospel," *JBL* 121 (2002): 3–21.

10. As George L. Parsenios, " 'No Longer in the World' (John 17:11): The Transformation of the Tragic in the Fourth Gospel," *HTR* 98 (2005): 14, says: "For, Jesus does not stand on the threshold between life and death, but on the threshold between life and glorification in new life—the resurrection and ascension."

11. These features will be discussed further in relation to the Gospel text.

John 13:1-38

Sophia's Gifts

Sophia will come to meet them like a mother . . . ,
She will feed them with the bread of learning,
and give them the water of wisdom to drink. (Sir 15:1-3)

There is narrative continuity between chapters 12, 13, and 14. In chapter 12 Jesus was in Bethany, and Mary, the sister of Lazarus, knelt at his feet and anointed them. In chapter 13 Jesus imitates her action by kneeling at the feet of disciples to wash their feet. Then chapter 14 announces the many dwellings in "my Father's house" (14:2), a term used earlier to refer to the Jerusalem temple (2:16). Prior to entering the temple, footwashing was required. This religious and cultural background needs to be part of an alert reading of John 13.

There are many different views on the sources, history of development, and structure of John 13.[1] Alongside these differing views are opinions

---

1. For a brief summary of the various approaches to John 13–17 within the past century, see Fernando F. Segovia, *Love Relationships in the Johannine Tradition: Agape/Agapan in 1 John and the Fourth Gospel*, SBLDS 58 (Missoula: Scholars Press, 1982), 82–96. For a discussion on the possible development of this passage from a pre-Johannine narrative to its current form, see Jean Zumstein, *Kreative Erinnerung: Relecture und Auslegung im Johannesevangelium*, ATANT (Zürich: TVZ, 2004), 168–76.

on how to understand Jesus's act of footwashing. The text itself appears to offer two different interpretations:[2]

1. Verses 6-11 promise understanding of the meaning later, a reference to a time after the events of Jesus's "hour" (see 2:22; 12:16). These verses also suggest that this act of footwashing enables the disciples to participate in Jesus's "hour."[3]

2. Verses 12-15 then appear to offer a second interpretation—that Jesus's action is a "model" that disciples are to emulate.

I begin by establishing a structure for the chapter, then I present a narrative reading of the text, and finally I offer an interpretation.

Structuring the Narrative[4]

The initial three verses of chapter 13 are a small prologue introducing the second part of the Gospel, the "hour" of Jesus (chaps. 13–20 [21]), and, more specifically, his final meal (13:1–17:26).[5] Following this "mini" prologue, the narrative proper starts with the action of Jesus washing the feet of his disciples (vv. 4-5). This action leads into the description of Jesus's final meal (vv. 6-38). The symbolism of the footwashing offers a theological introduction to the discourse and prayer that follow (14:1–17:26).

---

2. Raymond E. Brown, *The Gospel According to John*, 2 vols., AB 29–29A (New York: Doubleday, 1966, 1970), 2:558–62; Francis J. Moloney, *Glory not Dishonor: Reading John 13–21* (Minneapolis: Fortress, 1998), 1–2. For a summary of the discussions on these two views, see John C. Thomas, *Footwashing in John 13 and the Johannine Community*, JSOTSup 61 (Sheffield: JSOT Press, 1991), 11–17.

3. In R. Alan Culpepper's words, "The foot washing scene, therefore, functions metaphorically and proleptically in relation to Jesus' death" ("The Johannine *Hypodeigma*: A Reading of John 13," *Semeia* 53 [1991]: 133–52, here 139).

4. There is no agreement on the structure of this chapter. Although my proposal has been influenced by the work of Frédéric Manns ("Le Lavement des Pieds. Essai sur la structure et la signification de Jean 13," *RSR* 55 [1981]: 149–69), I differ from him in separating the action of the footwashing (vv. 4-5) from the subsequent discussion.

5. Both Manns and Culpepper liken these verses to a prologue; see Manns, "Le Lavement," 151; R. Alan Culpepper, *The Gospel and Letters of John*, IBT (Nashville: Abingdon, 1998), 203. For links between John 1:1-18 and 13:1-3, see Mary L. Coloe, "Welcome in the Household of God: The Footwashing in John 13," *CBQ* 66 (2004): 401.

The brevity of the description of the action (vv. 4-5) is not unusual in this Gospel in which Jesus's deeds are termed σημεῖα (signs, 2:11; 4:34) and a discourse follows the action to interpret the meaning of the signs.[6] This pattern continues in chapter 13, where, following the footwashing, the rest of the chapter is primarily discourse and dialogue showing a structure of reverse parallelism—A, B, C, C′, B′, A′. There are two major sections in the chapter: verses 6-20, which move from Peter to Judas, and verses 21-38, which move in reverse from Judas to Peter. Central to both sections are Jesus's teaching and gifts of a model (v. 15) and a new commandment (v. 34).

The diagram below shows this structure:

The Prologue to the "Hour" (vv. 1-3)

The Footwashing (vv. 4-5)

    A. Dialogue with Peter (vv. 6-11)

       B. Teaching and gift (vv. 12-15)

          C. The Betrayer (vv. 16-20)

          C′. The Betrayer (vv. 21-30)

       B′. Second Teaching and gift (vv. 31-35)

    A′. Dialogue with Peter (vv. 36-38)

Although most commentators conclude the footwashing at verse 30, following the departure of Judas, there are sound structural and thematic reasons for including verses 31-38 within the footwashing pericope.[7] The departure of Judas makes a break between verses 21-30 and what follows, but this break simply concludes the unit (vv. 21-30). Judas's departure sets in motion Jesus's arrest and crucifixion, which are presented in this Gospel as the "hour" of Jesus's glorification (12:23). His departure is the catalyst for Jesus's exultant cry to the Father (13:31), and it follows that Jesus's words to the Father, with their theme of glorification, are necessarily linked to Judas's betrayal and the cross.

---

6. John 5 and 9 show a similar brief description of Jesus's actions leading into a long discourse.

7. For arguments that tie vv. 31-38 to the discourse material, see, e.g., John Painter, "The Farewell Discourses and the History of Johannine Christianity," *NTS* 27 (1981): 526, 529–30; Brown, *The Gospel according to John*, 2:545–47; Segovia, *Love Relationships*, 136–79.

The discussion with Peter in verses 36-38, in which Peter queries Jesus's statement about following him, parallels the discussion in verses 6-11, in which Peter queries Jesus's action of washing his feet. The reference to the "giving" (δίδωμι) of the commandment in verse 34 recalls the giving (ἔδωκα) of the ὑπόδειγμα ("example, model") in verse 15. Frédéric Manns also argues for the unity of the entire chapter and points to an *inclusio* formed by the use of "lay down, or lay aside" (τίθημι, vv. 4 and 38).[8] These structural features situate verses 31-38 within the footwashing narrative as the pericope's conclusion. Verses 31-38 look back to the footwashing, and 14:1 initiates an *inclusio* with what follows, marked by the repetition of the phrase "Do not let your hearts be troubled" (14:1, 27). Even though there is no change in scene, time, or characters, 14:1 marks the beginning of a new stage in the discourse.

The Prologue to the "Hour" (13:1-3)

Throughout the first part of the Gospel, there have been many references to a future time called the "hour" (2:4; 7:30; 8:20; 12:23, 27), which is now mentioned here within the context of love. As 12:27 noted, this "hour" brings to a climax the purpose of Jesus's life, which has already been described as a gift of divine love (3:16). Now the fullness of that love is to be shown.[9] This is Sophia's banquet (Prov 9:1), where Jesus acts as both host and servant with no dichotomy in these roles because it is a meal of love. The prologue to the Gospel stated that "he came to his own [εἰς τὰ ἴδια], but his own did not receive him" (1:11; author's translation); now he gathers those of "his own" (τοὺς ἰδίους) who have received him (13:1). These have been promised that they would be given the "power to become children of God" (1:12), and the mention of "his own" recalls this promise, even as the reader waits to see how the narrative will show this being accomplished. The expression "his own" with its evocation of intimacy, trust, and friendship highlights the enormity of Judas's betrayal (13:2).

8. Manns, "Le Lavement," 151.

9. At this point I am giving the expression εἰς τέλος, which can be translated "to the end" or "to the full," its qualitative sense. The temporal sense of the root word is most profoundly revealed in Jesus's dying word, τετέλεσται, "It is finished" (19:30). According to Culpepper, "The *double entendre* serves the vital function of linking the footwashing to Jesus's death and interpreting Jesus's action as the culmination of his love for his own." Culpepper, "The Johannine *Hypodeigma*," 136.

John 13:1-3

¹³:¹Now before the festival of the Passover, Jesus knew that his hour had come to depart from this world and go to the Father. Having loved his own who were in the world, he loved them to the end. ²The devil had already put it into the heart of Judas son of Simon Iscariot to betray him. And during supper ³Jesus, knowing that the Father had given all things into his hands, and that he had come from God and was going to God,

Verse 2 contains two serious textual and grammatical difficulties: (1) the time of the footwashing in relation to the meal and (2) the identity of the one in whose heart (καρδίαν) the treachery is conceived. The expression δείπνου γινομένου does not necessarily mean that the meal has begun, and Rudolph Bultmann translates this phrase "on the occasion of a meal."[10] The meal may not yet have started, but the use of the term "again" (πάλιν) in verse 12 indicates that all have taken their places at the table. If one accepts Bultmann's translation on grammatical and contextual grounds, one could place the footwashing before the beginning of the meal. This interpretation makes better cultural sense, because it was customary for guests to have their feet washed prior to the meal (cf. Luke 7:44).

R. Alan Culpepper recognizes in verse 2 a Semitic idiom which he translates, "The devil had already made up his mind that Judas should betray him."[11] Culpepper's rendering makes clear that it is the *heart* of the devil (διάβολος), not Judas, that is the object of "had put into" (βεβληκότος εἰς). This reading also makes sense of verse 27, which reports that the devil entered into Judas "after the morsel." Furthermore, Culpepper's translation sets up the contrast between the mind/heart of Jesus (v. 1) and the mind/heart of the devil (v. 2).

10. Rudolph Bultmann, *The Gospel of John: A Commentary*, trans. G. R. Beasley Murray et al. (Oxford: Blackwell, 1971), 465 n. 2. Similarly, Édouard Delebecque, *Évangile de Jean: Texte traduit et annoteé*, CahRB 23 (Paris: Gabalda, 1987), 183.

11. Culpepper, "The Johannine *Hypodeigma*," 136; see also Moloney, *Glory not Dishonor*, 3 n. 39, and Marianne Meye Thompson, *John: A Commentary*, NTL (Louisville: Westminster John Knox, 2015), 284–85. For a discussion on this grammatical form and its background in Hellenistic Greek, see Delebecque, *Évangile de Jean*, 183. Delebecque states emphatically, "le cœur n'est pas celui de Judas, mais du diable." The conjunction ἵνα introduces a new clause about Judas, not linked grammatically to the word heart, καρδίαν.

The Footwashing (13:4-5)

The scene is described very sparsely in two parallel clauses:

[Jesus]
(v. 4) rose from the supper *and* laid aside his garments *and* taking a *towel girded* (διαζώννυμι) himself;
(v. 5) poured water into a bowl *and* began to wash the feet of his disciples *and* to dry them with the *towel* with which he was *girded* (διαζώννυμι).

In full awareness of the "hour" (v. 1), Jesus acts with a solemn and deliberative gesture toward the disciples who have spent time with him. The description of his "laying down" (τίθησιν) and later "taking up" (v. 12, ἔλαβεν) his garments recalls the image of Jesus the Good Shepherd, who is able to "lay down" (τίθησιν, 10:11, 15, 17, 18) and "take up" his life (λάβω, 10:17, 18). The laying down and taking up of life is a free and deliberate act by the shepherd, "No one takes it from me, but I lay it down of my own accord. I have power to lay it down, and I have power to take it up again" (10:18). These introductory words (13:4-5), overlaid with the words of the Good Shepherd, make it clear "that what follows is not simply a good example in humility but a prophetic action which will reveal the true meaning of Jesus's loving his own unto the end (13:1) in fulfillment of his mission to bring to completion the salvific intention of God's boundless love for the world (cf. 3:16-17)."[12]

Footwashing in the NT culture was performed on occasions such as "(1) cultic settings, (2) domestic settings for personal hygiene and comfort, and (3) domestic settings devoted to hospitality."[13] By the first century CE, while it may have been most unusual for a host to personally wash the feet of his guests, the action could be seen in the light of Abraham's hospitality. According to Manns, footwashing had a particular religious significance within Judaism as it recalled the hospitality shown by Abraham in welcoming his divine guests under the oaks of Mamre (Gen 18:4).[14] While the original Hebrew text portrayed Abraham merely

---

12. Sandra M. Schneiders, "The Foot Washing (John 13:1-20): An Experiment in Hermeneutics," *CBQ* 43 (1981): 76–92, here 81. The interpretation of this prophetic action will follow below.

13. Thomas, *Footwashing in John 13*, 27. So also Arland Hultgren, "The Johannine Footwashing (13.1-11) as Symbol of Eschatological Hospitality," *NTS* 28 (1982): 541.

14. Manns, "Le Lavement," 160.

John 13:4-5

⁴got up from the table, took off his outer robe, and tied a towel around himself. ⁵Then he poured water into a basin and began to wash the disciples' feet and to wipe them with the towel that was tied around him.

providing water for his guests to wash their own feet,[15] by the first-century Testament of Abraham, this tradition had developed to present Abraham himself washing the feet of the guests as an act of gracious hospitality.[16] Culturally, and within the Jewish religious traditions, there is evidence to suggest that a first-century community would understand the footwashing first as a gesture of hospitality and welcome.

Footwashing also had a cultic purpose, for it was necessary to wash one's feet before entering the precincts of the temple. The Mishnah records that a person could not enter the Temple Mount with staff, sandals, wallet, "or with the dust upon his feet" (m. Ber. 9:5). This cultic purpose predates the compilation of the Mishnah since the first-century Jewish philosopher Philo offers a number of comments on the practice of footwashing prior to entering the presence of God: "one should not enter with unwashed feet on the pavement of the Temple of God" (*QE Sup* 2.1.2). In a treatise on special laws commenting on the washing of the sacrificial victim Philo transfers the significance of the washing to the person offering the sacrifice. "By the washing of the feet is meant that his steps should be no longer on earth but tread the upper air" (*Spec. Laws* 1.207). These comments indicate that footwashing was a customary gesture in the first century prior to entering the temple, which the Mishnah will later encode.[17] The precedent for washing one's feet prior to entering the temple was established in Moses's instructions that Aaron and his sons should wash their hands and feet prior to entering the tent of meeting or approaching the altar (Exod 30:17-21; cf. 2 Chr 4:6; Ps 25:6).

15. "Let a little water be brought, and wash your feet, and rest yourselves under the tree" (Gen 18:4).

16. "Then Abraham went forward and washed the feet of the Commander-in chief, Michael. Abraham's heart was moved and he wept over the stranger" (T. Ab. 2:9).

17. This same conclusion is reached by Herold Weiss with regard both to Hellenistic synagogue practice and also the Jerusalem temple: "The notion that in order to walk on the pavement of the temple disciples were supposed to have washed their feet was a well-established and recognized one in the Judaism of the second temple" ("Foot Washing in the Johannine Community," *NovT* 21 [1979]: 298–325).

In discussing footwashing as a gesture of welcome into a house and also as the prelude to entering the temple, the artistry of the Fourth Evangelist is apparent, for these two aspects of "house" and "temple" come together in Johannine theology. In the OT, the most frequent name of the temple was the "house of God,"[18] and Jesus calls the temple "my Father's house" (2:16). Following the footwashing in chapter 13, Jesus will explain to his disciples the meaning of "my Father's house/hold" (14:2 and following). Washing the feet of the disciples he loved (chap. 13) prepared them for entering into the Father's house/temple (14:2) described in the following chapter. [19]

A. First Dialogue with Peter (13:6-11)

The meaning of Jesus's action is not clear to the disciples, and Peter's words could well voice the discomfort of the entire group, "Lord, *you* wash my feet?" Peter's difficulty is not with having his feet washed *per se* but with having them washed by Jesus. Peter perceives this as a degrading act for Jesus to perform, for it was customary that a slave would bring a bowl of water and a person would wash his or her own feet.[20] Jesus then states that his action will not be understood until a "later" time (v. 7).

On several occasions in the narrative, there have been indicators that the participants in the story will not fully understand their experience until after Jesus's death and resurrection (2:22; 12:16).[21] In both cases understanding occurs as a recollection, a remembering, and both cases also involve the Scriptures. This retrospective understanding is seen as a particular function of the Paraclete, who will "teach you everything, and remind you of all that I have said to you" (14:26). It is only in the "later" post-Easter time, when the community has the gift of the Paraclete, that the fullness of understanding will be possible. Jean Zumstein comments, "The Paraclete is the memory of Jesus in progress, the post-Easter ret-

---

18. The terminology בית יהוה (*bayt YHWH*) occurs 231 times while the expression היכל (*hekal*) occurs sixty times.

19. Remember that the Gospel was written without chapter divisions, so the footwashing flowed seamlessly into "my Father's house" (14:2).

20. In the scriptural instances, a person usually washes his or her own feet, whereas in the Greco-Roman world this act of washing would be done by a slave. See Thomas, *Footwashing in John 13*, 35–42, 46–56.

21. See also 8:27; 10:6.

⁶He came to Simon Peter, who said to him, "Lord, are you going to wash my feet?" ⁷Jesus answered, "You do not know now what I am doing, but later you will understand." ⁸Peter said to him, "You will never wash my feet." Jesus answered, "Unless I wash you, you have no share with me." ⁹Simon Peter said to him, "Lord, not my feet only but also my hands and my head!" ¹⁰Jesus said to him, "One who has bathed does not need to wash, except for the feet, but is entirely clean. And you are clean, though not all of you." ¹¹For he knew who was to betray him; for this reason he said, "Not all of you are clean."

rospect upon the incarnate Christ."²² In this pericope, the disciples will grasp the meaning of Jesus's act of footwashing only after his death.

In response to Peter's objection, Jesus begins to unfold the meaning *he* gives to this action. "Unless I wash you, you have no share [μέρος] with me" (v. 8). The term used here, μέρος, implies the sense of "share in my inheritance," "participate with," or "be drawn into my destiny."²³ Footwashing is an invitation to the disciples to become participants with Jesus in his "hour." As he, with deliberate foreknowledge, moves from this world to his Father, they too are invited to be involved. That the term μέρος involves Jesus's future death, presented as his departure (v. 1), is born out in the parallel section. Jesus says to Peter, "Where I am going, you cannot follow me now; but you will follow afterward" (v. 36). The "now" is the "hour" of Jesus, but by having a part/μέρος with him, disciples will also be included, in ways they do not yet understand.

B. Jesus's First Teaching and Gift (13:12-15)

The next section (vv. 12-15) and its parallel (vv. 31-35) introduce the idea of gift giving. In verses 12-15, Jesus says, "I have given [ἔδωκα] you

---

22. "Der Paraklet ist die im Vollzug begriffene Anamnese Jesu, die österliche Retrospektion des inkarnierten Christus" (Jean Zumstein, "Der Prozess der Relecture in der Johanneischen Literatur," *NTS* 42 [1996]: 394–411, here 410). Zumstein also notes that the small prologue (13:1-3) establishes that the footwashing needs to be understood retrospectively in the light of "the hour." See Zumstein, *Kreative Erinnerung*, 166.

23. Brown, *The Gospel according to John*, 2:565.

John 13:12-15

¹²After he had washed their feet, had put on his robe, and had returned to the table, he said to them, "Do you know what I have done to you? ¹³You call me Teacher and Lord—and you are right, for that is what I am. ¹⁴So if I, your Lord and Teacher, have washed your feet, you also ought to wash one another's feet. ¹⁵For I have set you an example, that you also should do as I have done to you.

a model,"²⁴ and he teaches, "what I have done, you also do" (v. 15). The parallel unit concludes with Jesus's giving (δίδωμι) a new commandment, "love each other as I have loved" (v. 34). A more precise translation shows this parallelism:

A model I have given to you	A new commandment I give to you—love one another
so that just as I did to you	so that just as I loved you
you also will do. (v. 15)	you also will love each other. (v. 34)

The two "gifts" link both units, as do Jesus's instructions—"as I have done [καθὼς] you also do" (vv. 15, 34); "wash each other's feet" (v. 14); "love each other" (v. 34).

Jesus instructs the disciples that they too should wash each other's feet, that what he has given them is a "model" (ὑπόδειγμα)—though what he means by this is not yet clear to them. In the New Testament, the term ὑπόδειγμα is found only here (John 13), in Hebrews (4:11; 8:6; 9:23), 2 Peter (2:6), and James (5:10). In these texts, it is usually translated as "example," which is commonly understood in ethical terms as a good example of humility or a model of exemplary death.²⁵ But it has a further usage in the Old Testament, which I consider to be even more significant for understanding why the Gospel uses this term to describe Jesus's action.

---

24. The NRSV translation *"set* you an *example"* does not accurately reflect the Greek ὑπόδειγμα γὰρ ἔδωκα ὑμῖν, "I have *given* a *model* to you."

25. In his discussion of the term ὑπόδειγμα, Culpepper cites a number of passages in Jewish literature, where the word is used "to exhort the faithful to mark an exemplary death": 2 Macc 6:28, 31; 4 Macc 17:23; Sir 44:16. See Culpepper, "The Johannine *Hypodeigma,*" 142–43; also Heinrich Schlier, "ὑπόδειγμα," *TDNT* 2 (1964): 32–33.

In looking to the OT background the words παράδειγμα and ὑπόδειγμα are interchangeable,[26] and in the LXX we find them used in two senses. They can be used to describe human behavior, and so Enoch is presented as an example of repentance (Sir 44:16), and similarly the Maccabean martyrs are held up as examples in their fidelity unto death (2 Macc 6:28, 31; 3 Macc 2:5; 4 Macc 6:19; 17:23).[27] This is the meaning discussed by Culpepper.

Apart from these usages, which refer to human behavior, there is a further use where the terms acquire the sense of a physical "model" or prototype from which something is to be built. Moses is shown the pattern (παράδειγμα) of the heavenly tabernacle and its furniture, which he is to make (Exod 25:9). David gives Solomon the model (παράδειγμα) of the temple that he is to build (1 Chr 28:11, 12, 18, 19). Similarly, Ezekiel is shown a vision of the temple as the model (ὑπόδειγμα) of the new house of God (42:15).[28] It is this meaning of ὑπόδειγμα as a prototype or physical model of the tabernacle and Father's House that I believe lies behind the Johannine use.[29]

C and C'. The Betrayer (13:16-20, 21-30)

The pivotal units in each parallel part concentrate on Judas, the betrayer. The *inclusio* formed by the double "very truly, I tell you" and the repetition of "the one who sent" (vv. 16, 20) indicate that verses 16-20 are a unit. In the center of both units the emphasis is on Judas's betrayal by eating the bread Jesus offers (vv. 18, 26). When the psalm (Ps 41:10) is cited in verse 18, the evangelist has made a significant change in the text. The Greek version of the Psalm reads, ὁ ἐσθίων ἄρτους μου, "the one *eating* [ἐσθίων] my bread," while the Gospel reads, ὁ τρώγων μου τὸν ἄρτον, "the one who *ate* [τρώγων] my bread." The Gospel's use of the

26. Schlier, "ὑπόδειγμα," 33. According to Schlier, the LXX "often employs ὑπόδειγμα and παράδειγμα as alternatives."

27. A similar sense relating to human behavior is found in Jeremiah 8:2 and Nahum 3:6, where παράδειγμα is used in the sense of public shame or exposure.

28. "When he had finished measuring the interior of the house, he led me out through the East gate and measured the model [ὑπόδειγμα] of the house around the outside" (Ezek 42:15, author's translation).

29. Jesus's identity as the living dwelling place or temple of God has been a dominant theme across the Gospel and this theme will be continued in John 14. See Mary L. Coloe, *God Dwells with Us: Temple Symbolism in the Fourth Gospel* (Collegeville, MN: Liturgical Press, 2001).

John 13:16-20, 21-30

¹⁶"Very truly, I tell you, servants are not greater than their master, nor are messengers greater than the one who sent them. ¹⁷If you know these things, you are blessed if you do them. ¹⁸I am not speaking of all of you; I know whom I have chosen. But it is to fulfill the scripture, 'The one who ate my bread has lifted his heel against me.' ¹⁹I tell you this now, before it occurs, so that when it does occur, you may believe that I am he. ²⁰Very truly, I tell you, whoever receives one whom I send receives me; and whoever receives me receives him who sent me."

²¹After saying this Jesus was troubled in spirit, and declared, "Very truly, I tell you, one of you will betray me." ²²The disciples looked at one another, uncertain of whom he was speaking. ²³One of his disciples—the one whom Jesus loved—was reclining next to

aorist τρώγων reflects Jesus's earlier teaching about "eating" his flesh, in 6:51c-58 where the same verb was used, and therefore makes the link between the morsel and the Eucharist.[30] These verses express the enormity of Judas's deed. Middle Eastern hospitality would require that even your enemy, if he has broken bread with you, should be safe within your home.[31] To turn against one who has welcomed you and given you bread to eat is the height of betrayal. The words of the psalm are fulfilled when Judas receives from Jesus the morsel of bread (vv. 26-27).[32] At this point of betrayal, Satan (ὁ Σατανᾶς) enters into Judas and he is now aligned with the powers of darkness.[33] In response to Jesus's words, he leaves

30. On this point, see Moloney, *Glory not Dishonor*, 20–22. Menken analyzes the possible sources for the Johannine version of the psalm and concludes that it is the evangelist's own translation of the MT based on Jewish exegetical methods of the time; see Maarten J. J. Menken, "The Translation of Ps 41:10 in John 13:18," *JSNT* 40 (1990): 61–79, here 62–63.

31. Bruce Malina, "The Received View and What It Cannot Do: III John and Hospitality," *Semeia* 35 (1986): 171–89, here 185. Malina comments, "Frequently the ritual of footwashing marks the movement from stranger to guest (see Gen 18:4; 19:2; 24:32)" (183).

32. The term ψωμίον need not necessarily mean bread; it could also be a morsel of meat. Given the link with Ps 41:10 and the use of the verb τρώγω with cross-reference to the discourse on the "Bread of Life" in 6:51c-58, however, ψωμίον is best understood as a morsel of bread.

33. For a critical discussion of the association of "darkness" with "evil," see David Goldenberg, "Racism, Color Symbolism, and Color Prejudice," in *The Origins of Racism in the West*, ed. Miriam Eliav-Feldon, Benjamin Isaac, and Joseph Ziegler (Cambridge: Cambridge University Press, 2009).

him; ²⁴Simon Peter therefore motioned to him to ask Jesus of whom he was speaking. ²⁵So while reclining next to Jesus, he asked him, "Lord, who is it?" ²⁶Jesus answered, "It is the one to whom I give this piece of bread when I have dipped it in the dish." So when he had dipped the piece of bread, he gave it to Judas son of Simon Iscariot. ²⁷After he received the piece of bread, Satan entered into him. Jesus said to him, "Do quickly what you are going to do." ²⁸Now no one at the table knew why he said this to him. ²⁹Some thought that, because Judas had the common purse, Jesus was telling him, "Buy what we need for the festival"; or, that he should give something to the poor. ³⁰So, after receiving the piece of bread, he immediately went out. And it was night.

the presence of Jesus, the light of the world (8:12; 9:5), and goes out; the terse statement "and it was night" (v. 30), is more than a time indicator. Judas has gone out into primal darkness, and in terms of Middle Eastern hospitality, Judas leaves the meal as enemy.³⁴

B'. Jesus's Second Teaching and "Gift" (13:31-35)

Chapter 13 symbolically anticipates the crucifixion; as Zumstein notes, "The footwashing scene is a metaphor for the cross."³⁵ In welcoming disciples into his "Father's house/temple" (14:2) by the act of footwashing, Jesus proleptically draws them into his own divine filiation within God's household. What is acted out here in symbol will be realized at the cross. Jesus is now the ὑπόδειγμα or prototype of the future house/ hold of God, which his disciples will become through their having a share (μέρος) in his hour and by their living out his new commandment of love. The love commandment identifies what is the essential structure of the ὑπόδειγμα/prototype of God's household, which is a communion-in-love (14:31; 15:9, 10; 17:23, 24, 26).

---

34. "The stranger-guest will leave the host either as friend or enemy" (Malina, "Received View," 186); Thompson, *John*, 294–95. On the theme of light and darkness in this Gospel, see Coloe, *John 1–10*, 26–27.

35. Zumstein, *Kreative Erinnerung*, 174. The link between the footwashing and Jesus's death was also noted by Hoskins who wrote, "The washing of the disciples' feet rests upon and interprets the death of the Lord, and is not a detached action containing in itself a merely ethical lesson." Edwyn C. Hoskyns, *The Fourth Gospel*, ed. F. N. Davis (London: Faber & Faber, 1947), 437.

John 13:31-35

³¹When he had gone out, Jesus said, "Now the Son of Man has been glorified, and God has been glorified in him. ³²If God has been glorified in him, God will also glorify him in himself and will glorify him at once. ³³Little children, I am with you only a little longer. You will look for me; and as I said to the Jews so now I say to you, 'Where I am going, you cannot come.' ³⁴I give you a new commandment, that you love one another. Just as I have loved you, you also should love one another. ³⁵By this everyone will know that you are my disciples, if you have love for one another."

Anticipating what will be achieved through his death, Jesus calls his disciples "little children" (v. 33), which recalls both the promise that those who receive the incarnate Word would become children of God (1:12) and the characterization of Jesus's task as gathering God's "scattered children" (11:52). In this unit, Jesus gives a new commandment to these little children to love one another *as* he has loved. The two instructions, featuring the verb "to give" (δίδωμι 15, 34), reciprocally interpret each other through their parallelism.³⁶ The action of Jesus in washing the feet of the disciples can now be seen as a model/prototype of loving "as I have loved." In both segments of these parallel statements, Jesus is the model or standard he proposes to his disciples: wash each other's feet *as* I have done; love each other *as* I have loved. Read this way, the footwashing is an expression of love. Peter considers Jesus's action as service, but in the experience of the one doing the deed, it is love.

Sandra Schneiders's work on "a phenomenology of service" has been particularly helpful in sharpening my interpretation of this text. She describes three models: (1) service between unequals, where one party has some rights over the other; (2) service given to another to meet some need within the one serving (even if this is an unconscious need); and (3) service between friends. It is this third model of service that Jesus enjoins on his disciples. It presumes the equality of server and served, unlike the first two models of service between unequals. The first model also

36. Although he presents a different structure, Yves Simoens also emphasizes the parallelism of these two gifts and the importance of relating them to each other in the process of their interpretation. Yves Simoens, *La gloire d'aimer: Structures stylistiques et interprétives dans le Discours de la Cène (Jn 13–17)*, AnBib 90 (Rome: Biblical Institute Press, 1981), 92.

includes enforced slavery and an abuse of the rights of the one forced into service.[37]

Furthermore, the placement of these two gifts highlights the extraordinary depths of Jesus's love as the Good Shepherd whose love entails the laying down of life (10:17; 15:13). In the structure I propose, the two units (vv. 12-15 and 31-35) in which Jesus speaks of his actions in terms of a gift are framed by description of two of "his own" who receive these gifts: Peter, who will deny him (vv. 6-11, 36-38), and Judas, who will betray him (vv. 16-20, 21-30). Truly, here is love displayed to the utmost (εἰς τέλος, v. 1), where love is given in the knowledge that those who receive it will fail to reciprocate that love. Such love is utterly gratuitous, given unreservedly—which shows that the dynamism of this love lies solely with the lover.[38] "It is precisely in his unconditional gift of himself to people who do not love him that Jesus reveals who he is and what he is doing. . . . Revealed here is God's love which transcends and challenges all human criteria and human experience."[39] Such love is not coerced. For it to be love it must be freely given and not responding to some inner distortion or for fear of the other. When service arises from fear or some inner compulsion, then love is overshadowed by what can only be named as evil, and the apparent giver of such service is victim. The dynamism of domestic abuse frequently distorts the true meaning of freely given love.

A'. Second Dialogue with Peter (13:36-38)

As in the first dialogue with Peter (vv. 6-11), Peter is portrayed as lacking understanding of the significance of Jesus's action. Peter asserts that he will lay down his life, which is the action of the Good Shepherd, symbolized in the footwashing, and soon to be realized at the cross. Again, the future events impinge on this occasion when Jesus speaks of the future failure of Peter when, rather than identifying with Jesus, he denies him, saying, "I am not" (οὐκ εἰμί, 19:17, 25, 27). The triple denial will be followed by Jesus's triple command that Peter be the shepherd in the postresurrection time (21:15-17).

37. Schneiders, "The Foot Washing," 81–86.
38. Moloney develops the three models of service proposed by Schneiders and suggests a fourth model: "a love unto death of friends who have betrayed and denied the one who loves still." Francis J. Moloney, "A Sacramental Reading of John 13:1-38," *CBQ* 53 (1991): 237–56, here 249 n. 4.
39. Ibid., 249.

John 13:36-38

[36]Simon Peter said to him, "Lord, where are you going?" Jesus answered, "Where I am going, you cannot follow me now; but you will follow afterward." [37]Peter said to him, "Lord, why can I not follow you now? I will lay down my life for you." [38]Jesus answered, "Will you lay down your life for me? Very truly, I tell you, before the cock crows, you will have denied me three times."

Conclusion

Love was apparent in the Bethany household of Mary, Martha, and Lazarus, shown especially when Mary anointed Jesus's feet (12:3), anticipating his entry into the "hour" of his return to God's presence. Now, Jesus kneels at the feet of his disciples in a gesture of love, and the self-surrender of his life, through which all of "his own" will join him within the household of God.

In laying down his garments and washing his disciples' feet, Jesus demonstrates the essential love relationship within God's "house." The model Jesus gives is not that of servitude but of the depths of his love (13:1) and of God's love (3:16). This love is willing to lay down (θῇ) life for friends (15:13), as the shepherd lays down his life for his sheep (τὴν ψυχὴν αὐτοῦ τίθησιν ὑπὲρ τῶν προβάτων, 10:11), shown symbolically here in Jesus laying down his garments (τίθησιν τὰ ἱμάτια). To an observer, love may appear to be service, but the experience of love transcends and transforms service. "By the foot washing Jesus has transcended and transformed the only ontologically based inequality among human beings, that between him and us."[40] This is why the attitude of love among disciples is so critical, for love is the essential dynamism of God's household.

Gail O'Day acknowledges that "the language of love is a different ethical language. . . . [I]t is language of fullness rather than language of emptying. One will give one's life for one's friends as an act of love (15:13), not as an act of self-denial and sacrifice. . . . [O]ne gives out of the abundance of one's love, not out of the denial of one's self."[41] Too often expectations are placed on women and girls to take on a role of service within the household at the cost of their own self-fulfillment through education or meaningful work. This type of "self-denial" can

40. See Schneiders, "The Foot Washing," 87.
41. Gail R. O'Day, "John," in *The Women's Bible Commentary*, ed. Carol A. Newsom and Sharon H. Ringe, exp. ed. (Louisville: Westminster John Knox, 1998), 391.

then mistakenly be idealized and held up as an example of love. With O'Day, I think that the Gospel of John challenges this ethos. There is a marked difference between servitude and the generosity born from love—even if they may appear to be the same on the outside.

At one level, Jesus's relationship with his disciples remains that of teacher, but as the "hour" approaches there is a deeper level of loving intimacy that he now reveals, knowing that it will not be understood until *later*. The prologue announced that Johannine Christology is incarnational (1:14), making possible the transformation of humanity into "children of God" (1:12). As Jesus gathers his own, the process of his "hour" begins, and Jesus enacts a loving welcome into the Father's household with the simple, homely implements of a towel, a basin, and water.

Service—or Servitude?

Modern Western society is slowly becoming aware of the coercive nature of unequal relationships that exist in the workplace and in some cultures in the home. When one person is either financially or socially dependent on another, there is necessarily inequality in the relationship that can, and often is, abused. The one in the dominant position may think the other is responding with full consent and freely offering service or affection, when in fact the one in the subservient position is enslaved to financial or social necessities.

Within the Catholic Church, canon law has established an unequal relationship between the cleric, who alone has powers of jurisdiction and sacramentality, and the laity; and between men who can become clerics and women who cannot. This leaves women doubly disenfranchised and reduced to volunteer ministry—and dependent on the goodwill of the local pastor. Elisabeth Schüssler Fiorenza is highly critical of a model of church emphasizing "servanthood" that often encourages women into self-giving as an act of spiritual commitment but that overlooks the injustices such service can and frequently does foster; "Servanthood without choice is not *diakonia* but becomes slavery (*douleia*)."[42] Servant ecclesiology can be fully Christian only when there is real choice—as modelled by Jesus's freely chosen agency as an act of love

---

42. Elisabeth Schüssler Fiorenza, " 'Waiting at Table': A Critical Feminist The*logical Reflection on Diakonia," in *Changing Horizons: Explorations in Feminist Interpretation*, ed. Elisabeth Schüssler Fiorenza (Minneapolis: Fortress, 2013), 218.

for those who were his own (13:1) and as an expression of God's love for the world (3:16). A second strategy for the recovery of servant ecclesiology that Schüssler Fiorenza proposes is redefining ministry in terms of the empowerment or building up of the community.[43] In John, Jesus empowers his disciples for ministry with the post-Easter gift of the Spirit (20:22).

The Characterization of Judas, Peter, and the Beloved Disciple

Three of Jesus's "own" play prominent roles in this chapter. The footwashing is framed by Jesus's dialogue with Peter (vv. 6-11, 36-38) who challenges Jesus, who in reply tells Peter that he will deny Jesus. At the center is Judas the one who will hand him over (vv. 16-30) and the Beloved Disciple (v. 23).

Peter has already emerged as the spokesperson for the disciples during the Bread of Life Discourse, where he expressed a degree of faith when he answered Jesus, "Lord, to whom can we go? You have the words of eternal life" (6:68). But now his words reveal hesitancy to trust and obtuseness. Michael Labahn describes him as an "ambiguous character."[44] In the Synoptics he is the first named and called to discipleship (Mark 1:16-20); not so in John, where it is Andrew and an unnamed disciple, considered by many to be the first appearance of the Beloved Disciple (1:35-40).[45] In John it is the Beloved Disciple who emerges as the leader in faith, particularly in chapters 20–21. He is the first to arrive at Easter faith (20:8) and the first to recognize the risen Lord on the shore of the Sea of Tiberias (21:7). But then, in chapter 21, it is Peter who is called to offer pastoral leadership, "Tend my sheep" (21:15-17). It seems the Gospel is balancing two trajectories: one, the local community's origins in the preaching of a disciple they came to call the Beloved

43. Ibid., 219.

44. Michael Labahn, "Simon Peter: An Ambiguous Character and His Narrative Career," in *Character Studies in the Fourth Gospel: Narrative Approaches to Seventy Figures in John*, ed. Steven A. Hunt, D. Francois Tolmie, and Ruben Zimmermann, WUNT 314 (Tübingen: Mohr Siebeck, 2013), 151. See also Michael Labahn, "Peter's Rehabilitation (John 21:15-19) and the Adoption of Sinners: Remembering Jesus and Relecturing John," in *John, Jesus, and History*, vol. 2: *Aspects of Historicity in the Fourth Gospel*, ed. Paul N. Anderson, Felix Just, and Tom Thatcher (Atlanta: SBL, 2009), 335–48.

45. See the discussion of the "authorship" of the Gospel in Coloe, *John 1–10*, liv–lviii.

Disciple; second, the wider church community looking to the leadership of Peter as depicted in Acts. While some see in Peter's characterization the gradual restoration of him as leader, I agree with Labahn who offers another, more nuanced, hermeneutical interpretation. Peter's failures occur when acting "on his own pre-Easter understanding."[46] His leadership emerges in response to Jesus's call and following the gift of the Spirit.[47]

When Jesus declares at the table that one in their midst will hand him over (13:21) Simon Peter defers to the Beloved Disciple to ask Jesus to whom he is referring. The Beloved Disciple is reclining on the breast (ἐν τῷ κόλπῳ) of Jesus (13:23), a place of heightened intimacy and love. This is the same closeness of the son in the embrace of the father's breast (εἰς τὸν κόλπον, 1:18). This disciple's primacy, both here and in later scenes (19:26; 20:4; 21:7), is based on love, and Peter's leadership emerges only after he confesses love, "Yes, Lord, you know I love you" (21:15-17). Jesus's action (13:5) and his command (13:34) stress the importance of love

within the community, and the brief comparison of the Beloved Disciple and Peter shows that love is the single criterion of leadership.

Apart from the Beloved Disciple, the characters in the Gospel who display love are primarily women: Mary in her lavish anointing of Jesus (12:1-8); the women who will stand faithfully with Jesus through the horror of his crucifixion (19:25); Mary the Magdalene, weeping at the tomb (20:11), then reaching out when her beloved speaks her name, "Μαριάμ" (20:16). From her study of the women in the Fourth Gospel, Sandra Schneiders proposes that their characterization "was the result of actual experience of Christian women who played prominent roles in the community of the Fourth Evangelist."[48] She further notes: "If leadership is a function of creative initiative and decisive action, the Johannine women qualify well for the role."[49] The strong, unconventional roles of these women characters, as witnesses (the Samaritan woman), evangelists (Mary Magdalene), prophets (Mary of Bethany), lead Schneiders to tentatively suggest that the

46. Labahn, "Simon Peter: An Ambiguous Character," 167.
47. More will be said on the relationship between Peter and the Beloved Disciple when examining chaps. 20 and 21.
48. Sandra M. Schneiders, *Written That You May Believe: Encountering Jesus in the Fourth Gospel*, rev. and exp. ed. (New York: Crossroad, 2003), 99.
49. Ibid., 101.

author of the Gospel may have been a woman, as embodied in the Samaritan woman.[50]

Judas is first introduced when Jesus identified him as "a devil" (6:70), and the narrator follows this by describing him as the one who will hand Jesus over (6:71). When Mary of Bethany anoints Jesus, Judas objects, and again he is said to be "the one who was about to betray him" (12:4). Then chapter 13 begins with the statement that the devil had already determined that Judas would hand Jesus over. Following the footwashing Jesus announces to the disciples that one of them will hand him over (13:22) and then indicates that it is the one who receives the morsel of bread from him, handing the morsel to Judas (v. 26). At this point the narrator states that "Satan entered into him" (v. 26). Judas's betrayal is heightened by the context of Jesus's love "to the end," indicating the depth of his love—and yet one of these he loves turns against him. No motive is given for this act, and the most sense a later community can offer is to quote a psalm (41:9): "But it is to fulfill the scripture, 'The one who ate my bread has lifted his heel against me'" (13:18).

A meal together around a table is recognized in many cultures as a sign of harmony. Table companions were bound by social conventions between host and guests and among guests. "The deeper the level of intimacy, the more that trust was a duty, and the more terrible its betrayal."[51]

The consistent comment on the heinousness of Judas's betrayal of Jesus sheds a light on the equivalent heinousness of abuse within a home, where table, bed, and lives have been shared. Calling violence within a home "domestic" tends to trivialize it, and such acts of violence do not attract the same penalties in law of acts of violence between strangers on the street. If violence happens beyond the home police lay charges; when violence happens within the home it is the victim who is asked, "Do you want to lay changes?" The walls of the home appear to offer sanctuary to violators. "A man's home is

---

50. Ibid., 251–53. While agreeing with Schneiders on the strong leadership roles of the women in the Gospel, and that this likely reflects their leadership in the community, I am not convinced that the Beloved Disciple was a woman, primarily because this disciple is named "son" (19:27). But read Schneider's response to such criticism: ibid., 241.

51. For details and examples of the honor codes around table fellowship, see Craig S. Keener, *The Gospel of John: A Commentary*, 2 vols. (Peabody, MA: Hendrickson, 2003), 2:912–14, here 912–13.

his castle" protects the rights of men,[52] but there is no equivalent statement concerning the rights of a woman.

> The sanctity of the family home and the charge that a "man's home is his castle" led to treating spouse abuse manifestly different than assaults between persons who were not intimates. Because the wife was viewed as belonging to her husband, what happened between them was regarded as a private matter and was not a concern to the criminal justice system.[53]

The betrayal of table fellowship by Judas elicits the harshest judgment by Jesus naming the betrayer a "devil" (6:70) and in this Gospel is identified as Satanic (13:27).

52. The statement was passed into English law by Sir Edward Coke in *The Institutes of the Laws of England*, 1628.

53. Lauren L. Baker, "Domestic Violence in the Domestic Church: An Argument for Greater Attention to Intimate Partner Abuse in Catholic Health Care," *Journal of Moral Theology* 7 (2018). Here, Baker is citing Edna Erez, "Domestic Violence and the Criminal Justice System: An Overview," *Online Journal of Issues in Nursing* 7 (2002): 4.

John 14:1-31

Sophia's Household

You have given command to build a temple on your holy mountain,
and an altar in the city of your dwelling [κατασκηνώσεώς]
a copy of the holy tent [σκηνῆς] that you prepared [προητοίμασας] from
*   the beginning.*
With you is wisdom, she who knows your works
and was present when you made the world. . . .
Send her forth from the holy heavens,
and from the throne of your glory send her,
that she may labor at my side,
and that I may learn what is pleasing to you. (Wis 9:8-10)

Introduction

As the second part of the original discourse (chaps. 13 and 14), this chapter continues to interpret the meaning of Jesus's departure to God through the cross, which will complete his mission and be his hour of exaltation. In the footwashing, the hour was symbolically enacted as Jesus's free laying down of life for his own, as the Good Shepherd willingly lays down his life for his sheep (10:15). And in this act the disciples are to have a part (μέρος). Now, with their feet washed, the disciples are welcomed into "my Father's house." When the phrase was first used it clearly referred to the temple building (2:16), where footwashing was a necessary preparation. But, for that culture, the term had a broader, figurative sense as "household."[1] In John 14 Jesus speaks the words of Sophia attempting to explain this double sense of Father's house/hold to the disciples, to prepare them for what will happen in "the hour." Sophia is most transparent across the discourse, as she adopts the genre of a παροιμία, that is, a proverb, parable, or figure of speech. "It [a παροιμία] states an experienced truth of popular wisdom in short and pointed form. . . . Often a concrete instance is set forth as typical, serving to represent the abstract thought contained in it. Since it only alludes to the example, the proverb can be rather enigmatic for those not acquainted with it."[2]

Chapters 14, 15, and 16 of the Fourth Gospel use a number of images (παροιμίαι, 16:25) such as the vine and the branches (15:1-11) and the woman in childbirth (16:21). The references to "my Father's house" (οἰκία τοῦ πατρός) and its "many dwellings" (μοναὶ πολλαί) belong to this same constellation of παροιμίαι and cannot simply be understood literally as Jesus's return to heaven and his preparation of a heavenly place for his disciples. Interpretations along these lines fail to give full weight to the figurative language of the verse and its context in a highly symbolic Gospel narrative. In what follows I will develop a reading of this verse that allows the Gospel itself to provide the primary hermeneutical clues to its interpretation. In the words of James McCaffrey, "The evangelist is his own best commentator."[3]

Structuring the Chapter

Chapter 14 develops around two statements of Jesus/Sophia (vv. 1-4, 18-21).[4] Following the statements there is a response by the disciples leading into a dialogue with Thomas and Philip (vv. 5-14), then with

1. Throughout the OT the expression "father's house" (בית אב) is frequently translated as "family," e.g., when Rahab protects Israelite "spies" seeking information in Jericho. Rahab says, "Now then, swear to me by the Lord that as I have dealt kindly with you, you also will deal kindly with my father's house, and give me a sure sign, and save alive my father and mother, my brothers and sisters, and all who belong to them, and deliver our lives from death" (Josh 2:12-13).

2. Friedrich Hauck, "παροιμία," *TDNT* 5 (1967): 854.

3. James McCaffrey, *The House with Many Rooms: The Temple Theme of Jn 14, 2-3* (Rome: Biblical Institute Press, 1988), 27.

4. There is no agreement among scholars about the structure of chapter 14. The structure I suggest is based on the patterns of speech and two different themes. Statement 1: I am going. Statement 2: I am coming.

Judas (vv. 22-24). Each of these dialogues concludes with the promise of the Paraclete (vv. 15-17, 25-26). The passage concludes with a summation repeating a number of themes already mentioned.

The structure can be shown as follows:

Statement 1: verses 1-17

  "Do not let your hearts be troubled" (vv. 1-4)

    Response: Dialogue with Thomas and Philip (vv. 5-14)

    Promise of the Paraclete (vv. 15-17)

Statement 2: verses 18-26

  "I will not leave you orphans" (vv. 18-21)

    Response: Dialogue with Judas (vv. 22-24)

    Promise of the Paraclete (vv. 25-26)

Conclusion: verses 27-31

  "Do not let your hearts be troubled" (v. 27)

  "I am going away" (v. 28; cf. vv. 2, 4, 12)

  "I am coming to you" (v. 28; cf. vv. 18, 24)

Two Paradoxes

The statements create two paradoxes. First, they speak of Jesus's going away: "I go to prepare a place for you" (v. 2), "the world will no longer see me" (v. 19), "I am going away" (v. 28). At the same time they promise a return to and presence with the disciples: "I will come again" (v. 3), "I will not leave you orphaned" (v. 18), "I am coming to you" (v. 28). But there is no sense that these two locations, Jesus's presence with the Father[5] and with the disciples, are mutually exclusive. God does not send Jesus again or gift the world a second time with the Son (3:16-17). The function of being the sent one and gift of God passes to the Paraclete (vv. 15, 25). In a way that is not yet clear, Jesus will be able to be present with the Father and with the disciples.

---

5. On Jesus's use of "Father" as personal image of God, refer back to the author's introduction, the excursus "The Iconic Father" at John 5, and the sidebar "The Symbol of the Father's Household" below.

The second paradox arises from the first. Even as the discourse promises a future presence, there is no denying that there will also be an experience of absence; "The approaching physical absence of Jesus is the substratum of the farewell discourse."[6] The function and tone of the discourse is to prepare the disciples for this absence and offer consolation. The second paradox is, therefore: How can there be presence in absence?

The key to penetrating the first paradox, of Jesus's presence simultaneously with the Father and with the disciples, lies in the Johannine concept of mutual indwelling, expressed in the verb "to dwell" (μένω) and its cognates. The key to the paradox of presence-in-absence lies in the role of the Paraclete. The two concepts are interrelated but will be dealt with separately.

Statement 1 (14:1-17)

The Divine Indwelling

Forms of the verb μένω (to dwell) occur primarily in chapters 14 and 15.[7] The mutual abiding of Jesus and the Father (14:10; 15:10) and Jesus and his disciples (15:4, 5, 6, 7, 9, 10) enables the evangelist to hold together the apparently contradictory statements of Jesus's presence with the Father and also with the disciples. The theology of mutual indwelling developed in chapters 14 and 15 is introduced in both chapters with an image (παροιμία): first, the father's house/hold and its many dwellings (μοναὶ πολλαί, 14:2),[8] and then, the vine and branches (15:1, 5). In chapter 14 the Father, Jesus, and the Paraclete are the ones abiding, with Jesus (v. 10) and also with the believer (vv. 17, 23, 25). In chapter 15 it is the believers who are called to abide in Jesus (vv. 4, 5, 6, 7, 9, 10). The first image, "my Father's house" and its many dwellings, introduces the theme of the abiding of the divine presence, and this image draws on and transforms Israel's temple traditions.

6. Robert H. Gundry, " 'In My Father's House Are Many *Monai'* (John 14:2)," *ZNW* 58 (1967): 68–69.

7. John 14:10, 17, 23, 25; 15:4 (x3), 5, 6, 7 (x2), 9, 10.

8. The text does not say "dwelling places" even though translations often add the word "places," or "rooms" or "mansions." Such poor translations obscure the Johannine theology.

14:1"Do not let your hearts be troubled. Believe in God, believe also in me. 2In my Father's house there are many dwelling places. If it were not so, would I have told you that I go to prepare a place for you? 3And if I go and prepare a place for you, I will come again and will take you to myself, so that where I am, there you may be also. 4And you know the way to the place where I am going." 5Thomas said to him, "Lord, we do not know where you are going. How can we know the way?" 6Jesus said to him, "I am the way, and the truth, and the life. No one comes to the Father except through me. 7If you know me, you will know my Father also. From now on you do know him and have seen him."

8Philip said to him, "Lord, show us the Father, and we will be satisfied." 9Jesus said to him, "Have I been with you all this time, Philip, and you still do not know me? Whoever has seen me has seen the Father. How can you say, 'Show us the Father'? 10Do you not believe that I am in the Father and

My Father's House

In chapter 14, the phrase "in my Father's house" (ἐν τῇ οἰκίᾳ τοῦ πατρός μου) needs to be interpreted in the light of a similar expression Jesus used to describe the Jerusalem temple as "my Father's house" (τὸν οἶκον τοῦ πατρός μου, 2:16). Even in this earlier scene, there was an obvious process of reinterpretation of the meaning of temple. The scene in chapter 2 began in the physical temple building but concluded with the enigmatic phrase "he was speaking of the temple of his body" (2:21). In the early part of the Gospel, beginning with the announcement of the Word tabernacling with us (1:14) and reiterated in 2:21, the function of providing a place for the divine presence shifted from a building to the living flesh of Jesus.

The choice of the term "house" (οἶκος, 2:16; οἰκία, 14:2) resonates with the dominant term for the Jerusalem temple in the Hebrew text—the House of the Lord (בית יהוה).[9] The very naming of this place as "House" indicates its function as a dwelling for the divine presence, appropriately furnished in all its accessories.[10]

The phrase "my father's house" is open to further levels of meaning. In the Scriptures this phrase means the group of people who make

---

9. The terminology בית יהוה occurs 258 times while the expression היכל, "temple" or "palace," occurs 69 times to refer to the temple and the nave of the temple.

10. Menahem Haran, "The Divine Presence in the Israelite Cult and the Cultic Institutions," *Bib* 50 (1969): 255.

the Father is in me? The words that I say to you I do not speak on my own; but the Father who dwells in me does his works. [11]Believe me that I am in the Father and the Father is in me; but if you do not, then believe me because of the works themselves. [12]Very truly, I tell you, the one who believes in me will also do the works that I do and, in fact, will do greater works than these, because I am going to the Father. [13]I will do whatever you ask in my name, so that the Father may be glorified in the Son. [14]If in my name you ask me for anything, I will do it.

[15]"If you love me, you will keep my commandments. [16]And I will ask the Father, and he will give you another Advocate to be with you forever. [17]This is the Spirit of truth, whom the world cannot receive, because it neither sees him nor knows him. You know him, because he abides with you, and he will be in you."

up the household, such as the parents, children, grandchildren, house servants, slaves, and even the future descendants.[11] In the OT, "the father's house" never means a building. In speaking of the temple as "my Father's house" in chapter 2, the evangelist began to move away from temple-as-building to something more personal and relational. In chapter 2 the image of temple shifted to a single person, Jesus (2:21). In chapter 14 this movement continues and extends beyond one person to a group of people in a household or familial relationship.

Chapter 14 develops this personal and relational understanding even further with the shift from the word οἶκος to οἰκία.[12] The term οἶκος is used only with the sense of a building, the temple (2:16, 17), and also the house at Bethany (11:20). The term οἰκία is used with a more fluid range of meanings in that it can mean both a physical building (11:31; 12:3) and also the household (4:53; 8:35).[13] Whereas in 2:16 the initial reference was to the οἶκος in the sense of a building, here in chapter 14, through the change of the word to οἰκία, there is a continuation of the movement begun in 2:21 to understand the phrase "my Father's house" not as a building but as a quality of personal relationships.[14] In Robert

11. E.g., Gen 24:38; 28:21; 46:31; Josh 2:13; Judg 6:15; 9:18; 16:31; 1 Sam 22:15; 2 Sam 14:9; 1 Chr 28:4. Often the expression "father's house" is translated as "family."
12. Otto Michel, "οἶκος, οἰκία," *TDNT* 5 (1967): 119–34.
13. Agreeing with Gundry, "'In My Father's House,'" 71.
14. McCaffrey, *The House with Many Rooms*, 31.

Gundry's words, "The father's house is no longer heaven, but God's household or family."[15]

Many Dwellings (μοναὶ πολλαί)

While μοναὶ can literally mean rooms within a house, the shift from a building to personal relationships suggested by the phrase "in my Father's household" requires a similar shift in understanding what the evangelist means by "dwellings" (μοναὶ). The chapter itself and chapter 15 provide the best interpretive clue to the particular Johannine meaning of this phrase. Chapters 14 and 15 use derivatives of μένω (to dwell) and μοναί (dwellings) to describe a variety of interpersonal relationships between the Father, Jesus, the Paraclete, and believers. The relationships are usually described with the translation "abiding" or "dwelling" or "remaining." These various relationships are appropriately introduced by the phrase "many dwellings." Chapter 14 focuses on a series of divine dwellings:

- the Father who dwells (μένων) in Jesus (v. 10)
- the Paraclete who dwells (μένει) *with* believers and who in the future will dwell *in* them (v. 17)
- the Father and Jesus who will make their dwelling (μονὴν) with the believer (v. 23)
- Jesus who dwells (μένων) with the disciples (v. 25)[16]

The subject of the verb μένω, throughout chapter 14, is not the *believer* but *God* (Father, the Paraclete, and Jesus). The action, therefore, is not the *believers* "going up" to dwell in God's heavenly abode but the *Father*, the *Paraclete*, and *Jesus* coming to dwell with the believers. It is a descending movement from the divine realm to the human, not an ascending movement from the human to the divine. In the words of Andreas Dettwiler

---

15. Gundry, " 'In My Father's House,' " 70.

16. The imagery of μοναὶ πολλαί continues into chapter 15, where the verb μένων is again used to describe the believers dwelling in Jesus. The shift to the community of believers is reflected by a shift in the metaphor from "house" to "vine," since the vine was a common image for the community of Israel. On the use of this image, see Anne Jaubert, "L'image de la Vigne (Jean 15)," in *Oikonomia. Heilsgeschichte als Thema der Theologie. Oscar Cullmann zum 65. Geburtstag gewidmet*, ed. Felix Christ (Hamburg-Bergstedt: H. Reich Verlag, 1967), 93–96.

it is "a great movement from the transcendence to the immanence of God."[17] Given that the emphasis in chapter 14 is on the divine dwelling with the believers, it is not surprising to find this theology introduced with an image that draws on Israel's symbol of the divine presence dwelling in its midst—the temple, Israel's House of the Lord, now renamed by Jesus as the "house of my Father" (2:16).

From the above analysis, the phrase "in my Father's household there are many dwellings" is best understood to mean a series of interpersonal relationships made possible because of the indwellings of the Father, Jesus, and the Paraclete with the believer. The divine indwelling in the midst of a believing community makes it appropriate to speak of the community as a living temple. The community is the House (household) of God.[18] David Aune goes so far as to claim that this image is so pervasive that it is the self-perception of the believing community.[19]

The familial language of the discourse supports this "household" interpretation. The discourse begins with Jesus gathering his own, and in 13:33 they are called children (τεκνία). These words recall the words of the prologue (1:11) and the affirmation that those of his own who do receive the *logos* are given the power to become the children of God (τέκνα θεοῦ). The language of family relationships continues in 14:18 with the word "orphaned" to describe a state of Jesus's absence, followed later by the allegory of the woman in childbirth (16:21). The believers will not be left without a "temple"; they themselves will be the living temple of God's indwelling presence.[20]

---

17. "Grosse Bewegung von der Transzendenz zur Immanenz Gottes." Andreas Dettwiler, *Die Gegenwart des Erhöhten: Eine exegetische Studie zu den johanneischen Abschiedsreden (Joh 13,31–16,33) unter besonderer Berücksichtigung ihres Relecture-Charakters* (Göttingen: Vandenhoeck & Ruprecht, 1995), 202.

18. To ensure that the term "house" has the more personal sense of family rather than building I will use the word "household," which is the more frequent meaning of οἰκία in the Fourth Gospel.

19. "It is probable that in John 14:2 (and also 8:35) the term οἰκία τοῦ πατρός reflects the self-designation of the Johannine community." David E. Aune, *The Cultic Setting of Realized Eschatology in Early Christianity*, NovTSup 28 (Leiden: Brill, 1972), 130. Other passages that reflect the use of οἶκος as an image of the community are 1 Pet 2:5; 4:17; 1 Tim 3:15; Heb 3:2-6.

20. The image of the community as a temple is not unique to the Gospel as it was an image developed earlier in the Pauline letters (1 Cor 3:16-17; 6:19; 2 Cor 6:16; Eph 2:21). For more on the Pauline image and its possible influence on the evangelist, see Mary L. Coloe, *God Dwells with Us: Temple Symbolism in the Fourth Gospel* (Collegeville, MN: Liturgical Press, 2001), 167–71.

To Prepare a Place for You (ἑτοιμάσαι τόπον ὑμῖν)

In the Hebrew text of the OT the terminology of a *prepared place* is used almost exclusively of the ark.[21] The LXX extends these references to include a place prepared for the building of the temple. "And Solomon began to build the house of the LORD in Jerusalem in the mount of Moriah where the LORD appeared to his father David, in the *place* which David had *prepared* in the threshing floor of Orna the Jebusite" (2 Chr 3:1).

The word "place" (τόπος) also has theological significance both in the Hebrew Scriptures and within this Gospel. The temple is frequently simply called "the holy place" (e.g., Exod 26:33; Lev 16; 1 Kgs 8:6, 8, 10), the place where God's name will be set (e.g., Exod 20:24; Deut 12:5, 11, 21), and God's dwelling place (e.g., Ps 74:7; 76:2; 132:7; Ezek 37:27). In chapter 11 Jesus's opponents are concerned that if they allow Jesus to continue, the Romans will destroy their "holy place" (John 11:48). The irony is that through their desire to protect their temple they become the destroyers of the new temple of Jesus's body.[22]

From this survey of the scriptural background, the phrase "to prepare a place for you" is a clear allusion to the Jewish temple traditions. There is also evidence from the targums testifying to a strong Palestinian tradition where the phrase "to prepare a place" is associated, first, with the exodus wanderings and then, by extension, with the temple sanctuary, the place where God's name and God's *Shekinah* would dwell.[23]

Taken together, the two key phrases of 14:2—"in my Father's house there are many dwellings" and "I go to prepare a place for you"—show a uniquely Johannine concern with the temple, reinterpreted in a radically new way as the *household of God*. When the disciples fail to understand Jesus's words (vv. 5-14), his explanation leads into the promise of the Paraclete (vv. 15-17) and an indication that "my Father's household" will be established through the indwelling of the Father, Jesus, and the Paraclete with the believer (14:17, 23, 25). In some way, the action of Jesus "going" to the Father is simultaneously the action when he "prepares/

21. The one exception is found in Exodus, where, in the context, the phrase refers to the land (Exod 23:20). All other references are to the ark. E.g., "David built houses for himself in the city of David, and he *prepared a place* for the ark of God and pitched a tent for it" (1 Chr 15:1; also 15:3, 12; 2 Chr 1:4).

22. For further examples of the use of the term "place" to designate a particular holy place such as the Mount of Moriah and Bethel, see Coloe, *God Dwells with Us*, 165–66.

23. Martin McNamara, " 'To Prepare a Resting Place for You': A Targumic Expression and John 14:2f.," *MilS* 3 (1979): 106–7. See also Coloe, *God Dwells with Us*, 166–67.

builds" the "place" (temple) for the disciples.[24] The *Father's house* will be no longer a construction of stones but a household of many interpersonal relationships (μοναὶ πολλαί) where the divine presence, the *Shekinah*, can dwell within believers.[25]

Promise of the Paraclete (vv. 15-17)

A new "character" is now introduced into the Gospel—the Advocate or Paraclete (παράκλητον). Jesus describes the role of the Paraclete as the "Spirit of truth," as yet unknown to the world, but one who dwells with the disciples and later will "be in" them. Jesus speaks of this Spirit of truth as *another* Paraclete; the Gospel describes the function of the Paraclete in almost identical words to the function of Jesus and thus identifies Jesus as the first Paraclete.[26] The Gospel is very careful to maintain the separate and distinct identities of both Jesus and the Paraclete even as it establishes a very close relationship between them. Spirit-Paraclete and Jesus are not assimilated into each other. Their close relationship is very like the intimacy of *logos* and *theos* (1:1). Jesus is the one on whom the Spirit descends and dwells (1:32), but Jesus is not the Spirit. Jesus is the incarnate *logos* (1:14), the Father's gift already given to the world (3:16), whereas in the time of Jesus's ministry the Spirit has not yet been given, for Jesus is not yet glorified (7:39). The distinctions between the Father, Jesus, and the Spirit-Paraclete are maintained even in the intimacy of their union.

Because Jesus is the bearer of the Spirit from the time of his baptism (1:32), Jesus can say to the disciples that the Paraclete is now with (παρά) them (v. 17). Jesus himself now mediates the presence of the Spirit-Paraclete to the disciples. But when Jesus returns to the Father,

---

24. Dettwiler, *Die Gegenwart des Erhöhten*, 148.

25. Stibbe's conclusion is along similar lines when he comments, "The realised eschatology in the rest of John 14 suggests that this house is not so much an eternal home in heaven as a post-resurrection, empirical reality for the true disciples." See Mark Stibbe, *John*, Readings: A New Bible Commentary (Sheffield: JSOT Press, 1993), 160.

26. "If the Paraclete is the Spirit of Truth, Jesus is the truth (xiv. 6). If the Paraclete is the Holy Spirit, Jesus is the Holy One of God (vi. 69). These observations, combined with those about Jesus' sending of the Paraclete, show that John shared the general New Testament picture of the Holy Spirit as the Spirit of Jesus." Raymond E. Brown, "The Paraclete in the Fourth Gospel," *NTS* 13 (1966–1967): 126–27. See also Gary H. Burge, *The Anointed Community: The Holy Spirit in the Johannine Community* (Grand Rapids: Eerdmans, 1987), 140–43.

the mediating roles are reversed. Jesus's role as Spirit-bearer ends, and in his Easter appearance he will gift the disciples with the Spirit (20:22). Within the discourse he can only promise a future time when the Paraclete will be in (ἐν) them (14:17). The Paraclete, dwelling in the disciples, will mediate a continuing presence of Jesus. The *immediate* experience of the postresurrection community is pneumatic, but the sole purpose of the gift of the Spirit is to mediate a presence of the now absent one, the risen Jesus. On this point of the presence and function of the Spirit, D. Moody Smith's comments indicate the experiential nature of the Fourth Gospel's pneumatology:

> The Spirit or Paraclete as the mode of Jesus' abiding with his disciples seems to be a *felt reality*, a presence regarded as given rather than imagined. It is not, in other words, a mere theological idea of the Evangelist or of his community. Exactly how the Spirit-Paraclete makes the presence of Jesus known and felt in the community is never stated in so many words. That is, the exact mode of his activity, the phenomenology of his presence, is not described, although its function is clear enough.[27]

Statement 2 (14:18-26)

The first statement made it very clear that Jesus was going away; the second statement gives more emphasis to Jesus's abiding presence: "I am coming to you" (v. 18); "you will see me" (v. 19); "I am in my Father, and you in me, and I in you" (v. 20); "I will reveal myself" (v. 21); "we will come and make our dwelling [μονὴν] with them" (v. 23). The promises of Jesus's abiding presence with the disciples are directed to a future time, "on that day" (v. 20). Before that day, Jesus's words cannot be understood, as Judas's question indicates. Understanding can happen only after the "hour" when the Spirit is given to them.

The Paraclete's role is further described. The Spirit will "teach" and will "remind" the disciples of Jesus's words. In looking at earlier Gospel references to the Spirit, there are clear associations with the community's worship. John witnesses the descent of the Spirit upon Jesus (1:32-33) at his baptism (v. 31), and Nicodemus was told of the necessity of birth by water and Spirit (3:5-6, 8). The Samaritan woman was told of an hour

27. D. Moody Smith, "The Presentation of Jesus in the Fourth Gospel," *Int* 31 (1977): 375, emphasis added.

¹⁸"I will not leave you orphaned; I am coming to you. ¹⁹In a little while the world will no longer see me, but you will see me; because I live, you also will live. ²⁰On that day you will know that I am in my Father, and you in me, and I in you. ²¹They who have my commandments and keep them are those who love me; and those who love me will be loved by my Father, and I will love them and reveal myself to them." ²²Judas (not Iscariot) said to him, "Lord, how is it that you will reveal yourself to us, and not to the world?" ²³Jesus answered him, "Those who love me will keep my word, and my Father will love them, and we will come to them and make our home with them. ²⁴Whoever does not love me does not keep my words; and the word that you hear is not mine, but is from the Father who sent me.

²⁵"I have said these things to you while I am still with you. ²⁶But the Advocate, the Holy Spirit, whom the Father will send in my name, will teach you everything, and remind you of all that I have said to you."

when worship will be "in spirit and truth" (ἐν πνεύματι καὶ ἀληθείᾳ, 4:24).[28] Following the discourse on the bread from heaven and its eucharistic allusions (6:51c-58), Jesus affirmed the life-giving role of the Spirit available in his words (6:63). At the Feast of Tabernacles, within the context of the Jewish water rituals, Jesus promised to be the one who would quench thirst; then, immediately, he spoke of the Spirit still to be given (7:39).

These earlier references link the Spirit-Paraclete with the community's celebrations of baptism and Eucharist. In the community's cultic *anamnesis*, the Spirit-Paraclete is present. The Paraclete will mediate the presence of Jesus primarily through the function of teaching and reminding (14:26). The human faculties of memory and insight, and the activity of worship, are named as the primary moments when the community experiences the gift of the Spirit, and, through the stirrings of the Spirit, these cultic moments become the special times of Jesus's presence.[29]

28. Reading the καὶ epexegetically, since the second noun has no definite article, this phrase about worship reads "a Spirit which is true" or "a true Spirit" or even "a Spirit of truth," which is very close to what is said in 14:17.

29. David Aune speaks of a "cultic vision" of Jesus, a *visio Christi*. "In our opinion, the 'coming' of Jesus in the relevant passages under discussion from John 14 refers primarily to the recurring cultic 'coming' of Jesus in the form of a pneumatic or prophetic *visio Christi* within the setting of worship 'in the Spirit' as celebrated by the Johannine community." See Aune, *Cultic Setting*, 89–135. The quotation is found on 129.

The nearest description of the felt experience of the Spirit in the community is found in the narratives of the African American ex-slaves who were affiliated with the Baptist Church in the southern states of the United States. "And then the Spirit lifted me up and I forgot all about the pain and just lost sight of the world and all things of the world. When the Spirit begins to work with one it don't have any cares for pain or anything of the world. My mind gets fixed on God and I feel a deep love, joy, and desire to be with God."[30]

Indigenous Australians have an immediacy of contact with the Spirit world of their ancestors. This Spirit is linked to particular places, and from the moment of birth-stirring the child receives the totem of that specific site.[31] For non-Indigenous people, and even uninitiated Indigenous people, awareness of the Spirit world is taboo. With such knowledge passed on through song and dance there is little written material available for study. What follows is an excerpt from a book written by a White woman and an Aboriginal man:

> For Gumbaynggirr people living in No Mans Land,[32] the knowledge of spirits in places belonged to the Old People. It was passed on through ceremony, particularly initiation ceremonies. This knowledge today is passed on in stories, in special places, and in the spirit presences of the Old People. These spirit presences visit people in their daily lives at the Old Camp by the Lake. People feel close to these spirits and welcome them as a sign of caring and protection.[33]

> Old Fred Laurie danced the brolga dance at the Old Camp as an initiated man. He painted himself up with white ochre from Corindi Beach and danced the brolga dance to teach the young men about the spirits of the brolga place. The dance, like the songs, holds some of the powers of the spirits of that place where the men changed into brolgas.[34]

If we non-Indigenous Australians could let go our presumption of cultural superiority, we would have much to learn from those who have lived in this land for over forty thousand years.

---

30. Clifton H. Johnson, ed., *God Struck Me Dead: Voices of Ex-Slaves* (Eugene, OR: Wipf & Stock, 2010), 23.

31. Graham Paulson, "Towards an Aboriginal Theology," *Pacifica* 19 (2006): 313–14.

32. No Mans Land [*sic*] is a coastal strip in northern NSW, Australia. It was called this because land further inland had been claimed by European settlers. No one had fenced in the sand dunes and the coastal strip.

33. Margaret Somerville and Tony Perkins, *Singing the Coast* (Canberra, ACT: Aboriginal Studies Press, 2010), 131.

34. Ibid., 133.

Conclusion (14:27-31)

The themes of the two statements about Jesus's going and his coming are summarized in the conclusion with an assurance of peace and a repetition of his earlier words beginning this section (14:1). The conclusion also adds the important hermeneutical information for making sense of these two chapters of the original discourse. They are words spoken *before* (v. 29) the event of Jesus's passion so that the disciples may understand the meaning of this event beyond the horrific execution by Rome of a Jewish troublemaker. The "hour" must be seen within the love of the Father and Son and also within the cosmic dimension of the conquering of one considered "the ruler of the world" (v. 30). Such understanding can happen only through the effects of the cross and the giving of the Spirit.

The first discourse, with its movement from the footwashing (chap. 13) into the Father's house (chap. 14), ends abruptly with Jesus's directive: "Rise, let us go from here." These words then lead directly into the beginning of the passion: "After Jesus had spoken these words, he went out with his disciples across the Kidron valley to a place where there was a garden, which he and his disciples entered" (18:1).

The Father's House/Household— A Johannine Symbol

In suggesting "household" as a possible symbol for the self-identity of the Johannine community, I am not suggesting that this gospel community organized itself along patriarchal lines. A proper understanding of symbol will liberate the term "household" from its cultural/sociological meaning and allow it to take on a theological meaning. In other words, the household model for the Johannine community is not to be found in the social sphere of the first century but to be located in the world of divine relationships.

In his work on symbol, Paul Ricoeur begins with examining the dynamics of a metaphor, which he describes as a linguistic double meaning. Two realities from different contexts or domains are brought together in such a way that simply, at a verbal level, the statement does not make sense.[35] The reader is then forced to grapple with the assimilation of these two realities into some meaningful relationship beyond the verbal

---

35. The following brief description of a metaphor and symbol draws upon Paul Ricoeur, *Interpretation Theory: Discourse and the Surplus of Meaning* (Fort Worth: Texas Christian University Press, 1976), 45–69.

John 14:27-31

[27]"Peace I leave with you; my peace I give to you. I do not give to you as the world gives. Do not let your hearts be troubled, and do not let them be afraid. [28]You heard me say to you, 'I am going away, and I am coming to you.' If you loved me, you would rejoice that I am going to the Father, because the Father is greater than I. [29]And now I have told you this before it occurs, so that when it does occur, you may believe. [30]I will no longer talk much with you, for the ruler of this world is coming. He has no power over me; [31]but I do as the Father has commanded me, so that the world may know that I love the Father. Rise, let us be on our way."

sense, creating something new out of what would otherwise be absurd. To speak of the Father's household we are speaking metaphorically. The theory of metaphor notes that there is both an *is* and an *is not* operating in this type of speech. Literally, "the Father," the full reality of divinity, is not a biological parent. The linguistic tension between the *is* and *is not* is the dynamic that enables a metaphor to create a new perception of reality. In a similar manner a symbol looks beyond its factual reality for its meaning; it refers to another level of reality and truth that is accessible only through the symbol. This last point is critical for understanding the theological necessity for symbols. Our primary way of knowing is mediated through sensory experiences: what we see, hear, taste, touch, and smell. In itself, however, the divine or spiritual world is beyond such sensory experience. For that reason, the process of revelation occurs through symbolic experience. God's presence is known through what God does, in creation, in the history of Israel, through prophetic teaching and writing, and, for Christians, in the incarnation of the divine Word. The reality of Jesus's humanity provides access to the reality of God. The transcendent is present in the symbol.[36]

In the Fourth Gospel, particularly in the last discourse, Jesus refers to aspects of his relationship with God as a

36. Sandra Schneiders's early work on symbolism in the Fourth Gospels remains foundational for appreciating the symbolic nature of biblical texts from a theological perspective, especially the Fourth Gospel. See Sandra M. Schneiders, "History and Symbolism in the Fourth Gospel," in *L'Évangile de Jean: Sources, rédaction, théologie*, ed. Marinus de Jonge, BETL 44 (Gembloux: J. Duculot, 1977), 371–76; and Sandra M. Schneiders, "Symbolism and the Sacramental Principle in the Fourth Gospel," in *Segni*

model for human relationships: "Holy Father, protect them in your name that you have given me, so that they may be one, as we are one" (17:11); "that they may all be one. As you, Father, are in me and I am in you, may they also be in us" (17:21, also 22).[37] This explicit comparison between human relationships and the divine world provides a hermeneutic for examining household, not in reference to Jewish/Greco-Roman patriarchal models, but using the relationships between the Father, Jesus, and the Spirit as the primary reference.[38] While the term "Father's house/hold" comes from the social context of the Gospel, it must be understood in a symbolic sense as referring to people who experience a relationship with God and with each other. Its reference is a household "not of this world."[39]

Dorothy Lee examines the meaning of "Father" within the Gospel text, allowing the evangelist to create his own world of meaning. In this way, fatherhood is properly interpreted by asking what kind of father figure is described in the Gospel. She points to the number of times in the Gospel where "the Father-symbol occurs in narrative contexts that are concerned with the surrender of power."[40] The Father's love for the world renders him vulnerable through the gift of his Son, given over to death. Power and authority are not held on to by the Father but are relinquished freely to the Son. This is in sharp contrast with the figure of the *paterfamilias* in the Greco-Roman world. Lee

---

E Sacramenti Nel Vangelo Di Giovanni, ed. Pius-Ramon Tragan, SA 67 (Rome: Editrice Anselmiana, 1977), 221–35. Since her work, there have been other studies of Johannine symbolism, including Craig Koester, *Symbolism in the Fourth Gospel: Meaning, Mystery, Community* (Minneapolis: Fortress, 1995) and Jörg Frey, Jan G. van der Watt, and Ruben Zimmermann, eds., *Imagery in the Gospel of John: Terms, Forms, Themes and Theology of Johannine Figurative Language*, WUNT 200 (Tübingen: Mohr Siebeck, 2006).

37. Other examples of this correlation between the divine world and the human world can be seen in John 6:57; 10:14-15; 13:15, 34; 15:9, 10, 12; 17:18; 20:21.

38. I am not suggesting here that the Fourth Gospel is already using a full trinitarian concept of God that will develop in later centuries.

39. In speaking of his kingship, Jesus says to Pilate, "My kingship is not of this world" (19:36). I am applying this same principle to the notion of household. While the metaphor of household or kingship uses the language of first-century culture, the reference is to the divine world.

40. Dorothy A. Lee, "The Symbol of Divine Fatherhood," *Semeia* 85 (1999): 180. Lee developed her critical understanding of the symbol of God as Father in Dorothy A. Lee, *Flesh and Glory: Symbolism, Gender and Theology in the Gospel of John* (New York: Crossroad, 2002), 110–34.

contrasts the gospel language of intimacy and mutuality with that of duty and fear associated with Roman family life and points out that the mutual love between Father and Son is opened out to include others. "Unlike patriarchal kinship, those outside the immediate family are drawn into the paternal embrace (*kolpon*, 1:18)."[41] Even the master-slave model is rejected and deconstructed by the model of friendship (15:11-17).

With Lee, I want to insist that the symbolism of the Gospel be taken seriously. God, in God's self, is beyond gender categories, beyond names and representations, and would be utterly unknowable without God's gracious self-revelation in ways accessible to human apprehension. Even then, the language used to speak of this revelation is necessarily metaphorical due to the limitation of language to express adequately the divine reality. The God we speak of always *is* and *is not* communicable. In

becoming flesh, the divine has allowed a specific particularity, Jesus, to be the means of God's presence in history. The male Jesus is symbol of the divine *Sophia/Logos*, and the Father in this Gospel is a symbol of the life-giving, self-surrendering God who invites all to be embraced as children (1:12). The "Father's house/hold" functions in the text as a way the evangelist tries to articulate the experience of being drawn into participation in God's own life mediated through Jesus and the Spirit. A father-son relationship becomes a symbol for the believer's post-Easter experience of life in Jesus. As Lee writes, "God's fatherhood operates in the Gospel by drawing others into the filial relationship between God and Jesus, so that it becomes symbolic of God's relationship to the world."[42] Ultimately, the challenge to the reader is not so much to see divinity in terms of fatherhood but to revision parenting in the light of the Gospel.

The Spirit/Paraclete[43]
The "Glue" of the Community
In the Fourth Gospel, the Spirit is named Paraclete (παράκλητος) by Jesus in five

distinct sections of the discourse (14:16, 26; 15:26; 16:7 [Spirit of truth]; 16:13-15). Others have provided a distinctly feminist exploration of the Spirit, noting

---

41. Lee, "Divine Fatherhood," 181.
42. Lee, *Flesh and Glory*, 126.
43. More will be said on the Spirit/Paraclete when examining specific passages.

that in the Hebrew the word "Spirit" (רוח) is feminine.[44] Here I ask, does the Fourth Gospel offer anything more?

When the Spirit/Paraclete first occurs in chapter 14, its role is one of mediation. The Paraclete will be the means of the community's ongoing experience of Jesus. The Jesus who becomes the absent-one in the post-Easter time can still be a presence in the lives of believers through the mediation of the Spirit. In one sense, the Spirit is the "glue" maintaining the interpersonal relationship between Jesus and believers. This "glue" image is readily visible in the place women have in families and communities. In commenting on the importance of African women in precolonial Zimbabwe, Barbara Moss writes: "However, women were the glue which bound communities together. Although men and women worked together, women spent most of their time in gender-segregated groupings where they performed most of the daily tasks which kept the household viable."[45] Women in this society also had significant roles in worship, which is a further role of the Spirit. "Those who could communicate with spirits were important to the living. Religious ritual was thus an ear to God and women did much of the whispering."[46]

A Voice for Women

In later chapters, the role of the Spirit/Paraclete shifts from mediating between Jesus and believer to a more forensic role of mediating in conflicts between believers and the synagogue (15:26), believers and the world (16:7-11, 13-15). In these conflict situations the Spirit/Paraclete will testify on behalf of Jesus, alongside the testimony of the disciples (15:26-27). This testimony will take place before Jews, and Jesus warns that on account of this testimony, "They will put you out of the synagogues" (16:2). Facing conflict from the wider politico-religious world of the Gentiles, where "world" refers to the mytho-cosmic world of the evil one, the Spirit/Paraclete will prove the world wrong (16:8), will offer guidance to the community (16:13), and will disclose to them the mind of Jesus (16:14-15).

This forensic aspect of the Spirit/Paraclete's role is well summed up in the phrase

---

44. See, for example, the excursus by Helen Bergin, "The Spirit as the 'Feminine Face of God'" in Barbara Reid and Shelly Matthews, *Luke 1–9*, WCS 43A (Collegeville, MN: Liturgical Press, 2020), 111–14.

45. Babara A. Moss, "'And the Bones Come Together': Women's Religious Expectations in Southern Africa, c 1900–1945," *The Journal of Religious History* 23 (1999): 110.

46. Ibid.

"speaking truth to power." Women in many cultures and localities have drawn strength from these four words to challenge the injustices that keep women subjugated and demeaned. In workplaces, families, churches, and societies, women find themselves voiceless and powerless. It is only when one woman dares to speak her truth that others draw the courage needed to face their abusers—be it sexual, economic, spiritual, or social. Journalist Peggy Guest writes, "As individual women had the courage to name their experience when raped or abused by strangers or by friends and relatives, the cultural systems changed."[47]

The inner movement propelling women to take such a risk, I would name the Spirit/Paraclete.

47. Peggy Guest, "The Personal Is Political: Women's Empowerment; Years of Speaking Truth to Power Have Improved the Legal System," *St. Louis Post-Dispatch*, May 24, 2011, A15.

John 15:1-17

Sophia's Friends

Therefore I prayed, and understanding was given me;
I called on God, and the spirit of wisdom [Sophia] came to me.

For she is a breath of the power of God,
and a pure emanation of the glory of the Almighty; . . .
For she is a reflection of eternal light,
a spotless mirror of the working of God,
and an image of God's goodness.
Although she is but one, she can do all things,
and while abiding [μένουσα] in herself, she renews all things;
in every generation she passes into holy souls
and makes them friends of God, and prophets. (Wis 7:7, 25-27)

Wisdom praises herself,
    and tells of her glory in the midst of her people. . . .
In the holy tent [ἐν σκηνῇ ἁγίᾳ] I ministered before him,
    and so I was established in Zion.
Like the vine [ἄμπελος] I bud forth delights,
    and my blossoms become glorious and abundant fruit. (Sir 24:1, 10, 17)

In the footwashing, disciples participated in a ritual act of welcome into the household of God. The "House of God," i.e., the temple, was renamed by Jesus as "my Father's house" (2:16), and in chapter 14 this terminology returned with a deeper, personalized image, which was more properly named "my Father's household" (τῇ οἰκίᾳ τοῦ πατρός).

Sophia's figurative language continues in John 15:1-17 with the introduction of a new image—the vine. Together, these two images of "household" and "vine" offer the distinctly Johannine perspective on salvation as a communion of life formed by the mutual indwelling of God and the believer. "On that day you will know that I am in my Father, and you in me, and I in you" (14:20). Where chapter 14 used the image of the household/temple of God to describe a series of *divine* indwellings, chapter 15 focuses on the indwelling of the *believer* in Jesus.

With chapter 15, a new complexity emerges. Jesus has just said, "Rise, let us be on our way" (14:31), and his words would lead seamlessly into, "After Jesus had spoken these words, he went out with his disciples across the Kidron valley to a place where there was a garden, which he and his disciples entered" (18:1). The placement of chapters 15 to 17 interrupts this narrative and raises many scholarly questions. Before examining John 15, it is necessary to consider the relationship between 13:1–14:31 and what follows.

John 15:1–17:26 within the Farewell Discourse

In looking at 15:1–17:26 scholars have differing opinions on its position in the discourse.[1] Recent European scholarship has been using the expressions *réécriture* (rewriting) and *relecture* (rereading) when considering the relationship between chapters 15–17 and 13–14. Jean Zumstein, Andreas Dettwiler, and Klaus Scholtissek have applied these literary and hermeneutical understandings in their analyses of the Gospel.[2] What

1. For a detailed discussion of scholarly views, see Fernando F. Segovia, *Love Relationships in the Johannine Tradition: Agape/Agapan in 1 John and the Fourth Gospel*, SBLDS 58 (Missoula: Scholars Press, 1982), 82–101; R. Bultmann, *The Gospel of John: A Commentary*, trans. G. R. Beasley Murray et al. (Oxford: Blackwell, 1971), 523; Rainer Borig, *Der Wahre Weinstock, Untersuchungen zu Jo 15:1-10*, SANT 16 (Munich: Kösel, 1967), 19; Raymond E. Brown, *The Gospel according to John*, 2 vols., AB 29–29A (New York: Doubleday, 1966, 1970), 2:658; Rudolph Schnackenburg, *The Gospel according to St John*, trans. K. Smyth et al., 3 vols., HTCNT (London: Burns & Oates, 1968–1982), 3:95; John Painter, "The Farewell Discourses and the History of Johannine Christianity," *NTS* 27 (1981): 526; Francis J. Moloney, *John*, SP 4 (Collegeville, MN: Liturgical Press, 1998), 416–17.

2. Jean Zumstein, *Kreative Erinnerung: Relecture und Auslegung im Johannesevangelium*, ATANT (Zürich: TVZ, 2004), 15–30; Andreas Dettwiler, *Die Gegenwart des Erhöhten: Eine exegetische Studie zu den johanneischen Abschiedsreden (Joh 13,31–16,33) unter besonderer Berücksichtigung ihres Relecture-Charakters* (Göttingen: Vandenhoeck & Ruprecht, 1995), 46–52; Klaus Scholtissek, *In Ihm sein und bleiben: Die Sprache der*

these new approaches add to earlier suggestions of different versions (Borig) and additions (Brown) is a more developed hermeneutical theory of a community guided by the Paraclete reinterpreting the Scriptures and their own tradition.[3] The hermeneutic of *relecture* accords well with feminist thinking as it proposes that a text develops because of later *experience*. When proposing a method for feminist interpretation, Elisabeth Schüssler Fiorenza states: "As a critical process of conscientization and emancipation, the spiraling dance of biblical interpretation begins with a hermeneutics of experience. From their beginnings, feminist theory and theology have understood experience as a central category and norm."[4] As the author engages with the later experience of the community, because of either changed historical circumstances or a deepening of the theology as new questions arise, the original text no longer suffices and so more is needed. Francis Moloney's summary of the process of *relecture* as articulated by Zumstein, Dettwiler, and Scholtissek is as follows:[5]

1. *Relecture* is an intertextual phenomenon that has to be analyzed both synchronically and diachronically.

2. The reread text (*der Rezeptionstext*) looks back on the original text (*der Bezugstext*) for its original meaning that it has further developed.

3. *Relecture* happens in the twofold action of further developing the original text and applying it to a different context.

Immanenz in den johanneischen Schriften, Herders Biblische Studien 21 (Freiburg: Herder, 2000), 131–39. Where Scholtissek relates 15:1-17 to John 8, and the saying about the son and slave in the household, Dettwiler argues that this passage is a *relecture* of the footwashing in 13:1-17.

A helpful summary of the processes of *réécriture* and *relecture* can be found in Raymond E. Brown, *An Introduction to the Gospel of John: Edited, Updated, Introduced and Concluded by Francis J. Moloney*, ABRL (New York: Doubleday, 2003), 291–92.

3. The role of the Paraclete, as the guide in the process of reflection and rearticulation of both the Scriptures and earlier aspects of the Gospel tradition, is described by Zumstein: "The Paraclete brings no new revelation, but reduplicates the eschatological event. He is the concrete remembrance of Jesus, the paschal retrospective of the incarnate Christ. He guides the *relecture* of the Jesus tradition." See Zumstein, *Kreative Erinnerung*, 29.

4. Elisabeth Schüssler Fiorenza, *Wisdom Ways: Introducing Feminist Biblical Interpretation* (Maryknoll, NY: Orbis Books, 2005), 169.

5. Brown, *An Introduction to the Gospel of John*, 291. This section is the work of Francis J. Moloney, added to Brown's original notes.

4. The final text is always to be understood as a *rereading* of the original text.

5. The reasons for *relecture* can, on the one hand, be a need for the further theological development of an original theological position within the narrative itself (synchrony), or, on the other hand, be needed because of a new historical or social situation of the community (diachrony).

6. The question of authorship plays little or no part in understanding the process of *relecture*.

The process of reinterpreting and revising earlier forms of the narrative does not necessarily require different authors. There is no need to postulate an original evangelist and a later editor when considering John 1–20. Even allowing for the process of *relecture*, the entire narrative could have been formulated by the creative theological reflection of one mind. The unity of theme, style, and theological perspective across these chapters argues for one author,[6] even though this author may have returned to his original narrative to offer further development in responding to the needs of his community. In the following discussion, I read chapters 13–17 as a coherent narrative by a single author.[7] Although some sections may be a later reformulation of an earlier discourse, I make no attempt to reconstruct a hypothetical historical situation that may have been the stimulus for these later reflections.[8] Instead, I postulate sections of the text based on their internal themes.

6. See Fernando F. Segovia, *The Farewell of the Word: The Johannine Call to Abide* (Minneapolis: Fortress, 1991), 320.

7. As Segovia (*The Farewell of the Word*, 48) states, "The present text of the farewell speech undoubtedly did represent to someone, somewhere, at some time, not only a unified and coherent literary whole but also a proper and meaningful form of communication."

8. One such reconstruction can be found in Painter, "The Farewell Discourses and the History of Johannine Christianity," 525–43. Painter bases his historical hypotheses on the three Paraclete sections found across the discourse. He suggests: the original discourse, 13:31–14:31; followed by a first revision, 15:1–16:4a; followed by a second revision, 16:4b-33. Chapter 17 is new material and not a revision of earlier material. Segovia also postulates a development in three stages but situates 15:1-17 as a final stage. His suggestion is: stage 1, 13:31–14:31; stage 2, 15:18–16:33 (with two small subdivisions); stage 3, 15:1-17. Stage 2 emerges in a situation of tension and conflict with the outside world, particularly with post-70 Judaism, while stage 3 reflects intramural tension and the possibility of community rupture; see Segovia, *The Farewell of*

There are two primary reasons why the majority of scholars take 15:1-17 as a distinct unit: First, the language associated with the vine, its branches, and fruit in verses 1-8 recurs in verse 16 as a way of expressing Jesus's teaching in verses 9-15. This language drawn from viticulture then disappears from the rest of the discourse. Second, verses 1-17 focus on the *internal* relationships between Jesus and the disciples while, beginning with verse 18, the remaining part of the discourse involves the relationship of disciples with the outside world.[9]

Structure of 15:1-17

Accepting 15:1-17 as a distinct unit, the next point of discussion is the unit's internal arrangement. Along with a number of scholars, I detect a parallelism across these verses forming two major units, verses 1-8 and verses 9-17. Verses 1 and 9 take their starting point in the relationship between Jesus and the Father expressed in images: "I am the vine and my father is the vinedresser" (v. 1); "As the Father has loved me" (v. 9). Both sections end with the assurance that disciples can "ask for whatever you wish" (v. 7), and "the Father will give you whatever you ask him in my name" (v. 16). The development of the vine imagery established in verse 1 temporarily concludes at verse 8, and verse 9 introduces the motif of "love," which extends through verses 9-17 (vv. 9, 10, 12, 13, 17).[10] In verses 14-15 the word "love" disappears and is replaced by "friend," which, according to Raymond Brown, is a term very close to "beloved"

---

the Word, 319–28. Along similar lines, Dettwiler (*Die Gegenwart des Erhöhten*, 100–107) makes the cautious suggestion that 15:1-17 arose out of a need to reaffirm the community's self-identity in the time after the destruction of the temple. In a situation of mounting tension with the synagogue, the text functions to remind believers that their identity rests solely on their relationship to Jesus and also that this relationship is conditional upon their remaining faithful (102). Dettwiler concludes thus: "historically we presuppose only the hypothesis of an extremely strained relationship between the Jewish synagogue and the Johannine community" (106). This statement represents my own position regarding the historical situation of the Gospel generally.

9. As well as Brown, some other scholars who read vv. 1-17 as a distinct unit are Marianne Meye Thompson, *John: A Commentary*, NTL (Louisville: Westminster John Knox, 2015), 322–30; Sharon H. Ringe, *Wisdom's Friends: Community and Christology in the Fourth Gospel* (Louisville: Westminster John Knox, 1999), 65–66; Dorothy A. Lee, *Flesh and Glory: Symbolism, Gender and Theology in the Gospel of John* (New York: Crossroad, 2002), 92; also by Lee, "Abiding in the Fourth Gospel: A Case-Study in Feminist Biblical Theology," *Pacifica* 10 (1997): 123–36.

10. The vine imagery appears again in v. 16, but it is not developed any further.

and so may be considered synonymous.[11] As well as the vine image in verses 1-8, these verses are also united by the constancy of the term μένω (dwell/remain/abide, vv. 3c, 4 [2x], 5, 6, 7 [2x]).[12] Within the two major sections, verses 1-8 and verses 9-17, the initial verses (vv. 1-3b, 9-11) establish a relational image that the rest of the section develops and applies to the disciples.

Part A	Part B
vv. 1-2 Viticulture image: The vine	vv. 9-11 Familial image: Jesus and the Father
vv. 3-8 Application to disciples	vv. 12-17 Application to disciples

The parallelism across these verses is shown in the following table:

A. vv. 1-8 Viticulture Image: The vine	B. vv. 9-17 Familial Image: Jesus and the Father
[1]"I am the true vine, and my Father is the vinegrower. [2]He removes every branch in me that bears no fruit. Every branch that bears fruit he prunes [καθαίρει] to make it bear more fruit.	[9]"As the Father has loved me, so I have loved you; abide in my love. [10]If you keep my commandments, you will abide in my love, just as I have kept my Father's commandments and abide in his love.
Aside[13] [3]You have already been cleansed [καθαροί][14] by the word that I have spoken to you.	Aside [11]I have said these things to you so that my joy may be in you, and that your joy may be complete.

---

11. Brown, *The Gospel according to John*, 2:664 n. 13. Similarly, Ringe, *Wisdom's Friends*, 65; and Lee, *Flesh and Glory*, 99.

12. Moloney sees the term "dwell" (μένω) as the controlling theme of the passage rather than the imagery of the vine and makes a break after v. 11 (Moloney, *John*, 417). He states that the vine "metaphor is not an end in itself but serves as a vehicle to articulate the importance of abiding." Francis J. Moloney, *Glory not Dishonour: Reading John 13–21* (Minneapolis: Fortress, 1998), 58. I consider that the parallelism across the section requires the first major break after v. 8 rather than after v. 11.

13. In his earlier work Segovia used the term "aside" to describe the function of vv. 3 and 11; Segovia, *Love Relationships*, 101, 110.

14. The same verb (καθαίρω) is used to speak of cleansing and pruning.

Teaching imperative: Dwell in me	Teaching imperative: Love one another
[4]Abide [μείνατε] in me as I abide in you. Just as the branch cannot bear fruit by itself unless it abides [μένη] in the vine, neither can you unless you abide [μένητε] in me.	[12]This is my commandment, that you love one another as I have loved you. [13]No one has greater love than this, to lay down one's life for one's friends.
Disciples: You are the branches	**Disciples: You are my friends**
[5]I am the vine, you are the branches. Those who abide [μένων] in me and I in them bear much fruit, because apart from me you can do nothing. [6]Whoever does not abide [μένη] in me is thrown away like a branch and withers; such branches are gathered, thrown into the fire, and burned. [7]If you abide [μείνητε] in me, and my words abide [μείνη] in you,	[14]You are my friends if you do what I command you. [15]I do not call you servants any longer, because the servant does not know what the master is doing; but I have called you friends, because I have made known to you everything that I have heard from my Father. [16]You did not choose me but I chose you. And I appointed you to go and bear fruit, fruit that will last,
Consequences[15]	**Consequences**
ask for whatever you wish, and it will be done for you.	so that the Father will give you whatever you ask him in my name.
Conclusion	**Conclusion**
[8]My Father is glorified by this, that you bear much fruit and become my disciples."	[17]I am giving you these commands so that you may love one another."

Literary Genre

The imagery of the vine and branches is difficult to categorize. In his review of previous scholarship, Fernando Segovia notes the following words used to classify the image: *Bildrede, mashal,* an extended metaphor, parable, and allegory.[16] Segovia favors the expression "sustained metaphor," while the complexity of the imagery in John 15:1-8 leads Jan van der Watt to speak of a "metaphorical network."[17] The Gospel itself

15. The term "consequences" comes from Segovia (*Love Relationships*, 107).

16. Segovia, *The Farewell of the Word,* 133–34. See also the summary table in Jan G. van der Watt, *Family of the King: Dynamics of Metaphor in the Gospel according to John,* BibInt 47 (Leiden: Brill, 2000), 29.

17. Segovia, *The Farewell of the Word,* 125; Van der Watt, *Family of the King,* 125.

states, "I have said these things to you in figures of speech" (παροιμίαις
λελάληκα, 16:25; see also 10:6; 16:29).[18] According to van der Watt the
term παροιμία implies a "double vision" or "two realities," which is very
close to the way he describes metaphor.[19] Awareness of the metaphorical
use of "vine" and "branch" requires an awareness of the other familial
metaphor of "father" and "son." Metaphors draw together in one statement two different realities while inviting the reader to see "an intuitive
perception of the similarity . . . in the dissimilars."[20] Metaphors tran-
scend the literalness of the words, creating an image in the mind that
defies exact translation.[21] This is particularly important when speaking
of the divinity in terms of "father" and "son." In reading "father/son"
terms in the Gospel, a caution is needed not to project backward from
later controversies the metaphysical language of "trinity." The Gospel
author is not making statements about the inner life of the Godhead but
rather bearing witness to the human experience of Jesus in his intimate
relationship with God and the post-Easter experience of the community
in their ongoing sense of a living, "enspirited" presence of the Christ.[22]

A writer who sees value in thinking of God as Trinity is Hannah Bacon.
She moves beyond the usual feminist critiques of trinitarian language
to argue that

> a discussion of what it might mean to think rightly about God and how
> this might impact feminist-Christian praxis is both timely and essential.
> This need not locate discussion of God in abstraction if the revelation of
> God in creaturely existence is taken as the foundation and Trinitarian
> thought is identified as principally a matter of thinking "back" from
> Christology to the wider doctrine of God. While in no way collapsing
> God the Father into God the Son, what this does assert with confidence
> is that there is no God outside the flesh and that the expansive, fleshy

---

18. Scholtissek describes these verses as a unique Johannine form that is *sui generis*
and suggests it can be compared only to other Johannine "figurative language" such
as the shepherd and sheepfold material in chap. 10. See Scholtissek, *Sein und Bleiben,*
278. He reads 15:1-8 as a *relecture* of 10:1-18.

19. van der Watt, *Family of the King,* 158–60.

20. Paul Ricoeur, *The Rule of Metaphor: Multidisciplinary Studies of the Creation of Meaning in Language* (London: Routledge & Kegan Paul, 1977), 23. For more on Ricoeur's
theory of metaphor, see excursus in chap. 14, "The Father's House/Household—A
Johannine Symbol."

21. See the work of Paul Ricoeur, *Interpretation Theory: Discourse and the Surplus of
Meaning* (Fort Worth: Texas Christian University Press, 1976), 45–69.

22. See the excursus below for particular feminist approaches to the Trinity.

space of the Trinity is big enough to embrace all bodies, in all their difference and particularities.[23]

Abiding

The vine metaphor functions to give expression to the Johannine theological word μένω (abide, abiding, dwell). Sometimes this is translated simply as "remain" or "stay," but its use primarily in a relational context lifts its meaning from such mundane uses. The Spirit is an abiding presence upon Jesus (1:32); the first disciples, responding to the testimony of John, follow Jesus and then "abide" with him (1:39). Dorothy Lee states, "Abiding belongs fundamentally to the divine realm."[24] In John 14, μένω was the term binding Father, Spirit, and Jesus with each other and with disciples. This term evoked the image of the many dwellings of the Father's household (14:2), as the triune God came to dwell in believers, making them into living temples. The active agent of this verb, "dwell," changes in John 15, where believers now are invited to dwell in the vine. The two chapters together express the mutual indwelling of God-believers in a communion of love. "Abiding defines the divine-human relationship as one of immanence: subject to subject, face to face, I-Thou. . . . It is mutual rather than condescending, co-operative rather than competitive, non-hierarchical rather than status-ridden. If abiding means kinship with God, it means simultaneous kinship with others who share similar yearnings."[25] The quality of the relationship expressed in this word "abiding" brings women and men together on the level, nonhierarchical, egalitarian plain of love.

Abiding, or dwelling, also reaches beyond humanity to respect the essential, yet fragile, relationship human creatures have with all creation. As long as we place ourselves "above" earth and her creatures we can find no ethic for sustainable and yet flourishing life. Here, we White Australians have much to learn from Indigenous Australians. They speak reverentially of "country," not "the country" as a thing, but "country" as an equal, living, spirit-filled being. They do not "own" land; in fact, it is as if country owns them as they respect her many seasons and faces.

23. Hannah Bacon, "Thinking the Trinity as Resource for Feminist Theology Today?," *Cross Currents* 62 (2012): 461–62.

24. Lee, *Flesh and Glory*, 89.

25. Dorothy A. Lee, "Abiding in the Fourth Gospel: A Case Study in Feminist Biblical Theology," in *A Feminist Companion to John*, vol. 2, ed. Amy-Jill Levine, FCNTECW 5 (London: Sheffield Academic, 2003), 75.

To describe this inter-dwelling of human and all nonhuman creation, Elizabeth Johnson speaks of pan*en*theism—all-in-God. "Panentheism entails a kind of asymmetrical mutual indwelling, not of two equal partners, but of the infinite God who dwells within all things sparking them into being and finite creatures who dwell within the embrace of divine love."[26] As the Fourth Gospel states, "Abide in me, as I abide in you" (15:4; μείνατε ἐν ἐμοί, κἀγὼ ἐν ὑμῖν).

John 15:1-17 as *Relecture* of 14:1-31

In examining the relationship between 15:1-17 and the preceding chapters, the process of *relecture* offers a helpful way of explaining both the disjunction at 14:31—"Arise, let us go"—and the repetitions of themes and words particularly across chapters 14 and 15:1-17. Within chapter 14 there are three occasions where disciples interrupt Jesus's discourse, revealing their lack of comprehension (14:5, 8, 22). In narrative time, these are issues raised by disciples prior to Easter, but these questions may also voice issues faced by the post-Easter believers who, puzzled by the delay of the parousia and troubled by tension with the local synagogue, are forced to clarify their own religious identity and to make a clear choice for Jesus. In chapter 14, an initial response is made to each of these interjections, but these responses are repeated and developed further in chapter 15, particularly in verses 9-17. I note the following themes:

the loving union of the Father and Jesus (14:10, 11, 21, 23, 25; 15:3c, 9, 10)

the glorification of the Father (14:13; 15:8)

asking in Jesus's name (14:13, 14; 15:7, 16)

keeping the commandments linked to love (14:21; 15:10)

These repetitions in such close proximity lead me to propose that 15:9-17, and its introductory image of the vine and the branches (15:1-8), is a *relecture* of 14:1-31.[27] Using the image of the temple/Father's house-

---

26. Elizabeth A. Johnson, *Ask the Beasts: Darwin and the God of Love* (London: Bloomsbury, 2014), 147. The title is taken from Job. "Asks the beasts and they will teach you" (Job 12:7).

27. Arguments relating 15:1-17 to the six aspects of a *relecture* as outlined by Moloney are detailed in Mary L. Coloe, *Dwelling in the Household of God: Johannine Ecclesiology and Spirituality* (Collegeville, MN: Liturgical Press, 2007), 157.

hold (14:2), chapter 14 emphasized God, Father, Jesus, Paraclete dwelling in the disciples (14:17, 23, 25), but as the interjections make clear, Jesus's words were not fully grasped. In chapter 15, using the image of the vine and the branches, the focus shifts to the disciples dwelling in Jesus and the reciprocal indwelling of Jesus and the Father. The intimate relationship between Jesus and the Father is not a new theme since it has been present across the Gospel (e.g., 1:1, 18; 5:20; 10:30, 38). What is new is the teaching that now disciples can also participate in this divine indwelling by their reciprocal indwelling in Jesus.

The image of the vine and the branches is a teaching tool to illustrate the close and necessary mutual indwelling of Jesus and disciples. Such mutual indwelling has no room for hierarchies of any kind, as Jesus says, "I no longer call you servants [δούλους]. . . . I have called you friends" (15:15). Egalitarian friendship created by bonds of love is the ethic called for by this image. Gail O'Day notes the organic nature of this image with "no individual a free agent, but is one branch of an encircling and intertwining vine whose fruitfulness depends on abiding with Jesus." This is in marked contrast to "Western models of individualism, privatism and success based on individual accomplishment. This metaphor assumes social interrelationship and accountability."[28] This is the one and only means that makes possible the mutual indwelling with the Father. By dwelling in Jesus, disciples will be enabled to dwell in the Father. Through keeping Jesus's command to love, disciples will dwell in Jesus's love and will in turn be loved by the Father, and the Father will dwell with them. Jesus's mission has been to reveal God. This is not simply intellectual knowing but an experience of a quality of God's own life, named in the Gospel as "eternity life" (e.g., 3:15, 16; 6:47, 54). Jesus is the singular way into the relationship with the Father and thus into the eternity life of God. The branches live only in their relationship to the vine. As a *relecture* of Jesus's response to the disciples' lack of comprehension in chapter 14, John 15:1-17 offers further clarification and development.

Viticulture Image (15:1-8)

The first part of this section (vv. 1-8) develops the imagery of the vineyard so familiar to people of that time.[29] Verse 1 begins by establishing

---

28. Gail R. O'Day, "John," in *The Women's Bible Commentary*, ed. Carol A. Newsom and Sharon H. Ringe, exp. ed. (Louisville: Westminster John Knox, 1998), 391.

29. See the excursus below on first-century viticultural practice. For a description of vine farming in antiquity, see van der Watt, *Family of the King*, 26–29. On the Jewish

John 15:1-8

15:1"I am the true vine, and my Father is the vinegrower. ²He removes every branch in me that bears no fruit. Every branch that bears fruit he prunes to make it bear more fruit. ³You have already been cleansed by the word that I have spoken to you. ⁴Abide in me as I abide in you. Just as the branch cannot bear fruit by itself unless it abides in the vine, nether can you unless you abide in me. ⁵I am the vine, you are the branches. Those who abide in me and I in them bear much fruit, because apart from me you can do nothing. ⁶Whoever does not abide in me is thrown away like a branch and withers; such branches are gathered, thrown into the fire, and burned. ⁷If you abide in me, and my words abide in you, ask for whatever you wish, and it will be done for you. ⁸My Father is glorified by this, that you bear much fruit and become my disciples."

the relationship between the vine and vinedresser and identifying the roles of Father and Son in this metaphor. The vinedresser's role is not mentioned after verse 2 as the metaphor concentrates on describing the relationship between the vine and the branches. By establishing the vine/vinedresser connection first, the metaphor grounds all further developments in this primary relationship. Verses 2 and 3 exploit the double meaning of the word καθαίρω, to make clean and to prune.[30] Stepping outside the imagery and speaking directly to his disciples, Jesus tells them that they are pruned/cleansed now through his word. In his discussion of verse 3, Klaus Scholtissek relates it to what was said by Jesus in chapter 8: "If you dwell [μείνητε] in my word, you are truly my disciples; and you will know the truth, and the truth will make you free" (8:31-32). And also his words to Peter in the footwashing scene: "One who has bathed does not need to wash, except for the feet, but is entirely clean [καθαρὸς]" (13:10).[31] While chapter 8, with its use of the future "will know," looks ahead to the time after the passion, 15:2 is said with the post-Easter perspective of disciples who *have* remained in Jesus's word

---

background for this image, see Schnackenburg, *The Gospel according to St John*, 3:104–7; Scholtissek, *Sein und Bleiben*, 279–81.

30. Johannes P. Louw and Eugene A. Nida, eds., *Greek-English Lexicon of the New Testament: Based on Semantic Domains*, 2nd ed., 2 vols. (New York: United Bible Societies, 1996), 1:699, §79.49: "In Jn 15.2 the meaning of καθαίρω may also be understood as 'to prune branches,' thus playing on two distinct meanings of καθαίρω."

31. Scholtissek, *Sein und Bleiben*, 288–90.

and who *have* therefore been cleansed/made free by their participation in his passion as symbolized in the act of footwashing.[32]

On Pruning and Cutting Away

To the non-gardener the words about cutting away and pruning (15:2) may sound threatening or judgmental, but in fact these actions are done to care for the life and fruitfulness of a plant. It is only by cutting away the no-longer-useful wood that new and more abundant growth is encouraged, with more prolific flowers.[33]

πᾶν κλῆμα ἐν ἐμοὶ μὴ φέρον
καρπὸν αἴρει αὐτό,
Every branch in me not
bearing fruit he removes
καὶ πᾶν τὸ καρπὸν φέρον
καθαίρει αὐτὸ ἵνα καρπὸν
πλείονα φέρῃ.
Every branch bearing fruit
he prunes so that it will
bear more.

In these verses (author's translation), a distinction is made between two types of branches in the vine. One is clearly a fruit-bearing branch; the other is not. The fruit-bearing branch is pruned so that it will be even more productive, while the non-fruit-bearing plant is treated differently. The verb αἴρει has many nuances of meaning, "to lift up, to carry, to move, to remove,"[34] and so, when used to speak of the branches, it is often translated "cut off," which can sound harsh. But understanding the first-century practice of viticulture may offer a less judgmental understanding. On this, the writing of Pliny offers a guide.[35] Pliny describes the different types of branches found on a vine

[a] The shoot which comes out of the hard timber and promises wood for the next year is called a leafy shoot or else when it is above the scar a fruit-bearing shoot,
[b] whereas the other kind of shoot that springs from a year-old branch is always a fruit-bearer.
[c] There is also left underneath the cross-bar a shoot called the keeper— this is a young branch, not

---

32. With Scholtissek, I also read the footwashing as a symbolic action drawing the disciples into the salvific meaning of Jesus's passion. For more on this, see the earlier discussion of John 13.

33. I write from my experience with roses and a row of espalier citrus trees: oranges, lemons, pomelos, and limes.

34. William Arndt, "αἴρω," in BDAG (2000): 28.

35. This passage is from Pliny's *Natural History* 17.35 as translated by Gary W. Derickson, "Viticulture and John 15:1-6," *BSac* 153 (1996): 46.

longer than three buds, which will provide wood next year if the vine's luxurious growth has used itself up—and another shoot next to it, the size of a wart, called the pilferer is also left, in case the keeper-shoot should fail.

From this description all the branches are kept but are treated differently depending on where they sprout from—the hard timber, or a year-old branch. Gary Derickson suggests that the image reflects the spring-time viticultural practice, which accords with the Passover timing:

> It would be better to see Jesus indicating what actually occurred during the spring, namely, certain non-fruiting branches were tied to the trellises along with the fruiting branches while the side shoots of the fruiting branches were being "cleaned up." The non-fruiting branches were allowed to grow with full vigor and without the removal of any side growth or leaves, since the more extensive their growth the greater the diameter of their stem where it connected to the vine, giving greater ability to produce more fruit the following season. Removing [or lifting] the non-fruiting branches from the ground and placing them on the trellis would allow the rows of plants to benefit from unhindered aeration, considered an essential element to proper fruit development. To see αίρει as removal (judgment or discipline) is to contradict the actual practice of the time. . . . Both kinds of branches may be in Christ and may be abiding, since they both existed, and were desired on every vine in Jesus' day.[36]

Following the harvest, a second type of pruning occurs as the plant moves into dormancy for the winter. At this time there is a more severe pruning, of the fruitful as well as the unfruitful branches, all done to encourage abundant fecundity. After this pruning, some branches are no longer connected to, or abiding, in the vine; they lie separated on the ground.

Rather than warning of discipline or judgment, verse 6 illustrates uselessness in light of dormant-season pruning. . . . Only at the end of the season would "branches" be removed, piled up, and burned. . . . In a vineyard anything not attached to the vine is useless and

36. Derickson, "Viticulture," 49.

discarded. A part of the discarding process at the end of the productive season is the burning of dry materials. The burning need not describe judgment; it is simply one step in the process being described. It is what happens to pruned materials. Their uselessness, not their destruction, is being emphasized.[37]

Before I leave the discussion of the practice of vinegrowing, the Bible provides evidence that women as well as men had

vineyards (Song 1:6), tended their vines (Prov 31:16), joined in the harvest festivals (Judg 21:21), and drank of the produce (Ruth 2:14; 1 Sam 1:9; Job 1:13). In the Song of Songs, the Shulammite woman claims her vineyard for herself: "My vineyard, my very own, is for myself" (Song 8:12). A community hearing the image of a vine, in the context of a meal of love (ἀγάπη), could enter into the image only with joyful memories of seeing the vines of ripening grapes and then the celebrations of the harvest.

The image resumes in verse 4 with the command, "Dwell in me as I in you" (μείνατε ἐν ἐμοί, κἀγὼ ἐν ὑμῖν). For the first time in this chapter the verb "dwell" (μένω)[38] is used, and this term will dominate the rest of the passage as a means of describing a number of relationships: between vine and branch (v. 4), disciples and Jesus (vv. 5, 6, 7), the word of Jesus and the disciples (v. 7), the disciple and Jesus's love (vv. 9, 10), Jesus and the Father's love (v. 10), and also the enduring quality of the fruit (v. 15). In verse 4 there is a uniquely Johannine shift in the vine imagery that was not foreshadowed in any previous Jewish literature. The image is now used to carry the meaning of reciprocal immanence and a profound divine/human intimacy, "dwell in me and I in you" (v. 4). The term "dwell" (μένω) was used in chapter 14 to describe the dwelling of the Father, Jesus, and the Paraclete with and in the disciples;[39] here in chapter 15 the subject of the verb changes to the disciples and the verb is used to describe a reciprocal abiding between disciples and Jesus. Through this

37. Ibid., 50.
38. The verb μένω can mean "abide" or "dwell" or "remain." In English translations interchanging these words can miss the continuity of the theme of "dwelling" and its rich theology. I prefer to use "dwell" in every use of μένω.
39. The verb dwell (μένω) is used in 14:10, 17, 25; the noun form "dwelling" (μονή) is used in 14:2, 23.

viticultural image of vine and branch, the reciprocity or intersubjectivity of the verb "dwell" is developed. The image is given a direct application to Jesus and his disciples in verse 5. Here the disciples are identified as the branches and Jesus as the vine. The consequences of dwelling or not dwelling in the vine are explained; the disciples who dwell in Jesus will bear fruit (v. 5) and their requests will be heard (v. 7), while the disciples who do not dwell in Jesus are cast away (v. 6).[40] The final verse in this section returns to the image of the vine, only now the relationship is directly between the disciples and the Father who will be glorified (ἐδοξάσθη) by the fruit-bearing of the disciples. While this section (vv. 1-8) speaks often of bearing fruit (vv. 2, 4, 5), there is no explanation of its meaning when applied to the disciples. This explanation requires a different image drawing no longer on nature but on the quality of the relationship between a father and son. In a sense, the vine image begins to break down from verse 4 when it begins to be utilized to express the mutual intimacy between Jesus and disciples. This intimacy, unlike the natural flow of life within a vine and its branches, is based on the divine choice to love (3:16) and will be expressed by Jesus in a love unto death (17:13). For disciples, it is conditional on their choice to remain faithful.

Familial Image (15:9-17)

The vine imagery in verses 1-8 gives way to a new image of the dynamic love relationship between parent and child. "Just as the Father has loved me, so I have loved you. Remain in my love" (v. 9). It is only when the image of the vine and branches is read in the light of the more personal familial image that its full emotive force is realized.

The imperative "Dwell in my love" (v. 9b) is revealed as the same love existing between the Father and Son (9a). Disciples are drawn into the very heart of the divine intimacy. The parallelism across the images now makes clear that the expression "bear fruit" means "keeping my commandments," which is to love as I have loved in laying down my life (v. 13). To speak of verses 9-17 as the ethical dimension of verses 1-8 misses the point of the image in verse 9 and its relationship to the vine image in verses 1-8.[41] It is not possible to differentiate between the

---

40. See the excursus above, "On Pruning and Cutting Away," for an explanation of this practice in viticulture.

41. Segovia (*Love Relationships*, 119–21) makes this distinction between "faith" and "ethic."

John 15:9-17

⁹"As the Father has loved me, so I have loved you; abide in my love. ¹⁰If you keep my commandments, you will abide in my love, just as I have kept my Father's commandments and abide in his love. ¹¹I have said these things to you so that my joy may be in you, and that your joy may be complete.

¹²"This is my commandment, that you love one another as I have loved you. ¹³No one has greater love than this, to lay down one's life for one's friends. ¹⁴You are my friends if you do what I command you. ¹⁵I do not call you servants any longer, because the servant does not know what the master is doing; but I have called you friends, because I have made known to you everything that I have heard from my Father. ¹⁶You did not choose me but I chose you. And I appointed you to go and bear fruit, fruit that will last, so that the Father will give you whatever you ask him in my name. ¹⁷I am giving you these commands so that you may love one another."

relationship of Father/Son and their mutual love. A definition of God that underpins the theology of the Fourth Gospel is *Being-in-Love*. God's "being" is God "loving"; the loving is not an ethical activity able to be distinguished from God's being, as the First Letter of John states: "God is love" (1 John 4:8, 16). This same mode of being is applied to the disciples, since remaining in the vine is to love one-another, as I have loved (v. 12). Love is to *be* the essence of Christian discipleship, not simply an ethical response.

The rich theology of divine/human intimacy that is the basis for the logic across these verses (14:1–15:17) is sustained by the word dwell/remain (μένω). In looking at the many places where this word is employed across the Gospel, it is difficult to determine when it has a theological use and when it can be understood in the neutral sense "to stay."[42] There have been a number of studies of the use of this expression in the Fourth Gospel,[43] and to my knowledge only Klaus Scholtissek has brought out

42. Scholtissek (*Sein und Bleiben*, 155–56) identifies only six places where μένω is used in a local sense meaning "stay" (2:12; 4:40; 7:9; 10:40; 11:6; 19:31) and thirty-two times in a theological sense: 1:32, 33, 38, 39 (2x); 3:36; 5:38: 6:27, 56; 8:31, 35 (2x); 9:41; 12:24, 34, 46; 14:10, 17, 25; 15:4 (3x), 5, 6, 7 (2x), 9, 10 (2x), 16; 21:22, 23; I would also add the use of μοναὶ (14:2) and μονὴν (14:23).

43. See, for example, Jürgen Heise, *Bleiben: Menein in den johanneischen Schriften*, HUT 8 (Tübingen: Mohr Siebeck, 1967); Lee, "Abiding in the Fourth Gospel," *Pacifica*, 123–36; Ignace de la Potterie, "L'emploi du verbe 'demeurer' dans la mystique johannique," *NRTh* 117 (1995): 843–59.

the ecclesial and soteriological meaning the Fourth Evangelist gives to this word.

Scholtissek perceives that in 15:1-17 the evangelist describes the ultimate revelation of Jesus's mission, which is to draw believers into the communion of life and love that he shares with God. The same dynamism of love existing between Father and Son now exists between Jesus and disciples. But whereas the relationship between Father and Son is constant, and so can be described using the verb "to be" (εἰμί), a verb expressing the reciprocal "being" of the Father in the Son, the relationship with believers is contingent upon their loving, and this could fail, so the verb "dwell" (μένω) is more appropriate.[44] The disciples' love for each other is the condition that determines their being caught up in the love, also described as friendship, of Jesus, who in turn exists in the love of the Father. Jesus is the mediator of this divine intimacy, for the believer does not dwell "immediately" in the Father; Jesus is "the Way," as he says to Phillip (14:6). Through friendship with Jesus, the disciple is drawn into the love existing between Jesus and God. Where Scholtissek uses the expression *vita communis,* I use the term "household," for this retains the image τῇ οἰκίᾳ τοῦ πατρός used in 14:2.[45]

The Vine of Woman Wisdom

The vine is a common image in the OT to represent Israel, as a people planted and nurtured by God in the land of Canaan (i.e., Ps 80:8-11; Isa 5:1-2; Jer 2:21). Many scholars look back to the Song of the Vineyard in Isaiah 5 or Psalm 80 as the likely background to the vine-and-branches metaphor, but this is not a satisfying comparison. In the Gospel, Jesus is never set up in comparison to Israel, and usually, when Israel is likened to a vine or vineyard, it is in a negative context of God's punishment for producing "wild grapes."[46] A more promising comparison is found in Sirach 24 when Sophia describes herself as a terebinth and a vine:[47]

---

44. Scholtissek, *Sein und Bleiben,* 365.

45. At times Scholtissek also uses "familial" terms recognizing that "household" is part of the metaphorical language of this Gospel: "Diese nachösterliche Glaubenserfahrung lotet Joh 14 *haus- und familienmetaphorisch* aus" (*Sein und Bleiben,* 374 also 265, 267).

46. Ben Witherington III, *John's Wisdom: A Commentary on the Fourth Gospel* (Louisville: Westminster John Knox, 1995), 255–57.

47. As well as Witherington, Rudolph Schnackenburg (*The Gospel according to St John,* 107) also notes the connection between John 15 and Sir 24:17: "The same elements

Like a terebinth I spread out my branches,
and my branches are glorious and bountiful [δόξης καὶ χάριτος].
Like a vine [ἄμπελος] I caused bounty [χάριν] to bud,
and my blossoms became glorious and abundant fruit [καρπὸς δόξης
καὶ πλούτου]. (Sir 24:16-17; author's translation)

In examining the possible scriptural echoes in the Pauline literature, Richard Hays proposes seven criteria to test the likelihood that the author is using such a technique: availability, volume, recurrence, thematic coherence, historical plausibility, history of interpretation, satisfaction.[48] Is it possible that Sirach 24 lies behind the vine imagery? The text of Sirach was available;[49] there are a number of words in these verses found in John 15,[50] particularly the word "vine" (ἄμπελος) rather than "vineyard"; the vine-branches imagery continues across 15:1-17; the theme of fruitfulness as a description of ministry is coherent with the earlier harvest imagery in John 4:35-38; the image of mutual indwelling enables the continuation of Jesus's mission in the mission of the disciples; it is therefore plausible for Jesus to console his disciples with this image in the context of his imminent absence. Given the strong allusions to Wisdom across the Gospel, particularly the description of Sophia tabernacling, pitching her tent (σκηνήν), in Jerusalem (Sir 24:8-11) as the likely background to the Gospel's description of the Word tabernacling (ἐσκήνωσεν) in the world (1:14),[51] it is plausible that first-century readers would look to Sirach rather than other "vine" passages that speak of God's displeasure with Israel.

In the book of Sirach, Sophia describes herself as a luxuriant plant bearing glorious and abundant fruit, but then, she is identified with

---

as those that occur in the figurative discourse in John 15 also appear here—the vine, buds (branches) and abundant fruit."

48. Richard B. Hays, *Echoes of Scripture in the Letters of Paul* (New Haven: Yale University Press, 1989), 29–32.

49. Parts of the book of Sirach were found among the Dead Sea Scrolls and also at Masada; Martin G. Abegg, Peter W. Flint, and Eugene Charles Ulrich, eds., *The Dead Sea Scrolls Bible* (Edinburgh: T&T Clark, 1999), 597–98.

50. Such as: vine, branches, glory, abundant fruit.

51. "Then the Creator of all things gave me a command, and my Creator chose the place for my tent.

He said, 'Make your dwelling in Jacob, and in Israel receive your inheritance.'

Before the ages, in the beginning, he created me, and for all the ages I shall not cease to be.

In the holy tent I ministered before him, and so I was established in Zion." (Sir 24:8-10)

Torah. "All this is the book of the covenant of the Most High God, the law that Moses commanded us as an inheritance for the congregations of Jacob" (Sir 24:23). The identification of Sophia-Vine-Torah may explain the assertion "I am the *true* vine" (John 15:1).[52] The addition of "true," meaning authentic, suggests a polemical contrast with a vine that is not authentic. The polemic between Jesus and Torah was established in the prologue with the description of two gifts—"a gift instead of a gift [χάριν ἀντὶ χάριτος[53]]" (John 1:16). The two gifts being compared are then identified, "The law indeed was given through Moses; the gift that is true [ἡ χάρις καὶ ἡ ἀλήθεια] came through Jesus Christ" (1:17). While Sirach identified Sophia and Torah, the Gospel refutes this to claim Jesus as the tabernacling presence (1:14) of divine Sophia, and so Jesus, not Torah, is the true vine and source of glorious fruitfulness.

Immediately following the description of Sophia's fruitfulness, she offers an invitation to come and "eat your fill of my fruits" (Sir 24:19). Wisdom's fecundity has the purpose of offering nourishment in the form of teaching for "future generations."

> I will again make instruction shine forth like the dawn,
>   and I will make it clear from far away.
> I will again pour out teaching like prophecy,
>   and leave it to all future generations.
> Observe that I have not labored for myself alone,
>   but for all who seek wisdom. (Sir 24:32-34)

Similarly in John 15, the vine-and-branches imagery has the purpose of mission. The disciples are "to go and bear fruit, fruit that will last," and in this "My Father is glorified." Across the discourse, Jesus has spoken of the Father being glorified in his person: "I will do whatever you ask in my name, so that the Father may be glorified in the Son" (14:13; see also

---

52. Ἐγώ εἰμι ἡ ἄμπελος ἡ ἀληθινή. The positioning of the adjective "true" following the noun "vine" gives an added emphasis to the authenticity of Jesus's claim to be the vine. It could be expressed as, "I am the vine, the true one."

53. These two words, χάριν and χάριτος, are also linked in Sirach 24:16 where the branches of the terebinth are described as χάριτος, which is usually translated as "graceful"; perhaps "bountiful" would be more accurate. In the following verse (Sir 24:17) the vine buds forth χάριν, usually translated "delights"; "exuberant gifts" or "bounty" would better convey both the fruitfulness of the vine and also maintain the sense of "gift" from John 1:16. Liddell and Scott provide the following translations of χάρις: "a favor done, a grace, kindness, boon . . . a gift." Henry G. Liddell and Robert Scott, *Greek-English Lexicon*, abridged ed. (Oxford: Clarendon, 1971), 778. As always, no translation is perfect!

13:31, 32). The vine imagery of chapter 15 adds how this will be possible in Jesus's absence. In the post-Easter time, through the mutual indwelling of Jesus and the disciples, the Father will continue to be glorified in the fruitful ministry of the disciples. The mission focus is clearly articulated by Ben Witherington who writes: "Abiding in Christ is not simply an end in itself, not just a means of maintaining unity in the community; it is also the necessary prerequisite to effective evangelism in a hostile world."[54]

The Vine and the Branches: A Covenant Community of Friends

The vine-branches metaphor defines Johannine discipleship and explains the Johannine understanding of the Christian community. The discourse in John 15:1-17 echoes a number of key elements associated with Israel's covenant relationship with God.[55] Johannine discipleship consists of covenant themes such as abiding in God's love, keeping the commandment of love, being chosen by God, being friends, glorifying God by bearing fruit, and having the joy of the chosen people of God.[56] When we look at these elements from the perspective of the Johannine ecclesiology, a paradigm of a new covenant community emerges. The discourse reveals the identity of the disciples as friends, their relationship with God as an experience of contemplation, their relationship with one another as a manifestation of communion, and the mission of glorifying God in the world as an expression of their commitment.

Being Chosen as Friends— Identity

Jesus calls his disciples his friends (φίλοι), and it is imperative for them to keep the commandments (15:12, 14) and to love one another (15:12, 17). As friends, the Johannine Jesus repudiates any form of relationship of domination, but with one condition, "You are my friends if you do what I command you" (15:14). So, it is clear that Jesus is not talking

54. Witherington, *John's Wisdom*, 257.

55. For a more detailed exposition of this theme, see Rekha M. Chennattu, *Johannine Discipleship as a Covenant Relationship* (Peabody, MA: Hendrickson, 2006), 89–137, esp. 111–18.

56. In this pericope (15:1-17), Jesus refers to God as "my Father" at vv. 1, 8, 10, 15 and "the Father" at vv. 9 and 16. See comments on the nonpatriarchal nature of fatherhood in this Gospel in the commentary on John 14, esp. the excursus "The Father's House/Household—A Johannine Symbol."

about some sentimental or emotional friendship but a covenant model of friendship in which God's command (God's will) takes priority over all else. The disciples are the friends for whom Jesus's love goes to the extent of laying down his life for them (15:13). They are chosen by Jesus to bear much fruit (15:16b).

Jesus's words, "I chose you . . . [a]nd I appointed you" (v. 16), remind the readers of the OT election of the people of Israel: "the LORD your God has chosen you out of all the peoples on earth to be his people, his treasured possession" (Deut 7:6). The concept of election is linked to the theology of covenant relationship in terms of both divine promises and human commitments; "Therefore, observe diligently the commandments—the statutes and the ordinances—that I am commanding you today" (Deut 7:11). As the election motif elicits the necessity for Israel to choose God and keep his commandments, the disciples are called to abide in Jesus's love and keep his covenant commandment (John 15:12). This is a choice that they must make to maintain the covenant relationship and engage in a fruitful mission (15:8). In sum, the disciples are friends (φίλοι) of Jesus; they are equal associates and partners in mission.

Abiding Relationship with the Father—Contemplation

The motif of abiding (μένω) is very significant in the covenantal language of the OT. The covenant relationship between YHWH and Israel demands that the latter abide in YHWH (Isa 30:18) and abide in obedience to the law (Deut 27:26). This abiding relationship implies fidelity to and communion with YHWH. Abiding in the word of Jesus becomes the hallmark of Johannine discipleship: "If you abide in my word, you will truly be my disciples" (John 8:31; author's translation).[57]

The evangelist develops the abiding motif further in the metaphor of the vine and the branches in 15:1-17 and teases out the intimate and binding covenant relationship between Jesus and his disciples. Jesus is presented as the true vine, and God, whom Jesus names "my Father," as the vinedresser who cares for the well-being of the vine by tending its branches, the disciples (15:1-2). The Johannine account proves faithful to Jewish traditions concerning YHWH when it ascribes to God the role of vinegrower (γεωργός, 15:1), but it reinterprets the identity

---

57. See also Edward Malatesta, *Interiority and Covenant: A Study of* εἶναι ἐν *and* μένειν ἐν *in the First Letter of Saint John*, AnBib 69 (Rome: Biblical Institute Press, 1978).

and designation of God's vine and vineyard.[58] By proclaiming, "I am the vine, you are the branches" (15:5), Jesus presents the disciples as the branches of a faithful and fruitful vine of God. The metaphor of vine and branches images the mutuality and binding force of the covenant relationship between Jesus and the disciples as well as that of the disciples and God, the vinegrower. Jesus encourages the disciples to turn to God in their need (15:16c). This abiding relationship implies fidelity, communion, and constant communication with Jesus and God.

Keeping the Love Commandment—Communion

According to the Johannine Jesus, if the disciples want to abide in his love and if they want to remain as his friends, they must keep his commandments.[59] By using these conditional clauses and the stipulation to keep the commandments, the evangelist parallels the abiding relationship and friendship between Jesus and his disciples with the OT

covenant relationship between YHWH and Israel. One needs to obey God's voice and keep God's covenant commandments in order to be God's vine (Jer 2:21; 3:13) and treasured possession (Exod 19:5). Similarly, the disciples are expected to keep the commandments in order to establish and maintain their friendship with Jesus and their covenant status in the community.

What is unique about the Johannine love commandment is the aspect of mutuality highlighted by the expression "love one another as I have loved you" (15:12). What is presupposed here is a community of equals, and their mutual love is modeled after the redemptive love of Jesus, with God as the source of this love (15:9). Jesus's love demands a loving service unto death—laying down one's life for her or his friends or covenant partners in the community (3:16; 10:11, 15, 17; 13:1; 15:13).[60] It implies disciples' participation in the paschal mystery of Christ—in the passion, death, and resurrection of Jesus.

58. According to the prophetic traditions, YHWH is the gardener and Israel is God's fruitful vine with many branches (Ezek 19:10; see also Ps 80:8-16 [LXX Ps 79:9-17]). Israel is also described as a choice vine (Jer 2:21) and God's vineyard (Isa 5:1-7; 27:2-6).

59. For the echoes of the OT covenant commandments (of Deuteronomy) in the Fourth Gospel, see Matthew J. O'Connell, "The Concept of Commandment in the Old Testament," *TS* 21 (1960): 351–403.

60. See also Francis J. Moloney, *Love in the Gospel of John: An Exegetical, Theological, and Literary Study* (Grand Rapids: Baker Academic, 2013), 99–133, esp. 117–21.

Mission of Bearing Fruit—Commitment

The organic oneness of the branches with the vine and with one another powerfully communicates the mutual indwelling of Jesus and his disciples. The disciples are called to be the fruitful branches of the vine; the model for their fruitfulness is Jesus's own committed life that springs from his abiding relationship with God. As the vine and its fruits are so intimately connected, so also the being of the disciples and their fruits/actions are inseparable. Johannine discipleship transcends the dichotomy traditionally attributed to one's being and one's doing. One's deeds are manifestations of one's true being, as was manifested in Jesus's life.

In the Johannine understanding of the Christian community, all members are branches; there is no superiority or hierarchy. The only distinction that one can make would be between the branches that bear fruit and those that do not. Distinctions made on the basis of power, position, or gender are foreign to Johannine discipleship. The mission is to build up an egalitarian community of covenant partners and friends that upholds justice, equality, and peace, thus or simultaneously revealing the glory (δόξα) or presence of God.

A New Covenant Community of Friends

The biblical metaphor of covenant defines the distinctive relationship between YHWH and the people of Israel. In and through the vine-branches metaphor, the evangelist presents the community of the disciples of Jesus as the new vineyard of YHWH, which is a new covenant community of friends. We have a paradigm of a Christian community characterized by contemplation, communion, and commitment. The discourse reveals a community of friends founded by an experience of God's abiding love, sharing a quality relationship of interdependence and reciprocal caring, and devoted to the mission of revealing God's life-giving presence in the world.

The experience of God's abiding love transforms the disciples—women and men—and makes them free. The members of the new covenant community thus value the other members as friends and equal partners, care for one another, and thus foster a relationship of reciprocity and interdependence. The covenant-friendship model of discipleship is other-centered and reciprocal. It implies respect and acceptance of one another as different and unique. This equality means not uniformity but an equity that by nature promotes diversity and plurality.

The community celebrates the freedom of being the children of God (1:12) and the chosen friends of Jesus (15:16). Only through joyful mutual appreciation do we become disciples of Jesus and show forth the glory of God.

The disciples' communion with God and closeness to one another are at the service of their mission. As covenant partners, we are called to participate in the ongoing struggle against all forms of discrimination and injustice, against all that impedes our quest for truth and wholeness. Women in India have taken up this challenge and are increasingly vocal in their demands for justice and equality. These women know that it is only when we create a new culture of human community marked by mutual respect, when we build up a new society that is more just and peaceful, when we take care of creation, a new human history manifesting God's glory is born. We shall then glorify God in our world.

Rekha M. Chennattu

The Household of God

Since the image used to describe the loving Being of God is the love between a father and son, it is appropriate to describe this as an image of the divine "household." The image of the household (14:2) thus unites the text of the Gospel across 13:1–15:17; chapter 13 is included here since in the ritual of footwashing disciples are welcomed in the household. Chapter 14 speaks of God's dwelling with believers and a future dwelling of the Spirit in believers. Chapter 15:1-8 employs an image from the natural world in order to describe the reciprocal indwelling of disciples and Jesus. Then 15:9-17 returns to the image of the household of God by applying the image of parental love to the love between Jesus and his disciples (15:9), adding the command that they live this love by loving "one another as I have loved you" (15:12). What Jesus meant by "bearing fruit" is clarified in these verses. When disciples love one another, their communion-in-love provides a living symbol in the world of the divine *communio*, the household of God.

Both the image of the vine and the model of familial intimacy directly engage the pre-Easter disciples present in the narrative and more especially the post-Easter believers. In Jesus's teaching, the sign of love is the readiness to gives one's own life for the beloved. This sign is realized only at the cross and so verse 13 presupposes that this event has already happened. Similarly, Jesus has made known all he has heard from his Father (v. 15); this statement also presupposes the completion of his revelation on the cross.[61] While the narrative setting is Jesus with his disciples prior to his arrest and crucifixion, the Johannine perspective is that of Jesus, the already risen and glorified Lord, encouraging post-paschal believers to remain faithful.[62] In Jesus's words, the relationship of love for his own can also be named as friendship.[63] "Greater love [ἀγάπην] than this has no-one than to lay down[64] his life for his friends [φίλων]. You are my friends [φίλοι]" (15:13-14a).

Friendship is born of Sophia, and these verses from the book of Wisdom also speak of mutual indwelling. Wisdom dwells in all things, and the one who dwells in Wisdom is loved by God.

> Being one, she is able to dwell [μένουσα] in all things,
> and in herself, all things are made new,
> In every generation she enters into holy souls
> and makes them friends of God [φίλους θεοῦ], and prophets.
> For God loves nothing so much as the one dwelling with Sophia [σοφίᾳ συνοικοῦντα]. (Wis 7:27-28; author's translation)

The reciprocal indwelling of Jesus/Sophia and the disciples will bring about a new dimension to the disciples' relationship with God. They will be "made new" as "friends" and "children of God" (John 1:12). Dwelling in Sophia, disciples will know through experience the love of God.[65]

In the ancient world friendship and household relationships overlap. "A man's friends are part of his *oikos*. They determine the social position

---

61. There is a mixture of present, perfect, and aorist forms of the verbs across vv. 1-17, indicating a retrospective telling of the story of Jesus's final meal. See Scholtissek, *Sein und Bleiben*, 277, 300.

62. Segovia, *The Farewell of the Word*, 327, suggests that the danger of falling away expressed in this section indicates the beginnings of an internal rupture that will lead to the situation of the Johannine letters.

63. On the meaning of friendship within Greco-Roman and Jewish philosophy, a helpful summary can be found in Ringe, *Wisdom's Friends*, 64–83, and Josephine Massyngbaerde Ford, *Redeemer—Friend and Mother: Salvation in Antiquity and in the Gospel of John* (Minneapolis: Fortress, 1997), 76–92.

64. Ringe, *Wisdom's Friends*, 67, translates τίθημι as "appoint," rather than "lay down," noting that the same verb is translated "appoint" in 15:16. She notes: "Clearly the assumption that v. 13 refers to Jesus' approaching death as his ultimate salvific act 'for his friends' has influenced translators in these different renderings of the same verb in this passage. Translating both occurrences by the same English verb 'appoint,' however, changes the emphasis of the first from death itself as the *purpose*, to death as the *consequence* of the intended 'appointment' or engagement of Jesus' life" (111 n. 9, emphasis original).

65. Similar theology of being drawn into God's household occurs in the Similitudes of *The Shepherd of Hermas*.

of the *oikos* and are determined by it."[66] Through friendship, someone beyond the household could be incorporated into the household. Sjef Van Tilborg describes Jesus's early activity in the Gospel as creating "an *oikos* of mutual friends who have found each other on the basis of freedom and kinship relationships."[67] Following the wedding at Cana, Jesus went with his mother, his siblings, and his disciples and dwelt (ἔμειναν) with them (2:12). Immediately after this, Jesus and his disciples entered his Father's house (2:16). Read against a first-century *oikos* ideology, disciples have been brought by the beloved Son into the household of God.[68] As members of the *oikos*, and because of their friendship with Jesus, they can make requests to the Father, in his Son's name, and be assured of them being granted (15:7, 16).[69]

The love-unto-death friendship Jesus proposes is the same as that discussed in Hellenistic philosophy.[70]

> To die for one another is only possible for people who love. (Plato, *Symp.* 179b)

> Truly, the honorable person does many things because of his friends and his country; if necessary, he will even die for them. (Aristotle, *Eth. nic.* 9.8.9)

> Epicurus on the wise man: And he will on occasion die for a friend. (Diogenes Laertius, *Lives* 10.120)

> Why do I seek someone's friendship? So as to have someone for whom I would be willing to die. (Seneca, *Ep.* 1.9.10)

---

66. Sjef Van Tilborg, *Imaginative Love in John*, BibInt 2 (Leiden: Brill, 1993), 149. On this point Tilborg cites a number of classical authors of *amicitia* literature.

67. Ibid., 116.

68. The *oikos* ideology described by Van Tilborg is further enriched by the narrative progression across these opening chapters using nuptial imagery as I proposed in discussing John 2. The Fourth Gospel may well provide the theological background for the parable in *The Shepherd of Hermas*, ca. 148, which describes a man leaving his vineyard in the care of his slave. While the owner is absent the slave takes great care of the vineyard, making it very fruitful and productive. On his return the owner consults with his beloved son and friends saying, "So in reward for this work which he has done I wish to make him joint heir with my son. . . . The Son of the master agreed with this plan, that the servant should be joint heir with the son" (Shep. *Sim.* 5.2.7-8, in *The Apostolic Fathers*. vol. 2: *The Shepherd of Hermas; The Martyrdom of Polycarp; The Epistle to Diognetus*, trans. Kirsopp Lake, LCL [London: William Heinemann, 1917]).

69. Van Tilborg, *Imaginative Love*, 150. See also the discussion in Mary Ann Beavis, "The Parable of the Slave, Son, and Vineyard: An Early Christian Freedman's Narrative" (Hermas *Similitudes* 5.2-11)," *CBQ* 80 (2018): 655-69.

70. I follow the translation offered by Van Tilborg (ibid., 150-53).

In the philosophical writings, to die for one's friend is presented as the ideal, but it is a *hypothetical* ideal. On the lips of Jesus, this statement of love moves from hypothesis to fact, from idea to reality. The depth of his love for his friends is shown by the extent to which he is prepared to go, that they too can become members of his *oikos* and "children of God" (1:12) and thus participate in the love shared between Father and Son. Where kinship is a matter of blood ties, friendship is a matter of free choice, as Jesus says, "I chose you" (v. 16).

Friendship speaks also of a free and reciprocal bond of the spirit between equals, rather than ties of blood or patronage. Although Jesus speaks frequently of his relationship with God using the metaphor of Father-Son, words such as "father," "household," and "son" can be used only analogically. Whether using the image of household or friendship, the creative dynamic at the heart of the Gospel is divine love, made possible by believers being drawn into God's own "Being-in-love." Believers are given a model of the relationships that exist in the divine household, and this model of love is to exist in their own communal relationships.

Conclusion

Situated on the eve of his return to his Father, Jesus gathers his own, those who have received his word (15:3) and who have abided with him. Now he discloses that through dwelling in him, his return to the Father will draw them into his own indwelling reciprocal love. Abiding in Jesus, disciples of all time will be able to participate in the loving and dynamic life of God in eternity. Participation in this communion of life and love is not relegated to the eschaton, but with the gift of the indwelling Spirit, this *communio dei* is a post-paschal reality. Participation in the divine "household" is the Johannine equivalent of salvation; this is the gift given in its fullness (1:16), enabling believers to become children of God (1:12). As Klaus Scholtissek states, "The reciprocal immanence between the Son and Christians articulates a living and relationship-rich salvation reality—the post-Easter union of the Christian with Christ. This reciprocal immanence is not only a praxis (namely, the presence of love), but it is the reality of salvation."[71] In the narrative, at this point, this revelation has still the character of a promise, but for the post-Easter community, it is the living experience that grounds their faith and praxis.

---

71. Scholtissek, *Sein und Bleiben*, 314.

The image of the vine and the branches (15:1-8), situated within passages that describe the abiding within the divine household (14:1-31; 15:9-17), invites disciples into a union with Jesus that will draw them into his own abiding as Son in the household of the Father for eternity (8:35). The initiative for this divine filiation is God. God comes to dwell with us in Jesus. Those who believe in him and become his friends can, in and through Jesus, experience his dwelling in the heart of God (1:18). This profound insight into the meaning of Jesus's mission must have been the post-Easter experience of the Johannine community, for only one who has experienced such union would be bold enough to propose such divine-human intimacy. I conclude with the words of Dorothy Lee, who succinctly expresses the meaning of 15:1-17:

> Abiding is a quality of the divine realm, an aspect of eternal life that in John's Gospel is offered to human beings. As a divine quality, abiding expresses the intimacy and reciprocity which, for John, lie at the heart of the universe. The relationship between God and Jesus, father and son, is the symbol and archetype of abiding. . . . To be a disciple means to be in union with Jesus, and through Jesus with God—a union that is reciprocal and oriented towards community.[72]

Feminist Adventures into the Trinity

In conventional trinitarian language of Father, Son, and Spirit, women are excluded. The constant repetition of this language in liturgy shifts these God-images to God-facts, so that any attempt to name the mystery of God using inclusive language meets very strong opposition. God can only be Father! Suggested alternatives such as Creator, Liberator, and Sanctifier are amorphous and expressive of primary beliefs about God in the Christian tradition, but the clerics in charge of liturgy fear losing male control of language and God images. In only using masculine terms, women, and their experience of God, are rendered invisible and insignificant.

Two scholars who have added significantly to God thinking and discourse are Catherine Mowry LaCugna (1952–1997) and Elizabeth Johnson.[73] LaCugna moves the discourse about God

---

72. Lee, "Abiding in the Fourth Gospel," 131.

73. Catherine Mowry LaCugna, *God for Us: The Trinity and Christian Life* (San Francisco: HarperCollins, 1991); Elizabeth A. Johnson, *She Who Is: The Mystery of God in Feminist Theological Discourse* (New York: Crossroad, 1992); idem., *Quest for the Living God: Mapping Frontiers in the Theology of God* (New York: Continuum, 2007).

from the neo-Platonic ontology of the early centuries, which attempted to name the inner life of God, to the phenomenological focus on how we experience God. Rather than imagine how God is in God's self, her approach, thoroughly biblical, proposes the Trinity as a communion of life-for-the-other. She writes, "The *archē*, the original and ruling principle of God's life with us is a person who unites himself or herself with another in the communion of love. . . . Mutuality rooted in communion among persons is a non-negotiable truth about our existence."[74] And, "Household is an appropriate metaphor to describe the communion of persons where God and creature meet and unite and now exist together as one."[75]

Johnson more explicitly critiques traditional male God-language—and how such language functions; exclusive male "speech about God serves in manifold ways to support an imaginative and structural world that excludes or subordinates women. Wittingly or not, it undermines women's human dignity as equally created in the image of God."[76] In a way similar to LaCugna, Johnson begins with Christian religious experience and finds in the symbol of Wisdom/Sophia a language of God that is more emancipatory for women. Her work also looks to the Scriptures for ancient experience and language of God. She writes, "The female figure of Wisdom is the most acutely developed personification of God's presence and activity in the Hebrew scriptures. Not only is the grammatical gender of the word for wisdom feminine (*hokmah* in Hebrew, *sophia* in Greek), but the biblical portrait of Wisdom is consistently female, casting her as sister, mother, female beloved, chef and hostess, teacher, preacher, maker of justice, and a host of other women's roles."[77] Rather than Father, Son, and Spirit, Johnson, starting with how we experience God, speaks of Spirit-Sophia, Jesus-Sophia,[78] and Mother-Sophia.

Both LaCugna and Johnson enrich Christian trinitarian theology and offer a more dynamic and inclusive way of imaging and speaking of God.

---

74. LaCugna, *God for Us*, 399.

75. Ibid., 411.

76. Johnson, *She Who Is*, 5.

77. Elizabeth A. Johnson, *Women, Earth, and Creator Spirit*, The Madeleva Lecture in Spirituality (Mahwah, NJ: Paulist Press, 1993), 52.

78. See also her article: Elizabeth A. Johnson, "Jesus, the Wisdom of God: A Biblical Basis for Non-androcentric Christology," *ETL* 61 (1985): 261–94.

John 15:18–16:4a

Sophia's Friends to Be Tested by the Synagogue

God tested them and found them worthy;
they were tried like gold in the furnace
and like a sacrificial burnt offering were accepted. . . .
Those who trust in God will understand truth,
and the faithful will abide with God in love,
because grace and mercy are upon the elect. (Wis 3:5-6, 9; author's translation)

The image of the vine and the branches, along with the image of Father and Son, addressed relationships within the Johannine community. The following section, 15:18–16:4a, looks beyond the community to the problematic relationship between the community and the "world." Once again, the literary explanation of *relecture* can help to understand how this section seems to repeat aspects of 14:1-31 but adds further teaching and more specific advice. This section is addressing a post-Easter situation of the community as evidenced by the use of verbs in the aorist and perfect tenses to speak of Jesus and present/future to refer to disciples.[1] The "world" in this section clearly refers to

---

1. I.e., hates you (ὑμᾶς μισεῖ), hated me (ἐμὲ . . . μεμίσηκεν); persecuted me (ἐμὲ ἐδίωξαν), will persecute you (ὑμᾶς διώξουσιν); kept my word (τὸν λόγον μου ἐτήρησαν),

431

the "world" of Judaism[2] and the conflict that belief in Jesus will bring with the synagogue.[3]

John Painter suggests that these verses became necessary as a further discourse following the destruction of the temple and Jerusalem in 70 CE.[4] Whereas the first discourse (John 13 and 14) needed to address the pain and loss from Jesus's absence, that loss is compounded by the growing strain with Judaism. The loss of temple, sacrifice, and priesthood thrust Judaism into a crisis of identity. How could Judaism survive? Gradually the heirs of the Pharisees assumed leadership and shifted the focus from cult to Torah. In the decades of struggle to redefine Judaism, a prayer was added to the synagogue morning "Blessings" that would identify those daring to profess something different from the tradition of the rabbis. This prayer was known as the *Birkat ha minim*, the "blessing" of the heretics. Those Jews who could not pray this "Blessing" would show that they no longer belonged within the Jewish synagogue community.

ἀποσυνάγωγος: *Being Put "Out of the Synagogue"*

Scholars are not in agreement about whether and how the *Birkat ha minim* was used against Jesus believers. Although it is attributed to the Jewish Council at Javneh in the 80s, Luke depicts some Jews, e.g., Jesus, Stephen, and Paul, as being driven out of the temple and synagogues prior to that time for being unorthodox in their thinking. Both Joel Markus and Pieter Van der Horst consider that by the end of the first century this prayer was being used in the synagogue as a tool for

---

will keep yours (τὸν ὑμέτερον τηρήσουσιν). Jean Zumstein, "Jesus' Resurrection in the Farewell Discourses," in *The Resurrection of Jesus in the Gospel of John*, ed. Craig R. Koester and Reimund Beiringer, WUNT 222 (Tübingen: Mohr Siebeck, 2008), 104.

2. John 16:2 makes this explicit with the reference to being "put out of the synagogues [ἀποσυνάγωγος]." See the excursus on this expression.

3. "If they persecuted me" (15:20) is evidenced by the earlier statement, "Therefore the Jews started persecuting Jesus, because he was doing such things on the Sabbath" (5:16). Jesus refers to the words spoken and works performed among *them* (15:22, 24). He speaks of "*their* law" (15:25), where in confrontation with "the Jews" he spoke of the law (7:19) and "your law" (8:17; 10:34). He also follows the requirement of Deuteronomy 19:15 by offering two witnesses to their sin, his words (v. 22) and his works (v. 24). Finally, he warns the disciples that "they will put you out of synagogues" (16:2). See Hans-Ulrich Weidermann, "Eschatology as Liturgy: Jesus' Resurrection and Johannine Eschatology," in Koester and Beiringer, *The Resurrection of Jesus in the Gospel of John*, 298–99.

4. John Painter, "The Farewell Discourses and the History of Johannine Christianity," *NTS* 27 (1981): 525–43.

identifying Jews considered to be apostates or heretics, as well as Christians.[5] If so, this could explain the use of ἀποσυνάγωγος in the Fourth Gospel (9:22; 12:42; 16:2).[6] Against this view Daniel Boyarin and Raimo Hakola question if the Javneh Council was the origin of this prayer and if the rabbis had achieved sufficient authority within the Jewish community post-70 to mandate its widespread use.[7] A third perspective is offered by Adele Reinhartz, who considers that the term ἀποσυνάγωγος was part of the author's rhetorical strategy for the community to disassociate itself from Judaism.[8] It is possible that the process of separating from each other was seen as necessary by both communities, as both are shaping and reshaping their identities within the Roman

Empire following the Jewish War (66–70 CE). In looking at the ἀποσυνάγωγος passages, Jonathan Bernier and Craig Evans do not see evidence of a formal, institutional mechanism. Instead, Bernier proposes that the term "is a retroactive awareness among emergent Christians that circa 30, in the land of Israel, Jewish persons could be driven out of the synagogue informally and with violence."[9] In a post-70 context when both the Jewish Jesus-followers and the rabbis are grappling with issues of continuity and identity, current tensions, coupled with earlier memories, could lead to the term ἀποσυνάγωγος *as if* this were a formal reality during Jesus's lifetime and a synagogue practice somewhere toward the end of the first century—as Evans explains, "a practice that

5. Joel Marcus, "*Birkat Ha-Minim* Revisited," *NTS* 55 (2009): 523–51; Pieter Van der Horst, "The Birkat Ha-Minim in Recent Research," *ExpTim* 105 (1994): 363–68.

6. Uri Ehrlich and Ruth Langer ("The Earliest Texts of the *Birkat Haminim*," *HUCA* 76 [2005]: 63–112) note that among the manuscripts, papyri, and prayer books found in the Cairo Geniza in the 1890s, "these versions of the *birkat haminim* explicitly included among the malefactors being cursed *noṣerim*, the common Hebrew term for Christians" (64).

7. Daniel Boyarin, *Border Lines: The Partition of Judaeo-Christianity* (Philadelphia: University of Pennsylvania Press, 2004), 68–71; Raimo Hakola, *Identity Matters: John, the Jews and Jewishness*, NovTSup 18 (Leiden: Brill, 2005), 45–61.

8. Adele Reinhartz, "Story and History: John, Judaism, and the Historical Imagination," in *John and Judaism: A Contested Relationship in Context*, ed. R. Alan Culpepper and Paul N. Anderson, RBS 87 (Atlanta: SBL, 2017), 125–26.

9. Jonathan Bernier, "Jesus, Ἀποσυνάγωγως, and Modes of Religiosity," in Culpepper and Anderson, *John and Judaism*, 131. Author's note: Geographically, the land between the Jordan River in the West and the Mediterranean in the East was known as Palestine, and in the 1st century CE it became the Roman Province of *Iudaea*, consisting of Samaria, Judea, and Idumea, with Galilee ruled by Herod Antipas as a client king. See Thomas R. Hatina, "Palestine," in *The World of the New Testament: Cultural, Social, and Historical Contexts*, ed. Joel B. Green and Lee M. McDonald (Grand Rapids, MI: Baker Academic 2013).

in time came to expression in the revised twelfth benediction."[10]

I find the Bernier-Evans position more convincing than other views, since the Gospels are retrospectives, relying on memory of events some fifty to sixty years earlier. Also, the *Birkat ha minim* was worded against members *within* the Jewish community who dared to stray from orthodoxy, not those outside Judaism. Following a study of all the Johannine writings, Evans concludes with a more nuanced understanding of the context giving rise to the term ἀποσυνάγωγος:

> The Fourth Gospel reflects a period of tension within the *Jewish* community that arose in the aftermath of the capture of Jerusalem and the destruction of the temple. It reflects the *intramural* conflict that at points recalls the

conflict the Jewish people experienced in the second century BCE at the time of the Maccabean revolt. The crisis of the destruction of the temple led to a conflict of ideologies and strategies as various groups called on the Jewish people to repent and embrace their respective theologies and religious practices. It is in this Jewish mix that the Johannine Christian community, as seen in the Fourth Gospel, should be viewed.[11]

Presenting the *Birkat ha minim* as an anti-Christian curse by the synagogue, and that this explains the term ἀποσυνάγωγος, I consider too extreme and open to fomenting anti-Semitism. We are trying to reconstruct the historical context when we have only the ideological faith perspective of the Gospel.

Structurally, the passage begins with a series of six conditional statements: "If the world hates you," "If you belonged to the world," "If they persecuted me," "If they kept my word," "If I had not come," "If I had not done" (v. 18, 19, 20c, 20d, 22, 24). This is followed by the promise of the Advocate (vv. 26-27) and the warning about expulsion from the synagogue and death (16:1-4a). The first four of these statements concern the world's hatred for the disciples (vv. 18-21). This is followed by verses where the focus shifts to the world's hatred of Jesus and Jesus's response in sending the Paraclete (vv. 22-25). The final verses return to

10. Craig Evans, "Evidence of Conflict with the Synagogue in the Johannine Writings," in Culpepper and Anderson, *John and Judaism*, 139.

11. Ibid., 154; italics added.

the world's hatred of the disciples, forming an *inclusio* around the ministry of Jesus and the Paraclete.

The World's Hatred for the Disciples (15:18-21)[12]

The "World" (ὁ κόσμος)

The "world," like the term "the Jews," has multiple meanings, and each occurrence needs to be understood in its own context.[13] First is the created world as distinct from the heavenly, uncreated realm of God. A second sense of the term "world" is "the theatre of human history. . . . The world is humanity's natural home, our only context."[14] Into this human and time-bound world, divine Sophia came in flesh (1:14).

A third meaning of "world" is associated with the humanity that God loves so that, through belief in Jesus, humanity can be drawn into God's own eternity life (3:16).

The fourth meaning has negative implications. Within the created world, humanity lives with freedom to make choices and, as an aspect of life in "the world," has ethical responsibility. In late Second Temple Jewish thought, a power of evil has taken dominion of this ethical world, influencing human choice and behavior in ways that set humanity against God, and so the Gospel speaks of "the sin of the world" (1:29). When individuals choose to reject God, and God's revelation in Jesus, then they live under the dominion of the "ruler of this world" (12:31; 14:30; 16:11). The disciples, who have chosen to believe in Jesus, still live within the created world loved by God and within the world that has rejected Jesus, but their choice to believe has taken them out from under the dominion of the evil one and into the life of the children of God.

12. This structure is also used by Fernando F. Segovia, *The Farewell of the Word: The Johannine Call to Abide* (Minneapolis: Fortress, 1991), 179. Segovia presents alternatives to this and his arguments in pp. 174–79.

13. As Sandra M. Schneiders shows, " 'World' in John is highly polyvalent. It is used with four distinct meanings running from the divine to the demonic" ("The Word in the World," *Pacifica* 23 [2010]: 256). For further discussion on the term "world," see Sandra M. Schneiders, *Buying the Field: Catholic Religious Life in Mission to the World*, Religious Life in a New Millenium 3 (New York: Paulist Press, 2013), 34–37; Margaret Daly-Denton, *John: An Earth Bible Commentary; Supposing Him to Be the Gardener*, Earth Bible Commentary (London: Bloomsbury T&T Clark, 2017), 192–93; and Adele Reinhartz, *The Word in the World: The Cosmological Tale in the Fourth Gospel*, SBLMS 45 (Atlanta: Scholars Press, 1992), 38–40.

14. Schneiders, "The Word in the World," 256.

18"If the world hates you, be aware that it hated me before it hated you. 19If you belonged to the world, the world would love you as its own. Because you do not belong to the world, but I have chosen you out of the world—therefore the world hates you. 20Remember the word that I said to you, 'Servants are not greater than their master.' If they persecuted me, they will persecute you; if they kept my word, they will keep yours also. 21But they will do all these things to you on account of my name, because they do not know him who sent me."

The section on the world's hatred for the disciples (15:18–16:4a)[15] follows on that which stressed the intimacy of Jesus and the disciples by using the image of the vine and the branches. It is because of that mutual indwelling of disciples in Jesus and Jesus in disciples (15:4) that the disciples will experience what Jesus has. Their relationship with Jesus means that they no longer belong to the world, and so the world responds to them as it responded to Jesus: with hate and persecution. These words are offered as consolation to disciples who experience conflict with the world of Judaism, particularly in the post-70 time when Judaism itself is in turmoil. In this time of conflict, they are told, "Remember the word that I said to you, 'Servants are not greater than their master.'" "Remembering the word" evokes the task of the Paraclete who is to "remind you of all that I have said to you" (14:26). The disciples are then reminded of the words Jesus spoke following the footwashing: "servants are not greater than their master" (13:16). In discussing the footwashing, I pointed out that the symbolism of this action proleptically presents the meaning of the crucifixion. In the laying aside and taking up of his garments, Jesus anticipates the laying down and taking up of his life. In the footwashing, disciples symbolically participated in the meaning of Jesus's crucifixion, just as in the Synoptics this is symbolically presented in the words over the bread and cup. The laying down and taking up of

15. The Gospel depicts a stark contrast between God's Word revealed in Jesus and a power at work that rejects this revelation. God's primary Word is love (3:16), and the rejection of this is described as hate. "The contrast ἀγαπᾶν/μισεῖν reaches a climax in Johannine thinking. The divine movement of love (ἀγάπη) here too comes into conflict with the cosmic movement of hate (μῖσος). . . . To hate is to live in hostility to the light, to reject it, to avoid its sphere" (Otto Michel, "Μισέω," TDNT 4 [1967]: 691). The Johannine community continues to experience rejection in their claim that Jesus is the Christ (9:22), and so the evangelist speaks of the "world's" hatred, whereas those who do accept the Gospel claims are drawn into a community where "love" is the sole command (13:34).

life that Jesus experienced is also to be the experience of disciples faced with the world's hatred. Where the vine-and-branches passage spoke of the intimate union of love, this passage now reminds the disciples of the intimate union with Jesus in suffering: "If they persecuted me, they will persecute you" (v. 20). The world did not recognize Jesus as the one sent from God and so considered him to be a blasphemer, as one leading the people astray, as one who could cause greater oppression by the Romans. These religious and political fears led to his death, and these same fears continue in the post-70 world of the disciples. The disciples cannot be removed from their world or protected from such religious and social suffering, but they can be consoled that such suffering does not indicate abandonment by Jesus; on the contrary, such struggle bears witness to their mutual indwelling in love and in pain.

Suffering

To speak of the union of disciples and Jesus in suffering is not to suggest any intrinsic or redemptive value in suffering *per se*. Suffering can lead to saintliness as it can lead to evil. Women have often been misled to endure suffering as a virtue. This is wrong; it demeans the value of other womanly virtues such as wisdom and courage. One theory of redemption that has dominated the West is that of Anselm of Canterbury (1033–1109), which postulated that Jesus's suffering was necessary to make satisfaction for sin's offense against God and to evoke God's forgiveness for sin. This is but one of many interpretations of the death of Jesus, but its simplicity has obscured others. This theory has no basis in the Gospel of John, nor does this Gospel interpret Jesus's death as a means of atonement for sin; this will become clear when discussing John 18 and 19.[16]

The World's Hatred for Jesus and His Response (15:22-27)

The focus shifts to Jesus in the following verses, expressing the world's hatred and its consequences in a series of parallel statements.

16. For a critique of the place of suffering and its abuse in women's spirituality, see Elisabeth Schüssler Fiorenza, *Jesus: Miriam's Child, Sophia's Prophet; Critical Issues in Feminist Christology*, 2nd ed. (London: Bloomsbury T&T Clark, 2015), 105–39.

John 15:22-27

22"If I had not come and spoken to them, they would not have sin; but now they have no excuse for their sin. 23Whoever hates me hates my Father also. 24If I had not done among them the works that no one else did, they would not have sin. But now they have seen and hated both me and my Father. 25It was to fulfill the word that is written in their law, 'They hated me without a cause.'

26"When the Advocate comes, whom I will send to you from the Father, the Spirit of truth who comes from the Father, he will testify on my behalf. 27You also are to testify because you have been with me from the beginning."

If I had not come . . . they would not have sin. (15:22)

If I had not done . . . they would not have sin. (15:24)

But the reality is that Jesus has come and has done works and so the world has (εἴχοσαν) sin. This sin is not only the hatred of Jesus but hatred of the Father revealed in Jesus's words and works. The rejection of Jesus and the One he revealed is seen as fulfilling Israel's (their) law: "They hated me without a cause." This citation may come from either Psalm 35:19 or Psalm 69:5, where the psalmist complains about the unrighteous hatred of his enemies.[17] Thus the "world," clearly some within Judaism, stands condemned by their own Scriptures. It is important to keep sight of the narrative context. Jesus is speaking these words to his disciples on the eve of his departure. These words are therefore meant to offer consolation and reassurance. When read decades later by the Johannine community, their experience of rejection from the synagogue is foreseen by Jesus, and, ironically, their struggle fulfills the Scriptures even as they are vindicated, for their persecution, like that of Jesus, is without cause.

> The world's hatred is inevitable, but Jesus encourages the disciples in two ways. First, he identifies with their experience. Second, he shows foreknowledge of what the future holds such that his credibility is high; so, if it is the case that what he says about the world's hatred comes to

17. Maarten J. J. Menken, *Old Testament Quotations in the Fourth Gospel: Studies in Textual Form*, CBET 15 (Kampen: Kok Pharos, 1996), 144, favors Psalm 69, as it has previously been referred to in John 2:17 and may lie behind the statement "I thirst" (John 19:28; cf. Ps 69:22). See also Bruce G. Schuchard, *Scripture within Scripture: The Interrelationship of Form and Function in the Explicit Old Testament Citations in the Gospel of John*, SBLDS 133 (Atlanta: Scholars Press, 1992), 119–23.

pass, it should also be the case that comforting promises (of an advocate, or eternal life, etc.) will likewise be fulfilled.[18]

As the disciples face the world's hatred in the future, they will not be alone, for Jesus will send the Paraclete from the Father.[19] In this third mention, the Paraclete is identified as the "Spirit of truth." To speak of the witnessing role of the Paraclete and the disciples continues to address the future situation of the believers who are called upon to defend their following of Jesus in the face of mounting hostility. Across the Gospel Jesus has defended his teaching and actions before Jewish opponents and will do so before Pilate. Believers will find themselves in similar situations, and, as the following verses indicate, the possibility is there that they will renege.

The World's Hatred for the Disciples (16:1-4a)

The ancient codex from Sinai shows no break in the text where today's versions place a significant chapter division at 16:1. From speaking about the sending and witnessing of the Paraclete and the witnessing of the disciples, Jesus explains his motive for speaking like this—to keep disciples from stumbling or falling away from their faith. In 6:61, following Jesus's teaching that he himself was the bread of life, that his flesh was to be eaten and his blood drunk as the means of eternity life, he had asked his disciples, "Does this offend [σκανδαλίζει] you?" (6:61). A more literal reading would be, "Does this scandalize you?" Will this teaching be a stumbling block for faith or cause you to fall away? In fact, some do turn back and do not stay with him (6:66). In the final discourse, the verb σκανδαλίζω (16:1) has this same sense. In the face of persecution and even death, some may fail, and the words Jesus has spoken promise that they will have the support of the Spirit of truth. Earlier in the discourse the task of the Spirit was "to teach you everything, and remind you of

---

18. Jaime Clark-Soles, "Scripture Cannot Be Broken: The Social Function of the Use of Scripture in the Fourth Gospel," in *Abiding Words: The Use of Scripture in the Gospel of John*, ed. Alicia D. Myers and Bruce G. Schuchard, RBL 81 (Atlanta: SBL Press, 2015), 108–15; quotation from p. 112.

19. While there is profound intimacy between the Paraclete and Jesus, and even a correspondence in their roles, they are not identical. As Ruth Sheridan states, "The Paraclete comes to witness to Jesus in Jesus's absence," and, "The Paraclete is presented as one quite distinct in character from Jesus." See Ruth Sheridan, "The Paraclete and Jesus in the Johannine Farewell Discourse," *Pacifica* 20 (2007): 138–39.

John 16:1-4a

16:1"I have said these things to you to keep you from stumbling. ²They will put you out of the synagogues. Indeed, an hour is coming when those who kill you will think that by doing so they are offering worship to God. ³And they will do this because they have not known the Father or me. ⁴But I have said these things to you so that when their hour comes you may remember that I told you about them."

all that I have said to you" (14:26). Once again it is the Paraclete's role to "testify about me [περὶ ἐμοῦ]" (15:26) to the disciples, helping them to remember Jesus's words in their time of trial. The disciples will testify in the public disputes; the Spirit of truth will testify interiorly, supporting the faith of the disciples.[20]

The unique Johannine expression "put out of the synagogue" has been discussed in earlier references (9:22; 12:42). What is new at this point is the reference to killing disciples as "worship of God." Within the OT, and in the writing of Philo, there are examples of killing fellow Jews, and Gentiles, apparently endorsed by God (e.g., Phinehas, Num 25:1-13; the Levites, Exod 32:17;[21] Mattathias, 1 Macc 2:24-26; and Abraham, Gen 22:1-10). Deuteronomy offers an extended basis for killing even members of one's family, if they entice to "worship other gods." "Even if it is your brother, your father's son or your mother's son, or your own son or daughter, or the wife you embrace, or your most intimate friend . . . But you shall surely kill them" (Deut 13:6, 9). Such murder is considered obedience to the voice of God and "keeping all his commandments that I am commanding you today" (Deut 13:18). Abraham's readiness to kill his own son is termed "worship" (Gen 22:5) and a "burnt offering" (Gen

---

20. This distinction between the public witness of the believers and the interior witness of the Spirit to the disciples is made by Ignace De La Potterie, *La Vérité dans saint Jean*, 2 vols., AnBib 73 (Rome: Biblical Institute Press, 1977), 1:396–97.

21. Philo commented on the killing of the idolaters by the Levites: "They began with their nearest and dearest, for *they acknowledged no love nor kinship but God's love*. This campaign, *waged spontaneously and instinctively on behalf of piety and holiness towards the truly existing God* . . . was *approved by none other than the Father of all* Who took it upon Himself to judge the cause of those who wrought the slaughter, declared them pure [καθαρούς] from any curse of blood guiltiness and gave them the priesthood as a reward for their gallantry" (*Spec.* 3.126–28). This translation from Jason J. Ripley, "Killing as Piety? Exploring Ideological Contexts Shaping the Gospel of John," *JBL* 134 (2015): 615; emphasis original.

22:2, 3, 6, 7, 8). While this religious justification for murder is presented in the OT, it is not the perspective of the Fourth Gospel, nor does it feature in post-70 Judaism.[22] Those who reject Jesus, both his own disciples (6:66), including Judas, and some of the Jews, are not met with violence. When Peter attempts to defend him from arrest, he is told, "Put your sword back in its sheath" (18:11). Nothing in this Gospel supports violence as a religious ideal.

22. Ripley states, "The configuration of violent Torah fidelity rejected in this Gospel bears little resemblance to the forms of Judaism that ultimately coalesced into rabbinic Judaism. Hence, John's polemic against 'the Jews' should not be construed as condemning the Judaism that developed after the wars with Rome, as it is directed against a religious ideology that the rabbis also rejected" (Ripley, "Killing as Piety?," 634). Further insight into post-70 Jewish interpretation of texts endorsing violence can be found in Beth A. Berkowitz, "Reconsidering the Book and the Sword: A Rhetoric of Passivity in Rabbinic Hermeneutics," in *Violence, Scripture and Textual Practice in Early Judaism and Christianity*, ed. Ra'anan S. Boustan, Alex P. Janssen, and Calvin J. Roetzel (Leiden: Brill, 2010).

John 16:4b-33

Sophia's Friends to Be Tested by the World

For though in the sight of others they were punished,
their hope is full of immortality.
[B]ecause God tested them and found them worthy. (Wisdom 3:4, 5c)

The discourse now turns to the conflict with the wider Greco-Roman world, and no longer addresses the intramural struggle with the synagogue. The theme of Jesus's immanent departure returns, and I consider, along with Andreas Dettwiler, that 16:4b-33 is a *relecture* of 13:31–14:31.[1] This indicates that a new historical situation has arisen and further teaching is required. As John Painter suggests, "The break from the synagogue probably lies in the immediate past as the community does not yet appear to have come to terms with the world. It can only be apprehensive at the hostility of the unknown."[2] Dettwiler situates the writing of this discourse between the Gospel and the first Epistle of John,

---

1. Andreas Dettwiler, *Die Gegenwart des Erhöhten: Eine exegetische Studie zu den johanneischen Abschiedsreden (Joh 13,31–16,33) unter besonderer Berücksichtigung ihres Relecture-Charakters* (Göttingen: Vandenhoeck & Ruprecht, 1995), 111, and in more detail 213–92. He considers that the first discourse (13:31–14:31) was primarily christological, whereas the second discourse (16:4b-33) is primarily concerned with ecclesial issues.

2. John Painter, "The Farewell Discourses and the History of Johannine Christianity," *NTS* 27 (1981): 357.

a position I agree with, where there are concerns about the community's self-identity and also about the "divine authenticity" of the Paraclete within the community.[3] Whatever the historical situation might be, this passage addresses the community's *angst*. Jesus's absence, now felt even more acutely following the break with Judaism, will thrust the disciples into sorrow, and the passage addresses their sorrow in three ways. First, they will have the consolation of the Paraclete (vv. 7-15). Then, Jesus uses an image of childbirth as the human equivalent of a time of pain followed by joy (vv. 16-24). Finally, Jesus offers the consolation of peace in his ultimate victory, through his return to the Father (vv. 25-33). I suggest the following structure:

Introduction (16:4b-6)

a. Consolation of the Paraclete who will act in two ways

—toward the world (vv. 7-11)

—toward the community (vv. 12-15)

b. Consolation of the "little while" of pain followed by joy (vv. 16-24)

c. Consolation of peace in Jesus's victory over the world (vv. 25-33)

Introduction (16:4b-6)

During Jesus's ministry there were veiled references to the events of his passion, using such terms as "the hour" and "lifted up."[4] During the Gospel narrative the disciples do not comprehend his meaning. Through the remembering and interpretive gift of the Spirit (14:26) in the postresurrection period, such terms will be understood. Jesus now states openly, "I go to the one who sent me." This statement repeats what was said earlier, "I am going to the Father who sent me" (14:12, 28). In response to Jesus's speaking of his departure, Thomas had asked earlier, "Lord, we do not know where you are going. How can we know the way?" (14:5). A new element that is named here is the experience of sorrow, where earlier there was simply confusion. The rest of the passage offers consolation in this sorrow.

3. Dettwiler, *Die Gegenwart des Erhöhten*, 290–92.
4. The hour is mentioned at 2:5; 7:8, 30; 8:20; 12:23; and 13:1. Jesus speaks of being lifted up or exalted in 3:14; 8:28; and 12:32. A further reference to his death is told through the parable of the grain of wheat that must die (12:24).

⁴ᵇ"I did not say these things to you from the beginning, because I was with you. ⁵But now I am going to him who sent me; yet none of you asks me, 'Where are you going?' ⁶But because I have said these things to you, sorrow has filled your hearts."

Sophia's Words of Consolation—The Paraclete (16:7-15)

In this passage, the Paraclete has two roles, one directed to the external world (vv. 7-11) and one toward the inner life of the community (vv. 12-15). Notice that the evangelist uses two different terms in describing these roles. In verses 7-11 the Advocate's role is described in forensic or legal terms of proving and convicting; further legal terms are used such as "righteousness," "judgment," and "condemned." Such forensic language is in keeping with the primary meaning of the word παράκλητος (Paraclete).[5] From verse 13, where the focus is on the community, it is the Spirit of truth who is described, in the role as guide.

The Paraclete, in a legal setting, was the one who spoke up for the defense before the accusers in a two-party controversy or before the judge if the situation later went to trial. But one strategy used by the defense in Jewish legal procedures was to show that the accuser is wrong, and so defense can shift to accusation.[6] Throughout Jesus's ministry he has been in conflict with people who believed that *they* were righteous and that Jesus was a sinner. They have made false judgments about Jesus to the point of trying to kill him (7:19; 8:59). Jesus's return to the Father will

5. Lochlan Shelfer, "The Legal Precision of the Term 'παράκλητος,'" *JSNT* 32 (2009): 131–50. Shelfer provides much evidence from both the secular and biblical worlds to show that the Roman legal term *advocatus* is the equivalent translation of the Greek παράκλητος. It was Origen who first introduced the meaning "Consoler" and "Intercessor" in his *De Principiis* (2.7.4) (132). The Advocate/Paraclete's legal position was to speak in defense, not in prosecution (141). The secular term was used to speak analogically of the divine world and this continued in Jewish practice where an angel could act as a Paraclete before a divine court (147). Shelfer asserts that "this [the Paraclete] is the technical term which John employs as a title of the Spirit of Truth. It is not exhaustive of the Holy Spirit's attributes, but is nevertheless a title with a precise legal meaning" (147).

6. Martin Asiedu-Peprah, *Johannine Sabbath Conflicts as Juridical Controversy*, WUNT 2/132 (Tübingen: Mohr Siebeck, 2001), 18–19, 28. The strategy of turning defense into accusation can explain the use of the term Paraclete in 16:7-11.

John 16:7-15

[7]"Nevertheless I tell you the truth: it is to your advantage that I go away, for if I do not go away, the Advocate will not come to you; but if I go, I will send him to you. [8]And when he comes, he will prove the world wrong about sin, and righteousness and judgment: [9]about sin, because they do not believe in me; [10]about righteousness, because I am going to the Father and you will see me no longer; [11]about judgment, because the ruler of this world has been condemned.

[12]"I still have many things to say to you, but you cannot bear them now. [13]When the Spirit of truth comes, he will guide you into all the truth; for he will not speak on his own, but will speak whatever he hears, and he will declare to you the things that are to come. [14]He will glorify me, because he will take what is mine and declare it to you. [15]All that the Father has is mine. For this reason, I said that he will take what is mine and declare it to you."

show that in fact *he* was the righteous one and those not believing in him were the sinners. Only one who is utterly righteous before God could, following death, send the Paraclete, the Spirit of truth. The presence of the Paraclete in the community will testify to Jesus's intimate and potent relationship with God. In this way the Paraclete will be an Advocate exposing (ἐλέγξει[7]) the false perceptions and accusations of the world.[8]

The Paraclete also has a role within the community and in this role is called "the Spirit of truth." In the original discourse the terms "Advocate" and "Holy Spirit" were interchangeable, and the Spirit was to be

7. The term ἐλέγξει is particularly difficult to interpret within the structure of this passage. The word was used by Jesus earlier in the Gospel, also in situations of conflict and judgment. Each time it was translated differently: "For all who do evil hate the light and do not come to the light, so that their deeds may not be *exposed*" (ἐλεγχθῇ, 3:20); "Which of you *convicts* me of sin? If I tell the truth, why do you not believe me?" (ἐλέγχει, 8:46).

8. A detailed exegesis of this passage can be found in Donald A. Carson, "The Function of the Paraclete in John 16:7-11," *JBL* 98 (1979): 547–66. In this article Carson sets out the text showing its balanced structure, which also causes some difficulties in the translation of ἐλέγξει. I follow his conclusions: "By his words and deeds, Jesus has set the world's self-vaunted righteousness against the backdrop of his own matchless righteousness and thereby brought home to the world the inadequacy of its own righteousness" (562). He continues: "The prime worker among them so far has been Jesus; the prime worker among them in the future will be the Paraclete" (564). In this way, the sending of the Paraclete will ensure the disciples are not abandoned as "orphans" but will have "another Paraclete" (14:16) bearing witness with them and through them to the world.

sent to "teach you everything, and remind you of all that I have said to you" (14:26). In this *relecture* of the original discourse, the term "Advocate" is used in a more precise forensic role, and it is the task of the Spirit of truth to "guide you into all the truth" and to "declare to you the things that are to come" (16:13). The wording of this role suggests that, in the postresurrection time, the Spirit will offer further revelations that are part of the "many things" Jesus wished to say to the disciples, but they were not yet ready to bear them, as Jesus had indicated (16:12). This sets up a comparison between the revelation Jesus can offer prior to his hour and the fullness of that revelation that can be known only when he has passed through the hour, returned to the Father, and sent the Spirit to the disciples. Having access to the fullness of Jesus's revelation is surely why Jesus tells the disciples, "it is to your advantage that I go away" (16:7). What the Spirit will bring is not a new revelation but the fullness of the revelation of Jesus. Twice the evangelist affirms this fact: "he will take what is *mine* and declare it to you" (16:14 and 15). In comparing the task of the Spirit in 14:26 and 16:3, Wilhelm Michaelis states, "Whereas 14:26 refers more to confirmation of the preaching of Jesus, 16:13 has in view its deepening and definitive completion."[9]

Sophia's Words of Consolation: The Pain and Joy of Birthing (16:16-24)

The second consolation that Jesus offers his disciples in their sorrow is that his "going" will only be for a "little while" and then they will see him again. This "little while," between not seeing and then seeing, is a reference to the time between his passion and resurrection.[10] These

---

9. Wilhelm Michaelis, "ὁδηγός, ὁδηγέω," *TDNT* 5 (1967): 101.
10. "The first μικρὸν refers to the death of Jesus; the second to his resurrection." Dettwiler, *Die Gegenwart des Erhöhten*, 240. Dettwiler presents arguments that the "little while" refers to the parousia (240–41) but then counters these with much stronger arguments in favor of the death/resurrection interpretation (241–42). He notes that the verb used to describe the "seeing" of the disciples (θεωρέω, vv. 16-19, 22) is the same verb used in the resurrection appearances in chap. 20 (20:18, 20, 25, 29); also the reference to "asking the Father" (v. 23) when they see Jesus again makes sense in the post-Easter period but would be meaningless after the parousia. Similarly, Jean Zumstein, *L'Évangile selon Saint Jean (13–21)*, CNT IVb 2nd ser. (Genève: Labor et Fides, 2007), 144–45; Francis J. Moloney, *John*, SP 4 (Collegeville, MN: Liturgical Press, 1998), 443–47. Moloney includes not only the resurrection appearances in John 20 and 21 but also the "seeing" associated with the worshiping community and the time of the Paraclete (447).

John 16:16-24

¹⁶"A little while, and you will no longer see me, and again a little while, and you will see me." ¹⁷Then some of his disciples said to one another, "What does he mean by saying to us, 'A little while, and you will no longer see me, and again a little while, and you will see me'; and 'Because I am going to the Father'?" ¹⁸They said, "What does he mean by this 'a little while'? We do not know what he is talking about." ¹⁹Jesus knew that they wanted to ask him, so he said to them, "Are you discussing among yourselves what I meant when I said, 'A little while, and you will no longer see me, and again a little while, and you will see me'? ²⁰Very truly, I tell you, you will weep and mourn, but the world will rejoice; you will have pain, but your pain will turn into joy. ²¹When a woman is in labor, she has pain, because her hour has come. But when her child is born, she no longer remembers the anguish because of the joy of having brought a human being into the world. ²²So you have pain now; but I will see you again, and your hearts will rejoice, and no one will take your joy from you. ²³On that day you will ask nothing of me. Very truly, I tell you, if you ask anything of the Father in my name, he will give it to you. ²⁴Until now you have not asked for anything in my name. Ask and you will receive, so that your joy may be complete."

verses (16:16-19) establish a contrast between not seeing and seeing, in response to the disciples' sorrow. The emotion associated with "seeing" is unspoken.

The stark contrast continues in the following verses (vv. 20-24) through the image of pain during a woman's labor, and her pain is then followed by joy when her child is born. The image first refers to the current sorrow of the disciples, to be followed later by their joy.

you will weep and mourn [κλαύσετε καὶ θρηνήσετε ὑμεῖς];
you will have pain [λυπηθήσεσθε], but your pain [λύπη] will turn into joy. (v. 20)
When a woman is in labor, she has pain [λύπην], because her hour has come. But when her child is born, she no longer remembers the anguish [θλίψεως] because of the joy of having brought a human being into the world. (v. 21)
So *you* have pain now. (v. 22)

For Jesus to use such a feminine image supports the claim that women were included in those of his own (τοὺς ἰδίους) whom he loved to the end (13:1) and with whom he shared this final supper.[11] Even the language used of the disciples, weeping and mourning, is most frequently descriptive of women at a time of death. At this point in the narrative, the "weeping" (κλαύσετε) of the disciples (16:20) is a term associated only with Mary of Bethany. At Lazarus's death the crowd thought Mary was going to the tomb to weep (κλαύσῃ) there (11:31), and then Jesus saw her weeping (κλαίουσαν, 11:33). Later, Mary (Magdalene) will also be found weeping (κλαίουσα) at the tomb of Jesus.[12] When Jesus weeps at the tomb of Lazarus, a different verb is used (ἐδάκρυσεν).[13]

The other expression of sorrow used of the disciples in verse 20 (θρηνήσετε) is a term associated with lamentations in the home when someone has died or more public mourning, such as with the singing of a funeral dirge. This term is used particularly about the lamentations of women in both the OT and NT.[14] Gustav Stählin's insight into the

---

11. Refer to the discussion of 13:1 earlier in this commentary where among "his own whom he loved" I proposed that the Bethany household were included—Mary, Martha, and Lazarus, "whom Jesus loved" (11:3); also "Jesus loved Martha and her sister and Lazarus" (11:5). At the cross other women are also named: "his mother, his mother's sister, Mary the wife of Clopas, and Mary Magdalene" (19:25). It would be wrong to presume that the "disciples" mentioned throughout the discourse refers only to male disciples, particularly with the use of such a feminine image as childbirth. This point is well argued by Dorothy A. Lee, "Presence or Absence? The Question of Women Disciples at the Last Supper," *Pacifica* 6 (1993): 13–15. See also the comments by Kathleen Rushton and references to the role of art in perpetuating the view of only "the twelve" present: Kathleen P. Rushton, *The Parable of the Woman in Childbirth of John 16:21: A Metaphor for the Death and Glorification of Jesus* (Lewiston, NY: Mellen, 2011), 84 n. 44.

12. The weeping woman named Mary, at the tomb of Lazarus and the tomb of Jesus, while frequently considered to be two different women, may in fact have been one woman named Mary. See the earlier discussion by Elizabeth Schrader when discussing Mary and Martha in John 11.

13. "To weep, with the clear implication of shedding tears." J. P. Louw and E. A. Nida, "δακρύω," in *Greek-English Lexicon of the New Testament: Based on Semantic Domains*, 2nd ed., 2 vols. (New York: United Bible Societies, 1996), 1:303.

14. "In the OT, too, women are particularly prominent in the exercise of θρῆνος [mourning/lamentation]. Jeremiah arranges for mourning women to accompany his θρῆνος (Jer 9:16-17), and he also calls all the women of the nation to θρῆνος (v. 19). Similarly, Ezekiel declares that the daughters of the gentiles will accompany his lament for Egypt (Ezek 32:16). In national mourning virgins play a predominant role (cf. Joel 1:8; Jdt 11:40; 3 Macc 4:6), as may also be seen from the symbolism of the weeping daughter of Sion (Jer 7:29 MT) and the mourning virgin of Samaria (Mic 1:8 LXX); cf. also the mourning of Rachel in Jer 31:15." See Gustav Stählin, "θρηνέω, θρῆνος," *TDNT* 3 (1965): 150–51.

weeping of Rachel (Matt 2:17-18, quoting Jer 38:15), shows a similar sorrow/joy contrast as found here in the Fourth Gospel. He writes, "The OT θρῆνος [lamentations] of the mother of Israel (Rachel) is applied to the mothers of Israel in the NT. But already in the OT the voice of the ἔλεος [mercy] of God rings out above the θρῆνος of Israel, and in the NT the divine redemption . . . arises out of the depths of the sorrow."[15]

The image of a woman's labor and childbirth is offered to console the disciples that their pain will be temporary and will "in a little while" be replaced by joy. In the narrative context, the image speaks not only of the disciples' experience but also of what awaits Jesus; in other words, this feminine image is both ecclesial, referring to the disciples, and christological, referring to "the hour" of Jesus's passion.[16] Josephine Massyngbaerde Ford provides three arguments that this image can also apply to Jesus:

(a) The context of the saying is within Jesus's prediction of his suffering, death, and resurrection;

(b) the suffering of the disciples is nearly always seen to be identified with the suffering of Jesus, especially in the Farewell Discourses;

(c) the explicit reference to "the hour" must be interpreted against the other saying about the "hour" in John's Gospel: all of them refer to Jesus's passion, death, and exaltation.[17]

In addition, the phrase εἰς τὸν κόσμον, "into the world," here describing the child newly born (16:21), is used repeatedly to speak of Jesus's coming "into the world" (1:9; 3:17; 6:14; 10:36; 11:27; 12:46). Judith Lieu considers that this phrase "more than any other is the Johannine Jesus's most significant epithet, affirmed by Jesus himself (9:39; 16:28; 18:37)."[18] The image linking childbirth and "coming into the world" (16:21) implies

---

15. Ibid., 153.

16. André Feuillet states this christological interpretation quite forcefully, in what he asserts as an undeniable fact (*le fait incontestable*); "in Jn 16.21 Jesus compares his hour to that of the woman." See André Feuillet, "L'heur de la femme (Jn 16:21) et l'heure de la Mère de Jésus (Jn 19:25-27)," *Bib* 47, no. 2 (1966): 171; author's translation. The article continues in *Bib* 47, no. 3 (1966): 361–80 and *Bib* 47, no. 4 (1966): 557–73. Some scholars also look to the Daughter of Sion imagery as background for this image, i.e., Rushton, *The Parable of the Woman in Childbirth*, 133–34. Here, I focus on the christological significance.

17. Josephine Massyngbaerde Ford, *Redeemer—Friend and Mother: Salvation in Antiquity and in the Gospel of John* (Minneapolis: Fortress, 1997), 163.

18. Judith Lieu, "The Mother of the Son in the Fourth Gospel," *JBL* 117 (1998): 72.

that God "mothered" in giving Jesus to the world (3:16), as a mother births her child into the world. This image challenges the more frequent image of a father sending a son (6:44; 8:16, 18, 42; 10:36; 12:49; 14:26).

In addition to these arguments, Barbara Reid notes the frequent "birthing" language used across the Gospel, even where the translations obscure this, particularly when translating γίνομαι and γεννάω.[19] Where the usual translations of John 1:3 read, "all things *came into being* through him," a more accurate translation of γίνομαι, which denotes the birth process, would read, "all things were birthed through him." Reid states: "There is an intriguing blurring of gender boundaries: the male *Logos* births all things (1:3) and *Theos* births the children of God (1:12-13)."[20] Our expressions of the Divinity, as seen in these texts, need to include male and female imagery and be expressed in language that includes all. This study has made it clear that feminine images and language can give expression to the Divine, so God's presence can be affirmed in titles such as Sophia and *Shekinah*. In an excursus titled "I Am Woman," I compared the "I am" statements of Jesus to the statement made to Abraham, "I am El Shaddai" (Gen 17:1). This title of God predates the name given to Moses, and the etymology of this ancient name is "God of the Breasts."[21]

Finally, the image of the woman in labor is used in the OT to speak of God's anguish when Israel was in exile. The exile suffering is likened to the pain of childbirth: "For a long time I have held my peace, I have kept still and restrained myself; now I will cry out like a woman in labor, I will gasp and pant" (Isa 42:14).[22] In other passages the woman's labor is linked to messianic resurrection imagery; as a woman gives birth to a child, so "the earth will give birth to those long dead" (Isa 26:17-19).[23]

This birth imagery means that when we speak of God in only male terms and images, we place limits on the Divinity, demanding that God

---

19. Barbara E. Reid, "Birthed from the Side of Jesus (John 19:34)," in *Finding a Woman's Place: Essays in Honor of Carolyn Osiek, R.S.C.J.*, ed. David L. Balch and Jason T. Lamoreaux (Eugene, OR: Pickwick, 2011), 192. Fernando F. Segovia, *The Farewell of the Word: The Johannine Call to Abide* (Minneapolis: Fortress, 1991), 254, also notes the importance of the "recurrent theme" of birth.

20. Reid, "Birthed from the Side of Jesus," 193.

21. See the excursus "I Am Woman" in Mary L. Coloe, *John 1–10*, WCS 44A (Collegeville, MN: Liturgical Press, 2021), 217.

22. Other images of a maternal God can be found in Deut 32:18; Ps 2:7; Job 38:28-29; Isa 49:15; 66:12-13. Reid also discusses the images of God as a midwife; Reid, "Birthed from the Side of Jesus," 199–200.

23. Edwyn C. Hoskyns, *The Fourth Gospel*, ed. F. N. Davis (London: Faber & Faber, 1947), 487–88.

only be considered "male." Not only is this an injustice to women and a denial of Genesis's clear statement that male and female image God (1:27), it is also heresy reminiscent of the Arian controversy in the early church. Whenever, because of our human limitations, we try to say God is "either/or," we confine God to our polarized perceptions, instead of giving God the freedom to be fully divine, to be "both/and," to be ineffable, indescribable, utterly transcendent, and utterly immanent. Israel's Shema proclaims accurately—"God is One." And it is a oneness that is all-inclusive. This is also true of the risen Christ who is no longer limited to the human body of a Jewish man named Jesus. The risen One cuts through the dichotomies of "slave or free," "Jew or Greek," "male and female"—as Paul states, "for all of you are one in Christ Jesus" (Gal 3:28).

From the birth of a child, the text moves to the assurance of the Father's attentive response to prayer, the fourth such promise (14:13-14; 15:7, 16). On that day, the day of Jesus's return, the disciples will not need him to intercede for them, for they will have they will have direct access to the Father. As the hour develops, it will become clear that the disciples enter into a new relationship with Jesus and the Father, becoming "children of God" (1:12-13), and there will be a moment of birth, even if it looks like a death.

The Woman in Labor
(John 16:21)

I have argued extensively, employing an interanimative theory of metaphor, that the parable of the woman in labor in John 16:21 functions in the Johannine text to make meaning of the death-glory of Jesus and the struggles of discipleship.[24] Among the associations this image evokes is the Isaian daughter of Zion whose depiction parallels that of the widely recognized "suffering servant" and is as extensive. The story of the female "suffering one" progresses from abandonment, childlessness, and suffering to joy at the birth of her children and a new creation drinking from her bosom (Isa 54:1; 66:11). Various biblical traditions distinguished and emphasized different facets of birth imagery, which are reducible to five metaphorical elements: the embodied woman, pain, the childbirth process itself, offspring, and joy after

24. See my PhD thesis (2000) published as Kathleen P. Rushton, *The Parable of the Woman in Childbirth of John 16:21: A Metaphor for the Death and Glorification of Jesus* (Lewiston, NY: Mellen, 2011).

childbirth. Only the Isaian daughter of Zion and the woman image of John 16:21 contain all five elements.

Any feminist reading of John 16:21 must be underpinned by a theory of parables that addresses the critical question of how it accesses the image of the parable theologically, because parables concern the relationship of God to world and creation. Otherwise, women are rendered invisible and their activities are not seen as a subject of theological reflection. The activity of the woman in the parable is participative action in the sphere of God's action. The bloody, messy phenomenon of natural childbirth is evoked by "a woman in labor" and "her child is born." The insertion of the term λύπη (pain), however, jolts the reader to seek new meanings because in the LXX λύπη is used in the creation account of Genesis 3:16-18. There is strong evidence that this word is used of mental pain, not physical pain.[25] It is not part of the specialized language of birth. In Genesis λύπη is not a birth image, and it is applied to both the woman (Gen 3:16) and the man (3:18). This suggests a semblance of equality exists,

even in that patriarchal text and society, between woman and man in sharing the unrelenting difficulties of the task of survival. This sense of equality matches the prominence of women in key points in the Johannine narrative.

Previously, I have attempted to examine tentatively factors that may have surrounded the Johannine community's original rhetorical reception of John 16:21, both culturally and biblically in the late first century.[26] The impurity/purity codes found in sacred texts are prescriptive and not necessarily descriptive. As a female-gendered image, ambivalence surrounds woman as birth giver. In one category of the Jewish and Christian traditions of birth imagery, birth itself, rather than pain, is the controlling image.[27] As opposed to the analogy that focuses on birth pain alone, a second category of images may be termed "productive" in that a new dynamic emerges: once pain erupts, it suggests a process, a cycle of recurring waves of pain that must run their course toward new life. Recognizable constructions of motherhood and of the longing of women to give birth to children are also found.

---

25. See my discussion of λύπη, Rushton, *The Parable of the Woman in Childbirth*, 124–28.

26. Kathleen P. Rushton, "The Woman in Childbirth of John 16:21: A Feminist Reading in (Pro)creative Boundary Crossing," in *Blood, Purity and Impurity: A Feminist Critique*, ed. Kristin de Troyer et al. (Harrisburg, PA: Trinity Press International, 2003), 77–96,

27. Such emphasis does not negate the pain.

One of these constructions is a recurring motif of the barren woman who conceives miraculously. The creative role is understood to lie with God.

Childbirth in the biblical tradition is imbued with paradoxes. Childbirth is women's domain at its most mysterious, being both powerful and frightening. It is distinctively female, yet it involves the power to give life, projecting the birthing mother into the image of the divine who creates. While previously, I have interpreted this parable along with 1:12-14; 3:5-8; 7:37-39; and 19:34 as part of a trajectory of birth imagery, now my interpretation has extended to include cosmological and ecological perspectives in which further cautions and new perspectives are disclosed. In dialogue with Claudia Bergmann's work on how biblical birth imagery is used for situations of local, universal, and international crisis, new thresholds emerge.[28] By relating *birth*, *crisis*, and *new beginnings* to the birth imagery in this Gospel, there are cosmic implications and parallels to the evolving processes of earth, e.g., earthquakes.[29]

Kathleen P. Rushton

Sophia's Words of Consolation—Peace in Jesus's Victory (16:25-33)

The final consolation Jesus offers to his sorrowing disciples is the assurance of his ultimate victory in which they can find peace.

These verses provide the conclusion to the discourses; in the following chapter Jesus turns from the disciples to speak directly to God. Jesus's words continue to offer consolation to the disciples, and they also offer an interpretation of the hour for the disciples in the postresurrection time, even if at this point this interpretation is not completely clear—in spite of the disciples' claim of knowledge (v. 30). The contrast is made between parabolic speech (παροιμίαι) and plain speech (παρρησία). The term παρρησία has the sense of one able to speak freely as with a friend,

---

28. Claudia D. Bergmann, *Childbirth as a Metaphor for Crisis: Evidence from the Ancient Near East, the Hebrew Bible, and 1QH XI, 1-18*, BZAW 382 (Berlin: de Gruyter, 2008).

29. Kathleen P. Rushton, "On the Crossroads between Life and Death: Reading Birth Imagery in John in the Earthquake-Changed Regions of Otautahi Christchurch," in *Bible, Borders, Belonging(s): Engaging Readings from Oceania*, ed. Jione Havea, David Neville, and Elaine Wainwright, SemeiaSt 75 (Atlanta: SBL, 2014), 57–72.

²⁵"I have said these things to you in figures of speech. The hour is coming when I will no longer speak to you in figures, but will tell you plainly of the Father. ²⁶On that day you will ask in my name. I do not say to you that I will ask the Father on your behalf; ²⁷for the Father himself loves you, because you have loved me and have believed that I came from God. ²⁸I came from the Father and have come into the world; again, I am leaving the world and am going to the Father."

²⁹His disciples said, "Yes, now you are speaking plainly, not in any figure of speech! ³⁰Now we know that you know all things, and do not need to have anyone question you; by this we believe that you came from God." ³¹Jesus answered them, "Do you now believe? ³²The hour is coming, indeed it has come, when you will be scattered, each one to his home, and you will leave me alone. Yet I am not alone because the Father is with me. ³³I have said this to you, so that in me you may have peace. In the world you face persecution. But take courage; I have conquered the world!"

with no fear of speaking frankly.[30] In the book of Wisdom the righteous can stand freely before God, and before their opponents, with utter confidence. "Then [on the day of judgment] the righteous will stand with great confidence [ἐν παρρησίᾳ πολλῇ] in the presence of those who have oppressed them and those who make light of their labors" (Wis 5:1). Then the unrighteous will ask: "Why have they been numbered among the children of God?" (Wis 5:5). The sage then states the reward of the righteous: "But the righteous live forever [αἰῶνα ζῶσιν], and their reward is with the Lord; the Most High takes care of them" (Wis 5:15). This will be the experience of Jesus in his hour and also the promise to those who believe that they too can be "children of God" (John 1:12-13) and be born into "eternity life" (3:15). The book of Job describes prayer as such free-speaking confidence before God: "then you will have boldness [παρρησιασθήσῃ] before the LORD, looking up cheerfully to heaven" (Job 22:26; LXX). The crowd considered that Jesus was speaking openly (John 7:26), and he spoke plainly to the disciples about Lazarus's death (11:14), but now the discourse suggests that such openness will be the experience of the disciples when they come before *their* loving Father in prayer. In the next chapter, Jesus will model such openness in prayer.

30. Heinrich Schlier, "παρρησία, παρρησιάζομαι," *TDNT* 5 (1967): 873.

The disciples respond, thinking that now they understand and profess their belief (vv. 29-30). But Jesus continues with a second warning that "the hour is coming" and that the disciples will fail. They will be scattered as a wolf scatters the sheep (10:12). Yet in spite of this Jesus claims victory, "I have conquered the world" (16:33). This terse saying needs to be understood as "shorthand" for announcing his victory over the "*ruler of this world*," not the world *per se*.[31] Jesus has already announced that the "ruler of this world will be driven out" (12:31), that "he has no power over me" (14:30), and that he "has been condemned" (16:11).

With this assurance of victory, the discourses come to an end. Across chapters 14, 15, and 16 the Gospel has shifted between the narrative time before the passion and the post-Easter time of the risen Jesus and the gift of the Paraclete/Spirit. These chapters presented Jesus offering consolation to his disciples as he speaks of his departure and also interpreting the meaning of his departure through death. This double perspective does bring some confusion of time (present and future), emotion (sorrow and joy), and what awaits the disciples (persecution and victory) while being "in the world" but no longer "of the world" (15:19). Much of these chapters remains obscure and can be fully understood only in the light of Jesus's exaltation on the cross, when the fullness of his revelation will be brought to completion, as he announces, "It is finished" (19:30).

31. For comments on the many different meanings of the term κόσμος in the Fourth Gospel, see the excursus on "The 'World' (ὁ κόσμος)" at 15:18-21.

John 17:1-26

Sophia's Prayer for Her Friends

Wisdom praises herself,
and tells of her glory in the midst of her people.
In the assembly of the Most High she opens her mouth,
and in the presence of the Mighty One she tells of her glory. (Sir 24:1-2)[1]

In John 17 we have the final words spoken by Jesus before his passion, and so these words provide the last glimpse into the Johannine understanding of the cross. At the heart of this chapter is Jesus communing with God who loves him (17:24, 26). In this communion he reflects on his mission, which had its origin in God's love for the world. Jesus has come into the world to embody that love, to make it visible and believable, but as the hour will demonstrate, God's love for the world is costly. Gathered now with his friends, Jesus offers prayers for those who have come and will come to believe in him. As did Woman Wisdom, Jesus has brought these friends of his (15:15) into friendship with God (Wis 7:27), but by so doing, they are alienated from the world that now hates them (17:14; also 15:13–16:3).[2] Jesus prays that they be

---

1. "In the presence of the Mighty One" is my own translation of ἔναντι δυνάμεως.
2. See my previous comments on the many different meanings of the term κόσμος in the Fourth Gospel; Mary L. Coloe, *John 1–10*, WCS 44A (Collegeville, MN: Liturgical Press, 2021), 221–22.

kept within the intimate friendship of God and kept from the harmful powers of the evil one (17:15), who still holds dominion over those in the world. Although mentioned only once (v. 26), the mutual love between God and Word (1:1, 18)[3] and between Jesus and his disciples pulsates through this chapter.

In narrative time, Jesus is at table with his disciples (13:4),[4] but even now he is moving toward the God he calls Father,[5] as he directs his gaze and his words heavenward.[6]

Outline

Various structures of the missionary prayer have been suggested, frequently based on the identity of the one spoken about, i.e., Jesus, the disciples, others who come to belief through the disciples;[7] more complex literary structures have also been proposed.[8] A structure that I will use looks at the function of each section. At the center of this chapter, verses

---

3. Love has dominated Jesus's final meal with his disciples. The love between Father and Son (14:31; 15:9, 10); between Jesus and his disciples (14:15, 21, 23; 15:9, 12, 13); the Father's love for the disciples (14:21, 23); and the disciples are to love each other (13:34, 35; 15:12, 17). A study of the "love" theme is richly expressed in Francis J. Moloney, *Love in the Gospel of John: An Exegetical, Theological, and Literary Study* (Grand Rapids: Baker Academic, 2013).

4. The gathering of Jesus with his friends at table recalls Wisdom's feast, where she sets her table and invites the townspeople to eat her bread and drink her wine (Prov 9:1-6). See comments at John 13:1 on these disciples comprising both females and males who are "his own."

5. God was imaged as "father" to the children of Israel: "For you are our father" (Isa 63:16; 64:8). God was also imaged as "mother": "As a mother comforts her child, so I will comfort you" (Isa 66:13; 49:15; 42:14; Deut 32:18). See the contribution by Dorothy Lee on "The Iconic Father" following John 5 in Coloe, *John 1–10*, 156.

6. From the time Jesus announced that "the hour has come" (12:23), a process has begun. Although not yet returned to God, "he is passing from this world to the Father." Francis J. Moloney, *John*, SP 4 (Collegeville, MN: Liturgical Press, 1998), 466.

7. E.g., Raymond E. Brown, *The Gospel according to John*, 2 vols., AB 29–29A (New York: Doubleday, 1966, 1970), 2:749; Moloney, *John*, 459; Andrew T. Lincoln, *The Gospel according to Saint John*, BNTC (London: Continuum, 2005), 434; Harold W. Attridge, "How Priestly is the 'High Priestly Prayer' of John 17?," *CBQ* 75 (2013): 9. Some, e.g., Moloney and Brown, are guided by the use of the verb "to ask," ἐρωτάω, found in 17:9, 15, and 20.

8. Edward Malatesta, "Literary Structure of John 17," *Bib* 52 (1971): 190–214; David A. Black, "On the Style and Significance of John 17," *CTR* 3 (Fall 1988): 141–59.

9-23, are three petitions, with an introduction naming those for whom Jesus prays and a conclusion where his prayer is extended to those later believers. These verses are the formal "petitionary prayer" of Jesus. The prayer section has a general introduction in terms of Jesus's identity and mission (vv. 1-8), and themes from this introduction return in verses 24-26 to conclude the chapter. This can be shown schematically:[9]

Introduction: vv. 1-8 Jesus/Sophia's identity and mission

   Petitions: vv. 9-23

      Introduction to petitions

         3 petitions: Keep them in your name

                        Keep them from the evil one

                        Consecrate them in the truth

      Conclusion to petitions

   Conclusion: vv. 24-26 Jesus/Sophia's identity and mission

At this point in the narrative, these are Jesus's final words on the eve of his passion. The prayer is a moment of intense communion revealing the intimate relationship between Jesus and God; the disciples, as members of the household, are privileged to "overhear" these words. Raymond Brown writes, "The disciple and the reader are party to a heavenly family conversation."[10] But this time-frame is the perspective from within the narrative. The time-frame of the actual Gospel places Jesus's passion in the past and his words *have been effective* for himself and *are being effective* for believers. Both time-frames need to be held, and at times they are blurred. George Parsenios describes this "as though two discourses have been blended together, one that Jesus delivers around the table on the night of his betrayal, and one that he delivers from the realm of the

9. The outline here is similar to the divisions made by Loren T. Stuckenbruck, "Evil in Johannine and Apocalyptic Perspective: Petition for Protection in John 17," in *John's Gospel and Intimations of Apocalyptic*, ed. Catrin H. Williams and Christopher Rowland (London: Bloomsbury T&T Clark, 2013), 208; it is also similar to Jean Zumstein, *L'Évangile selon Saint Jean (13–21)*, CNT IVb 2nd ser. (Genève: Labor et Fides, 2007), 160–61.

10. Brown, *The Gospel according to John*, 2:747.

Father after the Ascension. Jesus is alternately here and there, before and after, above and below."[11]

Introduction (17:1-8)

These introductory verses speak of Jesus's identity and relationship as Son (vv. 1, 4-5) and his mission (vv. 2-3, 6-8). He does not simply look "up" to heaven, but the expression εἰς τὸν οὐρανὸν has the sense of looking *into* heaven.[12] Jesus's relationship with God is expressed using a distinctively theological word, δόξα, "glory." Within the OT, the word כבוד, "glory," referred to the visible or invisible radiance of God's presence and being, as shown in creation and in the mighty acts of God. The most vivid expression of this glory was the revelation on Mount Sinai (Exod 19). Prior to the incarnation, the Word was fully present in God (John 1:1) and so participated fully in God's eternity life and glory. In taking flesh, this glory was visible in the person of Jesus, and at times this was recognized by his disciples (1:14; 2:11). Jesus, in his own being, made God present and known throughout his life, and so Jesus can say, "I glorified you on earth" (17:4). But the enfleshed glory is necessarily temporal and constrained by the mortal limitations of all flesh. When, through the crucifixion, Jesus returns to the presence of God, then he will assume the glory, the intimate presence of God, he once had. "So now, Father, glorify me in your own presence with the glory that I had in your presence before the world existed" (17:5). This glory no longer has the mortal limitations of flesh, and so the risen Jesus now participates

11. George L. Parsenios, " 'No Longer in the World' (John 17:11): The Transformation of the Tragic in the Fourth Gospel," *HTR* 98 (2005): 5. In 1965 a German scholar, Franz Mussner, presented a new hermeneutical approach for reading the Fourth Gospel based on the interpretive theology of Hans-Georg Gadamer. In his study, he used the term *johanneische Sehweise*, which I translate as a Johannine way of seeing, or Johannine perspective. This perspective merges the pre-Easter history of Jesus and the post-Easter experience of Jesus as the risen and glorified Lord—Gadamer's "fusion of horizons." Mussner's work has been significantly developed by another German scholar, Christina Hoegen-Rohls, who emphasizes the role of the Spirit-Paraclete. See Franz Mussner, *The Historical Jesus in the Gospel of John*, trans. W. J. O'Hara, QD 19 (New York: Herder, 1967), and Christina Hoegen-Rohls, *Der nachösterliche Johannes: Die Abschiedsreden als hermeneutischer Schlüssel zum vierten Evangelium*, WUNT/2 (Tübingen: Mohr Siebeck, 1996).

12. The phrase is similar to that in 1:18 describing the only-born son nestled in the bosom of the Father (μονογενὴς θεὸς ὁ ὢν εἰς τὸν κόλπον τοῦ πατρὸς). See the previous discussion of the prologue for the use of both maternal and paternal imagery of God.

John 17:1-8

¹⁷:¹After Jesus had spoken these words, he looked up to heaven and said, "Father, the hour has come; glorify your Son so that the Son may glorify you, ²since you have given him authority over all creation, to give eternal life to all whom you have given him. ³And this is eternal life, that they may know you, the only true God, and Jesus Christ whom you have sent. ⁴I glorified you on earth by finishing the work that you gave me to do. ⁵So now, Father, glorify me in your own presence with the glory that I had in your presence before the world existed.

⁶"I have made your name known to those whom you gave me from the world. They were yours, and you gave them to me, and they have kept your word. ⁷Now they know that everything you have given me is from you; ⁸for the words that you gave to me I have given to them, and they have received them and know in truth that I came from you; and they have believed that you sent me."

fully in the eternity life and glory of God. In summary, glory means the "divine mode of being."¹³ Because of his relationship as Son, the "divine mode of being" is now incarnate in Jesus.

Now that the hour has arrived, an hour through which Jesus will return to his Father, he asks that his Father will bring him back into the presence and relationship the Word experienced with God prior to the incarnation, i.e., that his Father will glorify him (17:1, 5). This will make manifest the presence of God in the hour of Jesus's passion. What might appear as degradation will in fact bring God's work and Jesus's mission to its completion and show the hour as the exaltation of Jesus and the definitive revelation of God's glory. This hour will thus mutually glorify the Father and the Son in the culmination of Jesus's mission (17:1). "The Son will be glorified by the Father, restoring him to the preexistent glory they shared, and the Father will be glorified by the completion of the Son's mission."¹⁴

The next verses (17:2-3) speak of the mission of Jesus to be the revelation of God in his very person and so make God known. As Son, he reveals God's love for the world and God's desire to draw all into God's own eternity life, which is to participate in the very being of God. Across

13. Gerhard Kittel, "δοκέω, δόξα, δοξάζω, συνδοξάζω, ἔνδοξος, ἐνδοξάζω, παράδοξος," *TDNT* 2 (1964): 247.

14. Adesola Joan Akala, *The Son-Father Relationship and Christological Symbolism in the Gospel of John*, LNTS 505 (London: Bloomsbury T&T Clark, 2014), 177.

these introductory verses, Jesus's words are not a request but impera-
tives—"glorify your Son" (vv. 1, 5)—spoken with utter confidence from
within the Son-Father relationship. For Jesus, this is a homecoming, and
there is no doubt that his words will be effective. Jesus's claim to authority recalls the words of the Sage, "The Lord created human beings out of
earth, and makes them return to it again. He gave them a fixed number
of days, but granted them authority over it (the earth)" (Sir 17:1-2).

The time frames are confused in verses 4-5, where Jesus speaks of
"finishing the work" when in fact that work will not be finished until
the passion, when Jesus announces, "It is finished" (19:30). Within the
narrative, the passion is yet to come, and so Jesus can say, "glorify me,"
when from the perspective of the postresurrection Gospel he has been
glorified and taken into the preincarnation experience of the Word in
and with God.

The final three verses of the introduction (vv. 6-8) again speak of Jesus's
mission of making God known, because as the Son who is close to his
Father's heart only he *can* make God known (1:18). In these verses the
term used is "name," which has similar theological force as "glory"
because the name expresses the essence of the person.[15] To avoid saying
"God," parts of the OT, particularly the Deuteronomistic History, use "the
name," as is the case in modern Judaism where *ha Shem* is a reverential
alternative to the word "God." The work given Jesus by his Father was
to reveal the God that only he knows from within the intimacy of his
relationship. And this work has been successful since the disciples have
received Jesus's teaching. They are the ones referred to in the prologue
who, because of their belief, will be given the power "to become children
of God" (1:12). This will be the task of the passion.

The Petitions of Jesus (17:9-23)

Introduction to His Prayer (17:9-11a)

Jesus's prayer begins formally in verse 9 as he names those for whom
he prays, "those who believed" (17:8) and who were given to him by

---

15. Hans Bietenhard, "ὄνομα," *TDNT* 5 (1967): 243–81. "Deuteronomic theology
expressed that presence of God as the presence of God's name. So the temple is that
place of which God has said, 'My name shall be there' (1 Kgs 8:29)"; Anthony F.
Campbell, *The Study Companion to Old Testament Literature: An Approach to the Writings
of Pre-Exilic and Exilic Israel*, OTS 2 (Wilmington, DE: Michael Glazier, 1989), 159–60.

⁹"I am asking on their behalf; I am not asking on behalf of the world, but on behalf of those whom you gave me, because they are yours. ¹⁰All mine are yours, and yours are mine; and I have been glorified in them. ¹¹And now I am no longer in the world, but they are in the world, and I am coming to you."

God. Once again, there is a blurring of time-frames in verses 10 and 11. In narrative time the disciples have not yet grasped the meaning of Jesus's words and have not yet received the Spirit-Paraclete that is still to come. It will be in the passion that they are drawn into the familial relationship with God that Jesus experiences. From within the unity of Father and Son, they will be able to manifest the divine presence and so glorify Jesus. It is only from the postresurrection perspective of the Gospel that the disciples can be said to have "glorified" Jesus. From this perspective, Jesus speaks of himself as "no longer in the world," but his disciples "are in the world." And so now the task of being and revealing the presence of God in the world falls to the disciples. In the postresurrection time they are the ones in whom Jesus is glorified, because they reveal his presence, while he has already passed through the passion into divine presence of God. After naming whom Jesus is praying for, he then makes three petitions.

Three Petitions (17:11b-19)

In these three petitions (vv. 11-13, 14-16, 17-19) Jesus reveals the intimate union between himself and his disciples. Just as Jesus does not belong to the world, neither do his disciples. Just as God sent Jesus into the world where he faced opposition, so now the disciples are sent into the world where they will also face opposition. As Jesus is consecrated, so he prays for the disciples.

The first two petitions are set in antithetic parallelism: keep them *in* (v. 11); keep them *from* (v. 15). Jesus prays that the disciples will be *kept in* (τηρέω) the Father's name, which means held within the very being of God, which will be the experience of the loving Father-Son relationship. There is some confusion in the manuscripts about the subject of the relative pronoun ᾧ, "that," in verses 11 and 12. Is it the "name" that has been given to Jesus or "the disciples"? Understanding that "the name" refers to the essence of a person, then Jesus, as Son, participates in the very

11b"Holy Father, protect them in your name that you have given me, so that they may be one, as we are one. 12While I was with them, I protected them in your name that you have given me. I guarded them, and not one of them was lost except the one destined to be lost, so that the scripture might be fulfilled. 13But now I am coming to you, and I speak these things in the world so that they may have my joy made complete in themselves.

14I have given them your word, and the world has hated them because they do not belong to the world, just as I do not belong to the world. 15I am not asking you to take them out of the world, but I ask you to protect them from the evil one. 16They do not belong to the world, just as I do not belong to the world. 17Sanctify them in the truth; your word is truth. 18As you have sent me into the world, so I have sent them into the world. 19And for their sakes I sanctify myself, so that they also may be sanctified in truth."

being of God (1:18) and so knows God's name and is able to reveal this. By sharing the being of God with disciples, Jesus gives them access to this same being.[16] They too can have the gift of the "eternity life" of God.

The second petition asks that the disciples not be taken from the world but be *kept from* the power of the evil one, and this creates a paradox. On the one hand, Jesus claims that the ruler of this world has no power over him (14:30) and has been condemned (16:11), and yet he prays that the disciples will be protected from this evil one. Also, the term "world" has multiple meanings. It is a world "loved" by God (3:16) and yet a world in opposition to Jesus and his disciples. We need to enter into the conceptual thinking of first-century Judaism to make sense of these conflicting ideas.

Within the OT there are no prayers requesting God's protection from an evil power in opposition to God, but within first-century Jewish literature there are numerous examples of such prayers. Loren Stuckenbruck examines a number of similar petitionary prayers from the Dead Sea Scrolls and the Book of Jubilees. He notes that such prayers presume the existence of an evil power at work in the world, even though the

16. The gift of participating in the being of God is possible only through Jesus and is known by the terms "theosis" or "deification." On this concept in the Christian tradition, see Stephen Finlan and Vladimir Kharlamov, eds., *Theōsis: Deification in Christian Theology* (Cambridge: James Clarke, 2006), and Michael J. Christensen and Jeffery A. Wittung, eds., *Partakers of the Divine Nature: The History and Development of Deification in the Christian Tradition* (Grand Rapids: Baker Academic, 2007).

presumption is that these powers have been defeated and await eschato-logical destruction.[17] From his study of these prayers, Stuckenbruck sees three ways in which they contribute to understanding John's Gospel:

> *First*, according to John's Gospel, "the world," which is under the do-minion of "the ruler of the world," is completely opposed to Jesus and his followers.
>
> *Second*, the confidence expressed in the petitionary prayers considered here, based on definitive acts of God in the past and the certain escha-tological defeat of demonic power in the future, is re-framed in John's Gospel around Jesus' death through which the world is already judged. Though the inimical world order holds sway, its days are numbered, and it already stands condemned.
>
> *Third* and finally, the petitions in search of protection are formulated in recognition that, in the meantime, a community which considers itself especially elect needs divine help in order to ward off the unabating influences of evil power.[18]

The third petition, that the disciples be "consecrated [ἀγίασον] in the truth," again addresses the intimate God-Jesus relationship. During the Jewish festival of Hanukkah recalling the reconsecration of the temple following the Maccabean victory over the Greeks, Jesus declares that he is the consecrated and sent one of God: "Can you say that the one whom the Father has consecrated [ἡγίασεν] and sent into the world is blaspheming because I said, 'I am God's Son'?" (10:36; author's translation). Because the glory of God dwells in Jesus (1:14), he can speak of his own body as a temple (2:21) and therefore as one already consecrated. In the hour of his passion, the temple of his body will be destroyed, but Jesus has promised that a new temple will be raised up (2:19). This new temple will be a new Father's house/hold of the disciples (14:2)[19] and so Jesus prays that they too, as living temples, will be consecrated by his return to his Father. This consecration will come about "in the truth," and this "truth" is identified as "your word" (ὁ λόγος ὁ σὸς ἀλήθειά ἐστιν, v. 17b). It is by participation "in" Jesus, in his filial relationship with God, that disciples will be drawn into his Father's household and into the holiness

17. Stuckenbruck, "Evil," 228.

18. Ibid.

19. Jesus had called the temple "my Father's house" (2:16), but this expression, when used in the OT, always meant the entire "household." See further comments above at John 14.

of God's being. Although they will remain in the world, they will no longer belong to the world and under the domain of the evil one.[20]

Some scholars, both ancient and modern, approach John 17 as the High Priestly Prayer and consider that when Jesus speaks of "consecration" he is speaking as a priest.[21] I disagree. Jesus's consecration is as the living temple (10:36), the dwelling of God, and this is what he prays for his disciples. Also, that Jesus makes an intercessory prayer for his disciples is not the prerogative of priesthood.[22] From his study of various OT figures who offered prayers for another, Samuel Balentine concludes: "It may be observed that although the responsibility for intercession appears to be relatively widely distributed among lay persons, kings, and prophets, the responsibility does not fall, according to the language examined thus far, to the priests."[23]

Some also write of Jesus as both priest and victim in a sacrifice,[24] but this particular cultic imagery is foreign to the theology of the Fourth Gospel. Jesus overturned the tables of those collecting the temple tax

---

20. Dorothy Lee writes, "To be a disciple of Jesus—to belong within the divine family—means to be hallowed, made holy, consecrated, in him and by him" (Dorothy A. Lee, *Hallowed in Truth and Love: Spirituality in the Johannine Literature* [Preston, VIC: Mosaic Press, 2011], 134).

21. A helpful survey of the history of this title can be found in Attridge, "How Priestly," 1–14; see also John P. Heil, "Jesus as the Unique High Priest in the Gospel of John," *CBQ* 57 (1995): 729–45. According to Attridge, Cyril of Alexandria, commenting on John 17:9-11, considered Jesus acted as a priest. "For he is the Sacrifice, and is Himself our Priest, Himself our Mediator, Himself a blameless victim, the true Lamb" (*In Joh.* 11.8; also *PG* 74:505). Attridge then states, "The tradition of labeling the chapter in this way is usally attributed to the Reformation theologian David Chytraeus, who lived from 1531–1600 and who called the passage the *praecatio summi sacerdotis*" (1).

22. Samuel E. Balentine, "The Prophet as Intercessor: A Reassessment," *JBL* 103 (1984): 163, examined intercessory prayer and, from just one type, using the verb פלל, he noted that "the role of intercessor is assumed by the following persons: Abraham (Gen 20:7), 'man of God' (1 Kgs 13:6), Nehemiah (Neh 1:6), Hezekiah (2 Chr 30:18), people (Jer 29:7; Ps 72:15), Moses (Num 21:7; Deut 9:20), Job (Job 42:8, 10), Samuel (1 Sam 7:5; 12:19, 23), Jeremiah (Jer 7:16; 11:14; 14:11; 37:3; 42:4; cf. 42:2; 42:20)."

23. Ibid., 164. A contrary view is held by Brown, who considers this prayer "high priestly" not in the sense of one about to offer sacrifice but as one making intercessory prayer, "before the throne of God" as in Hebrews and Romans 8 (Brown, *The Gospel according to John*, 2:747).

24. Frédéric Manns, *L'Evangile de Jean à la lumière du Judaïsme*, SBFA 33 (Jerusalem: Franciscan Printing Press, 1991), 397. By contrast, Brown comments, "There is no major or clear emphasis on the theme of sacrificial offering in xvii; Jesus does not say that he is laying down his life but that he is coming to the Father" (Brown, *The Gospel according to John*, 2:746).

and drove out the sacrificial animals (John 2:13-22). As I discussed earlier, this action is not a temple "cleansing" but an overturning of Israel's sacrificial system of worship and an indicator that Jesus is establishing a new manner of being in relationship with God. In Jesus's discussion with the woman of Samaria, this same point was made that God was not to be worshiped in temples "on this mountain or in Jerusalem," for "the hour is coming, and is now here, when the true worshiper will worship the Father in spirit and truth" (4:23). Through his passion, Jesus will establish a new form of worship, within a new "Father's house/hold."

During his "hour" Jesus is the active agent, not a sacrificial victim.[25] Recall his words in John 12:27, 31-32:

> Now my soul is troubled. And what should I say—"Father, save me from this hour"? No, it is for this reason that I have come to this hour. . . . Now is the judgment of this world; now the ruler of this world will be driven out. And I, when I am lifted up from the earth, will draw all people to myself.

These are the words, not of a victim, but of a victor. In his final prayer, Jesus is neither priest nor victim.

Conclusion to the Petitions (17:20-23)

The prayer comes to its conclusion by Jesus extending it beyond the immediate group of disciples to include future believers, i.e., the future readers of the Gospel. In this section it is clear that Jesus's desire for unity is not an end in itself but a critical aspect of continuing his mission in the world.[26] The union of "I in you" and "they also in us" is *so that* they may all be one."[27] The union Jesus prays for has a purpose. Jesus can be the true revealer of his Father only because of his union with God, and it is from this dynamic unity in love that he can make known the essence of God. Similarly, if disciples are to continue Jesus's mission and reveal God, then they too can do this only from within the union of Jesus and his Father. Jesus's desire that they all be one in him, in his Father, and among themselves is for the purpose of the mission. The revelation of God cannot occur from the outside, only from within the Father-Son-disciples relationship. Being one in God is the only way to reveal God.

25. The Passover Lamb imagery will be discussed further when examining John 19.

26. Francis J. Moloney, *Glory not Dishonour: Reading John 13–21* (Minneapolis: Fortress, 1998), 113.

27. Francis J. Moloney, " 'That All May Be One': The Theme of Unity in John 17," in *Johannine Studies 1975–2017*, WUNT 372 (Tübingen: Mohr Siebeck, 2017), 461–62.

John 17:20-23

[20]"I ask not only on behalf of these, but also on behalf of those who will believe in me through their word, [21]that they may all be one. As you, Father, are in me and I am in you, may they also be in us, so that the world may believe that you have sent me. [22]The glory that you have given me I have given them, so that they may be one, as we are one, [23]I in them and you in me, that they may become completely one, so that the world may know that you have sent me and have loved them even as you have loved me."

The communion in love that Jesus calls disciples to, in order to be agents of revelation, is particularly challenging for Christians today, living in a very fractured world—not just politically, religiously, and socially, but also in the essential meaning of "world" as God's good and blessed creation. We too are part of God's creation, not standing over, above, or against it. This Gospel takes as its point of origin "the beginning" and then proceeds to speak first of creation and then of incarnation. In the word *sarx* the two are essentially one.[28] By being in God, Jesus was able to be the revealer of God (1:18); by being *sarx*, the *logos* was able to reveal God to this cosmos. Theologians today are giving greater attention to this world we live in, to creatures who cohabitate with us, and to all the life-forms that give of their life so creatures, including humans, can live. Some look primarily at the ethical relationships that are needed for the world to continue to sustain life (ecology). Others consider how a greater cosmological awareness can be revelatory of God.[29] One such insight into God as a communion of life has come about through evolutionary sciences showing the interconnectedness of all living organisms with each other and with their local surroundings. Finding the whole of the natural world to be an interwoven web of life, a communion of life, establishes in our human experience a paradigm for imaging the relational nature of the God-life, called Trinity.[30]

28. Drawing on the teaching of Athanasius, the cosmic significance of the incarnation is richly explored in Denis Edwards, *Partaking of God: Trinity, Evolution, and Ecology* (Collegeville, MN: Liturgial Press, 2014), 152–63.

29. The cosmological theme was taken up by R. Alan Culpepper and Jan G. van der Watt, eds., *Creation Stories in Dialogue: The Bible, Science, and Folk Traditions*, BibInt 139 (Leiden: Brill, 2016), esp. chap. 1.

30. The relational life of God is central to the work of Elizabeth A. Johnson, *She Who Is: The Mystery of God in Feminist Theological Discourse* (New York: Crossroad, 1992), and

Conclusion to the Chapter (17:24-26)

With the formal prayer ended, Jesus now draws his time with his disciples and this "conversation" with his Father to conclusion. These verses echo many sentiments expressed in the introductory verses (vv. 1-8). The disciples are those given by God to Jesus (vv. 2, 6, 24), and they believe that Jesus has been sent by God (vv. 8, 25). The disciples are the ones to whom Jesus revealed the "name" or the very essence of God (vv. 6, 26). Jesus is able to be this revealer because of the preexistent love between Father and Son (vv. 5, 24). Because the disciples know his Father, they experience the eternity life and love of God (vv. 3, 26).

While echoing the earlier verses, these concluding words introduce something new. Jesus desires that the disciples may be with him, caught up in the divine love existing between *logos*/Sophia and *theos* before the foundation of the world (1:1). At this point Jesus/Sophia is most evident, for Sophia was present with God before the foundation of the world.

> The LORD created me [Sophia] at the beginning of his work,
> the first of God's acts of long ago.
> Ages ago I was set up,
> at the first, before the beginning of the earth. (Prov 8:22-23)

In this Sophia-*theos* intimacy they too will know God from the "inside" and know the divine love for themselves, and only then can they bear witness to God, from their own experience of love. In narrative time, this is not yet possible, but the fullness of love will be revealed in the "lifting up" that follows. In the exaltation of the crucified one, believers will, with Jesus, be drawn into his Father's household (14:2).

A Missionary Prayer[31]

The language of "union" and "consecration" can distract from the ultimate function of Jesus's words, which is to establish the foundation for the future mission of the disciples in his absence. While Jesus has been present, he is the one on mission from God, sent into the world loved by

---

"Jesus and the Cosmos: Soundings in Deep Christology," in *Incarnation: On the Scope and Depth of Christology*, ed. Neils Henrik Gregersen (Minneapolis: Fortress, 2015).

31. The missionary focus has come to the fore in some scholarship; e.g., Manns, *L'Evangile de Jean à la lumière du Judaïsme*, 383–400, names his study of chapter 17 as "La prière missionnaire de Jésus"; so also Moloney, " 'That All May Be One,' " 383–400.

[24]"Father, I desire that those also, whom you have given me, may be with me where I am, to see my glory, which you have given me because you loved me before the foundation of the world. [25]"Righteous Father, the world does not know you, but I know you; and these know that you have sent me. [26]I made your name known to them, and I will make it known, so that the love with which you have loved me may be in them, and I in them."

God.[32] But when he returns to God, the disciples are the ones who will continue his mission to reveal God's performative love for the world. For God's love is active; love enfolds believers into the Father-Son relationship, making them children of God (1:12) and freeing them from slavery to an evil power. By transferring paternity from "the devil" (John 8:44) to the Father of Jesus,[33] humanity is liberated to live with the freedom of children within the household and no longer as slaves (8:34-36). But, as John Painter notes, "The success of this mission remains totally dependent on the oneness of those who are sent with the source of divine love, which may yet transform the world from a place of darkness and terror."[34] Only the visible unity and love among believers can witness to and make present the divine love in the world.[35]

32. The verb ἀποστέλλω occurs six times in this chapter with reference to Jesus (vv. 3, 8, 18, 21, 23, 25) and once in reference to the disciples (v. 18), although the sending of disciples will not happen until after the resurrection (20:21).

33. The issue of paternity is a central part of the argument with "the Jews" in John 8. The logic is that "sons" do as their "father" does (8:40). "For Jesus the true criterion of paternity is conduct, not ethnic descent" (Brendan Byrne, *Life Abounding: A Reading of John's Gospel* [Collegeville, MN: Liturgical Press, 2014], 152). Sin enslaves, and only the Son can liberate to enable the believer a permanent place within the household (8:34-36) (Mary L. Coloe, *God Dwells with Us: Temple Symbolism in the Fourth Gospel* [Collegeville, MN: Liturgical Press, 2001], 138–40). Within a patriarchal worldview, only the father was considered as the origin of new life, but in the passion, the mother of Jesus will have a critical role in establishing the "children of God." For two contrasting views on this point, see Turid Karlsen Seim, "Descent and Divine Paternity in the Gospel of John: Does the Mother Matter?," *NTS* 51 (2005): 361–75, and Mary L. Coloe, "The Mother of Jesus: A Woman Possessed," in *Character Studies in the Fourth Gospel: Narrative Approaches to Seventy Figures in John*, ed. Steven A. Hunt, D. Francois Tolmie, and Ruben Zimmermann, WUNT 314 (Tübingen: Mohr Siebeck, 2013), 202–13.

34. John Painter, "Identity in the Fourth Gospel," *The Covenant Quarterly* 72 (2014): 258.

35. Zumstein, *L'Évangile selon Saint Jean (13–21)*, 185.

The High Priestly Prayer and Eucharist

Giving this prayer the title of "the High Priestly Prayer," without critical reflection, readily leads to false assumptions about the meal that Jesus shared with disciples before his death, and associating this prayer in John 17 with Jesus's actions with the bread and wine in the Synoptics establishes the wrong impression that this meal was the first Eucharist (even though Jesus had not passed through death and resurrection, nor had the Holy Spirit been given). Furthermore, the assumption that this was the occasion when he "ordained" "the twelve" sharing this meal is false. In popular imagination, helped by artistic representation, this is a very common misunderstanding—even though it has no critical textual basis, nor is it based on an accurate understanding of symbolism and sacramental theology. John Daly states this very clearly: "Was the Last Supper a Eucharist in this full sense of the word? Obviously not. This does not deny that Jesus instituted the Eucharist. What Jesus did at the Last Supper is obviously at least the generative moment of the institution of the Eucharist. But Eucharist in the full sense we have just described? No, that was still to come."[36]

The complexity of issues around the origins of the Eucharist, the "Lord's Supper" in the early church, its relationship to the Last Supper, and Passover goes well beyond what is possible in this commentary; all I can suggest here is some further reading.[37] What is clear, however, is that a simplistic equation of present practice as the intentional ritual instituted by Jesus can no longer be maintained in the face of better understanding of the nature of biblical writing; better awareness of what ritual is, in its dimensions of past, present, and future; and a phenomenology of "presence." Denying women the possibility of acting *in persona Christi* for the Eucharist in the *ecclesia* denies the theology of the community as the Body of Christ and the theology of the resurrected Jesus—the Christ, no longer confined or restrained by limits of mortality.

36. Robert J. Daly, "Eucharistic Origins: from the New Testament to the Liturgies of the Golden Age," *TS* 66 (2005).

37. Pitre Brant, *Jesus and the Last Supper* (Grand Rapids: Eerdmans, 2015); William R. Crockett, *Eucharist: Symbol of Transformation* (Collegeville, MN: Liturgical Press, 2017); Eugene La Verdiere, *The Eucharist in the New Testament and the Early Church* (Collegeville, MN: Liturgical Press, 1996).

John 18:1–19:42

Sophia's Hour Arrives

Let us test what will happen at the end of his life;
for if the righteous man is God's child, he will help him,
and will deliver him from the hand of his adversaries.
Let us test him with insult and torture,
that we may find out how gentle he is,
and make trial of his forbearance.
Let us condemn him to a shameful death,
for, according to what he says, he will be protected. (Wis 2:17-20)

Throughout the narrative there have been numerous references to "the hour," which had "not yet come" (2:4; 7:30; 8:20). This situation changes following the raising of Lazarus and the decision by Caiaphas (11:49-50). The final discourse begins with Jesus knowing that "his hour had come" (13:1), leading into his prayer, "Father, *the hour has come*; glorify your Son so that the Son may glorify you" (17:1). The Johannine passion, chapters 18 and 19, narrates this hour of Jesus's glorification. It is in this hour when all the themes and promises of the Gospel are fulfilled: Believers will become "children of God" (1:12); the temple ("my Father's house") will be raised up (2:19); the work for which Jesus was sent will be completed (4:34; 5:17); those who believe will have the gift of eternity life (4:14; 6:40); the Spirit will be given (7:39); the Son will liberate the slaves to live in the household (8:36), offering salvation and life in abundance (περισσός) (3:16; 10:9-10).[1] What has been glimpsed in fragments will now come together in a single whole. Throughout the narrative the reader has been looking at light refracted into its multiple hues through a prism; in the hour, the reader turns to look through the prism to the brilliant light source.

Arrest (18:1-14)

The Garden

A unique feature of the Johannine passion is the arrest of Jesus in a garden.[2] In the Synoptics the place of the arrest is Gethsemane (Mark 14:32; Matt 26:36) or the Mount of Olives (Luke 22:39), but John names it "a garden." Similarly, in John, the passion concludes in "a garden": "Now there was a garden in the place where he was crucified, and in the garden there was a new tomb in which no one had ever been laid" (19:41). Adding to the setting is the placement of Jesus's cross *in the middle*: "There they crucified him, and with him two others, one on either side, with Jesus in the middle [μέσον δὲ τὸν Ἰησοῦν]" (19:18). The overall setting of the passion recalls the iconography of the creation story (Gen 2:4b–3:24), where the "tree of life" is placed *in the middle* of a garden (ἐν μέσῳ, Gen 2:9; LXX). In the book of Proverbs, the tree of life is identified as Divine Wisdom: "She [Wisdom] is a tree of life to those who lay hold of her" (Prov 3:18). The placement of the cross in the middle of the garden means that the

---

1. περισσός in the Old Testament (LXX) meant the "superabundance of the age of salvation," and in the NT, forms of this word are "almost always used in contexts which speak of a fullness present and proclaimed in the age of salvation as compared with the old aeon. . . . To this extent περισσεύειν is an eschatological catchword." Friedrich Hauck, "περισσεύω," *TDNT* 6 (1968): 59.

2. On the garden symbolism, see Frédéric Manns, *L'Evangile de Jean à la lumière du Judaïsme*, SBFA 33 (Jerusalem: Franciscan Printing Press, 1991), 401–29; Ruben Zimmermann, "Symbolic Communication between John and His Reader: The Garden Symbolism in John 19–20," in *Anatomies of Narrative Criticism: The Past, Present, and Future of the Fourth Gospel as Literature*, ed. Tom Thatcher and Stephen D. Moore, SBLRBS 55 (Leiden: Brill, 2008), 221–35. While the Gospel uses the term κῆπος and not παράδεισος, which is the term used for "garden" in Genesis 2:8 (LXX), these two words are interchangeable and the word κῆπος, to mean the original garden, is found in Ezek 36:35; other Greek translations of the MT use κῆπος to translate the Hebrew גן (Aquila and Theodotion). On this point, see the arguments of Jeannine K. Brown, "Creation's Renewal in the Gospel of John," *CBQ* 72 (2010): 280; Edwyn C. Hoskyns, "Genesis I–III and St John's Gospel," *JTS* 21 (1920): 214; Manns, *L'évangile de Jean*, 405–7. Manns also notes a long patristic tradition of associating the garden of Jesus's arrest and burial with the Garden of Eden (402–7).

John 18:1-14

^{18:1}After Jesus had spoken these words, he went out with his disciples across the Kidron valley to a place where there was a garden, which he and his disciples entered. ²Now Judas, who betrayed him, also knew the place, because Jesus often met there with his disciples. ³So Judas brought a detachment of soldiers together with police from the chief priests and the Pharisees, and they came there with lanterns and torches and weapons. ⁴Then Jesus, knowing all that was to happen to him, came forward and asked them, "Whom are you looking for?" ⁵They answered, "Jesus of Nazareth." Jesus replied, "I am he." Judas, who betrayed him, was standing with them. ⁶When Jesus said to them, "I am he," they stepped back and fell to the ground. ⁷Again he asked them, "Whom are you looking for?" And they said, "Jesus of Nazareth." ⁸Jesus answered, "I told you that I am he. So if you are looking for me, let these men go." ⁹This was to fulfill the word that he had spoken, "I did

creative activity of Wisdom/Sophia is present at Golgotha. What appears to be a death will be transformed into a birth. Standing at the foot of the cross are a man (the Beloved Disciple)³ and a woman, named only in this Gospel as "woman" and "mother" (John 2:4; 19:26). Here again, Eden is recalled, where a man and a woman are depicted standing at the tree "in the middle of the garden" (Gen 3:3). In Genesis, Eve is at first named *"woman"* (Gen 2:23), and then later named *"mother* of all living" (Gen 3:20). These unique features, when taken together, suggest a deliberate evocation of the primordial garden of Eden and a theology of creation, which was introduced with the prologue, "in the beginning" (John 1:1).

When examining the prologue I argued that these eighteen verses are structured in two parallel arrays of three verses, as is the first creation account of Genesis (1:1–2:4a). While following the pattern of the Genesis creation narrative, the prologue has only six strophes and does not include the equivalent to the seventh day Sabbath rest when "the heavens and the earth were finished": "And on the seventh day God finished the work that he had done, and he rested on the seventh day from all the work that he had done" (Gen 2:1-2). I proposed that in its

3. See the author's introduction for comments on the identity and function of the Beloved Disciple, in Mary L. Coloe, *John 1–10*, WCS 44A (Collegeville, MN: Liturgical Press, 2021), liv–lviii. See Sandra M. Schneiders, *Written That You May Believe: Encountering Jesus in the Fourth Gospel*, rev. ed. (New York: Crossroad, 2003), 240, for the hypothesis that the Beloved Disciple is not a male follower; in 19:25-27, this disciple is embodied in the character of Mary Magdalene.

not lose a single one of those whom you gave me." ¹⁰Then Simon Peter, who had a sword, drew it, struck the high priest's slave, and cut off his right ear. The slave's name was Malchus. ¹¹Jesus said to Peter, "Put your sword back into its sheath. Am I not to drink the cup that the Father has given me?"

¹²So the soldiers, their officer, and the Jewish police arrested Jesus and bound him. ¹³First they took him to Annas, who was the father-in-law of Caiaphas, the high priest that year. ¹⁴Caiaphas was the one who had advised the Jews that it was better to have one person die for the people.

structure the prologue was presenting a theology that God's work was not yet finished and that the narrative would show that Jesus had come to bring God's work to its completion (John 4:34; 5:17). The return of the creation theme in the Johannine passion suggests that this is the "hour" when God's work will be finished.

The Nazarene[4]

A second unique aspect of the Johannine passion is the title given to Jesus. When Judas brings "a detachment of soldiers together with police from the chief priests and the Pharisees" (18:3) to arrest Jesus, he steps out (ἐξῆλθεν) and asks whom they seek. They answer, Ἰησοῦν τὸν Ναζωραῖον (v. 5; "Jesus the Nazarene," author's translation), which is then repeated (v. 7).[5] This designation is quite different from how Jesus is named in the Synoptic Gospels, where he is known as "Jesus of [or from] Nazareth" (Mark 1:24; 10:47; 16:6; Matt 21:11; 26:71; Luke 4:34), identifying Jesus in terms of his home village.[6] "The Nazarene" is used in John as a title and only in the hour. It is the unique Johannine title placed on the cross:

4. In John 18 and 19 where this title is used it has the definite article "the," so it should be translated "Jesus the [τὸν] Nazarene," not "Jesus of Nazareth" as in the Synoptics. This is quite significant in the Fourth Gospel, indicating that "Nazarene" is a title, not simply a place name.

5. For more detail, see Mary L. Coloe, "The Nazarene King: Pilate's Title as the Key to John's Crucifixion," in *The Death of Jesus in the Fourth Gospel*, ed. Gilbert van Belle, BETL 200 (Louvain: KUL, 2007), 839–48.

6. In John, the closest name to that found in the Synoptics is when Philip says to Nathanael, "We have found him about whom Moses in the law and also the prophets wrote, Jesus son of Joseph from Nazareth" (1:45).

"Pilate also wrote a title [τίτλον] and put it on the cross. It read, 'Jesus the Nazarene, the King of the Jews' " (19:19; author's translation).[7]

Nazarene and Nazareth are built on the Hebrew root נצר (*netzer*),[8] which describes the future royal shoot from the House of David: "A shoot shall come out from the stump of Jesse, and a branch [נצר] shall grow out of his roots" (Isa 11:1). While the term "branch," *netzer*, is not found in the OT as a direct messianic title, evidence from the Dead Sea Scrolls shows that by the first century this term has taken on messianic meaning in association with "the Branch" from Zechariah 3:8 and 6:12.

> The word of the LORD came to me: Collect silver and gold from the exiles—from Heldai, Tobijah, and Jedaiah—who have arrived from Babylon; and go the same day to the house of Josiah son of Zephaniah. Take the silver and gold and make a crown, and set it on the head of the high priest Joshua son of Jehozadak; say to him: Thus says the LORD of hosts: Here is a man whose name is Branch [צמח, *tzamah*]: for he shall branch out in his place, and he shall build the temple of the LORD. It is he that shall build the temple of the LORD; he shall bear royal honor, and shall sit and rule on his throne. (Zech 6:9-13)

Even though Zechariah uses צמח rather than נצר, first-century rules of interpretation allowed the substitution of equivalent words.[9] The community of Qumran looks to a future son of David and speaks of him with the symbolic name "Branch." When commenting on 2 Samuel 7:11, "YHWH declares to you that he will build you a house. I will raise up your seed after you and establish the throne of his kingdom forever. I will be a father to him and he will be a son to me," the Qumran scribe adds, "This refers to the Branch [צמח] of David" (4QFlor col 1:11); similarly, "Until the messiah of justice comes, the branch [צמח] of David" (4QpGen col 5:3-4).[10] Even more striking is the pesher on Isaiah 11:1-5

---

7. In Mark it is an inscription (ἐπιγραφή), "The King of the Jews" (15:26; similarly Luke 23:38); in Matthew it is a charge (αἰτίαν), "This is Jesus the King of the Jews" (27:37); in John it is a title (τίτλον; John 19:19). Again, the title is indicated by the use of the definite article, Jesus the Nazarene (Ἰησοῦς ὁ Ναζωραῖος), not Jesus of Nazareth, as it is often translated.

8. From the Greek, it was not clear if Nazareth would be spelled in Hebrew with a צ (*tz*) or the simpler ז (*z*). Excavations at Caesarea in 1962 found a clear Hebrew inscription referring to a family from Nazareth using the letter צ, thus clarifying that Nazareth is derived from נצר. Stephen Goranson, "Nazarenes," in *ABD* 4 (1992): 1049.

9. Hans H. Schaeder, "Ναζαρηνός, Ναζωραῖος," *TDNT* 4 (1967): 878.

10. The English text is taken from Florentino García Martínez, *The Dead Sea Scrolls Translated: The Qumran Texts in English* (Leiden: Brill, 1994), 136; the Hebrew from

where, following the quotation from Isaiah, the text is given a sectarian explanation.[11] The quotation follows the Hebrew text and uses נצר, but the following commentary, which speaks of the "branch of David," uses צמח from Zechariah.

These texts show that by the time of the Qumran writings the two terms meaning "branch," צמח and נצר, are being used synonymously. The man named "Branch" who will build the temple of the Lord, according to Zechariah 6, has been identified as the messianic shoot of David, the נצר (Isa 11:1).

Donald Juel examines the targum traditions where the temple-building role of "the Branch" in Zechariah 6 is linked to the Messiah.[12] "Thus says the LORD of Hosts: behold a man whose name is Branch [MT צמח]" (Zech 6:12). In the targum of this verse, the word Messiah (משיחא) is substituted for Branch (צמח). He concludes "that at some point in the development of the targumic tradition, it became customary to refer the prophecy in Zech 6:12-13 to the Messiah, and that at some point the phrase was added to Isa 53:5, reflecting the belief that the Messiah would rebuild the fallen temple."[13] The Qumran scrolls support Juel's conclusion and also indicate that the temple-building role of the Messiah was already in Second Temple Judaism and its literature prior to the Johannine writings. Evidence from the targums and Qumran scrolls support the hypothesis that by the first century CE the term "Nazarene" had developed associations with a Davidic Messiah who would build the eschatological temple.

In the Fourth Gospel, the term "Nazarene" is not a name derived from a place but a title that leads to Jesus's arrest and execution. It is the formal charge and final title applied to him in the pre-Easter narrative. Given this particular narrative usage, its historical background in contemporary Jewish literature, as well as the overall emphasis on the

Eduard Lohse, *Die Texte Aus Qumran: Hebräisch und Deutsch* (Munich: Kösel-Verlag, 1971), 256.

11. 4Q161 (4QpIsa[a] line 11). Florentino García Martínez and Eibert J. Tigchelaar, *The Dead Sea Scrolls Study Edition: 1Q1–4Q273* (Leiden: Brill, 1997), 1:316.

12. Dating of the targums is problematic since their text may be later than the first century CE. Even so, these texts reflect a liturgical origin making it possible that the targumic traditions predate the Johannine text. Where material from Qumran supports the targums, we can conclude we are dealing with material being used in a Jewish milieu prior to the written Gospel. On the issue of dating, see Geza Vermes, *Jesus and the World of Judaism* (London: SCM, 1983), 74–88, especially his conclusions on 85.

13. Donald Juel, *Messiah and Temple*, SBLDS 31 (Missoula, MT: Scholars Press, 1977), 189.

temple in the Gospel's narrative plot, I conclude that the title "Naza-rene" used by the arresting cohort and then Pilate is an ironic reference to Jesus's messianic role as builder of the eschatological temple. Jesus is condemned and dies as the Nazarene temple-builder. As his body is lifted up on the cross, his prophetic words in chapter 2 are fulfilled. The temple of his body is destroyed (2:19), but as "the Nazarene" he is also raising up a new temple.

Interrogations of Peter and Jesus (18:15-27)

Following Jesus's arrest the text describes some puzzling movements and titles. Jesus is sent to Annas (v. 13) who is called the father-in-law of Caiaphas the high priest. The reader is next told that the high priest questioned him (v. 19), but then Annas sends him to Caiaphas the high priest (v. 24). Annas was the high priest from 6–15 CE, and, although no longer officiating as the high priest, he still carried this title, with many rights and obligations,[14] so the high priest referred to in verse 19 is Annas. The interrogation of Peter in the outer courtyard frames the interrogation of Jesus. Where Jesus had twice affirmed his identity in the garden, stating, "I am [ἐγώ εἰμι]" (vv. 5, 7), Peter denies his identity as his disciple, stating, "I am not [οὐκ εἰμί]" (vv. 17, 25, 27). This triple denial around a charcoal fire fulfills Jesus's words, "before the cock crows, you will have denied me three times" (13:38).

The interrogation of Jesus before Annas reveals Jesus's innocence. Annas then sends him to the high priest Caiaphas, which reveals nothing further (v. 24).

The Trial (18:28–19:16)

The hearing before Annas and the trial before Pilate[15] were well established in the tradition, even before the first Gospel (Mark) was written.[16]

---

14. Emil Schürer, *A History of the Jewish People in the Time of Jesus Christ*, div. 2, vol. 1 (New York: Scribner, 1896), 203.

15. Andrew T. Lincoln, *Truth on Trial: The Lawsuit Motif in the Fourth Gospel* (Peabody, MA: Hendrickson, 2000), 137, suggests that the trial of Jesus before Pilate could be called "The Trial of Pilate and the Jews before Jesus." The text is ambiguous about who sits on the judgment seat—Pilate or Jesus. See below.

16. See the study by Marion Soards, "Appendix IX: The Question of a Premarcan Passion Narrative," in Raymond E. Brown, *The Death of the Messiah, from Gethsemane*

18:15–19:16

¹⁵Simon Peter and another disciple followed Jesus. Since that disciple was known to the high priest, he went with Jesus into the courtyard of the high priest, ¹⁶but Peter was standing outside at the gate. So the other disciple, who was known to the high priest, went out, spoke to the woman who guarded the gate, and brought Peter in. ¹⁷The woman said to Peter, "You are not also one of this man's disciples, are you?" He said, "I am not." ¹⁸Now the slaves and the police had made a charcoal fire because it was cold, and they were standing around it and warming themselves. Peter also was standing with them and warming himself.

¹⁹Then the high priest questioned Jesus about his disciples and about his teaching. ²⁰Jesus answered, "I have spoken openly to the world; I have always taught in synagogues and in the temple, where all the Jews come together. I have said nothing in secret. ²¹Why do you ask me? Ask those who heard what I said to them; they know what I said." ²²When he had said this, one of the police standing nearby struck Jesus on the face, saying, "Is that how you answer the high priest?" ²³Jesus answered, "If I have spoken wrongly, testify to the wrong. But if I have spoken rightly, why do you strike me?" ²⁴Then Annas sent him bound to Caiaphas the high priest.

²⁵Now Simon Peter was standing and warming himself. They asked him, "You are not also one of his disciples,

When compared to the Synoptic Gospels, John presents these quite differently. Little is made of the hearing before Annas, with the focus being on the contrast between the infidelity of Peter (Οὐκ εἰμί, 18:17, 25) and Jesus's affirmation of his open teaching to the world and to "the Jews" in their synagogues and temple. There is no charge brought against him in this Jewish context. The trial before Pilate is given much greater emphasis than the Synoptics' presentation, with significant differences: the Passover context, Jesus's royal status, and the portrayal of Pilate.[17]

---

to the Grave: A Commentary on the Passion Narratives in the Four Gospels, ABRL (New York: Doubleday, 1993), 2:1492–1524.

17. Pilate is not only a historical figure but also a character within this narrative. How he is portrayed by the evangelist serves his aim—"that you may believe that Jesus is the Christ, the Son of God" (20:31). Commentators have many varied opinions on the portrayal of Pilate in John. For a summary of various interpretations, see D. Francois Tolmie, "Pontius Pilate: Failing in More Ways Than One," in Character Studies in the Fourth Gospel: Narrative Approaches to Seventy Figures in John, ed. Steven A. Hunt, D. Francois Tolmie, and Ruben Zimmermann, WUNT 314 (Tübingen: Mohr Siebeck, 2013), 578–82; Ronald A. Piper, "The Characterisation of Pilate and the Death of Jesus in the Fourth Gospel," in The Death of Jesus in the Fourth Gospel, ed. Gilbert van Belle, BETL 200 (Louvain: KUL, 2007), 121–62. A recent study pits Pilate against

are you?" He denied it and said, "I am not." ²⁶One of the slaves of the high priest, a relative of the man whose ear Peter had cut off, asked, "Did I not see you in the garden with him?" ²⁷Again Peter denied it, and at that moment the cock crowed.

²⁸Then they took Jesus from Caiaphas to Pilate's headquarters. It was early in the morning. They themselves did not enter the headquarters, so as to avoid ritual defilement and to be able to eat the Passover. ²⁹So Pilate went out to them and said, "What accusation do you bring against this man?" ³⁰They answered, "If this man were not a criminal, we would not have handed him over to you." ³¹Pilate said to them, "Take him yourselves and judge him

according to your law." The Jews replied, "We are not permitted to put anyone to death." ³²(This was to fulfill what Jesus had said when he indicated the kind of death he was to die.)

³³Then Pilate entered the headquarters again, summoned Jesus, and asked him, "Are you the King of the Jews?" ³⁴Jesus answered, "Do you ask this on your own, or did others tell you about me?" ³⁵Pilate replied, "I am not a Jew, am I? Your own nation and the chief priests have handed you over to me. What have you done?" ³⁶Jesus answered, "My kingdom is not from this world. If my kingdom were from this world, my followers would be fighting to keep me from being handed over to the Jews. But as it is, my kingdom

The trial is framed by references to the Passover (18:28; 19:14), and this is the theological lens needed to read both the trial and subsequent crucifixion. More will be said on this below. The trial emphasizes Jesus's royal status using the word "king" (βασιλεύς, 18:33, 37 [2x], 39; 19:3, 12, 14, 15) and "kingdom" (βασιλεία, 18:36 [3x]), but his reign is not "of this world" (18:35), where power is exercised by fighting. The "royal" theme is introduced by Pilate, with "the Jews" simply accusing him of "evildoing" (κακὸν ποιῶν, 18:30). Pilate dismisses this charge as not needing his intervention, but "the Jews'" reply indicates that they are seeking the death penalty under Roman law, i.e., crucifixion.[18] To involve Roman law they need to bring a political, not a religious, accusation of evildoing.

---

the Jews, where he leads them to acknowledge the ultimate power of Caesar (19:15); Norman H. Young, "'The King of the Jews': Jesus before Pilate (John 18:28–19:22)," *ABR* 66 (2018): 31–42.

18. "The governor held power of life and death in a province" (Craig S. Keener, *The Gospel of John: A Commentary*, 2 vols. [Peabody, MA: Hendrickson, 2003], 1107–8). A governor could allow the Sanhedrin this power if a Gentile crossed beyond the boundary in the temple courtyard. These executions would be by stoning or beheading.

is not from here." [37]Pilate asked him, "So you are a king?" Jesus answered, "You say that I am a king. For this I was born, and for this I came into the world, to testify to the truth. Everyone who belongs to the truth listens to my voice." [38]Pilate asked him, "What is truth?"

After he had said this, he went out to the Jews again and told them, "I find no case against him. [39]But you have a custom that I release someone for you at the Passover. Do you want me to release for you the King of the Jews?" [40]They shouted in reply, "Not this man, but Barabbas!" Now Barabbas was a bandit.

[19:1]Then Pilate took Jesus and had him flogged. [2]And the soldiers wove a crown of thorns and put it on his head, and they dressed him in a purple robe. [3]They kept coming up to him, saying, "Hail, King of the Jews!" and striking him on the face. [4]Pilate went out again and said to them, "Look, I am bringing him out to you to let you know that I find no case against him." [5]So Jesus came out, wearing the crown of thorns and the purple robe. Pilate said to them, "Here is the man!" [6]When the chief priests and the police saw him, they shouted, "Crucify him! Crucify him!" Pilate said to them, "Take him your-

Pilate's first question to Jesus moves the charge from religious to political—"Are you the King of the Jews?" (18:33).[19] In reply, Jesus speaks not of himself but of his rule, which transcends this world and is the reason why he came into the world, to bear witness to the truth (v. 37). Jesus changes the direction of Pilate's inquisition to focus on his mission—to be revealer and savior. As the Word incarnate, Jesus embodies truth (1:14, 17), in contrast to Satan who is a liar with no truth in him (8:44). Instead of recognizing the truth in front of him, Pilate responds with a question, "What is truth?" then turns away to "the Jews" outside.

"The Jews" are then faced with the choice of Barabbas or Jesus. From his survey of Roman and Jewish amnesty/pardon parallels, Raymond Brown concludes that this release of a prisoner during the Passover festival was historically quite likely.[20] Dramatically, it highlights the contrast between the conviction of the innocent Jesus and release of the

19. Jesus has been called the "King of Israel" by Nathanael (1:49) and the Jewish crowd (12:13). Nothing in the immediate context explains Pilate's question, but since it is the first question asked in the three Synoptic accounts, the evangelist is probably following a traditional source.

20. Brown, *The Death of the Messiah*, 2:814–20.

selves and crucify him; I find no case against him." [7]The Jews answered him, "We have a law, and according to that law he ought to die because he has claimed to be the Son of God."

[8]Now when Pilate heard this, he was more afraid than ever. [9]He entered his headquarters again and asked Jesus, "Where are you from?" But Jesus gave him no answer. [10]Pilate therefore said to him, "Do you refuse to speak to me? Do you not know that I have power to release you, and power to crucify you?" [11]Jesus answered him, "You would have no power over me unless it had been given you from above; therefore the one who handed me over to you is guilty of a greater sin." [12]From then on Pilate tried to release him, but the Jews cried out, "If you release this man, you are no friend of the emperor. Everyone who claims to be a king sets himself against the emperor."

[13]When Pilate heard these words, he brought Jesus outside and sat on the judge's bench at a place called The Stone Pavement, or in Hebrew Gabbatha. [14]Now it was the day of Preparation for the Passover; and it was about noon. He said to the Jews, "Here is your King!" [15]They cried out, "Away with him! Away with him! Crucify him!" Pilate asked them, "Shall I crucify your King?" The chief priests answered, "We have no king but the emperor." [16]Then he handed him over to them to be crucified.

revolutionary (λῃστής). The Romans consider these bandits to be political criminals, and death was by crucifixion.[21]

When the crowd chooses to release Barabbas, Pilate hands Jesus over to his soldiers who beat him and mockingly dress him with a crown and the royal purple robe. When the soldiers return him to Pilate still wearing royal regalia, Pilate displays him to the crowd, saying, "Behold the man [ἰδοὺ ὁ ἄνθρωπος]" (19:5). This declaration is similar to that in Zechariah 6:12: "Behold a man [Ἰδοὺ ἀνήρ, LXX] whose name is Branch." Although the phrases are not identical, the similarity is such that, according to Jewish interpretive methods, they can be linked. Wayne Meeks also understands "man" to be a title, a "throne-name" given to the King of "the Jews." He argues that the title "the Man" was considered an eschatological title in Hellenistic Judaism and sees the links with Zechariah 6.[22] Also,

21. Karl H. Rengstorf, " λῃστής," *TDNT* 4 (1967): 259.

22. Wayne A. Meeks, *The Prophet-King: Moses Traditions and the Johannine Christology*, NovTSup 14 (Leiden: Brill, 1967), 70–72. Meeks writes, "A striking if perhaps accidental parallel to John 19:5 is found in Zech 6:12" (71). With Jesus already named "the Nazarene," the branch, I do not consider this parallel to be either "perhaps" or

since Jesus has already been introduced as "the Nazarene" (the Branch), and later Pilate will use this as his title on the cross, I consider that, for the Johannine audience, this announcement would continue the ironic thrust of this scene. "Behold the man" alludes to the announcement in Zechariah of the messianic Branch who will "build the temple of the LORD; he shall bear royal honor, and shall sit and rule on his throne" (Zech 6:13).

The chief priests and police then call for his crucifixion (19:6). When Pilate affirms for the third time that he finds no case against him (19:6; cf. 18:38; 19:4), they reply with a further accusation that Jesus "claimed to be the Son of God" (19:7). In the context of Roman imperial ideology, this claim is treasonous.[23] Julius Caesar was deified upon his death, and since then an emperor could be called a "Son of God." If Jesus is claiming divine status, then he is setting himself up in opposition to Caesar.

During the trial Pilate is depicted moving in and out of the Praetorium, to speak with Jesus and then with "the Jews." This movement and the questions he puts to "the Jews" could suggest that he is weak and vacillating, unsure what to do. He declares three times, "I find no case against him" (18:38; 19:4, 6), and attempts to release Jesus (19:12). Against this narrative characterization, the reader needs to be aware of the type of ruler Pilate was,[24] then they will appreciate the deep irony of this scene. Furthermore, while Pilate appears to be the judge, it is unclear who is seated on the judgment bench (19:13)—Pilate or Jesus.[25] The narrative calls for the readers to decide. I think Jesus is seated on the judgment

---

"accidental." It is a further aspect of the symbolic strata of the Gospel's theology that will continue into the crucifixion scene.

23. "Roman emperors were formally deified at their deaths, although imperial cults sometimes included living emperors in divine honors. After Julius Caesar was deified in the first century B.C. the title 'son of god' or 'son of the deified' was used for the emperors who succeeded him." See Craig R. Koester, "Why Was the Messiah Crucified? A Study of God, Jesus, Satan and Human Agency in Johannine Theology," in van Belle, *The Death of Jesus in the Fourth Gospel*, 168 n. 14; also Piper, "The Characterisation of Pilate," 125–27.

24. An inscription found at Caesarea Maritima in 1961 names Pilate as "Prefect of Judea," therefore he had military, financial, and judicial powers. Contemporary sources (Philo and Josephus) describe him as a ruthless administrator, and eventually he was withdrawn in 37 CE.

25. If it is Pilate, it means reading the verb ἐκάθισεν in an intransitive sense—Pilate sat himself. But it could also be read in a transitive sense with Jesus as the object—Pilate sat Jesus on the judgment seat (βῆμα). Grammatically, either sense is possible. The question is what the evangelist might have intended: to be historically plausible, in which case Pilate would sit in judgment; or to ironically stress that it is Jesus who

seat.[26] The final words in Jesus's public ministry are on judgment: "The one who rejects me and does not receive my word has a judge; on the last day the word that I have spoken will serve as judge, for I have not spoken on my own, but the Father who sent me has himself given me a commandment about what to say and what to speak" (12:48-49). In the "hour" of Jesus, the last day has come and so the "ruler of this world" now sits under the judgment of Jesus's word. Ernst Haenchen observes that it is not Pilate who is the judge but Jesus, and "he speaks in silence, by sitting on the seat of judgment with his mock crown, and purple mantle."[27]

What is at stake during the trial is the question of power or authority. "The Jews" claim they have no authority to execute Jesus (18:31), so they turn to Pilate. In the first dialogue between Pilate and Jesus (vv. 33-38), Pilate discovers no crime, but the confirmation that Jesus is King (v. 37). Pilate then hands Jesus over to his soldiers who scourge him and then return him to Pilate in the mocking garb of a king. Pilate parades Jesus before the crowd, stating again that he has not broken any law meriting execution (19:6). "The Jews" then raise the more serious charge that Jesus claimed to be the Son of God (19:7). Within the Roman Empire, the emperor could appoint client kings such as Herod; claiming kingship independent of imperial rule and then claiming divinity would be treasonable, as only Caesar could be hailed as "divine." Now Pilate has cause to act. Pilate returns inside for a second dialogue with Jesus asking about his origins—"Where are you from?" (19:9). Faced with Jesus's silence Pilate claims to have ultimate power—"Do you not know that I have power to release you, and power to crucify you?" (19:10). Jesus refutes this claim—"You would have no power over me unless it had been given you from above." This interchange is the crux of the scene. Where does power lie? With Pilate? With "the Jews"? With Jesus? Or is there some other cosmic dimension being reflected in this scene?

---

is making the judgment? For more detail on this extensive debate among interpreters, see Brown, *The Death of the Messiah*, 2:1388–93.

26. This position is well argued by Andrew T. Lincoln, *The Gospel according to Saint John*, BNTC (London: Continuum, 2005), 469. Here, Lincoln refers to Justin's *Apology* (1.35) where it is understood that Jesus sat on the judgment seat: "And as the prophet spoke, they tormented Him, and set Him on the judgment-seat, and said, Judge us."

27. Ernst Haenchen, *John 2: A Commentary on the Gospel of John Chapters 7–21*, trans. R. W. Funk, Hermeneia (Philadelphia: Fortress, 1984), 188. Haenchen also refers to Justin, *Apology* 1.35.6, and the Gospel of Peter 1:7 to show that this tradition of Jesus sitting on the judgment seat was known in the early centuries (187).

There have been hints in the narrative that there are cosmic powers penetrating the human drama. Jesus is the embodiment of holy Wisdom sent to bring salvation and eternity life to all who believe (3:16). Opposed to him is a power of evil called Satan (13:27), the devil (13:2), the evil one (17:15), and the ruler of this world (12:31; 14:30; 16:11).[28] Jesus is in the world but does not belong to this world as he says to "the Jews" opposed to him: "You are from below, I am from above; you are of this world, I am not of this world" (8:23). This power of evil influences the actions of the characters such as Judas, entering into him when he had received the morsel of bread (13:21). The harshest condemnation by Jesus is uttered in his confrontation with those "who had believed in him" (8:31), who had been his followers but, like Judas, turn against him. In rejecting Jesus's word these former followers have identified themselves as belonging to an evil power at work in the world (8:44-45).[29]

In the trial before Pilate Jesus testifies/witnesses to the truth (18:37), but Pilate and the Jewish authorities refuse to believe him. When the chief priests and police demand that he be crucified (19:6) and Pilate surrenders Jesus to them, these characters enact the desires of their "father, the devil" (8:44). On this human stage the power of God, incarnate in Jesus, confronts the cosmic power of Evil, embodied in Pilate, the chief priests, and police who call for his crucifixion (19:6). While Jesus sits in silence on the judgment seat, his judgment has already been proleptically given, "Now is the judgment of this world; now the ruler of this world will be driven out" (12:31). As Judith Kovacs states, "[T]he cross is not merely the metaphorical jumping off point for Jesus's reascent to his heavenly Father. It is the locus of a cosmic battle, in which Jesus achieves a decisive victory over Satan."[30]

---

28. On the power of evil operating in the crucifixion, see Koester, "Why Was the Messiah Crucified?"; Judith Kovacs, " 'Now Shall the Ruler of This World Be Driven Out': Jesus' Death as Cosmic Battle in John 12:20-36," *JBL* 114 (1995): 227–47; and John Dennis, "The 'Lifting up of the Son of Man' and the Dethroning of the 'Ruler of this World': Jesus' Death as the Defeat of the Devil in John 12:31-32," in van Belle, *The Death of Jesus in the Fourth Gospel*, 678–91.

29. The Qumran documents clearly show a first-century belief that the world was under the rule of demonic powers and needed the protection of God to be free from these powers. See the discussion of Jesus's prayer (John 17) in Cecelia Warren, "What Do Angels Have against the Blind and the Deaf? Rules of Exclusion in the Dead Sea Scrolls," in *Common Judaism: Explorations in Second-Temple Judaism*, ed. Wayne O. McGready and Adele Reinhartz (Minneapolis: Fortress, 2008), 115–29.

30. Kovacs, " 'Now Shall the Ruler of This World Be Driven Out,' " 246.

The Crucifixion (19:16b-25)

When Jesus is handed over to be crucified, the time is noted: "Now it was the day of Preparation for the Passover; and it was about noon" (19:14). At the time of Jesus, this was the hour when the priests in the temple would begin the slaughter of the lambs to be used in the Passover meal later that evening. Exodus 12:6 required that the lambs had to be killed "in the evening" of the Preparation day. In the first century, the large number of pilgrims meant that thousands of lambs needed to be slaughtered; rabbinic law, therefore, interpreted "evening" to begin at noon so that the necessary work could be completed before the Passover feast began at sundown.[31] At the same time that the lambs are being led to their slaughter in the temple, Pilate is handing over Jesus to his death.

Jesus carries his cross unaided; there is no Simon of Cyrene called on to assist, as in the Synoptics. This may well be a reference to the story of Isaac carrying the wood for his own sacrifice (Gen 22:6). According to the Book of Jubilees (ca. 160 BCE), the sacrifice of Isaac was regarded as the origin of the Passover (Jub. 18:17-19). According to Bruce Grigsby, "His [Isaac's] blood, not the Paschal Lamb's, was regarded by Yahweh on the first Passover night."[32] This indicates that by the first century the Isaac tradition and Passover are being linked. In the Fourth Gospel, however, this Isaac symbolism is lacking. Jesus walks to his death garbed in purple and wearing a crown of royal honors.

Unfortunately, most translations hide the theological themes that the evangelist is presenting. As noted earlier, Jesus is crucified "in the middle" (μέσον) of the two others, just as the "tree of life" was planted in the middle of the Garden of Eden; Pilate had a title (τίτλον) written, not an inscription, and this title reads "Jesus the Nazarene ['Ιησοῦς ὁ Ναζωραῖος], the King of the Jews." As explained earlier in discussing John 18:5, the word "Nazarene" is an allusion to Zechariah 6:12-13 where a man, Joshua, is introduced with the symbolic name "Branch" who will

---

31. Donald Senior, *The Passion of Jesus in the Gospel of John* (Leominister: Gracewing, 1991), 96; also Brown, *Death of the Messiah*, 1:847.

32. Bruce Grigsby, "The Cross as an Expiatory Sacrifice in the Fourth Gospel," *JSNT* 15 (1982): 59. The binding of Isaac became a highly developed theological motif called the *Aqedah* in rabbinic writings. Some attempts have been made to give a pre-Christian date to the *Aqedah* theology wherein Isaac is an adult who willingly moves to his death, but this pre-Christian dating of the *Aqedah* tradition has been challenged. See the discussion in Phillip R. Davies and Bruce D. Chilton, "The Aqedah: A Revised Tradition History," *CBQ* 40 (1978): 514–46.

John 19:16b-25

16bSo they took Jesus; 17and carrying the cross by himself, he went out to what is called The Place of the Skull, which in Hebrew is called Golgotha. 18There they crucified him, and with him two others, one on either side, with Jesus between them. 19Pilate also had an inscription written and put on the cross. It read, "Jesus of Nazareth, the King of the Jews." 20Many of the Jews read this inscription, because the place where Jesus was crucified was near the city; and it was written in Hebrew, in Latin, and in Greek. 21Then the chief priests of the Jews said to Pilate, "Do not write, 'The King of the Jews,' but, 'This man said, I am King of the Jews.'" 22Pilate answered, "What I have written I have written." 23When the soldiers had crucified Jesus, they took his clothes and divided them into four parts, one for each soldier. They also took his tunic; now the tunic was seamless, woven in one piece from the top. 24So they said to one another, "Let us not tear it, but cast lots for it to see who will get it." This was to fulfill what the scripture says,

"They divided my clothes among themselves,
and for my clothing they cast lots."

25And that is what the soldiers did.

build the eschatological temple.[33] Ironically, by this title, Pilate names Jesus as the royal temple-builder.

All the Gospels record the practice of dividing the clothes of the prisoner among the soldiers by casting lots. John gives a unique emphasis to the seamless tunic and provides an explicit and exact Scripture citation of Psalm 22:18: "They divide my clothes among themselves, and for my clothing they cast lots." For centuries there has been an interpretation of the seamless robe as a symbol of Jesus's priestly role.[34] In recent years scholars have moved away from this interpretation to seeing a symbol of church unity in the undivided tunic.[35] Both are possible, as symbols are frequently polyvalent, but the meaning may lie not in the undivided tunic but in the "fulfilment" theme introducing the citation.[36] The Gospel makes use of Scripture citations quite frequently, and they are introduced using two different expressions. Within the public ministry of Jesus

33. See further, Coloe, "The Nazarene King," 839–48.
34. See, for example, John P. Heil, "Jesus as the Unique High Priest in the Gospel of John," *CBQ* 57 (1995): 729–45.
35. For discussions on the tunic as a symbol of unity, see Bruce G. Schuchard, *Scripture within Scripture: The Interrelationship of Form and Function in the Explicit Old Testament Citations in the Gospel of John*, SBLDS 133 (Atlanta: Scholars Press, 1992), 125–32.
36. This point is made by Keener, *The Gospel of John*, 2:1140.

the Scripture is introduced "as *it is written*" (καθώς ἐστιν γεγραμμένον, 6:31, 45; 10:34; 12:14; also 2:17). When Jesus withdraws from his public ministry, the introduction changes to "*In order to fulfill* the word of Isaiah the prophet" (ἵνα ὁ λόγος Ἡσαΐου τοῦ προφήτου πληρωθῇ, similarly, 13:18; 15:25; 18:9; 19:24, 36, 37).[37] The fulfilment motif occurs five times in the passion, affirming that what happens to Jesus is not a tragic accident, or governed by historical/political purposes, but is part of the divine plan of God operative from the beginning of time and known particularly through the Scriptures of Israel. As the Gospel approaches the climactic moment of the cross, the evangelist testifies that in this death Scripture is brought to its fulfilment. In fact, the final word of the *Logos* is τετέλεσται, "It is finished" (19:30).

The Gospel's Climax (19:25b-30)

In my understanding, the Gospel reaches its climax in these verses, where all the promises of the prologue and following narrative are achieved. Once again weak translations obscure the meaning of this scene. Verse 27 uses an idiom, εἰς τὰ ἴδια, used earlier in the prologue, "he came to his own [εἰς τὰ ἴδια]" (1:11). As an idiom it cannot be literally translated, and so at times translators add words not in the original expression, hoping to give in English the sense of the phrase. In 19:27 translations add the word "home" when it is not in the original Greek. This addition incorrectly interprets the meaning of the scene as Jesus commending his mother into the care of his Beloved Disciple. This completely misses the point of the scene and of the deep theology of this entire narrative.[38] The idiom is better understood here to mean, "And from that hour the disciple took her *as* his own [mother]."

---

37. This distinction in the introductory formula and its theological function is the work of Andreas Obermann, *Die christologische Erfüllung der Schrift im Johannesevangelium*, WUNT 83 (Tübingen: Mohr Siebeck, 1996). Ruth Sheridan developed his study further in her examination of the way the Scriptures were used in the public ministry to bear witness to Jesus particularly in his interaction with "the Jews." See Ruth Sheridan, *Retelling Scripture: 'The Jews' and the Scriptural Citations in John 1:19–12:15*, BibInt 110 (Leiden: Brill, 2012).

38. This same position is taken by Dorothy A. Lee, *Flesh and Glory: Symbolism, Gender and Theology in the Gospel of John* (New York: Crossroad, 2002), 152–53, who considers that the traditional interpretation "makes little sense at the level of Johannine theology."

John 19:25b-30

^{25b}Meanwhile, standing near the cross of Jesus were his mother, and his mother's sister, Mary the wife of Clopas, and Mary Magdalene. ²⁶When Jesus saw his mother and the disciple whom he loved standing beside her, he said to his mother, "Woman, here is your son." ²⁷Then he said to the disciple, "Here is your mother." And from that hour the disciple took her into his own home.

²⁸After this, when Jesus knew that all was now finished, he said (in order to fulfill the scripture), "I am thirsty." ²⁹A jar full of sour wine was standing there. So they put a sponge full of the wine on a branch of hyssop and held it to his mouth. ³⁰When Jesus had received the wine, he said, "It is finished." Then he bowed his head and gave up his spirit.

When Jesus says to his mother, "Woman, behold your son," and then to the Beloved Disciple, "Behold your mother," he effects a change in their relationships. The woman is now mother to the disciple, and the disciple is now son to the mother of Jesus. In changing this relationship, Jesus creates a new relationship between himself and the disciple (and all disciples). The disciple is now brother/sibling of Jesus and is now drawn into Jesus's own relationship with God. This is the moment when disciples become children of God, as the prologue promised (1:12). In the prologue the expression εἰς τὰ ἴδια introduces the consequences of the *Logos* coming into the world.

> He came to his own [εἰς τὰ ἴδια], and his own did not accept him. But to all who received him, who believed in his name, he gave power to become children of God [ἔδωκεν αὐτοῖς ἐξουσίαν τέκνα θεοῦ γενέσθαι], who were born, not of blood or of the will of the flesh or of the will of man, but born of God [ἀλλ᾽ ἐκ θεοῦ ἐγεννήθησαν]. (1:11-13; author's translation)

The repetition of the phrase εἰς τὰ ἴδια here in the passion (19:27) creates a textual link between the statement of the prologue and its fulfilment in this scene. Those who believe are now reborn of God.[39]

The divine filiation brought about in this scene bring Jesus's work and mission to completion. Once again, the theme of the fulfillment of Scripture is stated. Following the received passion tradition, Jesus is given wine to drink (Mark 15:36; Matt 27:48), not on a reed, as in the Synoptics, but rather on a hyssop branch. Naming the reed as "hyssop" alludes to the hyssop used at the original Passover. When the lamb had

---

39. This is the rebirth that Nicodemus (chap. 3) could not understand and thought impossible.

been slaughtered, the blood was collected in a basin and then Moses said, "Take a bunch of hyssop, dip it in the blood that is in the basin, and touch the lintel and the two doorposts with the blood in the basin" (Exod 12:22). The action of passing the sponge to Jesus is introduced with the phrase "in order to fulfill the scripture." There is no explicit citation, but the naming of the "hyssop," along with the many other reminders of the Passover, provides an implicit allusion to this first salvific action for God's people.

At this point Jesus announces, "It is finished" (τετέλεσται), and hands over *the* Spirit (παρέδωκεν τὸ πνεῦμα).[40] The declaration that Jesus knew "all was now finished" (v. 28) makes verses 26 and 27 the climax and fulfilment of Jesus's mission. As Mark Stibbe remarks, this scene "really constitutes the climactic work in his ministry. John 19:25-27 is therefore a crucial narrative episode in the Johannine passion account."[41] In the hour, Jesus brings the work he was sent to accomplish to its conclusion. His final word, τετέλεσται (v. 30), echoes Genesis 2:1 when God "finished" (using a form of τέλεω, LXX) the work of creation.[42] Throughout the Gospel Jesus had claimed that God in fact was still working (5:17), that the creative work of God had not yet been completed, and that he has been sent to finish (τέλεω) this work (4:34; 5:36; 17:4). In the hour, as the sixth day comes to an end, Jesus announces the completion of God's creative work so that the Sabbath can truly begin (19:31). As one creative act "in the beginning" draws to its end, the new eschatological age is ushered in and its first gift is the Spirit. When Jesus dies, he inclines his head and hands over *the* Spirit to the small group of believers gathered at the foot of his cross. They are symbolically "reborn" from above, as children of God, enabling access to the reign of God as Jesus had told Nicodemus, "No one can see the reign of God without being born again" (3:3; author's translation).[43] This is a constitutive gift of the Spirit, drawing believers into Jesus's own divine filiation. Later in "the hour," the

---

40. The Greek clearly says "the Spirit" and not "his spirit" as a euphemism for death. The term "handed over" (παρέδωκεν) has occurred throughout the passion to describe Jesus being "handed over" to Pilate (18:30, 35; 19:11) or to "the Jews" (18:36; 19:16).

41. Mark Stibbe, *John as Storyteller: Narrative Criticism and the Fourth Gospel*, SNTSMS 73 (Cambridge: Cambridge University Press, 1992), 154.

42. Martin Hengel, "The Old Testament in the Fourth Gospel," in *The Gospels and the Scriptures of Israel*, ed. Craig Evans and W. Richard Stegner, JSNTSup 104 (Sheffield: Sheffield Academic, 1994), 393–94.

43. The Greek word ἄνωθεν can mean both born "from above" and born "again." When discussing the Nicodemus passage, I argue that in this verse it means to be

ministerial function of the Spirit will be emphasized (20:21-23). There are not two bestowals of the Spirit. I would rather speak of two moments within the *one* hour, one moment where the focus is on the believer's relationship to Jesus, and a second moment where the focus is on the believer's relationship to the world, as the agent of Jesus in the world.

The handing down of the Spirit completes the scene and clarifies the new relationship established through Jesus's words. From this moment, through the indwelling Spirit, the believer is drawn into the "house/hold of my father" (ἐν τῇ οἰκίᾳ τοῦ πατρός μου, 14:2). Even as the soldiers set about the task of crucifying Jesus, the Nazarene is building a new temple/household of God. As the soldiers destroy the body/temple of Jesus, the Nazarene temple-builder is in the process of raising up a new temple ("my Father's house," 2:16), thus fulfilling Jesus's words to "the Jews," "Destroy this temple and in three days I will raise it up" (2:19).

Scriptures Are Fulfilled (19:31-37)

The completion of Jesus's mission ushers in a great Sabbath (μεγάλη ἡ ἡμέρα ἐκείνου τοῦ σαββάτου), just as the completion of God's work of creation concluded with the Sabbath rest; this is yet another reminder that the creation theme suffuses the passion narrative, which is set within a garden. The Sabbath provides the reason for two unique Johannine additions to the crucifixion narrative—the piercing of the side of Jesus, and the breaking of the legs of the two criminals but leaving Jesus's legs unbroken. It was the usual practice to leave the bodies of those crucified on the cross as a warning to others. Because it was the Passover, and the Sabbath that falls within one of the pilgrim festivals is considered to be a Sabbath of extra solemnity, "the Jews" ask for the bodies to be removed. Death by crucifixion is a slow torture, as a criminal dies when he can no longer raise his body up in order to gasp for breath. This is why the legs were broken, so that the criminal would just hang suspended from his or her arms and would suffocate more quickly.[44] In coming to Jesus, the soldiers perceive that he is already dead and pierce his side to confirm this death.

---

born "again"; Nicodemus understands it in this sense when speaking about being born a second time (3:4). See Coloe, *John 1–10*, 88–89.

44. For references to the crucifixion of women, see Josephus, *Antiquities* 18.3.65-80 and Tacitus, *Annals* 14.45.

[31]Since it was the day of Preparation, the Jews did not want the bodies left on the cross during the sabbath, especially because that sabbath was a day of great solemnity. So they asked Pilate to have the legs of the crucified men broken and the bodies removed. [32]Then the soldiers came and broke the legs of the first and of the other who had been crucified with him. [33]But when they came to Jesus and saw that he was already dead, they did not break his legs. [34]Instead, one of the soldiers pierced his side with a spear, and at once blood and water came out. [35](He who saw this has testified so that you also may believe. His testimony is true, and he knows that he tells the truth.) [36]These things occurred so that the scripture might be fulfilled, "None of his bones shall be broken." [37]And again another passage of scripture says, "They will look on the one whom they have pierced."

The flow of blood and water from the side of Jesus is a multivalent symbol.[45] Since the narrator has identified the body of Jesus as "the temple" (2:21), the flow of blood and water from his side mirrors the action taking place in the temple on the other side of Jerusalem. The Passover lamb was slaughtered in the temple by the head of the household, and it was the role of the priests to hold basins to receive the blood. The priests would pass the basins along a line until the one nearest the altar received it and then tossed the blood on the altar (m. Pes. 5.5-6). The altar had two holes in one corner "like two narrow nostrils, through which the drops of blood which are tossed on the western foundation and on the southern foundation descend and mix together in the water channel" and flowed out into the Kidron brook (m. Mid. 3.2). As Preparation day drew to a close, quite literally, blood and water would flow from the side of the temple down into the Kidron.

The choice of the term πλευρά to describe the side of Jesus may be a deliberate allusion to God's work of creation. In the Yahwist's description of God's first creative activity in the Garden of Eden, he describes the birth of the woman as a birth from the side (LXX: τῶν πλευρῶν) of האדם, *ha adam* (Gen

45. A wide range of interpretations of the blood and water, as well as a list of patristic associations, can be found in Edward Malatesta, "Blood and Water from the Pierced Side of Christ (Jn 19,34)," in *Segni e sacramenti nel Vangelo di Giovanni*, ed. Pius-Ramon Tragan, SA 67 (Rome: Editrice Anselmiana, 1977), 165–81.

2:21).[46] The reminder that there were two others crucified with Jesus recalls that he, like the tree of life, is in the middle of the garden, and as the tree of life, Wisdom/Sophia (Prov 3:18) is manifest in him. The flow of blood and water from the side of Jesus/Sophia, seen against the Genesis background, symbolizes a moment of birth, a moment when new life comes into being. The concept of birth is not foreign to the Gospel. The gift of the Spirit has been described to Nicodemus as being born from above (3:3, 5, 7). Jesus hands down the Spirit to the mother and "son" who stand at the foot of the cross. The words to the Beloved Disciple and the mother of Jesus, who like Eve is called woman (19:26, cf. Gen 2:23) and mother (19:27, cf. Gen 3:21), create a new set of familial relationships. Jesus's words and the accompanying gift of the Spirit can be understood as a birth "from above," thus fulfilling the words to Nicodemus. Those who accept Jesus and receive the gift of the Spirit are "born of God" (1:13) and can now be called "children of God" (1:12). The first creative activity of God is brought to completion in Jesus's death, and the release of the Spirit ushers in the dawn of a new creation. An action that appears to be a confirmation of death is, from the Johannine perspective, a moment of birth.

Birthed from the Side of Jesus (John 19:34)[47]

Unique to the Gospel of John is the depiction of Jesus's death as a birthing of new life. In the crucifixion scene, when the soldier pierces Jesus's side with a spear, blood and water flow out (19:34)—the same liquids that accompany the birthing process. In addition to the blood and water, the presence of Jesus's mother at the foot of the cross (19:25-27) is evocative of birthing. The one who gave Jesus physical birth is also the one who helps, like a midwife, to birth his public ministry at Cana (2:1-11) and to bring forth the new life that is birthed at Jesus's death. The two scenes in which Jesus's mother appear form

---

46. When reading the Hebrew text, there is the clear pun on the earthling (הָאָדָם, *ha 'adam*) being made from the earth (הָאֲדָמָה, *ha 'adamah*) (Gen 2:7). At this point in the Genesis narrative the creature is not yet identified as "a man," nor is *"adam"* yet a personal name. It is only when the woman is created that the text speaks of a man (אִישׁ, *ish*) and a woman (אִשָּׁה, *ishah*) (2:23). The man and the woman come into existence together.

47. The content of this excursus is condensed from Barbara E. Reid, "Birthed from the Side of Jesus (John 19:34)," in *Finding a Woman's Place: Essays in Honor of Carolyn Osiek, R.S.C.J.*, ed. David L. Balch and Jason T. Lamoreaux (Eugene, OR: Pickwick, 2011), 191–214.

an *inclusio* and each provides interpretive clues for the other.[48]

The theme of birthing is introduced already in the prologue: "all things were birthed [ἐγένετο[49]] through him [ὁ λόγος, 'the Word']" (1:3) and "to all who received him, who believed in his name, he gave power to become [γενέσθαι] children of God, who were born [ἐγεννήθησαν], not of blood or of the will of the flesh or of the will of man, but of God" (1:12-13).[50] The prologue sets the stage for an understanding of discipleship that entails acceptance of one's birth as a child of God and empowerment to engender life in others through faith in the λόγος.

In the first scene with Nicodemus, Jesus says, "No one can see the kingdom of God without being born [γεννηθῇ] from above" (3:3). And further, "no one can enter the kingdom of God without

being born [γεννηθῇ] of water and the Spirit" (3:5). It is in the crucifixion scene that the meaning of birth in water and Spirit becomes clearer. At Jesus's death, he hands over the Spirit (19:30),[51] which is juxtaposed with flowing water from the pierced side of Jesus (19:34). Just as in Ezekiel 36:25-27, the symbols of water and spirit signal a rebirth accomplished by divine action.

The metaphor of birthing is nowhere more explicit than in the Farewell Discourse where Jesus likens his impending passion and the anguish of his disciples to the labor pains of a woman giving birth (16:20-22).[52] The focus is on the ensuing joy at the new life that will result, not on the suffering.

The theme of birthing, so carefully woven throughout the Gospel, climaxes in the crucifixion scene and its aftermath. The "power to

---

48. There are a number of verbal and thematic links: in both scenes Jesus addresses his mother as Γύναι, "woman" (2:4; 19:26); there is reference to "the hour" (2:4; 19:27) and to belief (2:11; 19:35); and water plays an important symbolic role in both.

49. The primary definition of the verb γίνομαι is "to come into being through process of birth or natural production, be born, be produced" (BDAG, 196–99).

50. The verbs γίνομαι and γεννάω each can connote both male begetting and female birthing; γίνομαι tends to be used more frequently for male begetting (e.g., Matt 1:2-20), and γεννάω for female birthing (e.g., John 3:4; 16:21). BDAG, 193–94.

51. In addition to the reasons given in the commentary above for why the expression παρέδωκεν τὸ πνεῦμα (19:30) should be understood as the giving of the Spirit rather than a euphemism for death, see Sandra M. Schneiders, *Written That You May Believe: Encountering Jesus in the Fourth Gospel*, rev. and exp. ed. (New York: Crossroad, 2003), 179, and James Swetnam, "Bestowal of the Spirit in the Fourth Gospel," *Bib* 74 (1993): 556–76.

52. The image is similar to Isa 42:14 depicting the divine anguish in rebirthing Israel after the exile.

become children of God" (1:12) is accomplished (19:30). The mother of Jesus, who gave him physical birth and who mediated the birth of his public ministry (2:1-11), is present again (19:25). Nicodemus returns and as he and Joseph of Arimathea wrap Jesus's body in linen cloths (19:40), images of death and birth meld, as they swaddle him like a newborn (Luke 2:7).[53] Jesus's promise of "living water" (4:10; 7:38) is brought to fulfillment as he hands over the spirit (19:30). His final declaration, "It is finished" (19:30), is that of a mother who cries out in joy when the birth pangs are over and her child is born.[54] Finally, the resurrected Christ breathes on the disciples (20:22) as a midwife blows breath into the nostrils of a newborn to help it to breathe on its own. There is an echo of how the Creator birthed the first human creature by breathing into its nostrils (Gen 2:7).

It is not a modern feminist invention to interpret Jesus's passion as labor pangs through which new life is birthed.[55] Clement of Alexandria (153–217)

wrote about "the body of Christ, which nourishes by the Word the young brood, which the Lord Himself brought forth in throes of flesh, which the Lord Himself swathed in his precious blood. . . . O amazing birth!" (*The Instructor* 1.6).[56] Similarly, Ambrose, bishop of Milan (d. 397), refers to Christ as the "Virgin who bare us, Who fed us with her own milk" (*On Virgins* 1.5).[57] In Syriac tradition there is a comparison made between Adam's side that gave birth to Eve and the pierced side of Jesus that gave birth to the church. In the sixth century, Jacob of Serugh wrote:

> For from the beginning God
>   knew and depicted
> Adam and Eve in the like-
>   ness of the image of his
>   Only-begotten;
> He slept on the cross as Adam
>   had slept his deep sleep,
> his side was pierced and from it
>   there came forth the Daughter
>   of Light,
> water and blood as an image of
>   divine children
> to be heirs to the Father who
>   loves his Only-begotten. . . .

53. Ingrid Rosa Kitzberger, "Transcending Gender Boundaries in John," in *A Feminist Companion to John*, vol. 1, ed. Amy-Jill Levine with Marianne Blickenstaff (London: Sheffield Academic, 2003), 173–207, here 204.

54. Josephine Massyngbaerde Ford, *Redeemer—Friend and Mother: Salvation in Antiquity and in the Gospel of John* (Minneapolis: Fortress, 1997), 196.

55. The following references and quotations are taken from Massyngbaerde Ford, *Redeemer—Friend and Mother*, 196–97.

56. See http://www.ccel.org/ccel/schaff/anf02.vi.iii.i.vi.html.

57. See http://www.ccel.org/ccel/schaff/npnf210.iv.vii.ii.v.html.

Adam's side gave birth to a
woman who gives birth to
immortals.
In the crucifixion he completed
the types that had been
depicted,
and the hidden mystery that
had been covered revealed
itself.[58]

The image of Jesus's death
as birth to new life offers
rich theological and pastoral
possibilities. One is that it enables
female disciples to identify more
fully with Christ, the Creator, and
the Spirit. Gender boundaries are
blurred and transcended in the
images presented of Jesus[59] who
gives birth to a renewed people,
of God who births believers
(1:13), and of the Spirit through
whom believers are born again/
from above (3:5).[60] In addition,
the metaphor of birthing gives
dignity to the bodily experience
of women and sees it as a locus
for the holy.[61] It also gives value
to suffering, as part of a natural
process but not as deserved or

desirable. Suffering is seen as the
consequence of a choice to entrust
oneself to love. This metaphor
enables us to understand Jesus's
self-gift as similar to that of lovers
who choose to make painful
sacrifices out of love for the other,
able to be endured because of
that love and because of the new
life that will result. Unlike the
kinds of economic transactions
between God and humanity that
are implied in sacrificial and
ransom metaphors, the birthing
image evokes an exchange of
love that is mutual and self-
replicating.

As empowering as is the
image of Jesus's death as birth,
there are also dangerous aspects.
Birthing and motherhood are
easily romanticized, masking the
reality that not all children are
conceived in love, that some are
unwanted, and that some are the
product of rape. In addition, not
all birth pangs give way to joy.
As Kathleen Rushton points out,
"Particularly for young women,

58. Quoted in Massyngbaerde Ford, *Redeemer—Friend and Mother*, 196.

59. See further Kitzberger, "Transcending Gender Boundaries," 193; María Clara Bingemer, "Mujer y Cristología. Jesucristo y la salvación de la mujer," in *Aportes para una Teología desde la Mujer*, ed. María Pilar Aquino, Nuevo Exodo 5 (Madrid: Editorial Biblia y Fe, 1988), 98–90. See also Elizabeth A. Johnson, "The Maleness of Christ," in *The Power of Naming: A Concilium Reader in Feminist Liberation Theology*, ed. Elisabeth Schüssler Fiorenza (Maryknoll, NY: Orbis Books, 1996), 307–15.

60. See María Pilar Aquino, "The God of Life and the *Rachamim* of the Trinity," in *Our Cry for Life: Feminist Theology from Latin America* (Maryknoll, NY: Orbis Books, 1993); María Clara Bingemer, "Reflections on the Trinity," in *Through Her Eyes: Women's Theology from Latin America*, ed. Elsa Támez (Maryknoll, NY: Orbis Books, 1989), 56–80.

61. See further Sallie McFague, *Body of God: An Ecological Theology* (Minneapolis: Fortress, 1993).

childbirth may be the result of lack of information and choice, poverty, exploitation, sexual and cultural violence. Hazards arise from fertility control, or lack of it, and the low priority given to diseases affecting women."[62] There can be increased anxiety about the ability to economically support more children and the impact of pregnancy and childrearing on one's ability to work. In addition, childbirth can result in death for the mother, the child, or both, a very high risk in biblical times. Consider too the anguish of a mother who endures agonizing labor, only to have her child stillborn or live only a brief time.

Another problematic aspect is when motherhood is seen as the epitome of woman's calling and "mother" is the only female image offered for God. Other images than mother, such as "sister," "midwife," "friend," are needed to speak of the ways that single women, vowed celibate women, childless married women, and widows incarnate divine being.[63] Another danger is the use of parental metaphors at all for God. Thinking of the divine in either maternal or paternal images can narrow our ways of relating to God, keeping us in perpetual childhood.[64]

The Fourth Gospel provides us with depictions of Jesus and his mother that provide potent images of God's power to birth new life out of death. Such portrayals give us an antidote to theologies that focus on God's wrath or human sinfulness. God's love, freely given, life-giving and productive, evokes from us a response in kind, transforming even the most hopeless of situations.

Barbara E. Reid

While the image of birth from the side of the male Jesus may seem discordant, this conflation of imagery was at home in the spiritual tradition of the church, as indicated in the passages cited by Barbara Reid above.[65]

62. Kathleen P. Rushton, "The (Pro)creative Parables of Labour and Childbirth (John 3:1-10 and 16:21-22)," in *The Lost Coin: Parables of Women, Work, and Wisdom*, ed. Mary Ann Beavis, BibSem 86 (Sheffield: Sheffield Academic, 2002), 208.

63. See Sallie McFague, *Models of God: Theology for an Ecological, Nuclear Age* (Minneapolis: Fortress, 1987), 97–123; Elizabeth A. Johnson, *She Who Is: The Mystery of God in Feminist Theological Discourse* (New York: Crossroad, 1992), 177–78.

64. Sallie McFague, "Mother God," in *Motherhood, Experience, Intuition, Theology*, ed. Anne Carr and Elisabeth Schüssler Fiorenza, Concilium 206, *Religion in the Eighties* (Edinburgh: T&T Clark, 1989), 139.

65. For numerous ancient quotations applying maternal imagery to Jesus, see Massyngbaerde Ford, *Redeemer—Friend and Mother*, 195–97; Reid, "Birthed from the Side of Jesus," 202–3. See also the discussion of "Motherhood as a trajectory in the tradition," in Lee, *Flesh and Glory*, 159–64.

Clearly the force of maternal symbolism in the Johannine text seemed more patent and less troublesome to earlier generations than to the modern world. . . . The fact that feminine symbolism was used of the male Christ was not problematic for generations who had a greater awareness of how symbols operate, both their iconic power and also their limitability.[66]

The piercing of the side is another action that fulfils the Scriptures, "They will look on the one whom they have pierced" (19:37). Scholars agree that the Scripture passage is Zechariah 12:10. Once again, the evangelist gives a free rendition of the Greek text as the LXX has "they shall look upon me because they have *mocked* me."[67] While citing only a phrase, the entire passage from Zechariah offers a Johannine understanding of the cross. The passage reads: "And I will pour out a spirit of compassion and supplication on the house of David and the inhabitants of Jerusalem, so that, when they look on the one whom they have pierced, they shall mourn for him, as one mourns for an only child, and weep bitterly over him, as one weeps over a firstborn" (Zech 12:10). From the cross, Jesus has just handed over the spirit, which the Zechariah passage describes as a spirit of compassion and supplication, on all Jerusalem, with the consequences that they will come to regret their action and experience a sadness like mourning for the death of a firstborn.

This Scripture is also linked to another citation since both are introduced by the one "fulfillment" theme: "These things occurred so that the scripture might be fulfilled, 'None of his bones shall be broken' " (John 19:36). Scholars look to two possible backgrounds for this second citation, namely, laws about the paschal lamb when not one bone shall be broken (Exod 12:46; Num 9:12), and a psalm depicting the suffering of the just one when God watches to see that not a bone will be broken (Ps 34:21). I think the Passover context, which names the household, is more significant: "It shall be eaten in one household [ἐν οἰκίᾳ μιᾷ]; you shall not take any of the animal outside the household, and you shall not break any of its bones" (Exod 12:46).

Jesus, the Passover Lamb

The Johannine Passion has emphasized the Passover, giving it far more attention than the Synoptics. The Jewish authorities do not enter

66. Lee, *Flesh and Glory*.
67. Brown considers that the LXX has "probably misread *dqr* ('pierce') as *rqd* ('skip about')" and that the evangelist may have been citing from another Greek form of the OT, not the LXX. Brown, *Death of the Messiah*, 2:1187.

the Praetorium to avoid ritual defilement that would prevent them eating the Passover (18:28); because it is Passover the crowd can choose between Barabbas and Jesus (18:39); at midday on the day of Preparation for Passover (19:14), when the first group of pilgrims enters the temple to slaughter the paschal lamb, Pilate hands Jesus over to be crucified (19:16). Jesus journeys to Golgotha carrying his own cross, as Isaac carried the wood of his own sacrifice, and in first-century Judaism, the sacrifice of Isaac was being linked to Passover. Wine was passed up to Jesus on a hyssop branch (19:29), the same plant that painted the blood of the original Passover lamb on the Hebrew houses in Egypt (Exod 12:22). Because the crucifixion happened on the day of Preparation (19:31) and the eve of the Sabbath, "the Jews" did not want the bodies to remain on the cross. This time detail led to the statement that Scripture is now fulfilled with a reference to the unbroken bones of the Passover lamb (Exod 12:46). Clearly, in the passion, Jesus dies as the Passover lamb.

By presenting Jesus as the new Paschal Lamb, the evangelist is giving the Christian community a symbolic interpretation of Jesus's death and testifying that this death has already been attested to by the Scriptures.[68] The Johannine emphasis is not a death to atone for sin, or a sacrifice of expiation, because the Passover lamb was not expiatory but a replacement; "its purpose was not sacrificial but apotropaic."[69] The purpose of the blood of the Passover lamb was to provide a salvific sign marking the households of the Israelites: "The blood shall be a sign for you on the houses where you live: when I see the blood, I will pass over you, and no plague shall destroy you when I strike the land of Egypt" (Exod 12:13).

The Johannine model of salvation is, in the light of the exodus, an act of liberation from the dominion of slavery under the ruler of this world,[70] to the freedom of children within the household of God. In this model there is a liberation from sin, where sin is perceived as a power that enslaves humanity, just as Israel was once held captive within the house of slavery.[71] With the incarnation of Jesus, God has entered the world offering life (John 10:10) and freedom. "Very truly, I tell you, everyone who commits sin is a slave to sin. The slave does not have a permanent

---

68. Obermann, *Die christologische Erfüllung der Schrift im Johannesevangelium*, 309–10.

69. John Ashton, *Understanding the Fourth Gospel* (Oxford: Clarendon, 1996), 491.

70. "By strength of hand the Lord brought us out of Egypt, from the house of bondage" (Exod 13:14).

71. "Take care that you do not forget the Lord, who brought you out of the Land of Egypt, out of the house of slavery. The Lord your God you shall fear; him you shall serve and by his name alone shall you swear. Do not follow other gods" (Deut 6:12-14a; cf. 5:6; 13:10).

place in the household; the son has a place there forever. So if the Son makes you free, you will be free indeed" (8:34-36). The contrast between slave and child is yet another way of expressing the idea of belonging to the ruler of this world or belonging to the household of God.

When John first sees Jesus, he identifies him as "the lamb of God who takes away the sin of the world" (ἴδε ὁ ἀμνὸς τοῦ θεοῦ ὁ αἴρων τὴν ἁμαρτίαν τοῦ κόσμου, 1:19). It is important to note that "sin" is not the personal sin of individuals but cosmic sin as a world power of evil. In the Fourth Gospel the term "world" has various meanings: both the world as the arena of God's creation and love and the world as an "inimical force" in opposition to God's purposes.[72] This force opposed to God is termed "sin," and it has power to enslave; "everyone who commits sin is a slave to sin" (8:34). To take away this world-sin requires more than atonement, or forgiveness; it is a power struggle between Jesus and the "ruler of this world," and Jesus is victorious. "Now is the judgment of this world; now the ruler of this world will be driven out" (12:31; also 16:18, 33). John's naming of Jesus as "the lamb of God" is fulfilled at Golgotha when Jesus dies as the Pass-over lamb, achieving for those who believe in him their liberation from the slavery of sin, to freedom to live as children in the household of God.

The emancipatory power of the Johannine crucifixion offers all people the promise that God is on the side of those in chains—economic, social, sexual, physical, psychological—whatever prevents the full flourishing of life. For centuries the major emphasis has been on atonement for sin, with women frequently being told, "You are the cause," or "You are the devil's gateway."[73] John's Gospel offers a liberative model, much needed particularly for women. The iconography of John's setting as a new Eden with the cross centered as the tree of life—this is an image promoting the full flourishing of life. As Hildegard of Bingen (1098–1179) sings, "The Word is living, being, spirit, all verdant greening, all creativity. This Word manifests itself in every creature."[74]

---

72. Loren T. Stuckenbruck, "Evil in Johannine and Apocalyptic Perspective: Petition for Protection in John 17," in *John's Gospel and Intimations of Apocalyptic*, ed. Catrin H. Williams and Christopher Rowland (London: Bloomsbury T&T Clark, 2013), 200–201. For a discussion of the multiple meanings of *the world* in John see Coloe, *John 1–10*, 221–22, and Sandra M. Schneiders, "The Word in the World," *Pacifica* 23 (2010): 254.

73. Tertullian (160–230): "Do you know that each of your women is an Eve? The sentence of God on this sex of yours lives in this age; the guilt must necessarily live too. You are the Devil's gateway; you are the unsealer of that tree; you are the first deserter of the divine law" (*The Dress of Women* 1.1.2).

74. Tim Wallace-Murphy, *Hidden Wisdom: Secrets of the Western Esoteric Tradition* (New York: Disinformation Co., 2010), 107.

A Royal Burial in a Garden (19:38-42)

The passion closes with Jesus once again among disciples, women as well as the two named men, within a garden. Joseph is described as a "secret" disciple, afraid of publicly acknowledging Jesus. Nicodemus is not said to be a disciple but the extraordinary amount of spices he brings suggests that he honors Jesus's royal status. In his first encounter with Jesus (3:1-12) Nicodemus was told that unless one was born again, one could not see the reign of God. The lavish anointing at least suggests that Nicodemus has been born again and can now see God's reign in Jesus. Without words to offer insight into his action, the meaning of Nicodemus's anointing is left to the reader.[75] The garden enfolds Jesus's passion.[76] In the scene of the arrest Jesus's sovereign control was much in evidence. In his burial, his sovereignty is recognized with a staggering amount of spices and his body is wrapped in linen, as befitting a king.

Conclusion

Familial and architectural imagery express the richness of the Johannine interpretation of Jesus's death. Jesus is the living temple of God's presence (1:14). "The Jews," through their priesthood, hand him over to Pilate and so carry out the destruction of the temple that Jesus had prophesied (2:19) and they had tried to avoid (11:50). At the same time as the Passover lambs are being sacrificed in the temple on Mount Moriah, Jesus is being handed over to death as the new Passover Lamb on a new Moriah (19:14). In the "hour" of his death Jesus is manifest as the royal temple-builder, the "Nazarene" (19:19), fulfilling the prophecy of Zechariah (Zech 6:11-12). The new temple is born through the creative Spirit released upon the nascent community by Jesus in his last breath (19:30). A new household of God comes into being at the foot of the cross when believers are drawn into Jesus's own filial relationship with the

---

75. For a discussion of the ambiguity of the character Nicodemus, see R. Alan Culpepper, "Nicodemus: The Travail of New Birth," in Hunt, Tolmie, and Zimmermann, *Character Studies in the Fourth Gospel*, 248–59.

76. Manns, *L'évangile de Jean*, 409. The theme of creation is very richly developed by Manns. He draws attention to many other Genesis motifs within the Johannine passion: the garden, the Kedron torrent (18:1), the tree of life in the middle of the garden (cf. 19:18), the rabbinic location of Eden beside the Jerusalem temple. See also Margaret Barker, *The Gate of Heaven: The History and Symbolism of the Temple in Jerusalem* (London: SPCK, 1991), 57–95.

John 19:38-42

³⁸After these things, Joseph of Arimathea, who was a disciple of Jesus, though a secret one because of his fear of the Jews, asked Pilate to let him take away the body of Jesus. Pilate gave him permission; so he came and removed his body. ³⁹Nicodemus, who had at first come to Jesus by night, also came, bringing a mixture of myrrh and aloes, weighing about a hundred pounds. ⁴⁰They took the body of Jesus and wrapped it with the spices in linen cloths, according to the burial custom of the Jews. ⁴¹Now there was a garden in the place where he was crucified, and in the garden there was a new tomb in which no one had ever been laid. ⁴²And so, because it was the Jewish day of Preparation, and the tomb was nearby, they laid Jesus there.

Father (19:26, 27) and are liberated from the power of the ruler of this world to live as children of God (1:12).

Jesus/Sophia has been put to the test with insult, torture, and a shameful death (Wis 2:17-20). As the readers know, he has been shown to be God's Son and has extended his own filiation to include all believers.

Women Crucified[77]

In the Fourth Gospel the cross, in the middle of the garden, is a tree of new life. For Jesus it is his moment of glorification (δοξάζω; 13:31; 16:14; 17:1, 5) and exaltation (ὑψόω; 3:14; 8:28; 12:32). He is not victim but conqueror of the "ruler of this world" (12:31). But if we look below the cross, we do see those crucified—the women.

"His mother, and his mother's sister, Mary the wife of Clopas, and Mary Magdalene" (19:25).[78] Mark's Gospel notes that there were women who followed him from Galilee (Mark 15:40-41), and it is possible that this description applies also to the Johannine group of women. Watching the torturous death of one they love, these women are the ones being crucified, and this

77. Tacitus (*Ann.* 14:45) and Josephus (*Ant.* 18:3) attest that women, usually slaves, were also punished by crucifixion in ancient Rome.

78. There is some uncertainly about the number of women present; the Greek text can be read to refer to two, three, or four women. The fact that there are four soldiers (19:23) suggests an equal number of women to balance the iconography. For further arguments, see D. Francois Tolmie, "The Women by the Cross: Creating Contrasts," in Hunt, Tolmie, and Zimmermann, *Character Studies in the Fourth Gospel*, 618–21.

crucifixion of women by proxy continues to happen. There are times, following a divorce or separation, when the male partner gets revenge by killing the children of the family: the man who poured petrol over his wife and children while they were in the car then set it ablaze;[79] the man who tossed his child over a bridge;[80] the former husband who killed his son to punish his ex-wife;[81] women who have no say when their daughter is given in marriage to a man twice her age.[82] These are women crucified by love.

When the figure of a Crucified Woman was placed below a cross in the Bloor Street United Church, Toronto, on Good Friday 1979, there were strong and conflicting reactions. One woman wrote:

> Having that beautiful sculpture—the Crucified Woman—in the front of the church on Good Friday and publicly giving support to battered women spoke to me more than you would realize. It is profoundly moving to see a female symbol as a crucifix. Women throughout the centuries have given of themselves as their way of caring—and all too often unrewarded and at great cost to all. It was very healing for me to have you recognize the pain of women.[83]

The painting by Arthur Boyd of a crucified young (pregnant) woman brings to the crucifixion the experience of many women around the globe—transfixed, not able to move, while horror happens around them. So while the Johannine crucifixion is a glorious interpretation of the meaning of Jesus's death, we must not forget the women, faithful, voiceless, and standing in their powerlessness.

79. Brisbane, Australia. February 2020. https://www.theguardian.com/australia-news/2020/feb/19/three-dead-including-children-after-car-allegedly-set-alight-in-brisbane.

80. Melbourne, January 29, 2009. https://www.abc.net.au/news/2011-03-28/dad-guilty-of-westgate-bridge-murder/2640356.

81. Melbourne, February 2014. https://www.abc.net.au/news/2014-02-13/mother-in-shock-after-son-killed-by-father-at-cricket-oval/5258252?nw=0.

82. See the report in the National Geographic, https://www.nationalgeographic.com/magazine/2011/06/child-brides/, and the statement by the United Nations: "If current levels of child marriages hold, 14.2 million girls annually or 39,000 daily will marry too young" (https://www.un.org/youthenvoy/2013/09/child-marriages-39000-every-day-more-than-140-million-girls-will-marry-between-2011-and-2020/).

83. Clifford A. S. Elliott, "Crucified Woman [a sculpture], Reprint, 1982," *International Review of Mission*, 71, no. 283 (1982): 335.

Arthur Boyd, Crucifixion, Shoalhaven, *1979–1980, oil on canvas. Reproduced with permission of Bundanon Trust; https://www.bundanon.com.au.*

John 20:1-31

Sophia's Radiance

Wisdom is radiant and unfading,
and she is easily discerned by those who love her,
and is found by those who seek her.
She hastens to make herself known to those who desire her.
One who rises early to seek her will have no difficulty,
for she will be found sitting at the gate.
To fix one's thought on her is perfect understanding,
and one who is vigilant on her account will soon be free from care,
because she goes about seeking those worthy of her,
and she graciously appears to them in their paths,
and meets them in every thought. (Wis 6:12-16)

The Johannine crucifixion is the culmination of Jesus's work and his hour of triumph. Jesus reigns from the cross as he displays a depth of love unto death for his friends, and God's love for the world (3:16). The cross, placed in the center of the garden, is a new tree of life;[1]

---

1. Ruben Zimmermann, "Symbolic Communication between John and His Reader: The Garden Symbolism in John 19–20," in *Anatomies of Narrative Criticism: The Past, Present, and Future of the Fourth Gospel as Literature,* ed. Tom Thatcher and Stephen D. Moore, SBLRBS 55 (Leiden: Brill, 2008), offers a rich interpretation of the garden theme across John 18–20 and links this theme with that of the temple, especially Jewish

Jesus, the Nazarene temple-builder, creates the Father's household as a community of beloved women and men disciples. Although only Mary the Magdalene is named in chapter 20, the four women at the foot of the cross may be presumed to be present, and perhaps Mary and Martha from nearby Bethany. The presence of women can be hidden within the generic term "disciples," so it is important to remember that in this Gospel it is the women who stand out as witnesses and prophets, e.g., the Samaritan woman, Mary of Bethany, the mother of Jesus, Mary the Magdalene.

In this garden, Jesus is the divine creator breathing the life-giving Spirit (19:30), and he is divine Sophia from whose side flows the blood and waters of new birth (19:34). As the Spirit is breathed onto this new creation, Jesus proclaims the divine judgment on this work—"it is finished" (19:30), recalling creation's completion in Genesis (Gen 2:1). In the theology of the Fourth Gospel, creation has only now been brought to completion in this holy Passover. The Sabbath can now begin (John 19:31).

With the cross as Jesus's hour of exaltation, the reader may wonder what more can follow. Unlike the Synoptics, where the resurrection is the vindication of Jesus following his apparent defeat, John 20 is not needed to witness to Jesus's triumph. Jesus has already been lifted up and glorified on the cross.[2] Resurrection in the Fourth Gospel has a different focus. In John 20 it is the disciples, the new "Father's household," who are resurrected as they move from mourning to faith in the risen One.

Structurally, John 20 has two locations: a garden scene and a household scene. There are two time-frames: the first day and the eighth day.

---

traditions of the eschatological temple. "Because the anticipation of the eschatological temple was, in early Judaism, explicitly connected to garden symbolism, one can conclude that the Evangelist in John 20 has created a conscious connection between the garden symbolism and temple metaphor. From John 20:21, it becomes clear that Christ is the new, eschatological temple, and this understanding must inform the scene of the first meeting with the Risen One in a garden" (232). While agreeing that the link is there between the garden and temple, I will argue that it is the community of disciples, now the sisters and brothers of Jesus, who are the eschatological Father's household (cf. 2:16; 14:2).

2. As Jörg Frey eloquently states: "Jesus's death is emphatically not a dying in God-forsakenness (so Mark 15:34-37) but rather the completion of the work given to him. It is not being conquered by the darkness (cf. John 1:5) but rather the victory over the world and its ruler . . . (16:11, 33)" (*The Glory of the Crucified One: Christology and Theology in the Gospel of John*, trans. Wayne Coppins and Christoph Heilig, BMSEC [Waco, TX: Baylor University Press, 2018]: 173).

Scene 1:   The garden tomb, the first day (20:1-10)

Mary Magdalene (20:11-18)

Scene 2:   The household (20:19-25)

The eighth day (20:26-29)

Conclusion (20:30-31)

Scene 1: The Garden Tomb, the First Day (20:1-10)

The Synoptic Gospels name women present when Jesus's body is laid in the tomb (Mark 15:47; Matt 27:61; Luke 23:55), and these same women return to the tomb bringing spices to anoint the body (Mark 16:1; Matt 28:1; Luke 23:56; 24:1). In the Fourth Gospel, lavish anointing has happened (19:39-40; also 12:1-8); Mary the Magdalene,[3] who was at the cross to witness the anointing, knows the place of burial. With no anointing necessary, the only reason for Mary to return to the darkness of the garden tomb is to mourn. Mary's being first reverses the order of entry into the Garden of Eden as recounted in the Book of Jubilees. There it describes the creation of Adam outside the Garden of Eden. "And after Adam had completed forty days in the land where he had been created, we brought him into the garden of Eden to till and keep it, but his wife they brought in on the eightieth day, and after this she entered into the garden of Eden" (Jub. 3:9). Now, the woman is first and she discovers the stone has been removed. She must have looked inside the tomb, as she announces to Peter and the Beloved Disciple that the body has been removed, leading to their rushing to the tomb. At this point there is no sense that Jesus is alive, more that someone has taken his dead body.

3. In all four Gospels Mary is named Mary *the* Magdalene (Μαρία ἡ Μαγδαληνή), and Luke actually says that Mary was the one called Magdalene (Luke 8:2), suggesting that μαγδαληνή was a nickname or title from the Aramaic *magdala* ("Mary the Tower" or "Mary the Great"), like "Simon called Peter" (Matt 10:2; Acts 10:32; 11:13; cf. John 1:42), "Simon called the Zealot" (Luke 6:15), or "Joseph called Barsabbas" (Acts 1:23); "Magdalene" was not a reference to her place of origin. Today there is a small village in Galilee called Migdal, but in the time of Jesus it was called Tarichea by Josephus, never Magdala. This nickname may have been a way to honor her greatness, as later on the church called her "Apostle to the Apostles." See Richard B. Vinson, "Magdala," *NIDB* 3 (2008): 766, and Mary Ann Beavis, "Reconsidering Mary of Bethany," *CBQ* 74 (2012): 286, 287. See further the excursus at John 11, "Mary, Martha, and Mary Magdalene: One Woman or Three?" by Elizabeth Schrader.

John 20:1-10

20:1Early on the first day of the week, while it was still dark, Mary Magdalene came to the tomb and saw that the stone had been removed from the tomb. 2So she ran and went to Simon Peter and the other disciple, the one whom Jesus loved, and said to them, "They have taken the Lord out of the tomb, and we do not know where they have laid him." 3Then Peter and the other disciple set out and went toward the tomb. 4The two were running together, but the other disciple outran Peter and reached the tomb first. 5He bent down to look in and saw the linen wrappings lying there, but he did not go in. 6Then Simon Peter came, following him, and went into the tomb. He saw the linen wrappings lying there, 7and the cloth that had been on Jesus's head, not lying with the linen wrappings but rolled up in a place by itself. 8Then the other disciple, who reached the tomb first, also went in, and he saw and believed; 9for as yet they did not understand the scripture, that he must rise from the dead. 10Then the disciples returned to their homes.

The details of time are significant. The setting in verse 1 is "the first day of the week," which, as the day after the Sabbath, can also be called the eighth day, marking the dawn of a new creation (more on this in the discussion of the scene with Thomas in 20:24-29). It is also "still dark." Throughout the narrative, light and darkness have had symbolic significance, with "light" identified with Jesus's presence (12:35) and "darkness" as a time of Jesus's absence, for example, "It was now dark and Jesus had not yet come to them" (6:17).[4] Mary the Magdalene and all the disciples are in this state of darkness, for the risen One has not yet come to them.[5] Mary reports what she has discovered to Simon Peter and to the "other disciple," also known as "the one whom Jesus loved" (13:23-25; 18:15-16; 19:25-27).[6] The plural "we do not know" may indicate that a source, which included a number of women at the tomb, is being used.[7]

4. See further comments on the symbolism of light and darkness in Mary L. Coloe, *John 1–10*, WCS 44A (Collegeville, MN: Liturgical Press, 2021), 26–27.
5. André Feuillet, "La recherche du Christ dans la nouvelle alliance d'après la Christophanie de Jo 20:11-18," in *Homme devant Dieu; Melanges offerts au Henri de Lubac*, Théologie 56 (Paris: Aubier, 1963), 95.
6. Lazarus, Mary, and Martha are also said to be loved by Jesus (11:3, 5, 36).
7. Francis J. Moloney, *John*, SP 4 (Collegeville, MN: Liturgical Press, 1998), 522. Alternately, the first-person plural makes Mary a representative character, voicing "the question of all disciples caught in the pre-dawn darkness of the scandal of the cross,

When these two disciples run to the tomb, the evangelist stresses that it is the Beloved Disciple who arrives first. This is not simply a physical description of a race but a theological statement that this disciple is the first to arrive at faith. This is the first hint of a comparison or even contention between these two disciples. Although the Beloved Disciple arrives first, he does not enter the tomb, and so can only know partially what lies within; he sees only the linen wrappings. This establishes a contrast between what he can see from the outside and what Peter sees from inside the tomb. Peter sees the linen wrappings and also the head cloth (σουδάριον) placed apart from the wrappings (v. 7). There is no indication that this "sign" leads Peter to faith. When the Beloved Disciple steps inside and sees the wrappings *and* the head cloth, he sees the "sign" and believes. He is the first to come to faith in the risen Jesus through seeing a sign.

What is the significance of the head cloth, the σουδάριον? When Lazarus came forth from the tomb, he too had a σουδάριον around his face that needed to be unbound (11:44). The σουδάριον therefore makes a textual link between the Lazarus event of being raised and what has happened to Jesus.[8] The verb "rolled up," ἐντετυλιγμένον, is in the perfect-passive form without a named subject, which in the Scriptures is often used to refer to divine action that has taken place.[9] As Sandra Schneiders has noted, there is a link between the head cloth now deliberately placed aside and the face veil Moses needed to wear to hide the radiance of his glorious face following his encounter with God (Exod 34:29-35).[10] When Moses was in the tent meeting with God, the face veil was not needed, but it was needed when he came out to the people. During Jesus's life, his divine glory needed to be veiled most of the time, being occasionally revealed in his signs (2:11); now that Jesus has definitively entered into

---

'Where is the Lord?' " (Sandra Schneiders, *Written That You May Believe: Encountering Jesus in the Fourth Gospel*, rev. and exp. ed. [New York: Crossroad, 2003], 213).

8. Brendan Byrne, "The Faith of the Beloved Disciple and the Community in John 20," *JSNT* 23 (1985): 88.

9. Daniel B. Wallace, *Greek Grammar Beyond the Basics: An Exegetical Syntax of the New Testament* (Grand Rapids: Zondervan, 1996), 437–38.

10. Sandra M. Schneiders, "The Johannine Resurrection Narrative: An Exegetical Study of John 20 as a Synthesis of Johannine Spirituality" (DST [unpublished], Pontificia Universitas Gregoriana, 1975), 310–11. Schneiders notes that in the Palestinian Targums, the face-veil of Exod 34:33 uses an Aramaic loan word from either Greek or Latin: *soudarion; sudarium*. See Sandra M. Schneiders, "The Face Veil: A Johannine Sign (John 20:1-10)," *BTB* 13 (1983): 96.

his glory, the "veil" of Jesus's mortal flesh is no longer needed.[11] The Beloved Disciple recognizes the discarded head cloth as a sign that the tomb has been left empty, not by grave robbers, but by an act of God, even though he does not yet fully understand its significance.

Mary the Magdalene (20:11-18)

When the two disciples leave, Mary is left alone weeping in the garden.[12] When she bends over to look inside the tomb, she now sees two angels at either end of the ledge where the body had been laid. The position of these angels is reminiscent of the golden cherubim carved above the ark of the covenant (Exod 25:19; 37:7; 1 Kgs 8:7) within the holy of holies.[13] This symbolism presents Mary as one who dares to enter into the holy of holies, an act reserved for the high priest, for it is only within the holy of holies that the ark can be seen. In the dispensation of this new creation Mary now assumes that priestly role. The two cherubim above the ark marked the place of God's invisible presence, and in the tomb the two angels mark where "the body of Jesus *had been* lying" (v. 12). The iconography of the scene marking the presence of God and yet

11. Schneiders, *Written That You May Believe*, 207; also Schneiders, "The Face Veil," 96, and Schneiders, "The Johannine Resurrection Narrative," 309–12.

12. The Gospel uses the term κῆπος (19:41) and not παράδεισος, which is the term used for the garden in Gen 2:8, but these two words are interchangeable (e.g., Eccl 2:5; Sir 24:30-31). The word κῆπος is used for the original garden in Ezek 36:35 (LXX) and other Greek translations of Genesis. See further Jeannine K. Brown, "Creation's Renewal in the Gospel of John," *CBQ* 72 (2010): 275–90; Edwyn C. Hoskyns, "Genesis I–III and St John's Gospel," *JTS* 21 (1920): 210–18; and Frédéric Manns, *L'Evangile de Jean à la lumière du Judaïsme*, SBFA 33 (Jerusalem: Franciscan Printing Press, 1991).

13. B. F. Westcott, *The Gospel according to St John: The Authorised Version with Introduction and Notes* (London: John Murray, 1890), 291. Many scholars disagree with this possible allusion to the cherubim over the ark. But given the original audience, who knew their OT and also the consistent use of cultic imagery across the Gospel (tabernacle, 1:4; temple, 2:21; etc.), I consider it quite likely that this is an allusion to the cherubim, which would make the tomb into "the holy of holies" where God is encountered. Eusebius (*Vita Constantini* 3.28) called the tomb the holy of holies; see supporting arguments in Izaak J. de Hulster, "The Two Angels in John 20:12: The Old Testament Background," *BN* 162 (2014): 97–120. Even though the body is no longer present, there is no doubt that God has been active in this tomb. Jan G. van der Watt, "Angels in the Gospel according to John," *JECH* 1 (2011): 191. Xavier Léon-Dufour, *Lecture de l'Évangile selon Jean*, vol. 4 (Paris: Éditions du Seuil, 1996), recognizes the possible allusion to the cherubim commenting that they mark the place where God is revealed to the people (218).

John 20:11-18

¹¹But Mary stood weeping outside the tomb. As she wept, she bent over to look into the tomb; ¹²and she saw two angels in white, sitting where the body of Jesus had been lying, one at the head and the other at the feet. ¹³They said to her, "Woman, why are you weeping?" She said to them, "They have taken away my Lord, and I do not know where they have laid him." ¹⁴When she had said this, she turned around and saw Jesus standing there, but she did not know that it was Jesus. ¹⁵Jesus said to her, "Woman, why are you weeping? Whom are you looking for?" Suppos-ing him to be the gardener, she said to him, "Sir, if you have carried him away, tell me where you have laid him, and I will take him away." ¹⁶Jesus said to her, "Mary!" She turned and said to him in Hebrew, "Rabbouni!" (which means Teacher). ¹⁷Jesus said to her, "Do not hold on to me, because I have not yet ascended to the Father. But go to my brothers and say to them, 'I am ascend-ing to my Father and your Father, to my God and your God.'" ¹⁸Mary Magdalene went and announced to the disciples, "I have seen the Lord"; and she told them that he had said these things to her.

the absence of Jesus's body raises the question, "Where is Jesus?"¹⁴ Mary still thinks of grave robbers and says again, "They have taken away my Lord" (cf. v. 2).

Following this statement she turns and sees a figure she supposes (correctly) to be the gardener. The first words spoken to Mary the Magdalene by the risen Christ echo the first words spoken by Jesus to the two disciples of John: "What are you looking for?" (1:38); "Who are you looking for?" (20:15). She asks again to know where Jesus is. Jesus now reveals himself by speaking her name in its Aramaic form, Μαριάμ, "Mariam." She is the first to experience the risen presence.

The Fourth Gospel is unique in placing the crucifixion, burial, and then the resurrection in a garden (18:1; 19:41). Mary rightly believes that the person she encounters near the garden tomb is a gardener, but there is great irony here, as the garden of the passion narrative had echoes of the Genesis garden of creation, with the tree of life planted in the middle. The original gardener of Genesis was God, who "planted a garden in Eden, in the east" (Gen 2:8), who cultivated it (Gen 2:9), and who walked in it "at

14. As Sandra Schneiders points out, "the 'where' of Jesus in John is not primarily spatial or geographical location. It denotes indwelling, the communion between Jesus and God and between Jesus and his disciples" (*Written That You May Believe*, 213).

the time of the evening breeze" (Gen 3:8).[15] Mary's perception that Jesus is the gardener is accurate.[16] The risen One has passed through death into the glory that was originally his, with God in the beginning. He returns to Mary as the divine Gardener walking in the garden of his creation (John 1:2).[17]

When Jesus speaks her name, the text states that Mary "turning around said" (στραφεῖσα, v. 16), and this is strange since she had earlier "turned around" (ἐστράφη, v.14) from looking into the tomb and saw Jesus. Seeing him was not enough for her to recognize him. When Jesus says, "Mariam," then it is as if her eyes were opened, and she experienced an inner "turning" from nonbelief to faith.[18] Now she knows who this gardener really is, and she repeats the title given to Jesus by the first two disciples: "my teacher" (Ραββουνι, v. 16; cf. 1:38).[19] The naming of each other is described by Schneiders as "a formula of mutual self-giving and

15. By the first century, the Garden of Eden was located in Jerusalem and identified with the temple, as the Book of Jubilees (ca. 150 BCE) makes explicit: "And he knew that the Garden of Eden is the holy of holies, and the dwelling of the Lord, and Mount Sinai the center of the desert, and Mount Zion the center of the navel of the earth" (Jub. 8:19).

16. "Mary's words are then true, the risen Lord is ὁ Κηπουρός, for he is Lord of the Garden, and once more He walks in His garden in the cool of the day, the early morning, xx i, and converses not with the fallen but with the redeemed." See Hoskyns, "Genesis I–III and St John's Gospel," 215.

17. In her fine study of the creation motif in John's Gospel, Jeannine Brown also makes the connection between the Garden of Eden and the garden of the resurrection in John 20. She considers that the evangelist is connecting Jesus "to that first gardener, Adam. At this point in the narrative, John implies an Adam Christology" ("Creation's Renewal in the Gospel of John," 281). *Contra* Brown, the biblical tradition presents *God*, not Adam, as the original gardener. It is God who plants the garden (Gen 2:8); in Gen 13:10 and Isa 51:3 there is the phrase "YHWH's garden," and in Ezek 31:8, "God's garden." As Mariusz Rosik writes, "In the Old Testament, Eden is thought of as a garden in which it is God, himself, who is the gardener" ("Discovering the Secrets of God's Garden: Resurrection as New Creation (Gen 2:4b–3:24; Jn 20:1-18)," *LASBF* 58 [2008]: 84). Ruben Zimmermann also adds that God is explicitly described as a "gardener" (Num 24:6; 4 Macc 1:29) ("Symbolic Communication," 229).

18. In both verses the aorist passive is used, which could have the sense "was turned around" by God, in the divine encounter with the angelic figures in the tomb (v. 14), and then by Jesus speaking her name (v. 16). Στρέφω can be used in the sense of "to experience an inward change"; BDAG, 948.

19. ῥαββουνί is a very personal affirmation meaning more than just "teacher," but "my teacher." "The pupil followed his teacher with obedience and respect and expressed this by addressing him as רבי, 'my master,' but also 'my teacher.' Since the student-teacher relation is determined by respect, and this is as great as the respect accorded to heaven, the student was bound to his teacher for the rest of his life" (Eduard Lohse, "ῥαββί, ῥαββουνί," *TDNT* 6 [1968]: 962).

mutual possession that brings to a culmination the most intimate OT expressions of the Covenant (e.g., Deut. 27:17-18; Hos. 2:23; Is. 54:5-8; Ezek. 16:60-63)."[20]

In the Royal Garden[21]

Mary Magdalene apparently mistaking the risen Jesus for "the gardener" (John 20:15) may well be the supreme moment of dramatic irony in the Gospel. The account of "the hour" has already mentioned the garden location several times, even twice in one sentence! (18:1, 26; 19:41). This is because the Fourth Evangelist believes that Jesus fulfills the Jewish hope for a restoration envisaged as a return of humankind to Eden. Israel's hoped-for restoration was imagined as renewal of the entire creation. This hope included the belief that, if Israel would recover wisdom and share that wisdom with all nations, then humankind would return to tending the garden of the Earth as the Creator originally intended (Gen 2:15). The Fourth Evangelist sees that hope now fulfilled in Jesus and the circle of those who belong to him.

For the Gospel's intended audience, mention of a garden just outside Jerusalem would have recalled the royal garden in the Kidron Valley. At a deeper symbolic level, however, it would have evoked memories of the Garden of Eden, known to readers of the Greek Scriptures as ὁ παράδεισος τῆς τρυφῆς, the Paradise of Delight. The Evangelist's use of the more unexceptional term κῆπος for the garden does not undermine this suggestion. In the Septuagint, an orchard (Song 4:13-15) and a grove of sacred oaks (Isa 1:29-30) can be at once a κῆπος and a παράδεισος. Josephus too wrote of the Roman destruction of the παραδείσοι of Judah—more likely to have been κῆποι (J.W. 6.6).

The Gospel's first hearers would have imagined Eden as an ancient Near Eastern king's pleasure garden: an enclosed park full of fragrant trees watered by elaborate, seemingly miraculous, irrigation systems that raised the water to the tops of stone-built structures so that when the king was about to promenade in the garden "at the time of the evening breeze" (see Gen 3:8), the water—in many cases brought from distant sources by aqueduct—could be released to flow into the garden as "living water" and intensify the garden's fragrance.

---

20. Schneiders, "The Johannine Resurrection Narrative," 438.

21. This comment is a brief synopsis of Margaret Daly-Denton, *John: An Earth Bible Commentary; Supposing Him to Be the Gardener*, Earth Bible Commentary (London: Bloomsbury T&T Clark, 2017).

At the time the Gospel was written, the famed Hanging Garden of Babylon—actually at Nineveh, it would seem—was still remembered and imitated. Obviously, such gardens were created by slave labor, but the king took all the credit for such a wondrous transformation of an arid environment and was accordingly celebrated as the royal gardener.

In the Fourth Evangelist's understanding of "the hour" of Jesus, Isaiah's vision of the wilderness turning into Eden and the desert into the Garden of the Lord is becoming a reality (Isa 51:3). When water gushes out of Jesus's opened side, a fountain is opened (Zech 13:1) and living streams flow into the garden "in the place where he was crucified" (John 19:41). In fact, that evocative scene where a man and a woman meet in a garden abounds in Edenic overtones, all pointing to the evangelist's awareness of the "return to Eden" motif widely used in Jewish writings of the late Second Temple period to describe the expected restoration of Israel. In these writings, Eden with its fragrant trees and limpid streams becomes a symbol of Earth as the Creator intended it to be. For the evangelist, "the hour" brings about nothing less than a re-creation of the whole Earth.

The Eden motif is inextricably bound up with the Johannine concept of "the temple of [Jesus's] body" (John 2:21) because of the strong symbolic association of the Jerusalem temple with Eden and the view of the temple as a representation of the universe and as the cosmic center from which life flowed to the entire creation. The Eden/temple/Earth-center motif is the wellspring for all the Johannine references to water. Water runs like "a silver thread" through the Gospel,[22] bringing with it its rich scriptural associations—in particular, the four rivers of Eden (Gen 1:10-14), reenvisaged by Ezekiel (47:1-12) as the life-giving streams flowing from the temple into all the earth to bring cleansing and fertility.

The ancient descriptions of Eden consistently feature its aromaticity. In some pseudepigraphical retellings of Genesis 1–3, Adam asks God's permission to gather fragrant spices before being banished from Eden. He uses these for an incense offering. It so happens that in several of these writings the trees of Eden produce exactly the ingredients that Moses specified for the temple incense! So whenever the aroma of incense wafts through the temple, it brings back memories of Eden. In a similar way, the precious spices that Mary provides and Nicodemus uses to honor the temple of Jesus's body (John 12:3; 19:39-40) ensure that the garden where Jesus lays

---

22. R. H. Lightfoot, *St. John's Gospel: A Commentary* (London: Oxford University Press, 1956), 121.

down his life and takes it up again (10:17) is redolent of the fragrant trees of Eden.

The Gospel, therefore, invites its readers to suppose that Jesus is the royal gardener, completing his day's work in the "garden" of the Earth, the work that God his Father gave him to do. The Johannine Jesus refers to the Father as a worker in the Earth— the literal translation of γεωργός (from the Greek γῆ and ἔργον), translated as "vinegrower" in John 15:1 by NRSV. So God is the "original" royal gardener who planted a garden in Eden (Gen 2:8). Noah was the first human γεωργός whose planting of a vineyard signaled a fresh start for the Earth after the flood. Jesus the gardener— someone totally aligned with

the Creator's intentions for the flourishing of Earth—the Son who does the Creator's ceaseless work of sustaining everything in being (John 5:17), can be a model and an inspiration for his twenty-first-century followers who are learning to see Earth-care and sustainable living as a constitutive part of their life as his disciples. To be seen in the garden with Jesus is to be recognized as one of them (John 18:26). Gardening Earth-care is the work of God (John 6:28) that disciples of Jesus are sent to do. In Jesus and in those he has sent as the Father sent him (John 20:21), Wisdom "reaches mightily from one end of the Earth to the other, and she orders all things well" (Wis 8:1).

Margaret Daly-Denton

Although there is no indication in the text that Mary has reached out to him or tried to cling to him, Jesus's first words are a command: "Do not touch me" (v. 17; author's translation).[23] This much discussed command may also echo aspects of the creation account. In Eden, God's command was not to eat from one tree (Gen 2:17); when the woman explains God's prohibition to the serpent, she adds "and you must not touch it" (LXX: οὐδὲ μὴ ἅψησθε αὐτοῦ, Gen 3:5). The LXX uses the verb ἅπτω, which is the same verb found in John 20:17 (μή μου ἅπτου).[24] Whereas the first woman's disobedience in touching the tree brought death, Mary Magdalene's obedience leads into the Easter proclamation of life as children

23. Artistic representations of this scene frequently have Mary clinging to the feet of Jesus, even though the text does not state this. Jesus says, "Do not touch [ἅπτου] me," with no suggestion that she is already touching him.

24. Sandra Schneiders notes that ἅπτω does not mean "cling" or "hold" (contrary to the NRSV translation, "hold on"), but rather "touch." In addition, it often connotes more than physical touching, as in being touched by a person's kindness (*Written That You May Believe*, 219).

of God.[25] "But go to my brothers and sisters and say to them, 'I am ascending to my Father and your Father, to my God and your God'" (v. 17).[26] This statement affirms the revelation in the passion narrative that, from the cross, Jesus changed the relationships between himself and his disciples.[27] They are now his sisters and brothers and therefore born as "children of God" as the prologue promised (1:12). This is the major revelation of the chapter. It affirms not only the living presence of Jesus but also that the promise of the prologue and the mission of Jesus has been accomplished—believers are now children of God (1:12).

Jesus speaks to Mary of "ascending:" "I have not yet ascended to the Father" and "I am ascending" (20:17). These words may conjure the two Lukan accounts of the disciples watching Jesus being "carried up into heaven" (Luke 24:51; also Acts 1:9), as well as numerous paintings of this "event" as if it were an instance in time and space as any ordinary human event. The Johannine language of "ascent" is a metaphorical and theological statement of Jesus being no longer present among the disciples in his mortality, as the incarnate Word. Jesus is now in the eternal presence of God. The language of ascending therefore marks an ending, but it also marks the beginning of a new mode of presence, for this Gospel was written from within the faith experience of a living, risen presence of Jesus. Without this experience of Jesus's presence, there would be no faith community and no Gospel. The narrative attempts to convey in words and visual images the experience of disciples that transcends ordinary mundane life; these original women and men disciples encountered a new experience of God in Jesus now risen through death, and former language conventions are no longer adequate.[28] Mary then leaves the emptied tomb,

---

25. Rosik, "Discovering the Secrets of God's Garden," 93.

26. ἀδελφοί is an inclusive plural meaning both brothers and sisters. See Henry G. Liddell, "ἀδελφός," in *A Lexicon: Abridged from Liddell and Scott's Greek-English Lexicon* (Oak Harbor, WA: Logos Research Systems, 1996). Similarly, Marianne Meye Thompson, *John: A Commentary*, NTL (Louisville: Westminster John Knox, 2015), 417 n. 20.

27. Sandra Schneiders points out that the emphatic placement of the pronoun μου, "me," at the beginning of the command suggests that it is not so much the touching itself that Jesus is forbidding but rather the object of touching, that is, Mary is being told not to try to continue to touch or encounter Jesus as if he were the earthly Jesus resuscitated. Jesus is redirecting Mary's desire for union with him from his physical earthly body (which no longer exists) to the new locus of his presence in the world: the community of his brothers and sisters (*Written That You May Believe*, 219–20).

28. A very rich exploration of the ascension, using the concept of a "saturated phenomenon" proposed by Jean-Luc Marion, can be found in Anthony J. Kelly, *Upward: Faith, Church, and the Ascension of Christ* (Collegeville, MN: Liturgical Press, 2014).

which has no further meaning for her, and she is the first to proclaim the Easter experience, "I have seen the Lord."[29] Mary has encountered the Divine and bears witness. The disciples will say the same to Thomas, "We have seen the Lord" (20:25). To have seen or to have heard establishes one's authenticity as a witness.[30] The next scene within a house expands the reality of Jesus's presence in the gift of the Spirit.

> ### Jesus, Mary, and the Song of Songs (John 12:1-8; 20:1-18)
>
> John's depiction of the anointing at Bethany by Mary the sister of Martha and Lazarus (12:1-8) and the postresurrection encounter between Jesus and Mary Magdalene (20:1-18) are rife with intertextual echoes with the Song of Songs (also known as the Canticle of Canticles)[31] that make them amenable to nuptial interpretations where Jesus the Bridegroom encounters Mary the Bride (compare with John 3:29a: "He who has the bride is the bridegroom"). The sensual scene where Mary anoints Jesus's feet with "a pound of costly perfume made of pure nard"

29. For this proclamation Mary was named *apostolorum apostola*, and within the Catholic Church her celebration now has the ranking of an annual feast. The title dates back to Hippolytus (ca. 170–235), who wrote in his commentary on the Canticle, "And after this with a cry the synagogue expresses a good testimony for us through the women, those who were made apostles to the apostles, having been sent by Christ" (*In Cant.* 25.6). There is a confusion in the text whether this title refers to Mary the Magdalene, or to Martha and Mary of Bethany, or to a collective of women who come to the tomb. In this section of the commentary there are clear references to the Fourth Gospel alongside phrases from the Synoptics, e.g., " 'Rabouni,' which means my Lord" (John 20:16; *In Cant.* 25.2); "And with a loud cry says to her, 'Do not touch me for I have not yet ascended to my Father' " (John 20:17). From this I conclude that the title refers to Mary the Magdalene of John 20, rather than Mary of Bethany. A study of the Canticle and its various forms can be found in Yancy Warren Smith, "Hippolytus' Commentary on the Song of Songs in Social and Critical Context" (PhD diss., Brite Divinity School, 2009); the citations from John are on p. 349.

30. Schneiders calls this "a credential formula" (*Written That You May Believe*, 222).

31. In assessing the likelihood of the Song of Songs allusions, it must be noted that the rabbinic council of Jamnia (c. 80 CE) gave this Canticle canonical status in their Scriptures. The council considered this to be the most sublime expression of Israel's covenant. The Mishnah records the famous declaration of Rabbi Aquiba at this council: "All the scriptures are holy, but the Canticle is the Holy of Holies" (m. Yad. 3.5). The great valuing of the Canticle in first-century Judaism may well have influenced the evangelist's construction of the scene with Mary Magdalene at the tomb. She is permitted within the holy of holies to see the two cherubim (20:12), and then she turns to find her beloved in the garden.

and wipes them with her hair so that "the house was filled with the fragrance of the perfume" (12:3) echoes Song of Songs 1:12: "While the king was on his couch, my nard gave forth its fragrance." In the late second or early third century, Hippolytus of Rome read Song of Songs 3:1-6 and John 20:11-18 intertextually, identifying the sisters at the tomb seeking Christ with the female lover separated from her beloved (*In Cant.* 24–25).

John's story of the meeting between Mary Magdalene and the resurrected Jesus (20:11-18) amplifies the intertextual echoes with the Canticle. In both:

A woman wakes early to seek a beloved man, but initially she does not find him:

> Early on the first day of the week, while it was still dark, Mary Magdalene came to the tomb and saw that the stone had been removed from the tomb. So she ran and went to Simon Peter and the other disciple, the one whom Jesus loved, and said to them, "They have taken the Lord out of the tomb, and we do not know where they have laid him." (John 20:1-2)

> Upon my bed at night I sought him whom my soul loves; I sought him, but found him not; I called him, but he gave no answer. "I will rise now and go about the city, in the streets and in the squares; I will seek him whom my soul loves." I sought him, but found him not. (Song 3:1-2)

The woman converses with men concerning the beloved's whereabouts:

> As she wept, she bent over to look into the tomb; and she saw two angels in white, sitting where the body of Jesus had been lying, one at the head and the other at the feet. They said to her, "Woman, why are you weeping?" She said to them, "They have taken away my Lord, and I do not know where they have laid him." (John 20:11b-13; cf. 20:2)

> The sentinels found me, as they went about in the city. "Have you seen him whom my soul loves?" (Song 3:3)

The woman joyfully encounters her beloved:

> When she had said this, she turned round and saw Jesus standing there, but she did not know that it was Jesus. Jesus said to her, "Woman, why are you weeping? For whom are you looking?" Supposing him to be the gardener, she said to him, "Sir, if you have carried him away, tell me where you have laid him, and I will take him away." Jesus said to her, "Mary!" She turned and said to him in Hebrew, "Rabbouni!" (which means Teacher). (John 20:14-16)

Scarcely had I passed them,
when I found him whom
my soul loves. (Song 3:4a)

The woman clings to her
beloved:

Jesus said to her, "Do not
hold on to me, because I
have not yet ascended to
the Father. But go to my
brothers and say to them, 'I
am ascending to my Father
and your Father, to my
God and your God.'" (John
20:17)

I held him, and would not
let him go until I brought
him into my mother's
house, and into the cham-
ber of her that conceived
me. I adjure you, O daughters of Jerusalem, by the
gazelles or the wild does:
do not stir up or awaken
love until it is ready! (Song
3:4b-5)

The embalming spices
mentioned in John 19:39-40
resonate with the myrrh, incense,
and spices of Song 3:6 (compare
1:13; 4:6, 14; 5:1, 13; 6:2), as does

the garden setting (John 19:41;
Song 4:12, 15, 16; 5:1; 6:2).

The affinities of the Song of
Songs with the sacred marriage
traditions of the ancient Near
East are well known,[32] and the
Fourth Gospel portrays Jesus as
bridegroom more extensively
than any other New Testament
text,[33] excepting perhaps
Revelation (19:7; 21:2, 9, 17). If,
as Kari Syreeni observes, the
Gospels' references to Jesus as
Bridegroom (Matt 9:15; 25:1-13;
Mark 2:19, 20; Luke 5:34, 35;
John 3:29; cf. John 2:9) are
reticent about the identity of the
Bride,[34] John is the only one to
allow a hint that she is Mary. The
blurring of the identities of Mary
of Bethany and Mary Magdalene
in John's Gospel enhances the
symbolism of Mary and Jesus as
beloved Bride and Bridegroom
(cf. John 11:1-5).[35]

John's sacred marriage motif
does not amount to historical
evidence that Jesus and Mary
Magdalene were literally
married. It does, however, figure
in the "bridegroom-messiah"

32. Martti Nissinen, "Song of Songs and Sacred Marriage," in *Sacred Marriages: The Divine-Human Sexual Metaphor from Sumer to Early Christianity*, ed. Martti Nissinen and Risto Uro (Winona Lake, IN: Eisenbrauns, 2008), 173–218.

33. Jocelyn McWhirter, *The Bridegroom Messiah and the People of God: Marriage in the Fourth Gospel*, SNTSMS 138 (Cambridge: Cambridge University Press, 2006), and Kari Syreeni, "From the Bridegroom's Time to the Wedding of the Lamb: Nuptial Imagery in the Canonical Gospels and the Book of Revelation," in *Sacred Marriages*, 343–70.

34. Syreeni, "From the Bridegroom's Time," 344.

35. Mary Ann Beavis, "The Deification of Mary Magdalene," *Feminist Theology* 21 (2012): 148–49.

Christology of John (compare
Jer 33:10-11; Ps 45:10-15; Gen
29:1-20). And, although more
difficult to pin down, I would
not be surprised if ancient
audiences heard in Mary's
weeping at the tomb echoes

of ancient myths of goddesses
mourning their murdered
consorts (cf. Ezek 8:14), like the
Daughter of Zion longing in
anguish for the restoration of
her king (Mic 4:8-13).
Mary Ann Beavis

Scene 2: The Household (20:19-25)

Later that same day, named again as the "first day," indicating not only
the first day of the week but also the first day of a new creation, the disciples are present within a house. While the motive appears to be "for fear
of the Jews," it is also appropriate that the group of disciples, the sisters
and brothers of Jesus, are gathered as a household. The "house" first
mentioned in the Gospel is the temple, "my Father's house" (2:16), and I
have shown that in John 14 this symbol of God's dwelling is transferred
to the community of believers in whom the Father, Jesus, and the Spirit
will dwell (cf. 14:2). Believers will be the newly raised up temple of the
Father's household. This scene witnesses to the resurrection of faith for
the disciples and to the reality of the new household of God promised
by the narrative plot as I have presented in this work.

When Jesus comes to the disciples, his first word is Εἰρήνη, "Peace."
The Hebrew word שׁלום, *shalom*, means far more than what is conveyed
by its English translation, "peace." *Shalom* in the OT carries the sense
of wholeness, or completion,[36] and is derived from the word שָׁלֵם, "to be
completed."[37] Thus there is continuity between the final words of Jesus
on the cross, τετέλεσται, "It is finished," and the first word of the risen
Jesus, Εἰρήνη, "Peace." In the Hebrew and Greek OT, the term also has a
sense of God's final eschatological salvation.[38] Not only does the word
look back to what has been brought to completion, but it looks ahead to
a future fulfillment. As Werner Foerster concludes from his study of the

36. As Joseph P. Healey notes, "In one form or another, the notions of wholeness,
health, and completeness inform all the variants of the word" ("Peace," *ABD* 5 [1996]:
206); see also Gerhard von Rad, "שָׁלוֹם in the OT," *TDNT* 2 (1964): 402–6.
37. Robert L. Thomas, "שָׁלֵם, Shalem," in *New American Standard Hebrew-Aramaic and
Greek Dictionaries*, updated ed. (Anaheim, CA: Foundation Publications, 1998), H7999.
38. Werner Foerster, "εἰρήνη," *TDNT* 2 (1964): 412.

John 20:19-25

[19]When it was evening on that day, the first day of the week, and the doors of the house where the disciples had met were locked for fear of the Jews, Jesus came and stood among them and said, "Peace be with you." [20]After he said this, he showed them his hands and his side. Then the disciples rejoiced when they saw the Lord. [21]Jesus said to them again, "Peace be with you. As the Father has sent me, so I send you." [22]When he had said this, he breathed on them and said to them, "Receive the Holy Spirit. [23]If you forgive the sins of any, they are forgiven them; if you retain the sins of any, they are retained."

[24]But Thomas (who was called the Twin), one of the twelve, was not with them when Jesus came. [25]So the other disciples told him, "We have seen the Lord." But he said to them, "Unless I see the mark of the nails in his hands, and put my finger in the mark of the nails and my hand in his side, I will not believe."

term "peace" in the OT and rabbinic usage: "εἰρήνη thus acquires a most profound and comprehensive significance. It indicates the eschatological salvation of the whole man [sic] which is already present as the power of God. It denotes the state of the καινὴ κτίσις [new creation] as the state of definitive fulfillment. In this sense salvation has been revealed in the resurrection of Jesus."[39]

When Jesus repeats his greeting, "peace," he breathes on the disciples and says, "Receive the Holy Spirit" (20:22). The word translated "breathed," ἐνεφύσησεν, recalls God's action in the garden of Genesis when God formed an earth creature from the dust and then "breathed [LXX: ἐνεφύσησεν] into his face" the breath of life, and the earth-creature became a living being.[40] When Jesus comes to his disciples and greets them the first time with "Peace," this could be understood as saying: God's first creation has been brought to completion. When he says to them again, "Peace," and breathes on them the Holy Spirit, this is an act of new creation, reaffirming Jesus's words and actions at the cross. The words of Jesus and the gift of the Spirit on Golgotha constituted the disciple as a child of God, drawing the disciple into Jesus's divine filiation. In John 20, the "hour" of Jesus continues, and when the group of disciples is gathered the Spirit is breathed, and the disciples are sent into the world, "As the Father sent me, even so I send you" (20:21). There are

---

39. Ibid., 414.
40. Zimmermann, "The Garden Symbolism in John 19–20," 233–34.

not two bestowals of the Spirit. Rather, there are two moments within the one hour: one moment where the focus is on the believer's relationship to Jesus, and a second moment where the focus is on the believer's relationship to the world, as the agent of Jesus in the world.[41] For this reason the narrative describes two moments in the giving of the Spirit to the believers, a moment of birth at the cross (19:30) and a moment of mission (20:21-23).

Jesus commissions his disciples to forgive sins. His own mission was to overcome the ruler of the world and in this way to take away "the sin of the world" (1:29); that has now been accomplished. The ruler can no longer completely dominate and enslave humanity, and yet individuals can still fail and not live up to their inheritance as "children of God." Sinfulness continues to exist in such human failure, but disciples, alive with the power of the Spirit, can now offer forgiveness of sins (note the plural, as distinct from the singular in 1:29).[42] This authority is clearly expressed in the first part of 20:23, which I translate awkwardly to match the original Greek pattern of words:

A: ἄν τινων ἀφῆτε τὰς ἁμαρτίας ἀφέωνται αὐτοῖς,
If of anyone you forgive the sins, they have been forgiven of them.

The second part of this verse has been very poorly translated in most English translations and is more literally rendered:

B: ἄν τινων κρατῆτε κεκράτηνται.
If of anyone you hold, they have been held.

The second part (B) does not mention the word "sins," nor is "retain" the best or only translation of the Greek κρατέω, which in the LXX most frequently means to be strong or "to have power over something."[43] In

---

41. For a very clear discussion on the use of the two different verbs in v. 21 for "send," ἀποστέλλω and πέμπω, as they apply to Jesus and the disciples, see Garry H. Burge, *The Anointed Community: The Holy Spirit in the Johannine Community* (Grand Rapids: Eerdmans, 1987), 200–204. Even in this missioning moment, the creation theme is still present as ἐνεφύσησεν (a *hapax legomenon* in the NT) refers back to Gen 2:7 as discussed above. On this, see also Martin Hengel, "The Old Testament in the Fourth Gospel," in *The Gospels and the Scriptures of Israel*, ed. Craig Evans and W. Richard Stegner, JSNTSup 104 (Sheffield: Sheffield Academic, 1994), 391.

42. Human sins are determined by belief or nonbelief in Jesus, as expressed in the Gospel: "I told you that you would die in your sins, for you will die in your sins unless you believe that I am he" (8:24; similarly 1 John 2:12).

43. Wilhelm Michaelis, "κράτος," *TDNT* 3 (1965): 911.

the NT the main meaning is "to seize" or "to hold." John 20:23b has been considered the one exception where κρατέω has been thought to refer to retention of sins.[44] This singular exception has come about by interpreting John 20:23b in the light of the Matthean episode where Jesus says to Peter: "I will give you the keys of the kingdom of heaven, and whatever you bind [δήσῃς] on earth will be bound in heaven, and whatever you loose [λύσῃς] on earth will be loosed in heaven" (Matt 16:19; similarly 18:18). In Matthew 18:18-20, the issue is Peter's authority, and this is followed by the command to forgive, "Not seven times, but, I tell you, seventy-seven times" (Matt 18:22). In both Matthew and John there is no mention of "retaining" sins! Taking the usual meaning of κρατέω with the genitive, the better translation is "hold fast"; "whomever you hold they are held fast."[45] As Sandra Schneiders asserts, "The community that forgives sins must hold fast those whom it has brought into the community of eternal life."[46]

Across the narrative so far, disciples have moved from death and nonbelief to the living presence of Jesus and faith, but their words are insufficient for Thomas. Before Thomas will believe the disciples' testimony, he demands that certain criteria be met. He places conditions on his believing—"Unless I see . . . and place . . . " (v. 25).[47] Being outside the household of disciples has placed Thomas outside the experience of Jesus's presence and outside their Easter faith.

The Eighth Day (20:26-29)

Thomas was absent from the first gathering of the household and in this situation, even having heard the Easter proclamation, "We have seen the Lord" (v. 25), Thomas voices the strongest rejection of faith in this Gospel, "I will not believe" (v. 25). Some are puzzled why there would be need for this final pericope:

44. Ibid., 912.
45. Sandra M. Schneiders, "The Resurrection (of the Body) in the Fourth Gospel: A Key to Johannine Spirituality," in *Life in Abundance: Studies of John's Gospel in Tribute to Raymond E. Brown, SS*, ed. John R. Donahue (Collegeville, MN: Liturgical Press, 2005), 186. This article is a synthesis of Schneiders's unpublished doctoral thesis on the resurrection, and in this thesis ("The Johannine Resurrection Narrative," esp. 528–52) she provides much further information and argument supporting her translation.
46. Schneiders, "The Resurrection (of the Body)," 186.
47. Ignace De La Potterie, "Genèse de la Foi Pascale d'après Jn. 20," *NTS* 30 (1984): 42.

John 20:26-29

²⁶A week later his disciples were again in the house, and Thomas was with them. Although the doors were shut, Jesus came and stood among them and said, "Peace be with you." ²⁷Then he said to Thomas, "Put your finger here and see my hands. Reach out your hand and put it in my side. Do not doubt but believe." ²⁸Thomas answered him, "My Lord and my God!" ²⁹Jesus said to him, "Have you believed because you have seen me? Blessed are those who have not seen and yet have come to believe."

> In a sense, we might well ask what is the point of the Thomas episode. Mary has seen Christ as he is about to ascend to the Father. The disciples have seen Christ risen and glorified. We have already reached the summit: the balance is perfect, the identity of the historical Christ with the eternal Word is fully manifest. What more is there to add?[48]

What more indeed! This Gospel has self-consciously testified to Jesus for the readers/hearers of this text.[49] The final scene continues this narrative device in its portrayal of Thomas. Through Thomas, the readers are not simply presented with a narrative of things past. Through Thomas, time is stretched and the past is brought into God's eternal present.

The second gathering of disciples, including Thomas, occurs "eight days later" (μεθ᾽ ἡμέρας ὀκτώ, rendered as "a week later" in NRSV), again making this the Sunday evening since the beginning and end day of a period of time are both counted.[50] Now Thomas is gathered within the household on the first/eighth day of the week, the day of later eucharistic gatherings. Ernst H. Riesenfeld suggests that the early Christian community chose the day after the Jewish Sabbath as the day for Christian worship to reflect their understanding that their worship was a continuation and fulfilment of their Sabbath worship.[51] The Sabbath was not only a day to celebrate God's initial creative activity; in postexilic

48. Liliane Dupont, Christopher Lash, and Georges Levesque, "Recherche sur la structure de Jean 20," *Bib* 54 (1973): 493. (Author's translation.)

49. Note the use of first-person pronouns in the prologue (1:14, 15, 16) and the testimony of the witness at the cross (19:35).

50. Rudolph Schnackenburg, *The Gospel according to St John*, trans. K. Smyth et al., 3 vols., HTCNT (London: Burns & Oates, 1968–1982), 3:331.

51. Ernst H. Riesenfeld, "Sabbat et Jour du Seigneur," in *New Testament Essays: Studies in Memory of Thomas Walter Manson*, ed. A. J. B. Higgins (Manchester: Manchester University Press, 1959), 212. Following their Sabbath worship in the temple

time it was also characterized by a strong eschatological hope in God's future act of re-creation/salvation of Israel.[52] In time the terminology of the "first day" shifted to the "eighth day" to reflect Christian belief that they were already living in the new eschatological age. The "eighth day" terminology first appears in Christian literature in the Epistle of Barnabas (ca. 95–135):

> He further says to them, Your new moons and Sabbaths I disdain. Consider what he means: Not the Sabbaths of the present era are acceptable to me, but that which I have appointed to mark the end of the world and to usher in the eighth day, that is, the dawn of another world. This, by the way, is the reason why we joyfully celebrate the eighth day—the same day on which Jesus rose from the dead; after which He manifested himself and went up to heaven. (Ep. Barn. 15:8-9)[53]

In the Gospel the disciples gather "on the first day" and then again, "eight days later." The eschatological new creation theme is suggested by these two details of time, "on the first day" and "eight days later" (20:1, 26), particularly given the placement of the crucifixion, burial, and resurrection in a garden (18:1; 19:41). "Augustine equated the number eight with the number one as a symbol of rebirth, which explains why Easter is always celebrated on a Sunday (it is both eighth and first day of the week). He points out that the mystery of this eighth day was known to the prophets and patriarchs and evident in their observation of circumcision on the eighth day. But the full meaning had been hidden until Christ's resurrection on the eighth day."[54] This "eighth day" symbolism has been preserved in church architecture even when it has been forgotten within the community. A study of baptismal fonts shows that many, particularly older ones, were designed to have eight sides or

---

(and possibly synagogue), the early Christians returned to their own homes (Acts 2:46; 5:42) to listen to apostolic teaching, for prayer, and for the breaking of the bread.

52. The Mishnah records: On the Sabbath day they did sing, "*A Psalm, A song for the Sabbath day* (Ps. 92)—A psalm, a song for the world that is to come, for the day which is wholly Sabbath rest for eternity" (m. Tam. 7.4).

53. The eschatological "eighth day" also appears in the Jewish apocalyptic source 2 Enoch (first century BCE), "And I appointed the eighth day also, that the eighth day should be the first-created after my work, and that the first seven revolve in the form of the seventh thousand, and that at the beginning of the eighth thousand there should be a time of not-counting, endless, with neither years nor months nor weeks nor days nor hours" (33:1).

54. Robin Margaret Jensen, *Living Water: Images, Symbols, and Settings of Early Christian Baptism* (Leiden: Brill, 2011), 246.

be within an eight-sided baptistery such as in Florence. In the ritual of baptism one is immersed beneath the water into the death of Jesus and then rises with him into a new creation.[55]

Thomas had earlier expressed his criteria for faith, but Jesus does not say, "Open your eyes and see"; rather, he says, "Put your finger here and see." On this eighth day, Thomas is given an opportunity to "see" with his sense of touch. He is challenged to come to faith by stretching out his hand and to "cast it" (βάλε) into the side of Jesus. This is how Thomas is to experience the presence of Jesus, where before he knew only absence. Thomas thus functions as a representative character who brings into the text the experience of future believers. They too are absent from the experience of the historical Jesus and his resurrection appearances. They too know the apparent absence of Jesus, but in the Johannine community's experience of Eucharist, future believers can, like Thomas, stretch out their hand in a physical act of faith. Thomas's words, the words of one not present for the initial Easter experience, now express the perfect act of faith, "My Lord and my God" (v. 28). Thomas has let go of his previous criteria for faith. There is no suggestion in the text that he did place his finger in the mark of the nails and his hand in Jesus's side. The sight of the risen One bearing the marks of the cross is sufficient. In this experience, he recognizes the true identity of Jesus and makes a personal commitment to him, "*my* Lord," "*my* God."[56] In seeing the risen Jesus, he now "sees" the invisible God. Future believers will be challenged to have this same faith, of "seeing" the divine presence in this world. "Their believing will be based on their 'seeing' him in sacramental signs, and 'hearing' him in the community's witness, and especially in the 'things written' in the gospel."[57]

Thomas voices an understanding not only of Jesus's identity but also of the significance of that identity for himself. In naming Jesus "my God" Thomas has moved away from strict Jewish monotheism, where YHWH alone is God, into a new faith community of the brothers and sisters of Jesus (20:17). Prior to Easter, disciples were outsiders to Jesus's experience of God. Through the death, resurrection, and gift of the Spirit,

---

55. On the recurring motif of "eight" associated with baptism, see chap 5. Jensen, *Living Water*, 179–232.

56. According to Brown, there are only three New Testament passages that indisputably call Jesus "God" (John 1:1; 20:28; Heb 1:8). See Raymond E. Brown, *Jesus: God and Man*, Modern Biblical Reflections (New York: Macmillan, 1967), 23–29.

57. Schneiders, "The Resurrection (of the Body)," 188.

outsiders have become insiders (12:32), participating in Jesus's own filiation, able to call God "my Father" (20:17) and to know themselves to be dwelling in the "Father's household" (14:2). In coming to know their own new identity as children of God, disciples come to know the identity of the one who made this possible, the Son, who has made them truly free (8:36). As Timothy Radcliffe comments, "It is only after the Resurrection that Jesus calls the disciples his brothers [and sisters], and it is only when they are called his brothers that they can call him God."[58] Thomas's confession is the high point of Johannine faith, giving voice to the community's faith in Jesus's identity and its own self-identity as the household of God.[59]

Then, from within this Easter household, symbolic of all eucharistic households, Jesus speaks from the narrative to the future believers. These are the final words of Jesus, now the risen Lord, and they are a beatitude spoken into history to all communities of faith, "Blessed are those who have not seen and yet believe." Raymond Brown draws the comparison with a stage play and writes evocatively:

> Throughout the Gospel, and more particularly in the Last Discourse, in what the evangelist has been describing on the stage of early 1st-century Palestine, he has had in mind an audience seated in the darkened theatre of the future, silently viewing what Jesus was saying and doing. True to the limitations and logic of the stage drama imposed by the Gospel form, the Johannine Jesus could address that audience only

---

58. Timothy Radcliffe, " 'My Lord and my God': The Locus of Confession," *NBf* 65 (1984): 61. In this article, Radcliffe discusses the different historical and religious contexts exhibited by the Pauline letters and the Fourth Gospel. He argues that in the early years believers saw themselves continuing within the faith of Judaism. Only when there had been a social transformation separating Jews and Christians, such as we find in the Gospel of John (9:22; 12:42; 16:2), could the early believers move away from strict Jewish monotheism. He speaks of an "ecclesial transformation" that made possible Thomas's confession. On the complex issue of Jewish-Christian relations in the first two centuries, see Judith M. Lieu, *Image and Reality: The Jews in the World of the Christians in the Second Century* (Edinburgh: T&T Clark, 1996); Judith M. Lieu, *Neither Jew nor Greek? Constructing Early Christianity*, SNTW (Edinburgh: T&T Clark, 2002).

59. With Brown (*Gospel according to John*, 2:1047) and Moloney (*John*, 537), I see Thomas's confession as the high point of Johannine faith, forming an *inclusio* with the pronouncement at the start of the prologue (1:1c) and appropriately bringing the Gospel to its conclusion. As a character in the narrative, Thomas, of course, has had the privilege of faith through seeing Jesus; the beatitude expresses that this privilege of seeing Jesus is not the only way of "possessing the joy and blessings of the risen Jesus" (Brown, *Gospel according to John*, 2:1049).

indirectly through the disciples who shared the stage and gave voice to sentiments and reactions that were shared by the audience as well. But now, as the curtain is about to fall on the stage drama, the lights in the theatre are suddenly turned on. Jesus shifts his attention from the disciples on the stage to the audience that has become visible and makes clear that his ultimate concern is for them—those who have come to believe in him through the word of his disciples (17:20).[60]

With this blessing on the future households of faith, the Gospel narrative ends.[61]

Conclusion (20:30-31)

The final two verses state the purpose of this Gospel: that readers would come to or continue to have faith in Jesus as Messiah and Son of God and, in this faith, attain life. There is a difficulty in the manuscript tradition, with some having "that you may come to believe [πιστεύσητε]," implying that the Gospel was written for nonbelievers. Other ancient manuscripts have "may continue to believe [πιστεύητε]," which implies that the readers already have faith in Jesus, and the Gospel aims to strengthen their faith.[62] I favor this second view that the Gospel is written for those who already have faith but who, toward the end of the first century, experience struggles with both the Jewish world and the Greco-Roman society (see 15:18-25 and 16:1-4). The images and language of the Gospel require knowledge of Judaism, its rituals, Scriptures, method of argument, and theology. Then, across the narrative, some symbols recur and develop (such as tabernacle, temple, marriage) in a manner that suggests an audience already familiar with the text and able to appreciate its meaning at a deeper level with each subsequent reading/hearing. In his work on interpreting texts, Paul Ricoeur speaks of a "second naïveté" to describe the process of returning to a literary work a second time, bring-

---

60. Brown, *Gospel according to John*, 2:1049.

61. Raymond Collins points to the gnomic character of beatitudes phrased in the third person, and that therefore have a general sense not limited to the immediate hearers of this Gospel; see Raymond F. Collins, " 'Blessed Are Those Who Have Not Seen': John 20:29," in *Transcending Boundaries: Contemporary Readings of the New Testament*, ed. Rekha M. Chennattu and Mary L. Coloe, Biblioteca di Scienze Religiose 187 (Rome: Libreria Ateneo Salesiano, 2005), 189.

62. According to Brown (*Gospel according to John,* 2:1056), two of the earliest manuscripts, Vaticanus and Sinaiticus, and probably 𝔓⁶⁶, have this reading.

30Now Jesus did many other signs in the presence of his disciples, which are not written in this book. 31But these are written so that you may come to believe that Jesus is the Messiah, the Son of God, and that through believing you may have life in his name.

ing to this second reading the insights gained from the first reading.[63] The second reading, therefore, has a certain level of perception that makes possible the disclosure of deeper levels of meaning. Thus, the reader is involved in an ongoing hermeneutical circle of reading, understanding, raising questions, new readings, new perceptions, and new questions. Such is the ongoing nature of interpretation.

The Gospel has told the story of Jesus by selecting signs that best express his identity and his mission, which are summed up in the final two titles, "Messiah" and "Son of God." Speaking of Jesus as "Messiah" places him firmly within the long history of his Jewish community and its faith in God's promises. These promises had become focused on a savior figure, an anointed one, "who would usher in the promised new age."[64] Studies of the Dead Sea Scrolls reveal that in some Jewish circles, this anointed one, "Messiah," was considered more a prophetic figure than a military, Davidic messiah. The prophetic Messiah would perform wonderful works as announced in Isaiah 61. John J. Collins concludes, "Since the works in question are typical of what is attributed to Jesus in the gospels, this text [4Q521] strengthens the case that the epithet 'anointed' or 'messiah' could have been attached to him because of his words and deeds."[65] The signs and words recorded by the evangelist legitimate the claim that Jesus is the Messiah, and his signs announce the arrival of God's reign.

The second title, "Son of God," also recapitulates what was announced in the prologue. Jesus can reveal God only because he is son "close to the Father's heart" (1:18). And only as son can Jesus draw believers into

63. Paul Ricoeur, *Interpretation Theory: Discourse and the Surplus of Meaning* (Fort Worth: Texas Christian University Press, 1976), 4.

64. Craig A. Evans and Peter W. Flint, *Eschatology, Messianism, and the Dead Sea Scrolls*, Studies in the Dead Sea Scrolls and Related Literature (Grand Rapids: Eerdmans, 1997), 2.

65. John J. Collins, "The Works of the Messiah," *DSD* 1 (1994): 110.

his own divine filiation, making them "children of God" (1:12). The title, Son of God, summarizes who he is and what his mission achieved. As children of God, believers now participate not in ordinary life but in the eternity life of God.

Toward the end of Second Temple Judaism, divine sonship was beginning to be attributed to the Messiah, drawing particularly on the promise to David. When commenting on 2 Samuel 7:11—"YHWH declares to you that he will build you a house. I will raise up your seed after you and establish the throne of his kingdom forever. I will be a father to him and he will be a son to me"—the Qumran scribe adds, "This refers to the Branch [*tzamah*] of David" (4QFlor col 1:11); similarly, "Until the messiah of justice comes, the branch [*tzamah*] of David" (4QpGen col 5:3-4).[66] These texts and others show that in late Second Temple Judaism some were considering a Davidic Messiah, who would also be appropriately called a Son of God (Pss 2:2; 89:20, 26). Sonship is attributed to Israel because of God's choice (Jer 31:20; Deut 14:1; Ps 82:6), and in the book of Wisdom the righteous one is considered a son of God (2:14) whose claim needs to be tested. Daniel Boyarin argues that by this time some Jews considered that the Godhead included figures such as the *Logos*, the *Memra*, *Sophia*, and the *Shekinah*, paradoxically maintaining God's transcendence while also affirming God's immanence within creation.[67] Boyarin states: "It is at least possible that the beginning of trinitarian reflection was precisely in non-Christian Jewish accounts of the second and visible God, variously, the Logos (*Memra*), Wisdom, or even perhaps the Son of God."[68] As the Word incarnate and the embodiment of Sophia, the risen Jesus can now be recognized as son in a unique manner (1:18).

---

66. The English text is taken from Florentino García Martínez, *The Dead Sea Scrolls Translated: The Qumran Texts in English* (Leiden: Brill, 1994), 136; the Hebrew from Eduard Lohse, *Die Texte Aus Qumran: Hebräisch und Deutsch* (Munich: Kösel-Verlag, 1971), 256.

67. "The idea that the Logos/Sophia (and other variants as well) was the site of God's presence in the world—indeed of God's Word or Wisdom as a mediator figure—was a very widespread one in the thought-world of first-century and even second-century Judaism" (Daniel Boyarin, "The Gospel of the Memra: Jewish Binitarianism and the Prologue to John," *HTR* 94 [2001]: 248; see also Daniel Boyarin, *Border Lines: The Partition of Judaeo-Christianity* [Philadelphia: University of Pennsylvania Press, 2004]).

68. Boyarin, "The Gospel of the Memra," 249. He provides further references "For the Logos as the 'first-begotten son of the Uncreated Father' in Philo" on 249 n. 21.

Across the Gospel narrative, Jesus's identity as the Christ has been at best ambiguous and frequently challenged.[69] Within Judaism at that time there were various understandings of who the Messiah could be—a royal son of David;[70] a priest like Aaron;[71] a sign prophet like Moses;[72] one who would heal, give sight to the blind, and raise the dead;[73] one who would rebuild the temple.[74] When characters such as Andrew (1:41), the Samaritan woman (4:25, 29), the disciples (6:69), some of the Jews (7:41), and Martha (11:27) name Jesus as the Christ, they would have been speaking within this constellation of Jewish figures. But now for the first time the narrator affirms that Jesus is *the* Christ (20:31)—where "Christ" is a title. This affirmation is possible only when the hour of Jesus's glorification has been completed. Jesus has passed through death and lives now participating in the eternity life of God. Jesus *is* the divine Messiah of late Second Temple hopes.[75] Jesus is so quintessentially the Christ that the narrator transforms the title into a name and speaks of "Jesus Christ"—a name at the end of the prologue (Ἰησοῦ Χριστοῦ, 1:17) and the self-designation by Jesus (Ἰησοῦν Χριστόν, 17:3).

The prologue concluded with naming "Jesus Christ" and then continues with the assertion that only Jesus can be the revelation of God as he is "the only Son" (1:18). These words that close the prologue are now repeated to bring the Gospel to closure—Jesus is the Christ, the Son of God.

John 20 brings the Gospel narrative of Jesus to its proper conclusion. The chapter shows the resurrecting of the disciples' faith, thus confirming that the temple/my Father's household has been raised (2:19) in a community of sisters and brothers of Jesus. While this concludes the mission of the incarnate Word, it is not the end of the story. More narrative is needed to show how this familial community continued.

69. See especially 7:25-31, 40-53.

70. Benjamin E. Reynolds and Gabriele Boccaccini, eds., *Reading the Gospel of John's Christology as Jewish Messianism: Royal, Prophetic, and Divine Messiahs*, AGJU 106 (Leiden: Brill, 2018), chaps. 7, 8 and 9.

71. The Qumran scrolls show that some looked to three separate figures: "the prophet, and the messiahs of Israel and Aaron" (1Qs 9:9-11). Ibid., 441.

72. Ibid., chaps. 10, 11, and 12.

73. Ibid., 442–43; Collins, "The Works of the Messiah," 98–112.

74. Donald Juel, *Messiah and Temple*, SBLDS 31 (Missoula, MT: Scholars Press, 1977), 171; see also Mary L. Coloe, *God Dwells with Us: Temple Symbolism in the Fourth Gospel* (Collegeville, MN: Liturgical Press, 2001), 171–72.

75. There are four chapters in Reynolds and Boccaccini (*Reading the Gospel of John's Christology*) discussing the concept of divinity applied to Jewish expectations of the Messiah, (chaps. 13, 14, 15, and 16).

Mary: The First Apostle of the Resurrection (The Gospel of Mary)

In the late nineteenth century, a fragment of an ancient Coptic codex was found in Egypt. The next century brought more ancient codices to light in Oxyrhynchus and in Nag Hammadi in Egypt. Among the later discoveries was a copy of the earlier Coptic document in Greek dating back to the second century; this document was called the Gospel of Mary (Magdalene). These documents revealed an ancient form of Christianity known as Gnosticism. An excerpt from this Gospel is given here showing that ongoing life of Mary.[76]

Chapter 5

1) But they were grieved. They wept greatly, saying, How shall we go to the Gentiles and preach the gospel of the Kingdom of the Son of Man? If they did not spare Him, how will they spare us?

2) Then Mary stood up, greeted them all, and said to her brethren, Do not weep and do not grieve nor be irresolute, for His grace will be entirely with you and will protect you.

3) But rather, let us praise His greatness, for He has prepared us and made us into Men.

4) When Mary said this, she turned their hearts to the Good, and they began to discuss the words of the Savior.

5) Peter said to Mary, Sister we know that the Savior loved you more than the rest of woman.

6) Tell us the words of the Savior which you remember which you know, but we do not, nor have we heard them.

7) Mary answered and said, What is hidden from you I will proclaim to you. . . .

Chapter 9

1) When Mary had said this, she fell silent, since it was to this point that the Savior had spoken with her.

2) But Andrew answered and said to the brethren, Say what you wish to say about what she has said. I at least do not believe that the Savior said this. For certainly these teachings are strange ideas.

3) Peter answered and spoke concerning these same things.

4) He questioned them about the Savior: Did He really speak privately with a woman and not openly to us? Are we to turn about and all listen to her? Did He prefer her to us?

5) Then Mary wept and said to Peter, My brother Peter, what do you think? Do you think that I have thought this up myself

---

76. The full text can be found at http://gnosis.org/library/marygosp.htm. For further information about the Gospel of Mary, see Karen L. King, *The Gospel of Mary of Magdala: Jesus and the First Woman Apostle* (Santa Rosa, CA: Polebridge, 2003).

in my heart, or that I am lying about the Savior?

6) Levi answered and said to Peter, Peter you have always been hot tempered.

7) Now I see you contending against the woman like the adversaries.

8) But if the Savior made her worthy, who are you indeed to reject her? Surely the Savior knows her very well.

9) That is why He loved her more than us. Rather let us be ashamed and put on the perfect Man, and separate as He commanded us and preach the gospel, not laying down any other rule or other law beyond what the Savior said.

10) And when they heard this they began to go forth to proclaim and to preach.

John 21:1-25

Sophia Has Built Her House—
The Gospel Continues

Wisdom has built her house,
she has hewn her seven pillars.
. . . she has mixed her wine,
she has also set her table.
She calls, "Come, eat of my bread
and drink of the wine I have mixed." (Prov 9:1-2, 5)

The Gospel narrative of Jesus's life, ministry, death, and resurrection came to its conclusion with chapter 20, especially
20:30-31. But the story of the community continued, witnessing to the
ongoing presence of Jesus/Sophia. Chapter 21 provides a glimpse into
the beginnings of this Gospel community and the issues it faced. Clearly,
this chapter comes some time later than the original Gospel, for it indicates that the Beloved Disciple has died (20:23-24) and that Peter has
also undergone martyrdom (20:18).[1] But while obviously a later addition,
this chapter brings the entire work to its completion, and there are no

---

1. See Jean Zumstein, *L'Évangile selon Saint Jean (13–21)*, CNT IVb 2nd ser. (Genève:
Labor et Fides, 2007), 299–300, who provides five arguments supporting the view
that John 21 is an addition to the Gospel.

manuscripts or papyri without John 21. Here we have the self-conscious reflection on the Johannine Jesus story, the Gospel, and how this relates to issues now facing the community. In the words of Michael Labahn, "The material in the new text [John 21] is not foreign to the older text [John 1–20]; rather, it reads and transforms the older text, filling its gaps by giving new answers or by actualizing the previous text while correcting or adding new insights. . . . The new text is intentionally based upon the older one and confirms its significance."[2] The Gospel's prologue (1:1-18) introduced the narrative by inviting the reader into the preexistence of Wisdom-Word; chapter 21 invites the reader into the postexistence of the Gospel's community. These verses are tied to the preceding narrative and are rightly called an epilogue.[3]

Structurally, the chapter has four sections:

21:1-14 The sign of an astounding catch of fish

21:15-19 Peter's rehabilitation and recommissioning

21:20-23 The Beloved Disciple

21:24-25 Conclusion

The Catch of Fish (21:1-14)

The passage begins in darkness; previously on the lake, darkness indicated the absence of Jesus (6:17). This absence may not be the reality but expresses the limited perception of the disciples. Elements not previously known are introduced: the sons of Zebedee, that the disciples were fishermen, and that Nathanael was from Cana. It appears as if the disciples have returned to the state and place before they met Jesus. The narrative opened with the activity of John baptizing in "Bethany across the Jordan" (1:28), but the exact location of this Bethany is not known. Some consider it to be the region of Batanea in Galilee, what was known

---

2. Michael Labahn, "Peter's Rehabilitation (John 21:15-19) and the Adoption of Sinners: Remembering Jesus and Relecturing John," in *John, Jesus, and History*, vol. 2: *Aspects of Historicity in the Fourth Gospel*, ed. Paul N. Anderson, Felix Just, and Tom Thatcher (Atlanta: SBL, 2009), 339.

3. In concluding that John 21 functions as an epilogue, Zumstein draws on the work of Gérard Genette and his theory of paratext. For further on this and how an initial text can generate further writings, see Gérard Genette and Marie Maclean, "Introduction to the Paratext," *New Literary History* 22 (1991): 261–72.

John 21:1-14

²¹˙¹After these things Jesus showed himself again to the disciples by the Sea of Tiberias; and he showed himself in this way. ²Gathered there together were Simon Peter, Thomas called the Twin, Nathanael of Cana in Galilee, the sons of Zebedee, and two others of his disciples. ³Simon Peter said to them, "I am going fishing." They said to him, "We will go with you." They went out and got into the boat, but that night they caught nothing.

⁴Just after daybreak, Jesus stood on the beach; but the disciples did not know that it was Jesus. ⁵Jesus said to them, "Children, you have no fish, have you?" They answered him, "No." ⁶He said to them, "Cast the net to the right side of the boat, and you will find some." So they cast it, and now they were not able to haul it in because there were so many fish. ⁷That disciple whom Jesus loved said to Peter, "It is the Lord!" When Simon Peter heard

as Bashan and described as "beyond the Jordan."⁴ In this state of "darkness" their work is fruitless—witnessing to the truth of the statement, "apart from me you can do nothing" (15:5). Peter takes the lead in this group of disciples.

As light begins to dawn, Jesus appears on the shore, but they fail to recognize him; then the stranger addresses them as Παιδία, "children" (v. 5). The disciples became "children of God" in the hour, when they became the "sisters and brothers" (20:17) of Jesus. In naming them "children" Jesus begins to affirm their post-Easter identity and reaffirm his own mission that believers would become "the children of God" (1:12). Following his words of instruction, they cast to the right side of the boat and this time catch an overwhelming number of fish.⁵

The bountiful catch, in response to the words of the stranger, acts as a sign to the Beloved Disciple, and s/he is the first to recognize Jesus's presence. "The disciples have seen such abundance before, in the signs that were performed in Galilee. . . . The changing of water into wine (2:1-11), and the feeding of the five thousand (6:1-14)."⁶ Now the Beloved

4. Rainer Riesner, "Bethany Beyond the Jordan," *ABD* 1 (1992): 704. Readers would be expected to know that Jesus's first disciples were Galilean fisherman, and in the Synoptics, fishing was a metaphor for their mission, to be "fishers of people."

5. The account of a wondrous draught of fish is similar to the miracle account in Luke 5:1-11. The similarities suggest that both draw on an oral tradition. It is not necessary to presume that the author of John 21 used Luke as a source.

6. Gail R. O'Day and Susan Hylen, *John*, WBC (Louisville: Westminster John Knox, 2006), 2001. The bread and fish were also provided in John 6.

that it was the Lord, he put on some clothes, for he was naked, and jumped into the sea. ⁸But the other disciples came in the boat, dragging the net full of fish, for they were not far from the land, only about a hundred yards off.

⁹When they had gone ashore, they saw a charcoal fire there, with fish on it, and bread. ¹⁰Jesus said to them, "Bring some of the fish that you have just caught." ¹¹So Simon Peter went aboard and hauled the net ashore, full of large fish, a hundred fifty-three of them; and though there were so many, the net was not torn. ¹²Jesus said to them, "Come and have breakfast." Now none of the disciples dared to ask him, "Who are you?" because they knew it was the Lord. ¹³Jesus came and took the bread and gave it to them, and did the same with the fish. ¹⁴This was now the third time that Jesus appeared to the disciples after he was raised from the dead.

Disciple offers leadership by acclaiming, "It is the Lord" (v. 7). At these words Peter responds by dressing himself more appropriately before his Lord and leaping into the sea.[7]

When the disciples reach the shore, they find Jesus, Peter, and a charcoal fire. This scene recalls the evening of Jesus's arrest when Peter was inside the high priest's house, warming himself at a charcoal fire (18:18). While Jesus is being questioned on his teaching and affirming it (18:19-24), Peter is denying his identity as "one of his disciples" (18:17, 25, 26). The setting prepares for the next scene when Jesus questions Peter three times on his relationship to him. Around this fire, Jesus takes the initiative, asking for some of the fish (v. 10), and again Peter responds by hauling in the net with the huge catch of 153 fish. Jesus then takes the bread and fish and gives these to the disciples, in almost identical manner to his taking bread and fish beside Galilee at an earlier Passover (6:13).

Sophia's Invitation

The symbolism of this passage (21:1-14) makes sense only in the light of the Johannine meaning of the cross and resurrection. At the cross, disciples became "children of God" (1:12), when the temple, the Father's house/hold, was raised (2:19). In this passage, Jesus calls the disciples

---

7. The word γυμνός can mean naked but also scantily dressed in a loin cloth—the simple clothes of a fisherman. Jerome H. Neyrey, *The Gospel of John*, NCBC (Cambridge: Cambridge University Press, 2007), 335.

"children" (Παιδία), not brothers and sisters (ἄδελφοι, 20:17), for he has now completed his ascension and has resumed his status as the divine Word/Wisdom, with God from the beginning (1:1; Prov 8:22; Sir 1:4; 24:9). He no longer speaks as the incarnate Jesus but as one participating again in the fullness of divine glory. Divine Sophia can address them now as "children" of God's house (21:5). The scene begins with a specific group of seven: Simon Peter, Thomas, Nathanael, the two sons of Zebedee, and two others. While this may simply refer to the disciples from Galilee such as Peter, Nathanael, and the sons of Zebedee, the number may also allude to the household that has been constructed. The seven "children" may portray the seven pillars of Wisdom's house (Prov 9:1). Jesus/Sophia then invites them, "Come and eat" (21:12), recalling Wisdom's invitation: "Come, eat of my bread and drink of the wine I have mixed" (Prov 9:5).

153 Fish

What can we make of this detail? Some consider it is just a way of saying "a great haul of fish." I disagree. John does not use numbers haphazardly (e.g., "the third day" [2:1]; "the sixth hour" [4:6]; "five husbands" [4:18]).[8] Jerome thought the number 153 represented the number of species of fish known at that time; without being a fish expert, I don't think this is the solution. John uses numbers for theological purposes, not for scientific information. In some way 153 expresses a Johannine theology of this episode.

The most plausible solution, I believe, can be found in the Jewish method of using numbers to indicate words—a method called gematria. In Hebrew there are no numbers. Instead, the first letter, *aleph*, represents the number 1; the second letter, *bet*, represents the number 2, and so on. So the name David, in Hebrew, would be represented by the numbers 4 (*dalet*), 6 (*vav*), and 4 (*dalet*), giving the total of 14. For instance, the genealogy in Matthew (1:2-17), with the emphasis on the number 14 (1:17), presents Jesus as the son of David (1:1). This is an example of gematria, which Jewish readers would understand—and enjoy.[9]

Across the Gospel, the temple has been a major symbol expressing both Jesus's identity (Christology) and salvific mission (soteriology).

---

8. See the discussion of these numbers earlier in this commentary.

9. For this discussion of David and gematria, see Neil J. McEleney, "153 Great Fishes (John 21,11)—Gematriacal Atbash," *Bib* 58 (1977): 413.

The "Father's house" first refers to the temple building (2:16), then to the temple "body" of Jesus (2:21), and points ahead to the household of the disciples, as the children of God.[10] The symbolism of the temple lies behind Jesus's teaching in John 7:37-38: "Let anyone who is thirsty come to me, and let the one who believes in me drink. As the scripture has said, 'Out of the believer's heart shall flow rivers of living water.'" Earlier in this commentary I argued that "his heart" refers to the heart of future believers to whom the Spirit has been given. When the temple of Jesus's mortal body is no longer available, then the community of the Father's household will be the future living temple, continuing to offer living waters. The background for this image lies in the description of waters flowing from the temple in Ezekiel 47:8-10:[11]

> He said to me, "This water flows toward the eastern region and goes down into the Arabah; and when it enters the sea, the sea of stagnant waters, the water will become fresh. Wherever the river [or the rivers, as it is in dual form נַחֲלַיִם] goes, every living creature that swarms will live, and there will be very many fish, once these waters reach there. It will become fresh; and everything will live where the river goes. People will stand fishing beside the sea from En-*gedi* to En-*eglaim*; it will be a place for the spreading of nets; its fish will be of a great many kinds, like the fish of the Great Sea.

In this passage two places are named—En-gedi and En-eglaim. Using the method of gematria, En-Gedi is the number 17 (גדי: *gimmel*, 3 + *dalet*, 4 + *yod*, 10 = 17) and En-eglaim is the number 153 (עגלים: *ayin*, 70 + *gimmel*, 3 + *lamed*, 30 + *yod*, 10 + *mem*, 40 = 153.[12] Mention of 153 fish, using this gematrian method of Jewish interpretation, directs the reader to the abundance of fish made possible by the waters flowing from the eschatological temple of Ezekiel and is consistent with the theology of the gospel.

The Hebrew MT describes the water from the temple flowing toward the eastern region known as *the Arabah* and then south into the Dead Sea (Ezek 47:8). The Arabah is a biblical term referring to all or portions of

---

10. Refer back to the discussion of John 14 and the expression, "In my Father's household."

11. Daniel Bodi, "The Double Current and the Tree of Healing in Ezekiel 47:1-12 in Light of Babylonian Iconography and Texts," *WO* 45 (2015): 25–26.

12. John A. Emerton, "The Hundred and Fifty-Three Fishes in John 21:11," *JTS* 9 (1958): 86–89. Emerton notes that the Hebrew word "En" is significant since it means "spring" and is to be thought of as an essential part of the proper names ("spring of Gedi, spring of Egliam"), and that 17 is a factor of 153: 9 x 17 = 153.

the Great Rift Valley in Palestine, running from the Sea of Galilee in the north, through the Jordan Valley to the Dead Sea.[13] Generally Arabah simply means desert or wilderness, but sometimes it is used to speak of a specific location along this rift valley.[14]

So when Ezekiel states that the rivers flow down into the Arabah, he simply describes the waters flowing east into the Jordan valley. It is naming the sea as "the sea of stagnant waters" that makes specific that the temple waters flow south to the Dead Sea. But while the translations speak of one river, the Hebrew is in dual or plural form[15]—"wherever the *rivers* go"—and this plurality gives rise to later elaborations.

The Aramaic Targum of Ezekiel describes the waters going to the Eastern region and down to the plain, what the MT calls the Arabah, but also flowing west into the Great Sea (the Mediterranean).

> And he said to me, "These waters go out to the eastern region and down to the plain, and enter into the sea; they spread to the Great Sea, and the waters become purified. And it shall be that every living creature that swarms, in every place where the waters of the river enter, shall live; and there will be very many fish, for these waters enter there and they are purified; and everything shall live in whatever place the waters of the river enter. There shall *be a place* to stand upon for fishermen, from En-gedi to En-eglaim; it shall be for fishermen to spread their nets; their fish shall be of various kinds, and very plentiful, like the fish of the Great Sea."[16] (Targum Ezekiel 47:8-10)

A further development of the Ezekiel tradition is recorded in the Tosefta,[17] which links the Ezekiel passage to Zechariah 14:8: "On that day, living

---

13. David R. Seely, "Arabah (Place)," in *ABD* 1 (1992): 321–22.

14. For example, in the distribution of land, Moses gives the region of the Arabah to the Reubenites and Gadites, naming its borders from Chinnereth, Lake Galilee, "as far as the sea of the Arabah, the Salt Sea" (Deut 3:17).

15. The dual form is indicated by the pointing in the Masoretic text. The original text would have simply shown the consonants and could be read as dual or plural.

16. Kevin Cathcart, Michael Maher, and Martin McNamara, eds., *The Aramaic Bible: The Targum of Ezekiel*, trans. Samson H. Levey, vol. 13 (Collegeville, MN: Liturgical Press, 1990), Ezek 47:8-10; emphasis added.

17. The Tosefta is a collection, in Hebrew, of earlier traditions that are not found in the Mishnah. There is a debate about which came first—the Tosefta or the Mishnah—and an approximate date is 200 CE. Like the Mishnah, these traditions in the Tosefta stretch back in time to when the temple existed. Daniel J. Harrington, "Can New Testament Interpreters Use Rabbinic Literature? Review Article," *STRev* 48 (2005): 335. This article reviews a six-volume project examining rabbinic traditions,

waters shall flow out from Jerusalem. Half of them to the eastern sea, and
half of them to the western sea." The rabbinic midrash on Ezekiel reads:

> Whither do the waters go? To the Mediterranean, and to the sea of Tibe-
> rias, and to the Dead Sea, that their waters may be healed, as it is said:

> And he said to me, These waters issue forth towards the eastern region
> that is the Dead Sea; and shall go down into the Arabah that is the Sea
> of Tiberias; and they shall go towards the other sea, that is the Mediter-
> ranean Sea; and waters shall be healed; and it shall come to pass that
> every living creature that swarms, in every place whither the river
> comes, shall live. (t. Sukkah 3:2)

The midrash understands that the river or rivers will separate into *three*
branches, one flowing into the Sea of Tiberias (Galilee); one flowing into
the Dead Sea; and the ultimate destination being the Great Sea (Mediterranean), encompassing the entire world. These writings suggest that
Jewish traditions elaborated on the torrents in Ezekiel to present a cosmic
river streaming from the temple to penetrate all the waters of the earth
and making them abundantly fertile.[18] The fertility reaches all along
the Arabah, from the northern sea of Tiberias to the southern Dead Sea.
While dating these traditions is problematic, it is possible that John 21
stands within this developing tradition from Ezekiel to the Tosefta.[19]

Understanding this Ezekiel background means that this scene enacts
the post-Easter fruitfulness of the disciples' mission.[20] The post-Easter

---

particularly in the Mishnah, and attempting to critically assess if these traditions
can be traced back to pre-70 CE. The first volume is David Instone-Brewer, *Traditions
of the Rabbis from the Era of the New Testament*, vol. 1: *Prayer and Agriculture* (Grand
Rapids: Eerdmans, 2004).

18. Other scholars also using gematria see Ezekiel as the most likely background for
this scene. Marc Rastoin, "Encore une fois les 153 poissons (Jn 21,11)," *Bib* 90 (2009):
84–92; Bruce H. Grigsby, "Gematria and John 21:11—Another Look at Ezekiel 47:10,"
ExpTim 95 (1984): 177–78; George J. Brooke, "4Q252 and the 153 Fish of John 21:11,"
in *Antikes Judentum und Frühes Christentum*, ed. Bernd Kollmann, Wolfgang Reinbold,
and Annette Steudel, BZNW 97 (Berlin: de Gruyter, 1999), 253–65.

19. John 7:38 uses the plural form "rivers"; John 21 uses the number 153, which
represents the word En-Eglaim, and locates this abundance in the northern Sea of
Tiberias, rather than the southern Dead Sea. To date, no Dead Sea Scroll has revealed
Ezekiel 47, which could show how this was read in the first century.

20. While I favor the link made between 153 and En-eglaim of Ezekiel 47, primarily
for its temple significance and coherence with the Christology of the Gospel, there
have been other suggestions. Joseph Romeo argues for "Children of God"; see Joseph
A. Romeo, "Gematria and John 21:11: The Children of God," *JBL* 97 (1978): 263–64.

community of the children of God forms a new "Father's household" (14:2), a living temple whose mission will fulfill the hopes for an eschatological temple expressed by Ezekiel 47. In this post-Easter mission, while the Beloved Disciple remains the model of perceptive faith, Peter steps forward into the role of leadership. But more is needed before Peter's leadership can be affirmed by Jesus.

Peter's Rehabilitation (21:15-19)

The last time there was a charcoal fire was after Jesus's arrest, and this marked a critical failure of Peter's faith (18:16-18). Three times Peter denied being a disciple of Jesus with his emphatic οὐκ εἰμί, "I am not" (18:17, 25, 27), and while the Beloved Disciple was present at the crucifixion, Peter was absent. When Jesus speaks to Peter, it is as if it is a first meeting, for he names him "Simon son of John," recalling his first encounter, when he renamed him "Cephas" (1:42).[21] Peter must begin his discipleship again.

Now, three times he is asked to affirm his loving commitment to Jesus. Does Peter love Jesus even more than he loves the other disciples? The triple question—Do you love me—when asked within a relationship must be disturbing, and Peter feels distressed.[22] Even though Jesus and Peter employ different verbs for "love" (ἀγαπάω and φιλέω),[23] these words are synonymous; the evangelist uses such minor variations for his own reasons.[24] During his final discourse, Jesus had described what love means when he said, "No one has greater love [ἀγάπην] than this, to lay

---

Yet another proposal by Margaret Starbird is that the Greek letters ἡ Μαγδαληνὴ (the Magdalene) also add up to 153; see Mary Ann Beavis, "From Holy Grail to The Lost Gospel : Margaret Starbird and Mary Magdalene Scholarship," *Journal of Religion and Popular Culture* 27 (2015): 139.

21. "You are Simon son of John. You are to be called Cephas" (which is translated Peter). The explanation is that the word for rock in Aramaic is *kepha*, and in Greek it is *petra*.

22. Labahn, "Peter's Rehabilitation," 343.

23. Jesus twice asks ἀγαπᾷς με; (vv. 15, 16) and then φιλεῖς με; (v. 17). All three times Peter responds, φιλῶ σε.

24. Donald A. Carson, *The Gospel according to John* (Grand Rapids: Eerdmans, 1991), 677. Carson provides a number of convincing reasons for not seeing the change of words as significant. Similarly, Francis J. Moloney, *John*, SP 4 (Collegeville, MN: Liturgical Press, 1998), 559; Zumstein, *L'Évangile selon Saint Jean (13–21)*, 312 n. 9. Similarly, the evangelist alternates between βοσκεῖν, "feed" (vv. 15, 17), and ποιεινεῖν, "tend" (v. 16), and ἀρνία, "lambs" (v. 15), and πρόβατα, "sheep" (vv. 16, 17).

John 21:15-19

15When they had finished breakfast, Jesus said to Simon Peter, "Simon son of John, do you love me more than these?" He said to him, "Yes, Lord; you know that I love you." Jesus said to him, "Feed my lambs." 16A second time he said to him, "Simon son of John, do you love me?" He said to him, "Yes, Lord; you know that I love you." Jesus said to him, "Tend my sheep." 17He said to him the third time, "Simon son of John, do you love me?" Peter felt hurt because he said to him the third time, "Do you love me?" And he said to him, "Lord, you know everything; you know that I love you." Jesus said to him, "Feed my sheep. 18Very truly, I tell you, when you were younger, you used to fasten your own belt and to go wherever you wished. But when you grow old, you will stretch out your hands, and someone else will fasten a belt around you and take you where you do not wish to go." 19(He said this to indicate the kind of death by which he would glorify God.) After this he said to him, "Follow me."

down one's life for one's friends" (15:13). Peter is asked if he has this depth of selfless love.[25]

On the strength of his affirmations that he has this depth of love, Peter is given the role of leading the community as a shepherd. Such a shepherding role calls Peter to nourish the community through his leadership,[26] but it will also demand of Peter his life, for Jesus has described and exemplified the model of being the good shepherd. "I am the good shepherd. The good shepherd lays down his life for the sheep" (John 10:11). That this will be Peter's path is indicated by Jesus's following words about Peter's death. While the narrative creates a time around the year 30 CE, when Pilate was governor, the Gospel was written decades later, and by this time Peter has died a martyr's death and legend has it that his hands "were stretched out" in crucifixion.[27] Like

25. By the time of the written Gospel, Peter's martyrdom has demonstrated that he has such love.

26. In his discussion of this passage Brown does not believe that this text alone supports the Catholic teaching on Petrine primacy. He also raises the question of why this text was needed for the community, when Peter "had already been dead for twenty or thirty years." Raymond E. Brown, *The Gospel according to John*, 2 vols., AB 29–29A (New York: Doubleday, 1966, 1970), 2:117. In a later book, Brown describes these verses as "plausibly the community acceptance of structured shepherding." Raymond E. Brown, *An Introduction to the Gospel of John: Edited, Updated, Introduced and Concluded by Francis J. Moloney*, ABRL (New York: Doubleday, 2003).

27. Acts of Peter 36–41; Tertullian, *Scorp.* 15.3; Eusebius, *Hist. eccl.* 2.25.8; 3.1.2. A helpful, critical evaluation of the texts about Peter can be found in John P. Meier, *A*

Jesus, Peter's death will glorify God, but until then he is commanded, "Follow me."[28]

The episode shows that Peter's triple denial of Jesus has been forgiven and that Jesus has entrusted Peter with pastoral leadership of the community. Without this scene, the narrative would have closed with the memory of Peter's denial and no plausible explanation for his later leadership role within the wider Christian community. The scene not only rehabilitates Peter but also enacts Jesus's commission to the community to forgive sin (20:23).

The Beloved Disciple (21:20-23)

The final scene of the Gospel concerns the fate of the Beloved Disciple, the primary witness in the community and authority behind the narrative. By the time of this writing, the Beloved Disciple is dead and this has caused anxiety within the community. We know from the Pauline letters that at first there was a sense of the imminent return of Jesus to the community, so that Paul, along with other believers, expected to be alive for the parousia. The Johannine community may have expected that their leader would remain with them until Jesus's return, so his death would have caused distress and possibly would have shaken their faith. The scribe behind John 21 has reprimanded the community through Jesus's reprimand of Peter. Jesus had not promised that the Beloved Disciple would remain alive until his return or that he would escape death.

It is possible such a rumor arose from the many references in the Gospel to eternity life. If this were taken, simplistically, to mean that physical death would not occur, it is a misunderstanding of Jesus's gift. Eternity life is the gift of a quality of divine life, enjoyed by the children of God, who are the brothers and sisters of Jesus. The text actually reminds the reader that believers are members of the Father's house—not simply a community, but brothers and sisters (ἄδελφοι, v. 23). Believers remain mortal and will experience physical death, as Jesus did, and they will

---

Marginal Jew: Rethinking the Historical Jesus, vol 3: *Companion and Competitors*, ABRL (New York: Doubleday, 2001), 221–45. The earliest account of Peter's death is in Clement's epistle to the Corinthians 5:1-17: "Peter, through unrighteous envy, endured not one or two, but numerous labors and when he had at length suffered martyrdom, departed to the place of glory due to him."

28. Philip is the only other disciple given such an explicit command/invitation in John's Gospel (1:43).

²⁰Peter turned and saw the disciple whom Jesus loved following them; he was the one who had reclined next to Jesus at the supper and had said, "Lord, who is it that is going to betray you?" ²¹When Peter saw him, he said to Jesus, "Lord, what about him?" ²²Jesus said to him, "If it is my will that he remain until I come, what is that to you? Follow me!" ²³So the rumor spread in the community, that this disciple would not die. Yet Jesus did not say to him that he would not die, but, "If it is my will that he remain until I come, what is that to you?"

experience the eternity life of God, to which Jesus's risen presence gives testimony.

Conclusion (21:24-25)

The chapter concludes almost prosaically, especially compared to the rich theological conclusion at the end of John 20. It affirms the reliability of the writer and alludes to his impossible task of selecting those things from the rich tradition and memory of Jesus to commit to writing. The chapter has expanded the Jesus story into his ongoing presence in the life of the community. As a late first-century document, it also witnesses that the Gospel has been received as authoritative. As Jean Zumstein states, "The process of canonization has commenced."[29] This chapter draws on the theology of the Gospel with its important imagery of the temple and its intertext with chapters 1–20; Peter is called "Simon son of John" (1:42; 21:15); it looks back to Peter's triple denial around a charcoal fire and his future martyrdom as predicted (13:36; 21:18). The chapter is firmly placed within the Jewish tradition of the targums and midrash, where Scripture is open to further exegesis and elaboration.

Postscript: Bread-Bakers

This final chapter depicts some of the disciples who are named in the boat with Peter. But there are unnamed others in this picture, who remain silent, whose presence is unacknowledged except by the work of their hands—the bread (vv. 9, 13). If there is bread, there are bread-bakers close by. The bakerwomen can be so much part of this scene that their presence

---

29. Zumstein, *L'Évangile selon Saint Jean (13–21)*, 300–301.

John 21:24-25

²⁴This is the disciple who is testifying to these things and has written them, and we know that his testimony is true. ²⁵But there are also many other things that Jesus did; if every one of them were written down, I suppose that the world itself could not contain the books that would be written.

is presumed and taken for granted in that first-century culture. But today their presence is forgotten and unknown. Here, midrash is needed. As Jewish feminist Judith Plaskow states: "Midrash expands and burrows, invents the forgotten and prods the memory, takes from history and asks for more. It gives us the inner life history cannot follow."[30] And in another article, she speaks of the "contradiction between the holes in the text and many women's felt experience."[31]

Women disciples today know that there were women disciples throughout the Gospel scenes, even when their presence has slipped through "the holes in the text," and many are not named.[32] But

> Why quibble with anonymity?
> For the mountain God remembers me; . . .
> My name is known on Horeb's heights
> and spoken in the love circle of home.[33]

30. Judith Plaskow, *Standing Again at Sinai: Judaism from a Feminist Perspective* (New York: HarperCollins, 1990), 59.

31. Judith Plaskow, "Standing Again at Sinai: Jewish Memory from a Feminist Perspective," *Tikkun* 2 (1986): 28.

32. This commentary has primarily followed conventions of biblical exegesis rather than feminist midrash. I hope that the "holes" in this text allow room for expansion and imagination to fill in the gaps, where the black marks on a manuscript leave empty space between.

33. Josephine Hoare, "Job's Wife," in *Selected Poems* (St Kilda West, VIC: Presentation Sisters, 2019), 26; used with permission.

Afterword

This is my first venture into explicit feminist writing. I have written on women's position in the church—but considered that an issue of justice. With the encouragement of Barbara Reid and my love of the Fourth Gospel, I dove in. Through previous work I was aware of the significance of the figure of Sophia and of the books of Sirach and Wisdom; as this commentary developed, I have become even more convinced that these books, particularly Wisdom, are essential intertext.

Through the experience of writing I have become more sensitive to a "boys' club" mentality in the church and, alas, in academia. I have been more vocal in demanding equal rights and participation and far less tolerant of excuses for misogyny.

Along the way I also experienced two brain aneurysms, and there were long months when I was unsure I could ever read again or hold a conversation. But here I am! Living life to the full with each day a gift.

Teaching, writing, zooming, and the Gospel still holds mystery and still draws me into its depths. I sense within another book beginning to make its presence felt—on John's model of salvation. As you read this work, you can probably already sense what I will emphasize—salvation as liberation into the fullness of life.

I finish with the words of John 15 that have always demanded my attention:

"Make your home in me—as I make mine in you" (15:4).

Works Cited

Abegg, Martin G., Peter W. Flint, and Eugene Charles Ulrich, eds. *The Dead Sea Scrolls Bible*. Edinburgh: T&T Clark, 1999.

Akala, Adesola Joan. *The Son-Father Relationship and Christological Symbolism in the Gospel of John*. LNTS 505. London: Bloomsbury T&T Clark, 2014.

The Apostolic Fathers. Volume 2: *The Shepherd of Hermas; The Martyrdom of Polycarp; The Epistle to Diognetus*. Translated by Kirsopp Lake. LCL. London: William Heinemann, 1917.

Aquino, María Pilar. "The God of Life and the *Rachamim* of the Trinity." In *Our Cry for Life: Feminist Theology from Latin America*, 130–38. Maryknoll, NY: Orbis Books, 1993.

Ashton, John. "The Transformation of Wisdom: A Study of the Prologue of John's Gospel." *NTS* 32 (1986): 161–86.

———. *Understanding the Fourth Gospel*. Oxford: Clarendon, 1996.

Asiedu-Peprah, Martin. *Johannine Sabbath Conflicts as Juridical Controversy*. WUNT 2/132. Tübingen: Mohr Siebeck, 2001.

Attridge, Harold W. "Genre Bending in the Fourth Gospel." *JBL* 121 (2002): 3–21.

———. "How Priestly Is the 'High Priestly Prayer' of John 17?" *CBQ* 75 (2013): 1–14.

Aune, David E. *The Cultic Setting of Realized Eschatology in Early Christianity*. NovTSup 28. Leiden: Brill, 1972.

Bacon, Hannah. "Thinking the Trinity as Resource for Feminist Theology Today?" *Cross Currents* 62 (2012): 442–64.

Baker, Lauren L. "Domestic Violence in the Domestic Church: An Argument for Greater Attention to Intimate Partner Abuse in Catholic Health Care." *Journal of Moral Theology* 7 (2018): 18–35.

Bakon, Shimon. "Creation, Tabernacle and Sabbath." *JBQ* 25 (1997): 79–85.

Balentine, Samuel E. "The Prophet as Intercessor: A Reassessment." *JBL* 103 (1984): 161–73.

Barker, Margaret. *The Gate of Heaven: The History and Symbolism of the Temple in Jerusalem*. London: SPCK, 1991.

Bauer, Walter, William F. Arndt, F. Wilbur Gingrich, and Frederick W. Danker. *Greek-English Lexicon of the New Testament and Other Early Christian Literature*. 3rd ed. Chicago: University of Chicago Press, 2000.

Beavis, Mary Ann. "The Deification of Mary Magdalene." *Feminist Theology* 21 (2012): 145–54.

————. "From Holy Grail to the Lost Gospel : Margaret Starbird and Mary Magdalene Scholarship." *Journal of Religion and Popular Culture* 27 (2015): 236–49.

————. "The Parable of the Slave, Son, and Vineyard: An Early Christian Freedman's Narrative (Hermas *Similitudes* 5.2-11)." *CBQ* 80 (2018): 655–69.

————. "Reconsidering Mary of Bethany." *CBQ* 74 (2012): 281–97.

Beavis, Mary Ann, and Ally Kateusz, eds. *Rediscovering the Marys: Maria, Mariamne, Miriam*, Scriptural Traces: Critical Perspectives on the Reception and Influence of the Bible 22. London: T&T Clark, 2020.

Bergmann, Claudia D. *Childbirth as a Metaphor for Crisis: Evidence from the Ancient Near East, the Hebrew Bible, and 1QH XI, 1-18*. BZAW 382. Berlin: de Gruyter, 2008.

Berkowitz, Beth A. "Reconsidering the Book and the Sword: A Rhetoric of Passivity in Rabbinic Hermeneutics." In *Violence, Scripture and Textual Practice in Early Judaism and Christianity*, edited by Ra'anan S. Boustan, Alex P. Janssen, and Calvin J. Roetzel, 145–73. Leiden: Brill, 2010.

Bernier, Jonathan. "Jesus, Ἀποσυνάγωγος, and Modes of Religiosity." In *John and Judaism: A Contested Relationship in Context*, edited by R. Alan Culpepper and Paul N. Anderson, 127–33. SBLRBS 87. Atlanta: SBL, 2017.

Bertram, Georg. "ἔθνος, ἐθνικός." *TDNT* 2 (1964): 364–69.

Beutler, Johannes. "Greeks Come to See Jesus (John 12:20 f.)." *Bib* 71 (1990): 333–47.

Bietenhard, Hans. "ὄνομα." *TDNT* 5 (1967): 243–81.

Bingemer, María Clara. "Mujer y Cristología. Jesucristo y la salvación de la mujer." In *Aportes para una Teología desde la Mujer*, edited by María Pilar Aquino. Nuevo Exodo 5. Madrid: Editorial Biblia y Fe, 1988.

————. "Reflections on the Trinity." In *Through Her Eyes: Women's Theology from Latin America*, edited by Elsa Támez, 56–80. Maryknoll, NY: Orbis Books, 1989.

Black, David A. "On the Style and Significance of John 17." *CTR* 3 (1988): 141–59.

Bodi, Daniel. "The Double Current and the Tree of Healing in Ezekiel 47:1-12 in Light of Babylonian Iconography and Texts." *WO* 45 (2015): 22–37.

Boismard, Marie-Emile. *Our Victory over Death: Resurrection?* Translated by Madeleine Beaumont. Collegeville, MN: Liturgical Press, 1999.

————. "Papyrus Bodmer II. Supplément de Jean." *RB* 70 (1962): 120–33.

Borgen, Peder. "The Use of Tradition in John 12:44-50." *NTS* 26 (1979): 18–35.

Borig, Rainer. *Der Wahre Weinstock, Untersuchungen zu Jo 15:1-10*. SANT 16. Munich: Kösel, 1967.

Boyarin, Daniel. *Border Lines: The Partition of Judaeo-Christianity*. Philadelphia: University of Pennsylvania Press, 2004.

———. "The Gospel of the Memra: Jewish Binitarianism and the Prologue to John." *HTR* 94 (2001): 243–84.

———. "How Enoch Can Teach Us about Jesus." *Early Christianity* 2 (2011): 51–76.

Brant, Pitre. *Jesus and the Last Supper*. Grand Rapids: Eerdmans, 2015.

Brooke, George J. "4Q252 and the 153 Fish of John 21:11." In *Antikes Judentum und Frühes Christentum*, edited by Bernd Kollmann, Wolfgang Reinbold, and Annette Steudel, 253–65. BZNW 97. Berlin: de Gruyter, 1999.

Brown, Jeannine K. "Creation's Renewal in the Gospel of John." *CBQ* 72 (2010): 275–90.

Brown, Raymond E. *The Death of the Messiah: From Gethsemane to the Grave*. ABRL. 2 vols. New York: Doubleday, 1994.

———. *The Gospel according to John*. 2 vols. AB 29–29A. New York: Doubleday, 1966, 1970.

———. *An Introduction to the Gospel of John: Edited, Updated, Introduced and Concluded by Francis J. Moloney*. ABRL. New York: Doubleday, 2003.

———. *Jesus God and Man*. Modern Biblical Reflections. New York: Macmillan, 1967.

———. "The Paraclete in the Fourth Gospel." *NTS* 13 (1966/1967): 113–32.

Bultmann, Rudolph. *The Gospel of John: A Commentary*. Translated by G. R. Beasley Murray et al. Oxford: Blackwell, 1971.

Burge, Garry H. *The Anointed Community: The Holy Spirit in the Johannine Community*. Grand Rapids: Eerdmans, 1987.

Byrne, Brendan. "The Faith of the Beloved Disciple and the Community in John 20." *JSNT* 23 (1985): 83–97.

———. *Lazarus: A Contemporary Reading of John 11:1-46*. Homebush: St. Paul, 1991.

———. *Life Abounding: A Reading of John's Gospel*. Collegeville, MN: Liturgical Press, 2014.

Campbell, Anthony F. *The Study Companion to Old Testament Literature: An Approach to the Writings of Pre-Exilic and Exilic Israel*. OTS 2. Wilmington, DE: Michael Glazier, 1989.

Carson, Donald A. "The Function of the Paraclete in John 16:7-11." *JBL* 98 (1979): 547–66.

———. *The Gospel according to John*. Grand Rapids: Eerdmans, 1991.

Cathcart, Kevin J., Michael Maher, and Martin McNamara, eds. *The Targum of the Minor Prophets*. The Aramaic Bible 14. Translated by Kevin J. Cathcart and Robert P. Gordon. Collegeville, MN: Liturgical Press, 1990.

———. *The Targum of Ezekiel*. The Aramaic Bible 13. Translated by Samson H. Levey. Collegeville, MN: Liturgical Press, 1990.

Charles, Robert Henry. "2 Bar 1:1–87:1." In *Pseudepigrapha of the Old Testament*. Bellingham, WA: Logos Research Systems, 2004.

Chennattu, Rheka M. *Johannine Discipleship as a Covenant Relationship*. Peabody, MA: Hendrickson, 2006.

Christensen, Duane L. "Nations." *ABD* 4 (1996): 1037–49.

Christensen, Michael J., and Jeffery A. Wittung, eds. *Partakers of the Divine Nature: The History and Development of Deification in the Christian Tradition*. Grand Rapids: Baker Academic, 2007.

Clark-Soles, Jaime. "Scripture Cannot Be Broken: The Social Function of the Use of Scripture in the Fourth Gospel." In *Abiding Words: The Use of Scripture in the Gospel of John*, edited by Alicia D. Myers and Bruce G. Schuchard, 95–117. RBS 81. Atlanta: SBL, 2015.

Collins, John J. *Jewish Wisdom in the Hellenistic Age*. Edinburgh: T&T Clark, 1997.

———. "The Works of the Messiah." *DSD* 1 (1994): 98–112.

Collins, Raymond F. " 'Blessed Are Those Who Have Not Seen': John 20:29." In *Transcending Boundaries: Contemporary Readings of the New Testament*, edited by Rekha M. Chennattu and Mary L. Coloe, 173–90. Biblioteca di Scienze Religiose 187. Rome: Libreria Ateneo Salesiano, 2005.

———. *These Things Have Been Written: Studies on the Fourth Gospel*. Louvain Theological and Pastoral Monographs 2. Louvain: Peeters Press, 1990.

Coloe, Mary L. *Dwelling in the Household of God: Johannine Ecclesiology and Spirituality*. Collegeville, MN: Liturgical Press, 2007.

———. " 'The End Is Where We Start From': Afterlife in the Fourth Gospel." In *Living Hope—Eternal Death?! Conceptions of the Afterlife in Hellenism, Judaism and Christianity*, edited by Manfred Lang and Michael Labhan, 177–99. Leipzig: Evangelische Verlagsanstalt, 2007.

———. "Gentiles in the Gospel of John: Narrative Possibilities—John 12:12-43." In *Attitudes to Gentiles in Ancient Judaism and Early Christianity*, edited by David C. Sim and James S. McLaren, 209–23. LNTS 499. London: T&T Clark, 2013.

———. *God Dwells with Us: Temple Symbolism in the Fourth Gospel*. Collegeville, MN: Liturgical Press, 2001.

———. *John 1–10*. WCS 44A. Collegeville, MN: Liturgical Press, 2021.

———. " 'A Matter of Justice and Necessity': Women's Participation in the Catholic Church." *Compass: A Journal of Topical Theology* 45 (2011): 13–18.

———. "The Mother of Jesus: A Woman Possessed." In *Character Studies in the Fourth Gospel: Narrative Approaches to Seventy Figures in John*, edited by Steven A. Hunt, D. Francois Tolmie, and Ruben Zimmermann, 202–12. WUNT 314. Tübingen: Mohr Siebeck, 2013.

———. "The Nazarene King: Pilate's Title as the Key to John's Crucifixion." In *The Death of Jesus in the Fourth Gospel*, edited by Gilbert van Belle, 839–48. BETL 200. Louvain: KUL, 2007.

———. "Welcome in the Household of God: The Footwashing in John 13." *CBQ* 66 (2004): 400–415.

Corley, Kathleen E. *Private Women, Public Meals: Social Conflict in the Synoptic Tradition*. Peabody, MA: Hendrickson, 1993.

Crockett, William R. *Eucharist: Symbol of Transformation*. Collegeville, MN: Liturgical Press, 2017.

Culpepper, R. Alan, and Jan G. van der Watt, eds. *Creation Stories in Dialogue: The Bible, Science, and Folk Traditions.* BibInt 139. Leiden: Brill, 2016.

Culpepper, R. Alan. *The Gospel and Letters of John.* IBT. Nashville: Abingdon, 1998.

———. "The Johannine *Hypodeigma*: A Reading of John 13." *Semeia* 53 (1991): 133–52.

———. "Nicodemus: The Travail of New Birth." In *Character Studies in the Fourth Gospel: Narrative Approaches to Seventy Figures in John,* edited by Steven A. Hunt, D. Francois Tolmie, and Ruben Zimmermann, 248–59. WUNT 314. Tübingen: Mohr Siebeck, 2013.

Daly, Robert J. "Eucharistic Origins: from the New Testament to the Liturgies of the Golden Age." *TS* 66 (2005): 3–22.

Daly-Denton, Margaret. *John: An Earth Bible Commentary; Supposing Him to Be the Gardener.* Earth Bible Commentary. London: Bloomsbury T&T Clark, 2017.

Davies, Phillip R., and Bruce D. Chilton. "The Aqedah: A Revised Tradition History." *CBQ* 40 (1978): 514–46.

De La Potterie, Ignace. "Genèse de la Foi Pascale d'après Jn. 20." *NTS* 30 (1984): 26–49.

———. "L'emploi du verbe 'demeurer' dans la mystique johannique." *NRTh* 117 (1995): 843–59.

———. *La Vérité dans saint Jean.* AnBib 73. 2 vols. Rome: Biblical Institute Press, 1977.

Dekle, George R., Sr. *The Case against Christ: A Critique of the Prosecution of Jesus.* Newcastle upon Tyne: Cambridge Scholars Publishing, 2011.

Delebecque, Édouard. *Évangile de Jean: Texte traduit et annoteé.* CahRB 23. Paris: Gabalda, 1987.

Dennis, John A. *Jesus' Death and the Gathering of True Israel: The Johannine Appropriation of Restoration Theology in the Light of John 11:47-52.* WUNT 2:217. Tübingen: Mohr Siebeck, 2006.

———. "The 'Lifting up of the Son of Man' and the Dethroning of the 'Ruler of this World': Jesus' Death as the Defeat of the Devil in John 12:31-32." In *The Death of Jesus in the Fourth Gospel,* edited by Gilbert van Belle, 678–91. BETL 200. Louvain: KUL, 2007.

Derickson, Gary W. "Viticulture and John 15:1-6." *BSac* 153 (1996): 34–52.

Dettwiler, Andreas. *Die Gegenwart des Erhöhten: Eine exegetische Studie zu den johanneischen Abschiedsreden (Joh 13,31–16,33) unter besonderer Berücksichtigung ihres Relecture-Charakters.* Göttingen: Vandenhoeck & Ruprecht, 1995.

Dodd, Charles H. *The Interpretation of the Fourth Gospel.* Cambridge: Cambridge University Press, 1970.

Douglas, Sally. *Early Church Understandings of Jesus as the Female Divine: The Scandal of the Scandal of Particularity.* LNTS 557. London: Bloomsbury T&T Clark, 2016.

Dupont, Liliane, Christopher Lash, and Georges Levesque. "Recherche sur la structure de Jean 20." *Bib* 54 (1973): 482–98.

Edwards, Denis. *Partaking of God: Trinity, Evolution, and Ecology*. Collegeville, MN: Liturgical Press, 2014.

Ehrlich, Uri, and Ruth Langer. "The Ealiest Text of the Birkat Haminim." *HUCA* 76 (2005): 63–112.

Elliott, Clifford A. S. "Crucified Woman [a sculpture], Reprint, 1982." *International Review of Mission* 71 (1982): 332–35.

Elnes, Eric E. "Creation and Tabernacle: The Priestly Writer's 'Environmental-ism.'" *HBT* 16 (1994): 144–55.

Emerton, John A. "The Hundred and Fifty-Three Fishes in John 21:11." *JTS* 9 (1958): 86–89.

Erez, Edna. "Domestic Violence and the Criminal Justice System: An Overview." *Online Journal of Issues in Nursing* 7 (2002).

Estes, Douglas. *The Questions of Jesus in John: Logic, Rhetoric and Persuasive Discourse*. BibInt 115. Leiden: Brill, 2013.

Evans, Craig. "Evidence of Conflict with the Synagogue in the Johannine Writings." In *John and Judaism: A Contested Relationship in Context*, edited by R. Alan Culpepper and Paul N. Anderson, 135–54. SBLRBS 87. Atlanta: SBL, 2017.

Evans, Craig, and Peter W. Flint. *Eschatology, Messianism, and the Dead Sea Scrolls*. Studies in the Dead Sea Scrolls and Related Literature. Grand Rapids: Eerdmans, 1997.

Feuillet, André. *Johannine Studies*. Staten Island: Alba House, 1965.

———. "L'heur de la femme (Jn 16:21) et l'heur de la Mère de Jésus (Jn 19:25-27)." *Bib* 47 (1966): 169–84.

———. "La recherche du Christ dans la nouvelle alliance d'après la Christophanie de Jo 20:11-18." In *Homme devant Dieu; Melanges offerts au Henri de Lubac*, 93–112. Théologie 56. Paris: Aubier, 1963.

Finlan, Stephen, and Vladimir Kharlamov, eds. *Theōsis: Deification in Christian Theology*. Cambridge: James Clarke, 2006.

Foerster, Werner. "εἰρήνη." In *TDNT* 2 (1964): 412–15.

Ford, Josephine Massyngbaerde. *Redeemer—Friend and Mother: Salvation in Antiquity and in the Gospel of John*. Minneapolis: Fortress, 1997.

Fortna, Robert T. *The Fourth Gospel and Its Predecessor: From Narrative Source to Present Gospel*. Philadelphia: Fortress, 1989.

Frey, Jörg. "Eschatology in the Johannine Circle." In *Theology and Christology in the Fourth Gospel: Essays by the Members of the SNTS Johannine Writings Seminar*, edited by Gilbert Van Belle, Jan G. van der Watt, and P. Maritz, 47–82. Leuven: Peeters, 2005.

———. *The Glory of the Crucified One: Christology and Theology in the Gospel of John*. Translated by Wayne Coppins and Christoph Heilig. BMSEC. Waco, TX: Baylor University Press, 2018.

Frey, Jörg, Jan G. van der Watt, and Ruben Zimmermann, eds. *Imagery in the Gospel of John: Terms, Forms, Themes and Theology of Johannine Figurative Language.* WUNT 200. Tübingen: Mohr Siebeck, 2006.

García Martínez, Florentino. *The Dead Sea Scrolls Translated: The Qumran Texts in English.* Leiden: Brill, 1994.

Genette, Gérard, and Marie Maclean. "Introduction to the Paratext." *New Literary History* 22 (1991): 261–72.

Goldenberg, David. "Racism, Color Symbolism, and Color Prejudice." In *The Origins of Racism in the West*, edited by Miriam Eliav-Feldon, Benjamin Isaac, and Joseph Ziegler, 88–108. Cambridge: Cambridge University Press, 2009.

Goranson, Stephen. "Nazarenes." In *ABD* 4 (1992): 1049–50.

Grabbe, Lester L. "Sanhedrin, Sanhedriyyot, or Mere Invention?" *JSJ* 39 (2008): 1–19.

Grigsby, Bruce H. "The Cross as an Expiatory Sacrifice in the Fourth Gospel." *JSNT* 15 (1982): 51–80.

———. "Gematria and John 21:11—Another Look at Ezekiel 47:10." *ExpTim* 95 (1984): 177–78.

Guest, Peggy. "The Personal Is Political: Women's Empowerment; Years of Speaking Truth to Power Have Improved the Legal System." *St. Louis Post-Dispatch.* May 24, 2011.

Gundry, Robert H. " 'In My Father's House Are Many *Monai'* (John 14:2)." *ZNW* 58 (1967): 68–72.

Haenchen, Ernst. *John 2: A Commentary on the Gospel of John Chapters 7–21.* Translated by R. W. Funk. Hermeneia. 2 vols. Philadelphia: Fortress, 1984.

Hakola, Raimo. *Identity Matters: John, the Jews and Jewishness.* NovTSup 18. Leiden: Brill, 2005.

Haran, Menahem. "The Divine Presence in the Israelite Cult and the Cultic Institutions." *Bib* 50 (1969): 251–67.

Harrington, Daniel J. "Can New Testament Interpreters Use Rabbinic Literature? Review Article." *STRev* 48 (2005): 335–40.

Hauck, Friedrich. "παροιμία." *TDNT* 5 (1967): 854–56.

———. " περισσεύω." *TDNT* 6 (1968): 58–61.

Hays, Richard B. *Echoes of Scripture in the Letters of Paul.* New Haven: Yale University Press, 1989.

Healey, Joseph P. "Peace." *ABD* 5 (1996): 206–7.

Heil, John P. "Jesus as the Unique High Priest in the Gospel of John." *CBQ* 57 (1995): 729–45.

Heise, Jürgen. *Bleiben: Menein in den johanneischen Schriften.* HUT 8. Tübingen: Mohr Siebeck, 1967.

Hengel, Martin. "The Old Testament in the Fourth Gospel." In *Scriptures of Israel*, edited by Craig Evans and W. Richard Stegner, 380–95. JSNTSup 104. Sheffield: Sheffield Academic, 1994.

Hens-Piazza, Gina. *Lamentations*. WCS 30. Collegeville, MN: Liturgical Press, 2017.

Hoare, Josephine. "Job's Wife." In *Selected Poems*. St Kilda West, VIC: Presentation Sisters, 2019.

Holst, Robert. "The One Anointing of Jesus: Another Application of the Form-Critical Method." *JBL* 95 (1976): 435–46.

Hoskyns, Edwyn C. *The Fourth Gospel*. Edited by F. N. Davis. London: Faber & Faber, 1947.

———. "Genesis I–III and St John's Gospel." *JTS* 21 (1920): 210–18.

de Hulster, Izaak J. "The Two Angels in John 20:12: The Old Testament Background." *BN* 162 (2014): 97–120.

Hultgren, Arland. "The Johannine Footwashing (13.1-11) as Symbol of Eschatological Hospitality." *NTS* 28 (1982): 539–46.

Instone-Brewer, David. *Traditions of the Rabbis from the Era of the New Testament*. Vol. 1: *Prayer and Agriculture*. Grand Rapids: Eerdmans, 2004.

Jaubert, Anne. "L'image de la Vigne (Jean 15)." In *Oikonomia. Heilsgeschichte als Thema der Theologie. Oscar Cullmann zum 65. Geburtstag gewidmet*, edited by F. Christ, 93–99. Hamburg-Bergstedt: H. Reich Verlag, 1967.

Jensen, Robin Margaret. *Living Water: Images, Symbols, and Settings of Early Christian Baptism*. Leiden: Brill, 2011.

Johnson, Clifton H., ed. *God Struck Me Dead: Voices of Ex-slaves*. Eugene, OR: Wipf & Stock, 2010.

Johnson, Elizabeth A. *Ask the Beasts: Darwin and the God of Love*. London: Bloomsbury, 2014.

———. "Jesus and the Cosmos: Soundings in Deep Christology." In *Incarnation: On the Scope and Depth of Christology*, edited by Neils Henrik Gregersen, 133–56. Minneapolis: Fortress, 2015.

———. "Jesus, the Wisdom of God: A Biblical Basis for Non-androcentric Christology." *ETL* 61 (1985): 261–94.

———. "The Maleness of Christ." In *The Power of Naming: A Concilium Reader in Feminist Liberation Theology*, edited by Elisabeth Schüssler Fiorenza, 307–15. Maryknoll, NY: Orbis Books, 1996.

———. *Quest for the Living God: Mapping Frontiers in the Theology of God*. New York: Continuum, 2007.

———. *She Who Is: The Mystery of God in Feminist Theological Discourse*. New York: Crossroad, 1992.

———. *Women, Earth, and Creator Spirit*. The Madeleva Lecture in Spirituality. Mahwah, NJ: Paulist Press, 1993.

Juel, Donald. *Messiah and Temple*. SBLDS 31. Missoula, MT: Scholars Press, 1977.

———. *Messianic Exegesis: Christological Interpretation of the Old Testament in Early Christianity*. Philadelphia: Fortress, 1988.

Keener, Craig S. *The Gospel of John: A Commentary*. 2 vols. Peabody, MA: Hendrickson, 2003.

Kelly, Anthony J. *Upward: Faith, Church, and the Ascension of Christ.* Collegeville, MN: Liturgical Press, 2014.

King, Karen L. *The Gospel of Mary of Magdala: Jesus and the First Woman Apostle.* Santa Rosa, CA: Polebridge Press, 2003.

Kittel, Gerhard. "δοκέω, δόξα, δοξάζω, συνδοξάζω, ἔνδοξος, ἐνδοξάζω, παράδοξος." *TDNT* 2 (1964): 232–55.

Kitzberger, Ingrid Rosa. "Transcending Gender Boundaries in John." In *A Feminist Companion to John*, vol. 1, edited by Amy-Jill Levine with Marianne Blickenstaff, 173–207. London: Sheffield Academic, 2003.

Koester, Craig R. *Symbolism in the Fourth Gospel: Meaning, Mystery, Community.* Minneapolis: Fortress, 1995.

———. "Why Was the Messiah Crucified? A Study of God, Jesus, Satan and Human Agency in Johannine Theology." In *The Death of Jesus in the Fourth Gospel*, edited by Gilbert van Belle, 163–80. BETL 200. Louvain: KUL, 2007.

Kossen, H. B. "Who Were the Greeks of John XII.20?" In *Studies in John: Presented to Dr. J. N. Sevenster on the Occasion of His Seventieth Birthday,* edited by J. N. Sevenster, 97–110. NovTSup 24. Leiden: Brill, 1970.

Kovacs, Judith. " 'Now Shall the Ruler of This World Be Driven Out': Jesus' Death as Cosmic Battle in John 12:20-36." *JBL* 114 (1995): 227–47.

Labahn, Michael. "Peter's Rehabilitation (John 21:15-19) and the Adoption of Sinners: Remembering Jesus and Relecturing John." In *John, Jesus, and History*, vol. 2: *Aspects of Historicity in the Fourth Gospel*, edited by Paul N. Anderson, Felix Just, and Tom Thatcher, 335–48. Atlanta: SBL, 2009.

———. "Simon Peter: An Ambiguous Character and His Narrative Career." In *Character Studies in the Fourth Gospel: Narrative Approaches to Seventy Figures in John*, edited by Steven A. Hunt, D. Francois Tolmie, and Ruben Zimmermann, 151–67. WUNT 314. Tübingen: Mohr Siebeck, 2013.

LaCugna, Catherine Mowry. *God for Us: The Trinity and Christian Life.* San Francisco: HarperCollins, 1991.

La Verdiere, Eugene. *The Eucharist in the New Testament and the Early Church.* Collegeville, MN: Liturgical Press, 1996.

Lee, Dorothy A. "Abiding in the Fourth Gospel: A Case-Study in Feminist Biblical Theology." *Pacifica* 10 (1997): 123–36.

———. "Abiding in the Fourth Gospel: A Case Study in Feminist Biblical Theology." In *A Feminist Companion to John*, vol. 2, edited by Amy-Jill Levine, 64–78. FCNTECW 5. London: Sheffield Academic, 2003.

———. *Flesh and Glory: Symbolism, Gender and Theology in the Gospel of John.* New York: Crossroad, 2002.

———. *Hallowed in Truth and Love: Spirituality in the Johannine Literature.* Preston, VIC: Mosaic Press, 2011.

———. "Presence or Absence? The Question of Women Disciples at the Last Supper." *Pacifica* 6 (1993): 1–20.

———. "The Symbol of Divine Fatherhood." *Semeia* 85 (1999): 177–87.

Léon-Dufour, Xavier. *Lecture de l'Évangile selon Jean.* Vol. 4. Paris: Éditions du Seuil, 1996.

Liddell, Henry G. "ἀδελφός." In *A Lexicon: Abridged from Liddell and Scott's Greek-English Lexicon.* Oak Harbor, WA: Logos Research Systems, 1996.

———. "χάρις". In *A Lexicon: Abridged from Liddell and Scott's Greek-English Lexicon.* Oak Harbor, WA: Logos Research Systems, 1996.

Lieu, Judith M. *Image and Reality: The Jews in the World of the Christians in the Second Century.* Edinburgh: T&T Clark, 1996.

———. "The Mother of the Son in the Fourth Gospel." *JBL* 117 (1998): 61–77.

———. *Neither Jew nor Greek? Constructing Early Christianity.* SNTW. Edinburgh: T&T Clark, 2002.

Lightfoot, John. *A Commentary on the New Testament from the Talmud and Hebraica.* 4 vols. Peabody, MA: Hendrickson, 1979.

Lightfoot, R. H. *St. John's Gospel: A Commentary.* London: Oxford University Press, 1956.

Lincoln, Andrew T. *The Gospel according to Saint John.* BNTC. London: Continuum, 2005.

———. *Truth on Trial: The Lawsuit Motif in the Fourth Gospel.* Peabody, MA: Hendrickson, 2000.

Loader, William. "Wisdom and Logos Tradition in Judaism and John's Christology." In *Reading the Gospel of John's Christology as Jewish Messianism: Royal, Prophetic, and Divine Messiahs,* edited by Benjamin E. Reynolds and Gabriele Boccaccini, 303–34. AGJU 106. Leiden: Brill, 2018.

Lohse, Eduard. *Die Texte Aus Qumran: Hebräisch und Deutsch.* Munich: Kösel-Verlag, 1971.

———. "ῥαββί, ῥαββουνί." *TDNT* 6 (1968): 961–65.

Louw, J. P., and E. A. Nida. "δακρύω." *Greek-English Lexicon of the New Testament: Based on Semantic Domains.* 2nd ed. 2 vols. New York: United Bible Societies, 1996.

———. "ἐμβριμάομαι." *Greek-English Lexicon of the New Testament: Based on Semantic Domains.* 2nd ed. 2 vols. New York: United Bible Societies, 1996.

———."καθαίρω." *Greek-English Lexicon of the New Testament based on Semantic Domains.* 2nd ed. 2 vols. New York: United Bible Societies, 1996.

Maier, Christl M. *Daughter Zion, Mother Zion: Gender, Space, and the Sacred in Ancient Israel.* Minneapolis: Fortress, 2008.

Malatesta, Edward. "Blood and Water from the Pierced Side of Christ (Jn 19,34)." In *Segni e Sacramenti nel Vangelo di Giovanni,* edited by Pius-Ramon Tragan, 165–81. SA 67. Rome: Editrice Anselmiana, 1977.

———. *Interiority and Covenant: A Study of εἶναι ἐν and μένειν ἐν in the First Letter of Saint John.* AnBib 69. Rome: Biblical Institute Press, 1978.

———. "Literary Structure of John 17." *Bib* 52 (1971): 190–214.

Malina, Bruce. "The Received View and What It Cannot Do: III John and Hospitality." *Semeia* 35 (1986): 171–89.

Manns, Frédéric. *L'Évangile de Jean à la lumière du Judaïsme*. SBFA 33. Jerusalem: Franciscan Printing Press, 1991.

———. "Le Lavement des Pieds. Essai sur la structure et la signification de Jean 13." *RSR* 55 (1981): 149–69.

Marcus, Joel. "*Birkat Ha-Minim* Revisited." *NTS* 55 (2009): 523–51.

Martínez, F. García, and Eibert J. Tigchelaar. *The Dead Sea Scrolls Study Edition: IQI-4Q273*. Leiden: Brill, 1997.

McCaffrey, James. *The House with Many Rooms: The Temple Theme of Jn 14,2-3*. Rome: Biblical Institute Press, 1988.

McEleney, Neil J. "153 Great Fishes (John 21,11)—Gematriacal Atbash." *Bib* 58 (1977): 411–17.

McFague, Sallie. *Body of God: An Ecological Theology*. Minneapolis: Fortress, 1993.

———. *Models of God: Theology for an Ecological, Nuclear Age*. Minneapolis: Fortress, 1987.

———. "Mother God." In *Motherhood, Experience, Intuition, Theology*, edited by Anne Carr and Elisabeth Schüssler Fiorenza, 138–42. Concilium 206: Religion in the Eighties. Edinburgh: T&T Clark, 1989.

McNamara, Martin. "'To Prepare a Resting Place for You': A Targumic Expression and John 14:2f." *MilS* 3 (1979): 100–107.

McWhirter, Jocelyn. *The Bridegroom Messiah and the People of God: Marriage in the Fourth Gospel*. SNTSMS 138. Cambridge: Cambridge University Press, 2006.

———. "Messianic Exegesis in the Fourth Gospel." In *Reading the Gospel of John's Christology as Jewish Messianism: Royal, Prophetic, and Divine Messiahs*, edited by Benjamin Reynolds and Gabriele Boccaccini, 124–48. AJEC 106. Leiden: Brill, 2018.

Meeks, Wayne A. *The Prophet-King: Moses Traditions and the Johannine Christology*. NovTSup 14. Leiden: Brill, 1967.

Meier, John P. *A Marginal Jew: Rethinking the Historical Jesus*. Vol. 2: *Mentor, Message, and Miracles*. ABRL New York: Doubleday, 1994.

———. *A Marginal Jew: Rethinking the Historical Jesus*. Vol 3: *Companion and Competitors*. ABRL. New York: Doubleday, 2001.

Menken, Maarten J. J. *Old Testament Quotations in the Fourth Gospel: Studies in Textual Form*. CBET 15. Kampen: Kok Pharos, 1996.

———. "The Translation of Ps 41:10 in John 13:18." *JSNT* 40 (1990): 61–79.

Metzger, Bruce M. *A Textual Commentary on the Greek New Testament: A Companion Volume to the United Bible Societies' Greek New Testament*. 4th rev. ed. London: United Bible Societies, 1994.

Michaelis, Wilhelm. "κράτος." *TDNT* 3 (1965): 905–15.

———. "ὁδηγός, ὁδηγέω." *TDNT* 5 (1967): 97–102.

Michel, Otto. "Μισέω." *TDNT* 4 (1967): 683–94.

———. "οἶκος, οἰκία." *TDNT* 5 (1967): 119–34.

Moloney, Francis J. "Can Everyone Be Wrong? A Reading of John 11:1–12:8." *NTS* 49 (2003): 505–27.

———. *Glory not Dishonor: Reading John 13–21*. Minneapolis: Fortress, 1998.

———. *The Johannine Son of Man*. Biblioteca di Scienze Religiose 14. 2nd rev. ed. Rome: LAS, 1978.

———. "The Johannine Son of Man Revisited." In *Theology and Christology in the Fourth Gospel*, edited by Gilbert Van Belle, Jan G. van der Watt, and P. J. Maritz, 177–202. BETL 184. Leuven: Peeters, 2005.

———. *John*. SP 4. Collegeville, MN: Liturgical Press, 1998.

———. *Love in the Gospel of John: An Exegetical, Theological, and Literary Study*. Grand Rapids: Baker Academic, 2013.

———. "The Parables of Enoch and the Johannine Son of Man." In *Parables of Enoch: A Paradigm Shift*, edited by James H. Charlesworth and Darrell L. Bock, 269–93. London: Bloomsbury, 2013.

———. "A Sacramental Reading of John 13:1-38." *CBQ* 53 (1991): 237–56.

———. "'That All May Be One': The Theme of Unity in John 17." In *Johannine Studies 1975–2017*. WUNT 372. Tübingen: Mohr Siebeck, 2017.

———. "Who Is the Reader?" *ABR* 40 (1992): 20–33.

Moss, Babara A. "'And the Bones Come Together': Women's Religious Expectations in Southern Africa, c 1900–1945." *The Journal of Religious History* 23 (1999): 108–27.

Mounce, William D. *Basics of Biblical Greek: Grammar*. Grand Rapids: Zondervan, 1993.

Neyrey, Jerome H. *The Gospel of John*. NCBC. Cambridge: Cambridge University Press, 2007.

Nissinen, Martti. "Song of Songs and Sacred Marriage." In *Sacred Marriages: The Divine-Human Sexual Metaphor from Sumer to Early Christianity*, edited by Martti Nissinen and Risto Uro, 173–218. Winona Lake, IN: Eisenbrauns, 2008.

O'Connell, Matthew J. "The Concept of Commandment in the Old Testament." *TS* 21 (1960): 351–403.

Obermann, Andreas. *Die christologische Erfüllung der Schrift im Johannesevangelium*. WUNT 83. Tübingen: Mohr Siebeck, 1996.

O'Day, Gail R. "John." In *The Women's Bible Commentary*, edited by Carol A. Newsom and Sharon H. Ringe, 293–304. Louisville: Westminster John Knox, 1992; exp. ed., 1998.

O'Day, Gail R., and Susan Hylen. *John*. WBC. Louisville: Westminster John Knox, 2006.

Painter, John. "The Farewell Discourses and the History of Johannine Christianity." *NTS* 27 (1981): 525–43.

———. "Identity in the Fourth Gospel." *The Covenant Quarterly* 72 (2014): 247–60.

Parsenios, George L. "'No Longer in the World' (John 17:11): The Transformation of the Tragic in the Fourth Gospel." *HTR* 98 (2005): 1–21.

Paulson, Graham. "Towards an Aboriginal Theology." *Pacifica* 19 (2006): 310–20.

Piper, Ronald A. "The Characterisation of Pilate and the Death of Jesus in the Fourth Gospel." In *The Death of Jesus in the Fourth Gospel*, edited by Gilbert van Belle, 121–62. BETL 200. Louvain: KUL, 2007.

Plaskow, Judith. "Standing Again at Sinai: Jewish Memory from a Feminist Perspective." *Tikkum* 2 (1986): 28–34.

———. *Standing Again at Sinai: Judaism from a Feminist Perspective.* New York: HarperCollins, 1990.

Pryor, John W. *John: Evangelist of the Covenant People; The Narrative and Themes of the Fourth Gospel.* London: Darton, Longman and Todd, 1992.

Radcliffe, Timothy. " 'My Lord and My God': The Locus of Confession." *NBf* 65 (1984): 52–62.

Ramos, Alex. "Bodmer Papyri." In *The Lexham Bible Dictionary,* edited by John D. Barry et al. Bellingham, WA: Lexham Press, 2016.

Rastoin, Marc. "Encore une fois les 153 poissons (Jn 21,11)." *Bib* 90 (2009): 84–92.

Reid, Barbara E. "Birthed from the Side of Jesus (John 19:34)." In *Finding a Woman's Place: Essays in Honor of Carolyn Osiek, R.S.C.J.,* edited by David L. Balch and Jason T. Lamoreaux, 191–214. Eugene, OR: Pickwick, 2011.

———. "The Spirit as the 'Feminine Face of God.' " In *Luke 1–9,* by Barbara E. Reid and Shelly Matthews. WCS 43A, p. 111. Collegeville, MN: Liturgical Press, 2020.

Reinhartz, Adele. "From Narrative to History: The Resurrection of Mary and Martha." In *A Feminist Companion to the Hebrew Bible in the New Testament,* edited by Athalya Brenner, 197–224. Sheffield: Sheffield Academic, 1996.

———. "Story and History: John, Judaism, and the Historical Imagination." In *John and Judaism: A Contested Relationship in Context,* edited by R. Alan Culpepper and Paul N. Anderson, 113–26. RBS 87. Atlanta: SBL, 2017.

———. *The Word in the World: The Cosmological Tale in the Fourth Gospel.* SBLMS 45. Atlanta: Scholars Press, 1992.

Rengstorf, Karl H. "λῃστής." *TDNT* 4 (1967): 257–62.

Reynolds, Benjamin E., and Gabriele Boccaccini, eds. *Reading the Gospel of John's Christology as Jewish Messianism: Royal, Prophetic, and Divine Messiahs.* AGJU 106. Leiden: Brill, 2018.

Ricoeur, Paul. *Interpretation Theory: Discourse and the Surplus of Meaning.* Fort Worth: Texas Christian University Press, 1976.

———. *The Rule of Metaphor: Multidisciplinary Studies of the Creation of Meaning in Language.* London: Routledge & Kegan Paul, 1977.

Riesenfeld, Ernst H. "Sabbat et Jour du Seigneur." In *New Testament Essays: Studies in Memory of Thomas Walter Manson,* edited by A. J. B. Higgins, 210–17. Manchester: Manchester University Press, 1959.

Riesner, Rainer. "Bethany Beyond the Jordan." *ABD* 1 (1992): 703–5.

Ringe, Sharon H. *Wisdom's Friends: Community and Christology in the Fourth Gospel.* Louisville: Westminster John Knox, 1999.

Ripley, Jason J. "Killing as Piety? Exploring Ideological Contexts Shaping the Gospel of John." *JBL* 134 (2015): 605–35.

Romeo, Joseph A. "Gematria and John 21:11: The Children of God." *JBL* 97 (1978): 263–64.

Rosik, Mariusz. "Discovering the Secrets of God's Garden: Resurrection as New Creation (Gen 2:4b–3:24; Jn 20:1-18)." *LASBF* 58 (2008): 81–98.

Rushton, Kathleen P. "On the Crossroads between Life and Death: Reading Birth Imagery in John in the Earthquake-Changed Regions of Otautahi Christchurch." In *Bible, Borders, Belonging(s): Engaging Readings from Oceania*, edited by Jione Havea, David Neville, and Elaine Wainwright, 57–72. SemeiaSt 75. Atlanta: SBL, 2014.

———. *The Parable of the Woman in Childbirth of John 16:21: A Metaphor for the Death and Glorification of Jesus*. Lewiston, NY: Mellen, 2011.

———. "The (Pro)creative Parables of Labour and Childbirth (John 3:1-10 and 16:21-22)." In *The Lost Coin: Parables of Women, Work, and Wisdom*, edited by Mary Ann Beavis, 206–29. BibSem 86. Sheffield: Sheffield Academic, 2002.

———. "The Woman in Childbirth of John 16:21: A Feminist Reading in (Pro) creative Boundary Crossing." In *Blood, Purity and Impurity: A Feminist Critique*, edited by Kristin de Troyer, Judith A. Herbert, Judith Ann Johnson, and Anne-Marie Korte, 77–96. Harrisburg, PA: Trinity Press International, 2003.

Sawicki, Marianne. *Seeing the Lord: Resurrection and Early Christian Practices*. Minneapolis: Fortress, 1994.

Schaeder, Hans H. "Ναζαρηνός, Ναζωραῖος." *TDNT* 4 (1967): 874–79.

Schlier, Heinrich. " παρρησία, παρρησιάζομαι." *TDNT* 5 (1967): 871–86.

———. "ὑπόδειγμα." *TDNT* 2 (1964): 32–33.

Schnackenburg, Rudolph. *The Gospel according to St John*. Translated by K. Smyth et al. HTCNT 3 vols. London: Burns & Oates, 1968–1982.

Schneiders, Sandra M. *Buying the Field: Catholic Religious Life in Mission to the World*. Religious Life in a New Millennium 3. New York: Paulist Press, 2013.

———. "The Face Veil: A Johannine Sign (John 20:1-10)." *BTB* 13 (1983): 94–97.

———. "The Foot Washing (John 13:1-20): An Experiment in Hermeneutics." *CBQ* 43 (1981): 76–92.

———. "History and Symbolism in the Fourth Gospel." In *L'Évangile de Jean: Sources, rédaction, théologie*, edited by M. de Jonge, 371–76. BETL 44. Gembloux: J. Duculot, 1977.

———. *Jesus Risen in Our Midst: Essays on the Resurrection of Jesus in the Fourth Gospel*. Collegeville, MN: Liturgical Press, 2013.

———. "The Johannine Resurrection Narrative: An Exegetical Study of John 20 as a Synthesis of Johannine Spirituality." DST [unpublished], Pontificia Universitas Gregoriana, 1975.

———. "The Resurrection (of the Body) in the Fourth Gospel: A Key to Johannine Spirituality." In *Life in Abundance: Studies of John's Gospel in Tribute to Raymond E. Brown, SS*, edited by John R. Donahue, 168–98. Collegeville, MN: Liturgical Press, 2005.

———. "Symbolism and the Sacramental Principle in the Fourth Gospel." In *Segni e sacramenti nel Vangelo di Giovanni*, edited by Pius-Ramon Tragan, 221–35. SA 67. Rome: Editrice Anselmiana, 1977.

———. "The Word in the World." *Pacifica* 23 (2010): 247–66.

————. *Written That You May Believe: Encountering Jesus in the Fourth Gospel.* Rev. and exp. ed. New York: Crossroad, 2003.

Scholtissek, Klaus. *In Ihm sein und bleiben: Die Sprache der Immanenz in den johanneischen Schriften.* Herders Biblische Studien 21. Freiburg: Herder, 2000.

Schrader, Elizabeth. "Was Martha of Bethany Added to the Fourth Gospel in the Second Century?" *HTR* 110 (2017): 360–92.

Schuchard, Bruce G. *Scripture within Scripture: The Interrelationship of Form and Function in the Explicit Old Testament Citations in the Gospel of John.* SBLDS 133. Atlanta: Scholars Press, 1992.

Schürer, Emil. *A History of the Jewish People in the Time of Jesus Christ.* Division 2, vol. 1. New York: Scribner, 1896.

Schüssler Fiorenza, Elisabeth. *In Memory of Her: A Feminist Theological Reconstruction of Christian Origins.* New York: Crossroad, 1983.

————. *Jesus: Miriam's Child, Sophia's Prophet; Critical Issues in Feminist Christology.* 2nd ed. London: Bloomsbury T&T Clark, 2015.

————. " 'Waiting at Table': A Critical Feminist The*logical Reflection on Diakonia." In *Changing Horizons: Explorations in Feminist Interpretation*, edited by Elisabeth Schüssler Fiorenza, 213–22. Minneapolis: Fortress, 2013.

————. *Wisdom Ways: Introducing Feminist Biblical Interpretation.* Maryknoll, NY: Orbis Books, 2005.

Seely, David R. "Arabah (Place)." *ABD* 1 (1992): 321–22.

Segovia, Fernando F. *The Farewell of the Word: The Johannine Call to Abide.* Minneapolis: Fortress, 1991.

————. *Love Relationships in the Johannine Tradition: Agape/Agapan in 1 John and the Fourth Gospel.* SBLDS 58. Missoula, MT: Scholars Press, 1982.

Seim, Turid Karlsen. "Descent and Divine Paternity in the Gospel of John: Does the Mother Matter?" *NTS* 51 (2005): 361–75.

Senior, Donald. *The Passion of Jesus in the Gospel of John.* Leominister: Gracewing, 1991.

Shelfer, Lochlan. "The Legal Precision of the Term 'παράκλητος.' " *JSNT* 32 (2009): 131–50.

Sheridan, Ruth. "The Paraclete and Jesus in the Johannine Farewell Discourse." *Pacifica* 20 (2007): 125–41.

————. *Retelling Scripture: 'The Jews' and the Scriptural Citations in John 1:19–12:15.* BibInt 110. Leiden: Brill, 2012.

Simoens, Yves. *La gloire d'aimer: Structures stylistiques et interprétives dans le Discours de la Cène (Jn 13–17).* AnBib 90. Rome: Biblical Institute Press, 1981.

Sinnott, Alice. "Wisdom as Saviour." *ABR* 52 (2004): 19–31.

Smith, D. Moody. "The Presentation of Jesus in the Fourth Gospel." *Int* 31 (1977): 367–78.

Smith, Yancy Warren. "Hippolytus' Commentary on the Song of Songs in Social and Critical Context." PhD diss., Brite Divinity School, 2009.

Soards, Marion. "The Question of a Premarcan Passion Narrative." In *The Death of the Messiah, from Gethsemane to the Grave: A Commentary on the Passion Narratives in the Four Gospels*, edited by Raymond E. Brown, 2:1492–1524. ABRL. New York: Doubleday, 1993.

Somerville, Margaret, and Tony Perkins. *Singing the Coast*. Canberra, A.C.T: Aboriginal Studies Press, 2010.

Stählin, Gustav. "θρηνέω, θρῆνος." *TDNT* 3 (1965): 148–55.

Stibbe, Mark. *John*. Readings: A New Bible Commentary. Sheffield: JSOT Press, 1993.

———. *John as Storyteller: Narrative Criticism and the Fourth Gospel*. SNTSMS 73. Cambridge: Cambridge University Press, 1992.

Strack, H., and P. Billerbeck. *Kommentar zum Neuen Testament aus Talmud und Midrasch*. 6 vols. Munich: C. H. Beck, 1922–1961.

Stuckenbruck, Loren T. "Evil in Johannine and Apocalyptic Perspective: Petition for Protection in John 17." In *John's Gospel and Intimations of Apocalyptic*, edited by Catrin H. Williams and Christopher Rowland, 200–232. London: Bloomsbury T&T Clark, 2013.

———. " 'Protect Them from the Evil One' (John 17:15): Light from the Dead Sea Scrolls." In *John, Qumran, and the Dead Sea Scrolls: Sixty Years of Discovery and Debate*, edited by Mary L. Coloe and Tom Thatcher, 139–60. EJL 32. Atlanta: SBL, 2011.

Swetnam, James. "Bestowal of the Spirit in the Fourth Gospel." *Bib* 74 (1993): 556–76.

Syreeni, Kari. "From the Bridegroom's Time to the Wedding of the Lamb: Nuptial Imagery in the Canonical Gospels and the Book of Revelation." In *Sacred Marriages: The Divine-Human Sexual Metaphor from Sumer to Early Christianity*, edited by Martti Nissinen and Risto Uro, 343–70. Winona Lake, IN: Eisenbrauns, 2008.

Thomas, John C. *Footwashing in John 13 and the Johannine Community*. JSOTSup 61. Sheffield: JSOT Press, 1991.

Thomas, Robert L. "שָׁלֵם, Shalem." In *New American Standard Hebrew-Aramaic and Greek Dictionaries: Updated Edition*. Anaheim, CA: Foundation Publications, 1998.

Thompson, Marianne Meye. *John: A Commentary*. NTL. Louisville: Westminster John Knox, 2015.

Tolmie, D. Francois. "Pontius Pilate: Failing in More Ways Than One." In *Character Studies in the Fourth Gospel: Narrative Approaches to Seventy Figures in John*, edited by Steven A. Hunt, D. Francois Tolmie, and Ruben Zimmermann, 578–97. WUNT 314. Tübingen: Mohr Siebeck, 2013.

———. "The Women by the Cross: Creating Contrasts," in *Character Studies in the Fourth Gospel: Narrative Approaches to Seventy Figures in John*, ed. Steven A. Hunt, D. Francois Tolmie, and Ruben Zimmermann, 618–21. WUNT 314. Tübingen: Mohr Siebeck, 2013.

Trocmé, Etienne. *The Passion as Liturgy: A Study in the Origin of the Passion Narratives in the Four Gospels*. London: SCM, 1983.

Van der Horst, Pieter. "The Birkat ha-minim in Recent Research." *ExpTim* 105 (1994): 363–68.

van der Watt, Jan G. "Angels in the Gospel according to John." *JECH* 1 (2011): 185–204.

———. *Family of the King: Dynamics of Metaphor in the Gospel according to John*. BibInt 47. Leiden: Brill, 2000.

Van Tilborg, Sjef. *Imaginative Love in John*. BibInt 2. Leiden: Brill, 1993.

Vermes, Geza. *Jesus and the World of Judaism*. London: SCM, 1983.

Vinson, Richard B. "Magdala." *NIDB* 3 (2008): 766.

von Rad, Gerhard. "שָׁלוֹם in the OT." *TDNT* 2 (1964): 402–6.

Voorwinde, Stephen. *Jesus' Emotions in the Fourth Gospel*. LNTS 284. London: T&T Clark, 2005.

Wallace, Daniel B. *Greek Grammar Beyond the Basics: An Exegetical Syntax of the New Testament*. Grand Rapids: Zondervan, 1996.

Wallace-Murphy, Tim. *Hidden Wisdom: Secrets of the Western Esoteric Tradition*. New York: Disinformation Co., 2010,

Warren, Cecelia. "What Do Angels Have against the Blind and the Deaf? Rules of Exclusion in the Dead Sea Scrolls." In *Common Judaism: Explorations in Second-Temple Judaism*, edited by Wayne O. McGready and Adele Reinhartz, 115–29. Minneapolis: Fortress, 2008.

Weidermann, Hans-Ulrich. "Eschatology as Liturgy: Jesus' Resurrection and Johannine Eschatology." In *The Resurrection of Jesus in the Gospel of John*, edited by Craig R. Koester and Reimund Beiringer, 277–310. WUNT 222. Tübingen: Mohr Siebeck, 2008.

Weiss, Herold. "Foot Washing in the Johannine Community." *NovT* 21 (1979): 298–325.

Westcott, B. F. *The Gospel according to St John: The Authorised Version with Introduction and Notes*. London: John Murray, 1890.

Willett, Michael E. *Wisdom Christology in the Fourth Gospel*. San Francisco: Mellen Research University Press, 1992.

Williams, Catrin H. "Isaiah in John's Gospel." In *Isaiah in the New Testament*, edited by Steve Moyise and Maarten J. Menken, 109–15. NTSI. London: T&T Clark, 2005.

Winston, David. *The Wisdom of Solomon*. AB 43. New York: Doubleday, 1979.

Witherington, Ben, III. *John's Wisdom: A Commentary on the Fourth Gospel*. Louisville: Westminster John Knox, 1995.

Yamaguchi, Satoko. *Mary and Martha: Women in the World of Jesus*. Maryknoll, NY: Orbis Books, 2002.

Young, Norman H. " 'The King of the Jews': Jesus before Pilate (John 18:28–19:22)." *ABR* 66 (2018): 31–42.

Zimmermann, Ruben. *Christologie der bilder im Johannesevangelium: Die Christo-poetik des vierten Evangeliums unter besonderer Berücksichtigung von Joh 10.* WUNT 171. Tübingen: Mohr Siebeck, 2004.

———. "Symbolic Communication between John and His Reader: The Garden Symbolism in John 19–20." In *Anatomies of Narrative Criticism: The Past, Present, and Future of the Fourth Gospel as Literature,* edited by Tom Thatcher and Stephen D. Moore, 221–35. SBLRBS 55. Leiden: Brill, 2008.

Zumstein, Jean. " Der Prozess der Relecture in der Johanneischen Literatur." *NTS* 42 (1996): 394–411.

———. "Jesus' Resurrection in the Farewell Discourses." In *The Resurrection of Jesus in the Gospel of John,* edited by Craig R. Koester and Reimund Beiringer, 103–26. WUNT 222. Tübingen: Mohr Siebeck, 2008.

———. *Kreative Erinnerung: Relecture und Auslegung im Johannesevangelium.* ATANT. Zürich: TVZ, 2004.

———. *L'Évangile selon Saint Jean (13–21).* CNT IVb 2nd ser. Genève: Labor et Fides, 2007.

Index of Scripture References and Other Ancient Writings

Genesis

1	91
1:1–2:4a	18–19, 475
1–3	316, 516
1:2	95
1:3-5	10
1:3	24–25, 214, 231
1:10-14	516
1:27	lxv, 5, 452
2:1-2	475
2:1	491, 508
2:2	337n9
2:4b–3:24	474
2:7	85, 496
2:8	111–12, 512n12, 513, 514n17, 517
2:9	513
2:15	515
2:17	517
2:21	493–94
2:23	5, 475, 494
3:3	475

3:5	517
3:8	514–15
3:16	453
3:18	453
3:20	475
3:21	494
6:17	85n3
7:22	85n3
9:8	58
12:6-7	119
12:7	494n46
13:10	514n17
15:18	58
17:1-2	218
17:1	25, 219n67, 229, 451
17:22	25
18:4	364, 365n15
22:1-10	440–41
22:6	487
24:10-33	110
24:10-21	111
24:38	386n11
25:24	230

26:24	167n14
28:3	219n67
28:12, 18-19	46
28:16-17	119
28:21	386n11
29	252
29:1-20	522
29:1-14	110
29:1-9	110
29:6	253n45
29:10	114–15
30:24	252
32:28	44
33:18-20	119
35:9-12	219n67
35:10	44
35:11	218, 229
46:31	386n11
48:3-4	219n67
48:15	275
49	358
49:10-12	54n3
49:10	197
49:24	275
49:25	218–19

Exodus

2:4	233
2:5	128
2:7-9	233
2:15-22	111
2:15-18	252
2:16-21	253n45
4:16	277n17
4:24-26	253
3:6	229
3:14	120–21, 167
4:1-9	163
4:30-31	163
6:3	229
7:1	277n17
7:3	71, 88, 152, 170
10:1-2	30
12:1-13	67
12:6	487
12:13	500
12:14-20	67
12:22	39, 491, 500
12:46	39, 499–500
13:14	276, 500n70
13:21	205, 217
14:24	217
14:26	197
15:1-18	233
15:6	276
15:20	233
15:21	233
16	181, 205
16:4	171n21, 172, 174
16:7	154, 181
16:8	181
16:10	154, 217
16:15	176
16:16	176
16:20	169
17	205
17:1-17	173
17:5-6	211
17:6	215
19–24	60
19:1	59
19:3	62
19:4	187
19:5	423
19:6	62, 138
19:9-12	62
19:9	217
19:10-11	58
19:15	58, 62–63
19:16	27, 58, 217
19:21	62
20:8-11	142
20:13	266
20:24	389
23:14-17	269
23:16	59n19, 195, 202
23:20	389n21
24	205
24:3	58
24:4	187, 357
24:15-16	337
24:15	217
24:16, 17	58, 154
25:1	337n9
25:8-9	337
25:9	369
25:19	512
26:33	389
27:21	142
28:3	96
30:11	337n9
30:14-16	68
30:17-21	365
30:17	337n9
30:22	337n9
30:23	338
30:34	337n9
31:1	337n9
31:12	337n9
32:17	440
33:7-11	65
33:17	250
34:10-16	61n27
34:22-23	162
34:22	59n19, 195, 202
34:29-35	511
35:5	337
37:7	512
40:9	337
40:33-34	338
40:33	337n9
40:34-38	217
40:34-35	278
40:34	23, 205
40:35	338

Leviticus

4:1-31	37
16	389
17:11	184
20:10	264
21:17-25	240n16
21:17-23	240
23:9-14	164
23:17	59n19
23:34-36	209
23:36	199, 210
23:40	227n89
24:3	264n7
24:16	203n28

Numbers

9:4-5	162
9:9-14	68
9:10-12	162–63
9:12	499
9:15, 17	217

11:16	65, 239n42	14:1	532	**Ruth**	
11:24	65	14:23	23	1:11	231
12:4-5, 10	65	15:21	240n16	2:14	415
14:27	181	16:6	23		
14:36	181	16:10	59n19	**1 Samuel**	
15:36	264n7	16:13	209	1	269
16:11	181	16:14	227n89	1:9	415
17:5	181	16:16	269	10:10	95
20:1	233	17:1	240n16	16:13	95
20:2	233	18:15-18	166	22:15	386n11
20:7-16	211	18:18	36,	28:7	128
20:9-11	215		118n28,		
21:6-9	100		200	**2 Samuel**	
21:16-18	197	19:15	152,	1:19	274
24:6	514n17		432n3	5:2	275
25:1-13	440	22:24	264	5:8b	240
26:10	30	27:17-18	515	7:7	275
27:18	95	27:26	422	7:11	477, 532
28:2-6	38n6	28:4, 11	230	12:1-14	251
28:26	59n19	31:14	65	14:2	127
		32:18	451n22	14:9	386n11
Deuteronomy		33:3	317	16:10	56n10
1:19	144n11	32:18	11, 458n5	19:22	56n10
1:41, 42	144n11	34	358		
2:14	144	34:9	96	**1 Kings**	
3:17	543n14	34:11	30	1	343n21
4:12	152			3:2	23
4:34	170	**Joshua**		4:25	44
5:6	500n71	2:12-13	74n23,	8:4-11	217
5:10	61n27		382n1	8:6, 8, 10	389
5:12-15	141	2:13	386n11	8:7	512
6:12-14	500n71	7:19	243n21	8:10-11	338
7:6	422	7:25	264n7	12:18	264n7
7:11	422	14:3-4	123n39	17:17-24	132n5
8:3	172, 174			17:18	56n10
8:16	174	**Judges**		18:12	95
12:5	23, 389	4:4	233n100	21:13	264n7
12:11	389	6:15	386n11		
12:21	389	9:18	386n11	**2 Kings**	
12:23	184	9:37	119	3:13	56n10
13:6, 9	440	11:12	56n10	4:23	141n3
13:10	500n71	16:31	386n11	4:42-44	164
13:18	440	21:21	415	14:25	216n59

22:14	233n100	22	256	**Proverbs**	
		22:18	488	1:1	258n67
1 Chronicles		23:1, 2	275	1:20	8
15:1	389n21	25:6	365	1:21	352
15:3, 12	389n21	28	199	2:1	103,
28:4	386n11	29:2	xlvi		318n14
28:11, 12, 18,		34:21	499	3:18	276, 474,
19	369	35:19	438		494
30:6-9	243n21	41:9	378	3:19	4
		41:10	369	4:23	211
2 Chronicles		45:4	278	5:15	211
1:4	389n21	45:10-15	522	8	xlvi, 2,
3:1	389	65:7	167		11n28
4:6	365	68	218	8:1	352
5:13	338	69	256	8:4	4
7:3	278	69:5	438	8:22-31	95, 276
7:20	278	69:7	256	8:22-29	4
10:18	264n7	74:7	389	8:22-23	2–3, 469
24:21	264n7	76:2	389	8:22, 25	1
30:8	278	77:19	167	8:22	xlvi, 4,
35:21	56n10	78:15-16	211		280, 541
		78:24-25	173	8:23-25	xlvi
Nehemiah		78:24	171n21,	8:23	318
6:14	233n100		173	8:27-31	318
8:1-3	24	80:1-16	423n58	8:27-30	276
8:8	23n59, 24	80:1	275	8:30-31	2–3, 318
8:13-18	195	80:8-11	418	8:31-36	4
		80:38	256	8:35	276
Job		81:6	272, 277	9:1-6	174–75,
1:13	415	82:6	532		231, 318,
1:21	231	89	347n35		458n4
3:11	231	89:9-10	167	9:1-3	xlvi
22:26	455	89:20, 26	532	9:1-2	537
28	2	107:23-30	166–67	9:1	362, 541
38:16	167	109	11n28	9:5-6	53, 168–69
38:28-29	451n22	113–118	196	9:5	xlvi, 537,
38:29	11	118:2	340		541
		118:15	276, 340	18:4	211
Psalms		118:25	198	26:7	258n67
2	11n28	118:26	341	31:16	415
2:2	532	120–134	198		
2:7	451n22	132	152	**Ecclesiastes**	
18:2	lxv	132:7	389	2:5	512n12

Song of Songs
1:2   61
1:5-8   253n45
1:5-6   27
1:6   415
1:12   520
2:3   61
2:4   353
3:1-6   520–21
4:12   116, 521
4:13-15   515
4:15   116, 521
4:16   521
5:1   521
6:2   521
8:12   415

Isaiah
1:13   141n3
1:29-30   515
2:2-4   196
5:1-7   423n58
5:1-2   418
6:10   348, 350
8:3   233n100
8:6   239
11:1-5   477
11:1   45, 477–78
11:2   96
11:11   122n36
12:3   211
25:6   61
26:17-19   451
26:19   151
27:2-6   423n58
27:12   122n36
30:18   422
40:3   37
40:6-9   13
40:11   256
41:4   220n69
41:10   167n14
41:14   186n58

41:16   186n58
41:18   197
41:20   186n58
42:1   349
42:14   11, 451, 458n5, 495n52
43:3   186n58
43:10   220n69
43:14   186n58
43:16   167
43:20   197
43:25   167n14, 220n69
44   215
44:3   214
44:28   275
45:18   220n69
45:19   167n14
46:4   220n69
48:13   276
49:9-10   256
49:15   17, 451n22, 458n5
50:10   348n36
51:3   514n17, 516
51:10   167
51:12   167n14, 220n69
51:15   167
52:6   210n31, 220n69
52:13–54:12 256
52:13   349
52:15   349
53   38
53:1   348–49
53:3   349
53:5   478
53:7   256n63
53:8-9   349

53:11   349
53:12   349
54:1   452
54:4-8   61n27
54:5-8   515
54:5   58
54:13   182
55:1-3   174n37
55:5   342n18
55:10-11   2
56:6-8   196
56:7   342n18
56:10   236n5
58:11   211
60:4   122
60:5-6   342n18
61:10   58
63:16   458n5
64:8   458n5
66:9a   11
66:11   452
66:12-13   451n22
66:13   11, 17, 458n5

Jeremiah
2:2   61n27, 62
2:21   418, 423
3:1-10   62
3:4-6   256
3:13   423
8:2   369n27
11:15   61n27
13:16   243n21
13:17   256
15:16   174
17:21-22   145
23:1-18   252n39
23:1, 2   275
23:3   122n36, 256
23:4   275
26:28   167n14

29:14	122n36
31:10	256
31:15	252
31:20	532
31:32	58
33:10-11	522
38:15	450
43:5-7	67n2
49:11-12	61
49:11	167n14
50:6	275
51:12	167n14

Ezekiel

2:2	95
3:3	174n37
8:4	23
8:14	522
8:16	199, 246n26
10:18-19	279
11:23	279
13:17	233n100
16	58
16:8-13	61n27
16:60-63	515
18:20	237
19:20	423n58
20:34	122n36
22:26	2
31:8	514n17
34	252n39, 256–57
34:2	275
34:4-5	251
34:5	255n59, 275
34:7-10	275
34:11-13	252
34:12	255n59, 275
34:13	122n36
34:15	275

34:23	256, 275
34:24	275
34:30-31	253n46
36:25-27	495
36:25-26	214
36:35	474n2, 512n12
37	123–25
37:1-10	95
37:14	2
37:21-22, 24	256
37:21	122n36
37:27	389
38:12	119
42:15	369
43:5	23
45:17	141n3
47	195, 208–9, 212–13, 215, 542–45
47:1-12	516
47:1	209, 211, 213
47:1, 3, 5, 8-9, 12	112
47:2	213
47:8-10	542–43
47:8	113
47:9	213

Daniel

7:13	46n34, 51–52
7:14	51
9:24	71
9:26	71
12:2-3	315
13	265

Hosea

1:2-9	61n27
2	58

2:2-10	61n27
2:2-5	117
2:13	141n3
2:16	117n24
2:23	515
6:11–7:1	122
11:1-4	10

Joel

2:28	233n100
3:1	214
3:8	197
4:18	61

Amos

8:5	141n3
8:11	174
9:11, 13-14	54n3

Micah

3:8	95
4:4	44
4:8-13	522
5:2-4	256
7:12	342n18

Nahum

3:6	369n27

Habakkuk

1:5	170n17

Zephaniah

3:8	341
3:9	342
3:14	341n17, 342
3:16	341, 343n21

Zechariah

2:11	342n18
3:8-10	44–45

3:8 477
3:9 46
3:10 44
6:9-13 477
6:11-12 502
6:12-13 478, 487
6:12 45, 477–78, 483
6:13 484
7:12 95
8:21-23 342n18
9–14 216
9:9 341–43
9:10 343
10:2-3 252n39
12:10 499
13:1 211, 516
14 212
14:8 211, 213, 543–44
14:16-19 196
14:16 342n18
14:20 196n9
14:21 70

Malachi
4:5 36
4:6 15n41

Tobit
2:1 59n19
6:11 12n29
13:16-18 71
14:4 71
14:5 71

Wisdom
1:7 4
1:13-14 131
1:13 176
1:15 91, 177
2:12-13 333

2:12 334
2:13 91, 103, 318n14
2:14 532
2:16-17 280, 333, 352
2:16 91
2:17-20 473, 503
2:23 91, 177, 313, 316
3:1-4 313
3:1 91, 316–17
3:2 91, 177, 316
3:4 443
3:5-6 431
3:5 443
3:9 317, 431
3:23 317
4:10-14 316
4:20–5:13 92
5:1 455
5:5 330, 455
5:9, 11 88n6
5:15 xlvii, 91, 99, 317, 318n16, 319, 328, 455
6:12-16 507
6:12 276
6:17-20 92
6:18 xlvii
7 2
7:7 401
7:22-27 276
7:22-24 1
7:22 xlix n12, 95–96
7:24-26 269
7:24 4
7:25-27 401
7:25-26 3, 4, 276

7:25 270n3, 278
7:26 217
7:27-28 426
7:27 xlvi, 3, 4, 11, 74, 318, 457
7:29-30 217
8:1 4, 96, 517
8:3 318
8:4-6 4
8:4 318
8:5-6 150
8:6 96n33
8:13 lxxvi n105, 177, 183, 319, 328
8:17-18 83, 105
8:17 xlvii, lxxvi n105, 96, 107, 317
8:21 xlvii, 3, 316
9:1 96
9:8-10 381
9:11 270n3, 278
9:17 96
9:18 96, 318
10:1 96
10:4 96
10:5 96
10:10 xlvii, 46, 93, 96, 318n16
10:13 96
10:15-21 xlvii
10:15-19 20
10:15 96, 193, 195, 258
10:17 139n6, 193, 195, 217, 232, 258–59

10:21	96n34
11:1-14	xlvii
11:4	96, 193, 195, 232, 258
11:6	259
11:7	96, 139n7
11:17	276
11:25	4
12:1	91, 96, 99, 177, 316–17
14:2	96n33
14:5	166n11, 167
14:6	276
15:16-17	150n28
16	181
16:2	96, 181
16:3	181
16:5-6	100
16:6	102
16:7	101
16:15	276
16:20-21	161, 177
16:20	96, 139n5, 171n21, 173, 176, 181
16:21	139n8
16:26	177n46
18	20
18:14-16	21
19:8	276
19:21	173, 176, 177

Sirach
1:1	318
1:4	4, 541
1:9-10	4
1:14-20	4
2:1	103, 318n14

4:10-11	103, 318n14
4:14	186n58
6:18-31	4
6:26-27	35
6:35	258n67
8:8	258n67
15:1-8	4
15:1-3	359
15:2-3	231
16:24–17:7	4
17:1-2	462
18:29	258n67
24	xlvi, 2, 3, 15, 418
24:1-34	20
24:1-17	95
24:1-2	457
24:1	401
24:2	278
24:3-5	276
24:3	4
24:4	3
24:7	4
24:8-18	278
24:8-12	xlvi, 318
24:8-11	3, 65, 419
24:8-10	230, 276
24:8	270n3, 352
24:9	541
24:10	14, 66, 193–94, 235, 270n3, 401
24:12	4
24:16-17	419–20
24:17	401, 418n47
24:18	218
24:19-33	4
24:19-22	4, 318
24:19-20	168, 187
24:19	231

24:21	175, 180, 183, 231
24:23	3, 65, 139n8, 141n1, 155, 175, 193, 259, 420
24:26-29	109
24:26	126
24:30-33	211
24:30-31	512n12
24:32-34	420
39:3	258n67
44:16	369
45:5	352n40
47:17	258n67
51	358
51:23	318

Baruch
3:9–4:4	155n39
3:36–4:1	175n38, 318
3:37–4:1	235
4:1	3, 66, 139n8, 155, 259

1 Maccabees
1:11-15	273
1:20-28	273
1:54	273
1:59	273
2:24-26	440
4:48	278
9:21	274
4:36-51	273
13:41	341
14:12	44

2 Maccabees
1:18-36	273
4:7-10	273

6:28	369	16:19	525	6:30-44	163–64
6:31	369	16:23	226	6:51	255n57
7:9	86, 90n15,	18:18-20	525	7:29	134
	315	18:22	525	7:33	132
7:10-11	86	20:61	66	7:34	132
7:14	315	21:2	340	8:1-10	163
10:1-6	273	21:11	476	8:6	164
10:36	272n6	21:12-13	66	8:33	226
12:32	59n19	24:20	356n5	10:17	170n17
		25:1-13	49n43, 521	10:45	40
3 Maccabees		25:31-46	316	10:47	476
2:5	369	26:6-13	335	11:1	340
2:9	278	26:20	355	11:15-19	66
2:16	278	26:26	356	14:3-9	335
		26:36	474	14:12, 13,	
2 Esdras		26:61	71	14, 16	187
1:19	174n36	26:71	476	14:14	356
		27:37	45n32,	14:17	187, 355,
4 Maccabees			477n7		356
1:29	514n17	27:48	490	14:20	187
6:19	369	27:55-56	188	14:32	187, 356,
17:23	369	27:61	509		474
		28:1	509	14:57	66
				14:58	71
New Testament				15:24	256n63
Matthew		**Mark**		15:26	45n32,
1:2-20	495n50	1:1-11	36		477n7
1:2-17	542	1:16-20	376	15:34	256n63
2:17-18	450	1:24	56n10, 476	15:36	256n63,
2:18	252	1:30	47		490
3:1-17	36	1:31	134	15:40-41	188, 355,
5:37, 47	255n57	1:41	132		503
6:3	170n17	2:19, 20	521	15:47	509
8:5-13	131n1	2:24	170n17	16:1	509
8:26	167	3:13-19	187	16:6	476
8:29	56n10	3:22	40		
9:15	521	4:39	167	**Luke**	
9:18	131n1	5:7	56n10	2:7	496
10:1-11	187	5:29	134	2:36-38	189
10:2	321, 509n3	5:40	134	2:41	269
10:25	40	5:41	132	3:1-22	36
11:19	313	5:42	134	4:24	125
13:57	125	6:4	125	4:34	56n10, 476
14:13-21	163–64	6:6-13	43	5:1-11	539n5
15:32-39	163	6:7-13	187		

5:34, 35	521	8:32	256n63	3:29	245n23
6:12-16	187	10:14	331	6:11	liv n32
6:13	356n5	10:32	321, 509n3		
6:15	321, 509n3	11:13	321, 509n3	**Ephesians**	
7:1-10	131n1	12:12	188n63	2:21	388n20
7:4	131n1	16:14-15	188n63	5:2	259
7:36-50	335	17:31	151n30	5:22–6:9	74n22
7:44	363	18:2	189n65		
8:2	321, 509n3	18:19	189n65	**Philippians**	
8:25	167	19:1-7	li	2:9	40
8:28	56n10	21:9	189		
9:1-6	187	26:24	258n66	**Colossians**	
9:1	356n5			3:19–4:1	74n22
9:10-17	163	**Romans**		4:15	188n63
9:10	356n5	2:6-10	151n30	4:18	liv n32
10:38-42	321, 322n23	3:1	255n57		
		3:24	40	**2 Thessalonians**	
13:13	134	3:25	259	3:17	liv n32
15:1-2	106	5:6-7	40		
16:1	356n5	8:32	40	**1 Timothy**	
17:5	356n5	9:6-8	245n23	2:1, 8-15	74n22
19:30	340	10:9	40	3:1-13	74n22
19:45-48	66	16:1-2	lvi, 188	3:15	388n19
21:38	261	16:3	189n65		
22:3	355	16:7	188n64	**2 Timothy**	
22:11	356n5			4:1	151n30
22:14	356n5	**1 Corinthians**		4:19	189n65
22:20	356	3:16-17	388n20		
22:30	355	6:19	388n20	**Titus**	
22:39	356n5, 474	10:21	165	2:1-19	74n22
		11:5	189		
23:38	45n32, 477n7	11:20	165, 357	**Philemon**	
		16:1	liv n32	1:2	188n63
23:55	509	16:18	189n65		
23:56	509			**Hebrews**	
24:1	509	**2 Corinthians**		1:8	528n56
24:51	518	5:10	151n30	2:17	260
24:53	261	5:19	40	3:2-6	388n19
		6:16	388n20	4:11	368
Acts of the Apostles		9:1	255n57	7:11, 15, 17	188n60
1:9	518			8:6	368
1:23	321, 509n3	**Galatians**		9:23	368
2:46	527n51	3:6-7	245n23	9:26	260
5:42	527n51	3:28	452	10:12	260

James
5:10 368

1 Peter
2:5 388n19
4:5 151n30
4:17 388n19

2 Peter
2:6 368

1 John
1:1-3 31
2:2 259
2:18-19 lx
2:18 226n86
2:22 226n86
4:8 417
4:10 259–60
4:16 417

2 John
7 226n86

Revelation
19:7 521
21:2, 9, 17 521

Old Testament Pseudepigrapha
2 Baruch
29:3 52n3, 165, 171, 274n12
29:5 54n3, 61, 274n12
29:6-8 174
29:8 165, 171, 274n12
30:1-2 347
77:11, 13-16 258–59

1 Enoch
42 280
42:1-2 318, 352

89:12-27 252n39

2 Enoch
33:1 527n53

Jubilees
1:4 182n52
1:5 154
1:7 154
1:20 40
1:26-27 154
1:28 71
3:9 509
6:1, 18 59
6:11 59
8:19 514n15
10:7 40
11:5 40
15:1 59
15:34 40
16:20 227
16:25 227
16:26 227
16:27 227
16:30 201, 221
18:17-19 487
32:27-29 199n19
49:2 40
50:10 141n3

Pss. Sol.
17:32 182n52

Mishnah, Talmud, and Related Literature
t. Abot
2.9 365n16

m. Berakot
9:5 365

t. Berakot
28b lii n23

m. Bekorot
8:7 68n4

m. Middot
3.2 493

b. Pesahim
5.5-6 493
68b 59

m. Qiddušin
1:7 138

m. Šabbat
7:2 241n18
8:1 241n18

m. Šeqalim
1:3 68
6:3 212–13

m. Sukkah
4:1 210
4:3, 5-7 197
4:5 196–97
4:6 198
4:8 210
4:9 195–96
5:3 198
5:4 198n18, 199, 205, 246
18:3 204

t. Sukkah
3:2 544
3:3 212–13

y. Sukkah
55a 215n55

m. Ta'anit
1:2 210

m. Tamid
7.4   527n52

m. Yadayim
3.5   27n71,
               519n31

m. Yoma
8:6   145n13

Targumic Texts
**Targum Neofiti
Genesis**
1:1   lv, 24

Targum Neofiti Exodus
24:17   24
40:34   23

Josephus
Antiquities
12.325   272
17.253-254   78n39
18.2   78n39
18.3   503n77
18.4.1   118n27
20.43   78n39
Jewish Wars
6.6   515

Dead Sea Scrolls
4Q174
1:1-3   71

11Q19
col. 29   119

4QFlor
1:11   477, 532

4QpGen
5:3-4   477, 532

1 QS
4:4   170n17
9:9-11   533n71

1 QH
5:36   170n17

Apostolic Fathers
Letter of Barnabas
12:5-7   101n43
15:8-9   527

1 Clement
34.7   165

Didache
9.3   165n8
9.4   165
10.7   357
13.3   357

Damascus Rule
1:1   170n17
2:14   170n17
13:7   170n17

**Shepherd of Hermas,
Similitudes**
5.2.7-8   427n68

Nag Hammadi
Acts of Peter
36–41   546n27

*Classical and Ancient
Christian Writings*
**Ambrose of Milan, On
Virgins**
1.5   496

Aristotle
Ethica nicomachea
9.8.9   427

*De generatione
anamalium*
1.20   5n11, 21

**Apostolic
Constitutions**
2.24   266

Augustine, *Homilies on
the Gospel of John*
48.9   277–78

Clement of Alexandria,
The Instructor
1.6   496

Diogenes Laertius,
Lives
10.120   427

*Didascalia
Apostolorum*
7.2.23   266

Epistle to Diognetus
6.3   lii–liv
10.2   liv

Eusebius
Historia ecclesiastica
2. 25.8   546n27
3.1.2   546n27
3.39.4   liv
3.39.16   261
6.14.7   28
Vita Constantini
3.28   512n13

Hippolytus, *In
Canticum canticorum*
25.3   189n64
25.6.7   lxxiv n98
25.6   188n64

Ignatius, *To Polycarp*
4.2   165

**Irenaeus, *Adversus
haereses***
3.1.1   liv

**Origen, *Commentary
on John***
13.169   126–27

Philo
On Flight and Finding
52   21
Leg All
3.162   173n30

De Fuga
137   175–76
139   176
QE Sup
2.1.2   338n11,
      365

Spec. Laws
1.207   365

Plato, *Symposium*
179b   427

**Seneca, *Epistulae
morales***
1.9.10   427

Tacitus, *Annals*
14.45   503n77
22.54   78n39

Tertullian
De Pudicitia
17.7   190
Scorpiace
15.3   546n27

**Theophylact
of Bulgaria,
*Joan.***
4.28ff.   127

Index of Modern Authors
and Subjects

Aaron, 365, 533

abiding, 158, 384, 387, 391, 406, 409–10, 415–18, 421–24, 428–29

aborigines, xlv, 26–27

Abraham, lxviii, lxxi, 16, 25, 41, 58, 119, 194, 201, 218, 221–30, 245, 254, 364–65, 440, 451

absence of Jesus, 26, 211, 314, 323–28, 354, 384, 388, 391, 419, 421, 432, 444, 460, 513, 528, 538

abundance, 149

abuse, 39, 75, 102, 375, 378–79

Adam, 96, 496, 509, 516

adoption, 10–11, 74

adultery, 117, 261–67

Advocate, 390, 434, 445–47

Alexandria, li

allegory, 29, 254, 407

Ambrose, 321, 496

Andrew, lv, 43, 47, 59, 125, 355, 376, 533

androcentrism, lxvi, 264

Annas, 479–80

anointing
    of Jesus's body at burial, 502, 509
    of Jesus's feet, 313–14, 319, 326, 333–39, 374, 377–78, 519–20

anonymity, 127–29

Anselm, 39, 437

anthropology, 5, 26, 91

anthropomorphism, 24–25

anti-Judaism, lxii–lxiii, lxxiii, 77–81, 227, 434

Antioch, li

Antiochus IV, 270, 272–73, 277

Antiochus Epiphanes, 274

apocalyptic, 40–41, 51, 71, 73

apostle(s), lvii, lxxiv, 126–27, 187

Arabah, 542–44

Aramaic language, xliii, 23, 25, 50–51, 114, 117, 211, 321

archaeology, 72, 75, 143

Arianism, 452

Aristotle, 189

ark of the covenant, 14, 112, 389, 512

arrest of Jesus, 205, 219, 272, 278–79, 334, 354, 361, 426, 441, 474–79, 540, 545

Ashton, John, lxxii

Assyrian Empire, 113

Astarte, 20

atonement, 39–41, 437, 500–501

Attridge, Harold, 358

audience, xliii, 7–8, 43, 236, 515

Augustine, Saint, 277–78

Aune, David, 388

Australia, xlv, 26–27, 409

author, Johannine, l, liv–lviii, lxxv, 8, 26, 50, 404, 408

authorities, Jewish, lxxiii, 66, 70, 78–79, 152, 243, 346, 486, 499–500

authority, lxviii, lxx, lxxiv, 70–71, 133–34, 142, 147, 152, 156, 158, 170, 194, 200, 204, 243, 351, 462, 485

Babylon(ians), 2, 20, 123, 142, 252, 270, 279, 516

Bacon, Hannah, 408

Balentine, Samuel, 466

baptism, li, 35–37, 48, 71, 93, 272, 390–92

Barabbas, 482–83, 500

Barnabas, li

Barrett, C. K., lx, 93

basileia, 97, 105–7, 481; *see also* reign of God, kindom of God

Bassler, Jouette, 103

Bathsheba, 127

Beavis, Mary Ann, xliv, 321, 519–22

Beck, David, 128

Bechtel, Lyn, lxii–lxiii

Beelzebub, 40

beginning, 1, 4, 9, 15, 17, 20

Beirne, Margaret, lxiii–lxiv

Belial, 40, 221, 346

belief, 8, 13, 18, 26, 33, 43, 83, 98–99, 103, 123, 150–51, 170, 180, 187, 219, 223, 226, 228, 246, 251, 257, 328, 348, 435, 457, 525

believer(s), xliv, liii, lix, lxviii–lxix, lxxvi, lxxx, 8, 10–12, 23, 41, 74, 77, 79, 81, 102–3, 105, 154–55, 159, 180, 182, 184, 207–10, 214–15, 228, 242–43, 245, 384, 387–90, 397–98, 402, 409, 418, 425, 428, 439, 457–71, 473, 491–92, 528–29, 547–48

Beloved Disciple, liv–lviii, lix–lx, lxiii, lxxx, 43, 62, 186, 376–79, 475,

489–90, 494, 509–12, 537, 539–40, 545, 547–48

Bergmann, Claudia, 454

Bernier, Jonathan, 433–34

Bethany, lv, lxxiv, 35, 102, 272, 315, 322–23, 335–36, 359, 374, 386, 508, 538–39

Beth-el, 46, 115, 119–20

Bethesda, lv, 134, 193, 200, 243

Bethsaida, 47, 125

Biale, David, 218–19

Bible, 8, 74–75

Bildrede, 407

birth(ing), xlviii–xlix, lxvii, lxx, lxxvi, 10–11, 17, 22–23, 63, 83–107, 117, 120, 148, 190, 197, 231, 444, 447–54, 494–98, 502, 508

blasphemy, 147, 203, 271, 276–78, 437

Blickenstaff, Marianne, lxiii

blindness, 31, 44, 200, 205, 216–17, 235–59, 348, 350

blood, 169, 184, 231, 253, 281, 439, 491, 493–95, 500, 508

Bloor Street United Church (Toronto), 504

Boyd, Arthur, 504–5

Boismard, Marie-Émile, 321

Book of Glory, lxxix, 313, 345, 353

Book of Jubilees, 145, 154, 464, 487, 509

Book of Signs, lxxviii–lxxix, 313, 339, 345, 353

Borig, Rainer, 403

Boyarin, Daniel, 16, 242–43, 433, 532

Branch, 44–45, 477–78, 483–84, 487–88

bread, lxiii, 31, 96, 139, 164, 278, 392, 548–49

    of life discourse, 168–86, 210, 376, 439

    unleavened, 66–68, 163

Brenner, Athalya, lxii

bride, 61

bridegroom, Jesus as, xliii, li, lxxix, 48–49, 54–56, 61, 103, 110, 118, 124–25, 132

Brown, Raymond, lix, lx, 93–94, 184, 403, 405, 459, 482, 529–30
Bultmann, Rudolph, lx, 79–80, 323, 363
Burge, Garry, 215
Byrne, Brendan, xliv

Cady Stanton, Elizabeth, lxi–lxii
Caiaphas, 329, 334, 473, 479
Cana, lv, lxii–lxiii, lxxiv, lxxviii–lxxix, 36, 47, 53–64, 94, 111, 118, 125, 132–33, 135, 494, 538
Canaan, 20, 418
Capernaum, 60–61, 72–73, 104, 132–33, 168
Chennattu, Rekha, xliv, 421–25
chief priests, 205, 216, 476, 484, 486
children, 10, 39, 102
    of God, xlix, lxix, lxxvi, lxxx, 8, 10–11, 16, 23, 41, 159, 210, 224, 228, 245, 329–30, 372, 375, 388, 425–26, 428, 435, 452, 455, 470, 473, 490–91, 494, 496, 503, 517–18, 523–24, 532, 539–41
    of Israel, lxviii, lxxi, 11, 20, 24, 44, 47, 62, 165, 252, 343
    of the devil, 223, 226
Christ, 120–21
Christianity, lii–liv, lxiv, lxxii–lxxiii, 8, 12–13, 27, 39–40, 42, 73, 79–80, 138–39, 151, 155, 245
Christology, xlviii, li, lix–lx, lxxv, 22, 25, 40, 74, 157, 211, 239, 375, 408, 450, 522, 541; *see also* Wisdom: Christology
circumcision, 204–5, 253, 273
class, lxxvi, 73
Clement of Alexandria, 496
Collins, John, J. 531
Collins, Raymond, 97
command(ment), 368, 371–72, 377, 410, 416, 421–23, 425
community, Johannine, lix–lx, 4, 9, 15–16, 48, 71, 73, 79, 81, 92, 102, 120, 135, 137–39, 150, 155, 168, 182,

185, 187, 210–11, 214, 236, 243, 245, 249, 279, 314, 348, 350–51, 355, 377–78, 391, 394–97, 408, 423–25, 429, 431, 438, 443–47, 453, 518, 528, 533, 537–49
Constantine, emperor, 74, 190
Conway, Colleen, lxiii, lxiv
cosmos, 7, 9, 10, 15, 17, 39, 221–22, 344
covenant, 58–60, 62–63, 65–66, 119, 124–26, 187, 205, 218, 273, 356–57, 421–25, 515
creation, xliv, xlv–xlvi, lxxvi, 2–5, 10–12, 18–20, 22–23, 91, 95–96, 111–13, 154, 196, 214, 231, 276, 281, 316, 318, 337, 409–10, 460, 468, 474–76, 491–94, 508, 515, 517, 523, 526–27
cross, xlix, lvi, lxix, lxxiv, 11, 20, 40, 45, 55, 57, 63, 94, 102, 231, 326, 338, 354–55, 361, 371, 373, 381, 394, 425–26, 457, 474–75, 479, 487, 489–92, 494, 499–500, 502, 507–8, 523, 540
crowd, 163–67, 169–72, 183–85, 202–5, 215–16, 226, 237, 264, 266, 328, 334, 340–41, 343–44, 347–48, 455, 485, 500
crucifixion, lvii, 39–40, 102, 210, 220, 259, 346, 354, 361, 371, 426, 436–37, 460, 481, 483–84, 486–89, 492–96, 500–505, 513, 527, 545
Culpepper, Alan, lxi, 97, 363, 369
Cyprian of Carthage, 260
Cyril of Alexandria, 321
Cyrus, King, 275

Daly, John, 471
Daly-Denton, Margaret, xliv, 515–17
D'Angelo, Mary Rose, lxix
darkness, 1, 10, 18, 26–27, 103, 235, 258, 270, 278, 323, 348, 351, 370–71, 510, 538
David, King, lix, 113, 119, 127, 251, 256, 274, 341, 369, 477–78, 532–33; *see also* messiah

da Vinci, Leonardo, 356
day(s), lxxix, 35–48, 53 58–60, 509–12, 522, 525–30
Day of Atonement, 72
Deacon Sophia, 190–91
dead, the, 149–51
Dead Sea, 113, 116, 542–44
Dead Sea Scrolls, l, lv, 23, 145, 464, 477, 531
death, 13, 42, 86, 90–93, 132, 148–49, 151, 183, 197, 264, 316–17, 323–29, 333–39, 423, 547–48
    of Jesus, lxix, 39–40, 57, 70, 73, 97, 154–55, 184, 199–200, 203, 220, 246, 256, 259–60, 272, 279, 313–15, 344–46, 351, 357–58, 366–67, 423, 437, 450, 452, 456, 465, 473–505, 518, 528–29, 533
Dedication, lxxix, 138, 269–81, 465
demon(s), lxviii
departure of Jesus, lxxx, 270, 314, 323, 352, 354, 367, 381, 438, 444, 456
Derickson, Gary, 414–15
Dettwiler, Andreas, 387–88, 402–3, 443–44
Deuteronomic tradition, 23
Deuteronomistic History, 262
Deutero-Isaiah, 182
devil, 40, 77, 221, 346, 363, 378–79, 486
Dewey, Johanna, 259
Didache, 357
Diocletian, emperor, 190
disability studies, 239–40
disciples, xlv, xlix, li, lvi, lxviii, lxxiv, lxxvii, lxxix–lxxx, 11, 32, 35–52, 66, 70–71, 79, 102–5, 121–22, 126, 163–67, 184–87, 211, 226, 237–38, 240, 314, 318, 323, 328, 338, 340, 352, 354–56, 364, 366–67, 371–79, 381–84, 387, 390–91, 394, 405–6, 409–12, 415–27, 435–41, 444, 447–52, 454–56, 457–71, 508, 510, 518–19, 522–30, 533, 537–49

former, 194, 226
    Wisdom's, 175–77, 180, 318
    wives of, 47
    women, 47, 188, 355, 508, 549
discipleship, lvi–lvii, lxv, 43, 47, 244–45, 355, 417, 421, 452, 495, 545
discourses, lxxviii, 11, 255, 354–55, 381–99, 401–30, 431–41, 443–56, 473, 495, 545–46
divine presence, 3, 4, 14, 195, 209, 214, 384–85, 388, 390, 463, 528
Dodd, C. H., 147, 157, 238
doubt, 121, 315
Douglas, Sally, xlvii, 4–5
dualism, l, 13–14, 18
Dunn, James, 226
dwelling, lxvii, lxix, lxxvi, 2–3, 14–15, 20, 23–26, 42–43, 47, 60–62, 65–81, 104, 124–26, 154, 193, 214, 231, 246, 270, 276, 278, 280, 384–85, 387–89, 409, 415–18, 425–29

earth, 112, 119
Easter proclamation, lxxiv
eating, 164, 168–69, 183–85, 187, 369–70, 500
ecclesiology, 9, 375–76, 421, 450
ecology, xliv, 468
eco-theology, 14, 468
Edwards, Matthew, 96
Egypt, xlvii, liii, 20, 39, 41, 141, 187, 252, 276, 500, 534–35
Eighteen Benedictions, lii
El'azar ben Pedath, Rabbi, 59
Elijah, 36–37, 88
El Shaddai, 218–19, 229, 451
Enoch, 369
Ephesus, li
epilogue, lxxix–lxxx, 538
Epistles, Johannine, lx, 74
eschatology, xlviii, lxxvi, 36–37, 42, 45, 51, 71, 86, 91–93, 96, 105, 118, 122, 148–49, 151, 165, 174, 180, 196–97,

199, 210–11, 214–15, 316–18, 324,
343, 346, 351, 428, 465, 491, 522, 527
realized, l, 51, 70, 99, 149, 151, 255,
318
resurrection, 316
eternity life, xlviii–xlix, lxxvi, lxxix,
22–23, 33, 51, 83, 91–92, 98–101,
103, 105, 114–16, 122, 124, 149, 151,
153, 155–56, 162, 169, 180–82, 184–
86, 229, 255, 276, 316–19, 324–29,
351, 411, 435, 439, 455, 460–64, 469,
473, 486, 532–33, 547–48
Eucharist, 161–62, 165, 184, 188–90,
260, 357, 370, 392, 471, 528
Eusebius, 261
evangelization, 48
Evans, Craig, 25, 433–34
Eve, 475, 494, 496, 517
evil, 13–14, 26, 36, 38, 40, 51, 86, 102,
346, 435, 437, 458, 464–66, 470, 486,
501
exaltation of Jesus, 57, 101–2, 220,
327, 345–46, 349, 381, 450, 456, 469,
503, 508
exile, 2, 11, 15, 20, 95, 114, 123, 182,
198–99, 237, 251–52, 256, 451
exodus, 65, 166, 187, 195, 232, 269,
273, 389, 500
exorcism, lxxv
Ezekiel, 95, 119, 123–24, 213, 237, 251,
255–57, 369
Ezra, 24

faith, 9–10, 47, 83, 95, 121, 131–35,
170, 185, 202, 249, 258, 273, 314–15,
323, 326–29, 416, 439, 508, 511, 514,
525, 528, 530
Father, lxvii–lxxi, 9, 11, 22, 62, 120,
142, 147–48, 156–59, 169–70, 172,
180, 182, 185, 194, 220–21, 224–25,
229–30, 255, 257, 275–76, 278, 280,
327, 383, 394–97, 405, 409, 411,
415–21, 427–29, 438–39, 444, 447,

452, 455, 458, 461–63, 467, 469–70,
503, 517, 529, 531–32
Father's house/hold, my, lxvii, lxix,
lxxvii, 60–61, 69–70, 74–76, 104,
125, 224, 231, 338, 359, 365, 369,
371, 375, 381–99, 409–11, 427,
465–67, 469, 473, 492, 508, 512,
529, 533, 540–42, 545, 547; *see also*
household of God
fatherhood, 194
feeding, 163–66, 168–69, 171
Fehribach, Adeline, 57
feminism, xliv, xlvii, lviii, lxiv, lxvi,
8, 14, 39–40, 47–48, 52, 127–28,
429–30
feminist criticism, lxi–lxvii, 156,
314–15
fertility, 197, 219
festivals/feasts, lxxi, lxxvii, lxxix, 58–
59, 66–67, 137–39, 141, 162, 194–95,
210, 269–71, 279–80
First Fruits. *See* Weeks
flesh, 12–14, 17, 32, 71, 89–90, 94, 157,
159, 169, 183–85, 214, 246, 279, 370,
385, 439, 460, 468
flood, 112
Foerster, Werner, 522–23
food, 122, 143, 168–69, 173–74, 193
footwashing, 313–14, 336–37, 354,
359–79, 381, 394, 412–13, 425, 436
forgiveness, 265–67, 278, 437, 501,
524, 547
Fortna, Robert, 321
friendship, 11, 62–64, 74, 105, 411,
418, 421–29, 457–58

Gadamer, Hans-Georg, 42
Galilee, l–li, lv, lxxviii–lxxix, 9, 23, 43,
78, 110, 120, 125–26, 162–63, 181,
200, 202, 216, 238, 540
Garden of Eden, 475, 487, 493, 501,
509, 514–17, 523
Garden of Gethsemane, 187, 474

garden, 474–76, 492, 502, 507–14, 515–17, 520, 527
gate, 251, 253–55
gematria, 541–45
gender, xlix, lxii–lxiv, lxvii, lxxv–lxxvi, 17, 20–21, 55, 73, 76, 94, 126, 190, 231–32, 497
  dualism, xlix
  of God, 156, 159, 397
Gentiles, xlv, lix–lx, 21, 72, 163–64, 343–46, 349–51, 398, 440
gift, 14–16, 18–19, 40, 96, 103, 122, 183–84, 205, 367–69, 371–73, 390, 494, 519, 528–29
glorification of Jesus, 57, 215, 314, 322–23, 340, 345, 349, 351, 358, 361, 390, 410, 420–21, 452, 461, 473–505, 508, 512, 514, 533
glory, 13–14, 23–24, 26–27, 31–32, 58, 60, 153–54, 270–72, 278–80, 322, 337–38, 350, 424–25, 460–62, 465, 541
Gnostics, Gnosticism, liv, lvii, 534–35
Golgotha, 102, 475, 500–501, 523
Good Shepherd, 255–56, 259–60, 364, 373, 381
Gospels, canonical, 4–5
grace, 14–15
Great Rift Valley, 543
Greek language, xliii, xlvi, lxxvi, 9, 12, 14–15, 17, 84, 94, 111, 114, 211, 233, 320, 522, 524
Greeks, lxxi, 86, 91, 343–47, 351
Green, Yosef, 252
Gregory of Nyssa, 27, 156
Grelot, Pierre, 212
Grigsby, Bruce, 487
Grills, Dorothy, 28
Guest, Peggy, 399
Gundry, Robert, 385–86
Günther, Eva, 4–5

Hadewijch of Brabant, 27
Haenchen, Ernst, 485
Hagar, 223–24

Hakola, Raimo, 433
Hanna, 269
Hanukkah. *See* Dedication
Haran, 115
harvest, 122–23, 126, 195, 419
Hasmonean period, 78
Hays, Richard, 419
healing, lxxv, 16, 32, 131–35, 142, 143–47, 152, 193, 204–5, 238–41, 245, 249
heaven, l, 3, 17–19, 46, 51, 99, 112, 119, 169, 171–81, 183–86, 209, 317, 347, 382, 387, 460, 518, 525
Hebrew language, xliii, xlvi, 12, 23–25, 45–46, 114, 185, 220–21, 233, 385, 389, 398, 477–78, 522, 541, 543
Hellenization, 272–73
heretics, lvii
hermeneutics, lx–lxvii, 22, 50, 77–81, 183, 402–3, 531
Herod, lv, 71, 104, 485
heterarchy, 75
hierarchy, 13, 72–76, 158, 411, 424
high priest, 138, 273, 479
Hildegard of Bingen, 501
Hippolytus of Rome, 520
historical-critical method, lx–lxi, lxvi, 77
holy of holies, lxxvii, 27, 72, 112, 199, 281, 512
Holy Spirit, 12, 446, 523
hour, lxxx, 55, 57, 94, 120, 203, 210, 214–15, 220, 314, 327, 338–39, 344–46, 351, 353–54, 360–64, 367, 371, 374–75, 381–82, 391, 394, 444, 447, 450, 452, 454–56, 461, 467, 473–505, 515–16, 523, 533
house church, 72–73
household, 142–43, 224, 374, 382, 386, 418, 499, 522–26
household of God, lxix, lxxvii, 41, 371, 374, 381–99, 425–28, 459, 501–2; *see also* Father's house/hold

humanity, lx, 3–4, 18, 26, 84, 120, 134,
157, 246, 375, 409, 435, 470, 497,
500, 524
human-one, 51–52, 99–101, 105, 169–
70, 184, 220, 246, 345
hyssop, 39, 490–91, 500

"I Am" sayings, lxiii, 120–21, 125,
167, 180–81, 201, 217–21, 229, 240,
280, 324
iconography, 156–59, 512
identity of Jesus, lvi–lvii, lxx, lxxiv,
lxxix, 44, 50, 54, 71, 104–5, 110, 118,
121, 193, 199–202, 205–6, 215–17,
219–21, 229, 241, 250, 271, 274,
277–78, 323, 339, 347, 458–60, 528,
531, 533, 541
idolatry, 156, 199, 270, 280
illness, 131–35, 145, 236, 238, 322–23,
328
imagery, xlvii, lxvi–lxvii, lxxvi, 5,
11, 17, 23, 58, 61–62, 112, 117, 122,
156–58, 183, 213–14, 255, 260, 342,
382, 405, 407, 411, 415–16, 419–21,
451–54, 466, 498, 502, 548
immersion. *See* baptism
immortality, 91–92, 107, 173, 176–77,
183–84, 316, 328
impurity, 68, 113, 453
incarnation, 4, 12–14, 23, 32, 46, 69,
92, 99, 157, 246, 460–61, 468, 500
inclusio, lxxvii–lxxviii, 362, 369, 435,
495
India, 425
Indigenous people, 26–27, 393, 409;
see also aborigines
indwelling, 63, 184, 384, 388–89, 402,
409, 411, 419–21, 424, 425–26, 428,
436–37
injustice, 188, 264, 375, 399, 425, 452
intertextuality, lxxvii
Irarrázaval, Diego, xlvii
Irenaeus, li, liv
irony, lxxviii, 244, 389, 484, 488, 513, 515

Isaac, 110, 487, 500
Isis, 20
Islam, lxiv
Israel, xlvii, lxvi, 2–4, 10–11, 14–16,
20–21, 24, 44, 57–58, 62, 66, 68, 71–
72, 86, 95, 99, 113, 123–25, 155, 170,
175, 181, 187, 195, 205, 255–57, 272,
275–77, 279, 318, 350, 418, 422–25,
438, 451, 515, 527, 532

Jacob, 3, 11, 44, 46, 96, 110, 114–16,
119–20, 124, 214, 218–19, 228–29,
231–32, 250, 252, 357
well of, 110–12, 115, 124
Jacob of Serugh, 496
Jamnia, li–lii, 137
Jeremiah, 252
Jerome, 541
Jerusalem, lv, lxxi, 37, 65–68, 83, 113,
119, 125, 138, 143, 152, 162, 190,
193–94, 196, 200, 202–3, 205, 269,
278–79, 323, 334, 339–51, 419, 499,
515
destruction of, 20, 142, 226, 236,
245, 249, 432
Jesus ben Sirach, 358
Jewish War, 138
"Jews," the, xliv, lii–liii, lxii, lxxi–
lxxix, 70–71, 73, 76–81, 105, 135,
137, 145–46, 169, 181–83, 185, 194,
202–4, 225–29, 236, 238, 242–45,
270–72, 276–80, 314, 350, 435,
480–81, 484–86, 492, 500, 502
Jews, lix, 20, 69, 112–13, 119–20, 203–
4, 314–15, 319, 323–28, 440, 533
leaders, 155, 215–17, 236, 258, 314–
15, 330, 333–34
John Chrysostom, 321
John, son of Zebedee, lv
John the Baptist, li, lv, lxxix, 10, 15,
18–19, 35, 36–37, 42–43, 46, 48–50,
54, 59, 61, 70, 103–5, 111, 135, 152,
272
disciples of, lix, 42, 47, 49

John Paul II, Pope, 331
Johnson, Elizabeth, 410, 429–30
Jonathan, 274
Jordan River, lv, 272, 278–79, 314,
    538–39, 543
Joseph, 96, 125
Joseph of Arimathea, 496, 502
Joseph, son of Jacob, 219, 252
Josephus, 118, 272, 515
Judah, 123–24, 515
Judaism, xliii, l, lii, lv, lx, lxii–lxv,
    lxxi–lxxiii, lxxvii, 4, 8–9, 12, 25, 36,
    40–41, 56, 66, 69, 73, 76–81, 85–88,
    90, 99, 105, 118, 132, 135, 138–39,
    145–46, 151, 172–77, 185, 194–99,
    204, 227, 245, 249, 273, 279, 236,
    348–49, 357, 364–65, 432–34, 436,
    438, 441, 444, 464–65, 483, 530, 533
Judas, 47
Judas Iscariot, lxiii, 47, 185, 337–38,
    354, 361–63, 369–71, 373, 376–79,
    383, 391, 441, 476, 486
Judas Maccabeus, 272
Judas Matthias, 273–74
Judea, l–li, lix, lxxi, 9, 23, 78, 102, 110,
    113, 120, 122, 124–26, 200, 272, 314
Judeans, 120
judgment, 51, 86, 92, 98, 103, 146–51,
    156, 158, 249–51, 265–66, 317,
    484–86, 508
Juel, Donald, 256, 478
Julius Caesar, 484
justice, 8, 86, 237, 316

Kidron Valley, lv, 402, 493, 515
kindom of God, 105–7
Kitzberger, Ingrid Rosa, lxxv
knowledge, 84, 95–96, 98
Koester, Craig, 44–45
Kopas, Jane, 56
Kovacs, Judith, 486
kyriarchy, xlix

Labahn, Michael, 376–77, 538

LaCugna, Catherine Mowry, 429–30
lamb, paschal, 37–39, 41–42, 46, 67–
    68, 162, 355, 487, 491, 493, 499–502
Lamb of God, lvi, 43, 499–502
language, xlvi–xlvii, xlix, lxiii, 17, 21,
    79, 84, 382, 402, 429–30, 449, 451
    "father," lxvii–lxxi, lxxvi, 156–59
    inclusive, 11, 52
    Johannine, lxii
    masculine, 17, 22, 52, 75
    sacramental, 183
last day, 151, 169, 180, 182, 200, 207,
    209–11, 213–15, 351, 485
Last Supper, 187, 355–57
Law, 11, 15, 73–74, 141–59, 164, 170,
    193–94, 200, 204, 238, 422, 438
Lazarus, xliv, lvii, lxxiv–lxxv, lxxx, 62,
    134, 279, 313–31, 334–40, 347, 359,
    374, 449, 455, 473, 511, 519
leadership, 236, 250–52, 254–55, 275,
    377, 546–47
Lee, Dorothy A., xliv, lxx, 13, 22, 63–
    64, 84–85, 148, 156–59, 247, 396–97,
    409, 429
letters, NT, 5, 10
Levine, Amy-Jill, lxiii
Levites, 195–96, 198, 239, 281, 440
liberation, 5, 22, 40–42, 105, 186, 223,
    252, 270, 473, 500–501
Lieu, Judith, xlviii, lii–liii, lxii, 245,
    450
life, lxiii, lxxvi, 7–8, 14, 21, 22, 32, 42,
    89–93, 95–96, 104, 116, 133, 146–51,
    155–56, 158, 180, 184, 197, 259, 278,
    317, 328, 474, 500
    after death, 86, 315–16, 319, 329
    Jesus as, 324–26
    of Jesus, 154–55
    See also water: living
light, lxiii, lxxix, 1, 10, 12, 14, 18–19,
    21, 26–27, 33, 97–103, 139, 193–94,
    198–99, 201, 210–11, 217, 236, 238,
    258–59, 270, 274, 280, 323, 348–49,
    351, 370–71, 510

Lincoln, Andrew, lxi
Lindars, Barnabas, 266
liturgy, lxx, 58–62
Logos, 17, 20–22, 25, 51, 134, 229, 246,
    390, 468–69, 489–90, 532; *see also*
    Word
Lord, title, 185, 246
Lord's Supper, 188
Lot, 96
love, lxx, 32, 42, 62–64, 102, 158–59,
    255, 257, 322, 353, 362, 364, 371–75,
    377–78, 405, 410–11, 415–18, 421,
    423, 425–26, 428, 437, 457–58, 461–
    62, 464, 469–70, 497, 507, 545–47
Lowe, Malcom, 78

Maccabees, 86, 138, 270, 278, 341, 369
Magdala, 335
maleness of Jesus, 5, 13, 21
man born blind, lxiii, 32, 51, 128, 134,
    194, 235–47, 278
manna, 161–62, 165, 169, 171, 172–77,
    180–81, 183–86, 205, 232
Manns, Frédéric, 26, 196, 362, 364
Manoah's wife, 127
manuscript tradition, 207–8, 224–25,
    319–21, 530, 538
Mark, 40
Markus, Joel, 433
marriage, 48, 61–62, 70, 74, 76, 103,
    110–11, 116–17, 124, 519–22
Martha of Bethany, xlv, lvi–lvii, lxii–
    lxiii, lxxiv–lxxv, 47, 62, 134, 186,
    314–31, 336–37, 355, 374, 508, 519,
    533
Martyn, J. Louis, lii–liii, 79, 137, 236
Mary Magdalene, xlv, xlix, lvi–lvii,
    lxiii, lxix, lxxiv, 47, 56, 61, 76, 134–
    35, 186–87, 210, 319–22, 334–35,
    355, 377, 449, 508–10, 512–22
Mary of Bethany, xliv, lvi–lvii, lxii–
    lxiii, lxxiv–lxxv, 47, 61–62, 76, 134,
    186, 314–31, 334–39, 355, 359, 374,
    377–78, 449, 508, 519, 521

mashal, 407
Masoretic Text, 350, 542–43
Massyngbaerde Ford, Josephine, 450
Mastema, 40
McCaffrey, James, 382
McWhirter, Jocelyn, 61, 256
meal, lxxx, 106, 188, 354, 356, 362–63,
    378, 449, 471
Mediterranean, 20, 543–44
Meeks, Wayne, 483
Meier, John P., 321
Memra, 24–26, 532
men, xlvii, l, lxiii–lxiv, lxvi, 5, 13, 40,
    50, 61–62, 72, 94, 106, 269, 281, 415
Méroz, Christianne, 233
messiah, lix, lxxiv, 37, 43, 120–21, 124,
    174, 217, 229, 271, 274–76, 347, 478,
    530–33
metaphor, lxiii, lxxi, 10–11, 17, 26–27,
    73, 107, 159, 183–85, 255–56, 394–
    97, 407–9, 411–13, 452, 495, 497
Meyers, Carol, 75–76
Michaelis, Wilhelm, 447
Michelangelo, lxxvi
Middle East, 111
Midian, 252
midrash, xlix–l, 232, 252, 544, 548–49
ministry
    of disciples, 421, 424
    of Jesus, xliv, 66, 70, 122, 137, 214,
        270, 272, 314, 348, 351, 390, 444–
        45, 489, 494
miracles, lxxviii–lxxix, 115, 131–32
Miriam, 197, 232–33
Mishnah, 68, 145, 195, 198, 210, 212–
    13, 273, 365
misogyny, lxvi, 5
mission, 5, 43, 76, 102, 126, 420, 422
    of disciples, 419, 425, 469–70, 524,
        544–45
    of Jesus, 129, 158, 255, 314, 334,
        350–51, 364, 381, 418–19, 429,
        457, 459, 461–62, 467–68, 482,
        490, 518, 531, 541

misunderstanding, lxxviii
Modein, 273
model, 359–79
Moloney, Francis, xliv, lxi, 256, 326–27, 403–4
money changers, 66, 68–69
morality, 117, 145–46
Mosaic law, lxxi–lxxii, 16, 18–19, 59, 204, 245, 263, 265
Moses, lix, lxxi, 3, 15–16, 36, 43, 58, 62–63, 71, 88, 99, 110, 118, 120–21, 127, 139, 152, 154–55, 162–63, 167, 170–73, 180, 187, 194, 197, 200–201, 203–5, 215, 221, 228–29, 232–33, 244–45, 250, 252–54, 337–38, 356–57, 365, 369, 451, 491, 511, 516, 533
  prophet-like-Moses, 37, 118–19, 166, 171, 197, 200, 216
Moss, Barbara, 398
mother(ing), lxviii, 9, 11, 17, 84–85, 94, 97, 105, 451, 453, 497–98
mother of Jesus, xlv, lxiii, lxxi, lxxiv, lxxix, 53–64, 66, 76, 104–5, 128, 132, 134–35, 227, 269, 427, 475, 489–90, 494, 508
mountain, 163
Mount Gerizim, 118–19
Mount Moriah, 389, 502
Mount of Olives, 199, 263, 279
Mount Sinai. *See* Sinai
Mount Sion, 119
mourning, 327, 448–49, 499, 508–9
mutuality, 63, 148, 158, 276, 397, 423, 430
mysticism, 26–27

Nag Hammadi, 534–35
narrative criticism, lxi, lxvii
Nathan, 251
Nathanael, lvii, 43–47, 59, 125, 155, 355, 538, 541
nations, 113, 123, 196, 217, 224, 256, 341–43, 349, 351, 515

nature, 13
Nazareth, 45, 125, 476–79
Nazarene, 476–79, 484, 487, 492, 502, 508
Neoplatonism, 14
Neusner, Jacob, 69
New Testament (NT), lxvii, 5, 8, 39, 40, 74, 76, 187–90, 357, 368, 449–50, 520
Nicodemus, xlviii, lxiii, lxxiv, lxxviii–lxxix, 83–107, 114, 117, 120, 135, 144, 183, 207, 216, 219, 231, 255, 391, 491, 494–96, 502, 516
Niditch, Susan, 224
night, 88, 103, 238, 370–71
Nineveh, 516
Noah, 58, 96, 112, 276, 517
Northern Kingdom, 113

obedience, 170, 238, 260
O'Day, Gail, lxii, 17, 262, 374–75, 411
Old Testament (OT), lv, 4, 8, 10, 12–13, 18–22, 25, 27, 30, 36, 40, 44, 58, 61, 86, 92, 110–11, 123–25, 154, 174, 211, 250, 256, 368–69, 386, 389, 418–22, 440–41, 449–51, 460, 522
oppression, lxiv, lxxiii, 102, 273
oral tradition, 86
ordination, 188, 357, 471
Origen, 126–27, 321
other disciple, lv–lvi, lviii, 43
Oxyrhynchus, liv

Painter, John, 432, 443, 470
Palestine, 25, 114, 543
Papias, liv, 261
parable, lxxviii, 147–48, 224, 236, 248, 250–51, 253–60, 323, 345, 382, 407, 452–53
Paraclete, 62, 70, 366–67, 383–84, 387–92, 397–99, 403, 411, 415, 434–36, 439–40, 444, 445–47, 456, 463
Park, In-Hee, 106–7
parousia, 410, 547

Parsenios, George, 459–60
paschal mystery, 42, 423
passion of Jesus, xliv, lxix, lxxviii, 23,
    57, 158, 238, 232, 358, 394, 412–13,
    423, 444, 447, 450, 456, 457, 459,
    461–63, 465, 467, 473–505
    narrative, 39, 335–36, 513, 518
Passover, lxxix, 38–39, 66–69, 83, 138,
    161–62, 164, 171, 186, 194, 210, 228,
    269, 278–80, 333–34, 353, 355–56,
    480–83, 487, 490–92, 499–502, 508,
    540
paterfamilias, 158, 396–97
patriarchy, xlv, xlix, lxiv–lxvi, 5, 11,
    22, 42, 44, 61–62, 72, 75–76, 150,
    157–58, 265, 394, 396
Paul, li, 10, 15, 40, 102, 316, 350–51,
    452, 547
Peacore, Linda D., 47–48
Peninnah, 269
Peter, lvi, lxiii, lxxx, 43, 47, 59, 125,
    185–86, 354, 361–62, 366–67,
    372–73, 376–79, 412, 441, 479–80,
    509–11, 525, 537, 539–41, 545–48
    mother-in-law, 134
Pharaoh's daughter, 128
Pharisees, xlviii, lxxi–lxxiii, 78, 85, 89,
    92, 103, 138, 205, 216, 219, 240–42,
    247–59, 263, 265–67, 329, 336, 343,
    345, 432
Philip, 43–44, 47, 59, 125, 155, 164,
    343, 382, 418
Phillips, Peter, 264–65
Philo, 21, 25, 172–73, 175–77, 365, 440
philosophy, 5, 12–14, 25, 150, 189,
    427–28
Phoebe, lvi
Photina, 127, 129; *see also* Samaritan
    woman
Pilate, lxiii, lxxi, 39, 45, 102, 277, 439,
    479–88, 500, 502, 546
Plaskow, Judith, l, 549
Pliny, 413–14
Plotinus, 13–14

pneumatology, 390
Poe, Garry, 27
Pollard, T. E., 148
pool of Siloam, lv, 195, 236, 238–39,
    258
postexilic period, 2–3, 86, 196, 256
postresurrection time, 70–71, 150,
    155, 159, 214, 373, 412, 425–26, 428,
    444, 447, 454, 456, 462–63, 544–45
power, 41, 75, 102, 128, 149–51, 157–
    59, 485–86, 501
prayer, 354, 452, 455, 457–71
presence
    in absence, 211, 384
    of God, 65–66, 71, 86, 120, 146, 202,
        270, 388, 460–61, 502, 512
    of Jesus, 26, 125, 323–28, 392, 469,
        518–19, 528, 549
priesthood, lxxi, 73, 138, 143, 188, 357,
    466, 471, 502, 512
Priestly tradition, 23
prologue, xlviii, lxvii, lxix, lxxvi,
    lxxix–lxxx, 1–33, 36–37, 46, 50, 69,
    71, 94, 103, 127, 154, 183, 202, 246,
    276, 280, 318, 329, 351, 362, 375,
    388, 420, 475–76, 489–90, 495, 518,
    531, 533, 538
prophets, 2, 65, 70–71, 95, 174, 256
    Jesus as, 117–21, 200, 217, 229, 241
    women, 134–35, 508
Prophets, Law and, 11, 155
purification, 36, 38, 68, 273, 337

Q source, 106
Qumran, 118–19, 477–78, 532

rabbis, 27, 59, 68, 73, 79, 137–39
    Jesus as, 85, 169
race, lxxvi, 27, 126
Rachel, 110–11, 114–16, 119, 124, 252,
    450
Radcliffe, Timothy, 529
Rahlfs, Alfred, 218
reader-response criticism, 81

Rebecca, 110–11
rebuke, 132
reconciliation, 40
Redman, Judith, 128
Reid, Barbara, xliv, 63, 451, 494–98
reign of God, xlviii, lxxviii, 36, 42, 86–87, 89–93, 98–99, 102–7, 346, 531
Reinhartz, Adele, liii, lxii, lxxii–lxxiii, 9, 56, 81, 127–28, 137–38, 326, 433
rejection, 10, 18, 21, 153, 158, 181, 205, 225, 250, 270–72, 279–80, 318, 350–52, 435, 438, 441, 486
relecture, 254, 402–4, 410–11, 431, 443, 447
remain(ing), 412–13, 416
resurrection, lxxx, 43, 73, 95, 149, 151, 154–55, 184, 210, 257, 279, 313, 326, 354, 366, 423, 447, 450, 508, 513, 527–29, 540
  bodily, 151, 184, 315–18, 329
  Jesus as, 324–26
  of the righteous, 86–87, 90, 92, 99, 103, 315, 328, 347
  on the last day, 180, 182, 317, 324
revelation, lxv, lxxii, 2, 4, 32, 51, 63, 99, 115, 121, 154, 159, 169, 180, 185, 447, 456, 461–62, 467–68, 518
rhetoric, 77, 80, 87, 121, 139, 177, 226, 314
Ricoeur, Paul, lxv, 42, 50, 394, 530–31
Riesenfeld, Ernst H., 526
righteous, xlviii, 3, 10, 40, 66, 86, 89–93, 98–99, 177, 237, 280, 315–17, 329, 445–46, 455, 532
Ringe, Sharon, xlviii, lxvi, 2
Roman Empire, 138, 433, 485
Romans, lxxi, 69, 71, 73, 329, 389, 437, 483
Rome, 138, 315, 394
royal official, lvii, lxiii, lxxi, lxxix, 131–35
Rubenstein, Jeffrey, 213
Ruel, 252

Ruether, Rosemary Radford, 48
ruler of this world, 40–41, 51, 221, 344–46, 394, 456, 464–65, 485–86, 500–501, 503, 524
Rushton, Kathleen, xliv, 107, 452–54, 497–98
Russell, Letty, 73

Sabbath, lxxix, 16, 18, 20, 138, 141–47, 148–49, 155–56, 193–94, 197, 200, 203–5, 209–10, 241, 255, 269, 278–79, 475–76, 491–92, 500, 508, 510, 526
sacrament, 29, 471
sacrifice, lxxi, 37–40, 67–70, 73, 138–39, 188, 259–60, 432, 500
Sadducees, 329
sages, 2, 4, 15, 65
salvation, 5, 21, 23, 32, 39–40, 95–96, 99–102, 105, 114, 120, 255, 276, 279, 318, 351, 402, 428, 473, 486, 500, 541
Samaria, lxxix, 9, 109–29
Samaritans, lix, lxxi, 112–13, 118–19, 120, 123, 125, 272
Samaritan woman, xlv, lvi–lviii, lxiii, lxxiv–lxxv, lxxviii–lxxix, 47, 56, 61, 76, 109–29, 131, 134–35, 172, 186–87, 208, 215, 228, 240–41, 378, 391–92, 467, 533
  as disciple, 121
Samson, 127
Sanhedrin, 138, 329
Sarah, 223–24
Satan, 26, 40, 221–22, 346, 370, 379, 482, 486
Saul, 274
Schnackenberg, Rudolph, 182, 254
Schneiders, Sandra, xliv, lvi–lviii, lxv, 28–33, 42, 48, 90–93, 222, 316, 326, 372, 377–78, 511, 514–15, 525
Scholtissek, Klaus, 402–3, 412, 417–18, 428
Schrader, Elizabeth, xliv, 319–22

Schüssler Fiorenza, Elisabeth, xlix, lxii, lxiv–lxv, 21–22, 39–40, 326, 375–76, 403

Scott, Martin, xlviii, 218–19

scribes, 263, 265–67

Scriptures, lxxvii, 4, 8, 11, 21, 23, 25, 36, 86, 95, 114, 138, 141, 152–55, 179, 182, 204, 211–14, 251, 256, 272, 277, 315, 340–43, 349, 354, 366, 385–86, 389, 403, 438, 488–89, 492–500

Sea of Galilee, 163, 166, 543

Sea of Tiberius, lv, 163, 184, 376, 544

Second Temple period, lxxvi, 23, 86, 90, 139, 172, 175, 213, 217, 221, 227, 259, 274, 280, 315, 435, 478, 516, 532–33

Segovia, Fernando, 407

seeing/sight, lx, 47, 83, 95, 98, 132, 194, 235–59, 348, 350, 447–48, 511, 514, 528

Septuagint, 30, 56, 86, 91, 93, 100, 120, 173, 185, 220, 277, 315, 350, 369, 389, 499, 515, 517, 524

serpent, 98–101

Servant Song(s), 256, 349–50

seven, 132–33

sexuality, 116

Shechem, 119

sheep, 236, 247–60, 275, 374

Shekinah, 23–26, 389–90, 451, 532

Shema, 452

Sheol, 86, 317

shepherd, 236, 247–60, 271, 274–76, 374, 546–47; *see also* Good Shepherd

Sheridan, Ruth, xliv, 76–81

signs, lviii, lxxviii–lxxix, 29–33, 53, 71, 83, 88, 95, 100, 105, 121, 123, 132, 135, 152, 163, 170–71, 180, 184–85, 250, 274–75, 339, 343, 361, 425, 511, 531

Simon Peter. *See* Peter

Simon of Cyrene, 487

sin, 12–13, 36–41, 46, 135, 145, 237, 240, 243–45, 250, 265–67, 435, 438, 500–501, 524–25

Sinai, xlvii, 14, 27, 58–60, 62, 154, 187, 277, 337–38, 356, 460

Sion, 112

slavery, 40, 42, 141, 186, 223–25, 252, 373, 470, 500–501, 516

slaves, lxxviii, 41, 366, 473, 500–501 ex-, 393

Smith, D. Moody, 391

Sobrino, Jon, xlvii

Solomon, 96, 113, 177, 338, 369

Son, 416–18, 427–29, 460–64, 467, 469–70, 473, 517, 529 of God, lxii, 43, 101, 133, 150, 277, 325–26, 484–85, 503, 530–33 of Man, 50–52, 246; *see also* human-one

Song of the Vineyard, 418–19

sonship, 224, 228

sons of Zebedee, 538, 541

Sophia, xlvi–l, lxii, lxxv, lxxvi, lxxix, 2–9, 14–15, 17, 20–24, 28, 40, 44, 46–47, 61, 66, 69, 73–74, 83, 91–92, 95–96, 101, 105, 107, 126, 141–59, 166–67, 175, 177–84, 187, 190, 193–233, 258–59, 269–81, 313–31, 333–52, 381–99, 401–30, 431–41, 443–56, 457–71, 473–505, 507–35, 537–49

Southern Kingdom, 113

Spirit, li, 62, 89–90, 93–96, 98–99, 102–4, 115, 120, 124, 159, 209–11, 214–15, 376, 393–94, 397–99, 409, 444, 463, 473, 491–92, 494, 508, 519, 522–25, 528–29 of truth, 390–92, 439, 445–47

spirituality, 13, 33

Stählin, Gustav, 449–50

St. Ann's Church, 190

Stephanus, Robert, 53

Stibbe, Mark, 491

structure, 5, 9, 12, 18–20, 59–60, 87, 142, 162, 168–69, 177–79, 181, 199–202, 236, 248, 271, 314–15, 333–34, 339, 360–62, 382–83, 405–7, 444, 458–60, 508–9, 538

Stuckenbruck, Loren, 464–65

suffering, 39, 102, 437, 450, 497

suffering servant, 38, 452

Sukkot, lxxix, 138, 193–233, 235–59, 262, 269, 276, 278–80, 392

supercessionism, 16, 71

Susanna, 265

Sychar, 112

symbol(ism), lxxvii–lxxviii, 23, 26–27, 28–33, 48–49, 70, 79, 100–102, 105, 111, 115–18, 122, 156–59, 208, 213, 230, 271, 394–97, 471, 488, 493, 499–501, 512, 527, 540–45

synagogue, li–lii, lix, 23, 25–26, 81, 114, 138–39, 155, 242–43, 245, 350, 398, 410, 431–41, 443, 480

Synoptic Gospels, li, lvii, lxxv, lxxviii, 28, 35–36, 43, 47–48, 66, 78, 86, 92, 105, 134, 163, 186, 263, 316, 339–40, 355–57, 376, 471, 474, 476, 480, 487, 490, 499, 508–9

Syreeni, Kari, 521

Syrophoenician woman's daughter, 134

tabernacle, 3, 8, 14–15, 20, 23, 46, 71, 143, 214–15, 231, 278, 337–38, 385, 419

Tabernacles. *See* Sukkot

Tannen, Deborah, 55–57

targum(s), lv, 23–26, 60, 114–15, 197, 211–12, 389, 478, 543, 548

teaching of Jesus, 95, 105, 162, 183, 185–86, 194, 200, 203–5, 265, 323, 334, 352, 354, 361, 367–69, 371–73, 480

temple, 4, 14, 23, 39, 45, 112–13, 138, 197–99, 270, 273, 278–81, 366,

371, 381–82, 384–85, 388–89, 410, 541–42

community as, l, 215, 388, 465, 522, 545

destruction of, 9, 59, 71, 73–74, 138–39, 211, 258, 432

eschatological, 195, 208–9, 213, 478–79, 488, 542–45

Jerusalem, lii, lv, lxvii–lxix, lxxi, lxxvii, 46, 65–74, 119, 143, 163, 203, 213, 263, 275, 338, 359, 365, 480

Jesus as, xliv, lxxvi–lxxvii, 23, 69, 71, 110–13, 116, 125–26, 213–16, 230, 278, 329, 385–86, 389, 465–67, 492, 502, 508, 516, 542

Temple Mount, 229, 279, 365

tent, 14–15, 20, 28, 65; *see also* tabernacle

Tertullian, 5, 321

testimony, 5, 12, 15, 18–19, 47–49, 59, 103–5, 123, 152, 187, 219, 245, 398, 409, 440, 489, 548

theodicy, 237

theology, xlv–xlviii, l, lxxv, lxxvii, 13–15, 19–20, 22, 29, 33, 36, 40, 44, 48, 66, 69–70, 86, 110, 126, 142, 146, 154, 156, 190, 221, 235, 246, 255, 260, 315–18, 388, 409, 417, 487, 489–90, 508, 511, 518, 541–45, 548

Theophylact of Bulgaria, 127

Theos, 17, 390, 469

Thomas, lviii, lxiii, 47, 187, 211, 323, 382, 444, 519, 525–30, 541

Thompson, Marianne, lxi

time, 49, 200, 209, 214, 238, 314, 333, 354, 456, 459, 462, 508, 510, 526

Toensing, Holly, 264

tomb

Jesus's, lvii–lviii, lxxiv, 40, 210, 339, 449, 509–14, 518–19, 522

Lazarus's, 326–28, 449, 511

Torah, lxxi–lxxii, 3–4, 15, 59, 73, 92, 138–39, 155, 161–62, 165, 172, 175,

182, 185–87, 197, 200, 205, 260, 279, 420, 432

Tosefta, 212–13, 543–44

Trinity, 63, 408, 429–30, 468

Trocmé, Etienne, 335

truth, 14, 32, 482

Twelve, the, lvii, 187, 355–57

type scene, 110–11

unbelief, 13, 18, 26, 33, 98–99, 150–51, 153, 348, 525

Underhill, Evelyn, 27

unity, 148, 421, 463, 467, 470, 488

Van der Horst, Pieter, 433

van der Watt, Jan G., 170, 407–8

Van Tilborg, Sjef, 427

Vermes, Géza, 50

Via Dolorosa, 190

vine and branches, 384, 402, 405–7, 409, 411–16, 418–25, 429, 436–37

violence, lxiv, 39, 227, 260, 330, 378–79, 433, 441, 498, 504

Von Baer, Karl Ernst, 189

von Wahlde, Urban C., 78

water, lxxix, 10, 18, 27, 31, 36, 57, 89–90, 93–94, 98–99, 111–29, 139, 143–44, 193–99, 205, 230–32, 236, 239, 258, 280, 391, 493–96, 508, 515–16

living, 113–17, 200–201, 206–15, 496, 515, 542

Water Gate, 195, 212–13

Way, 418

wedding at Cana, lxii, 36, 53–64, 103, 111, 427

Weeks, 58–60, 138, 194

weeping, 252, 327, 377, 449–50, 499, 512, 522

Westcott, Brooke F., lv

wilderness wanderings, 20, 28, 99, 144–46, 152, 173–74, 181, 195, 200, 205, 215–17, 232–33, 258, 389

Willett, Michael, 318

wind, 95, 98

wine, 31, 54–56, 61, 168, 490, 500

Wisdom, xlvi–xlvii, lxxv, lxxix, 2–11, 15, 20–21, 23, 31–32, 47, 66, 92, 95–96, 115, 155, 161–62, 168–69, 172–77, 180, 183, 185–86, 230–32, 258–59, 276, 280, 313–31, 352, 418–21, 426, 457, 474–75, 486, 515, 517, 538, 541

banquet, 169, 174, 353–58, 362

Christology, xlviii–xlix, lxii, 20, 139, 276, 319

wisdom literature, xlvi, xlviii–xlix, 8, 95, 126, 168, 174, 183

wisdom tradition, xlviii–xlix, 2, 180, 183, 232, 316, 318

wise woman of Tekoah, 127

witch of Endor, 128

Witherington, Ben, III, xlviii, lxii, 116, 421

witness, 10, 12, 15, 18, 35–37, 47–49, 54, 61–62, 70, 76, 98, 103–4, 109–29, 152–53, 219, 228–29, 254, 271–72, 275, 277, 470, 508, 519

woman caught in adultery, 56, 261–67

woman with hemorrhage, 134

woman with infirmity, 134

womb, 207–10, 230–32, 281, 345

women, xlv–xlvii, l, lvi, lxii–lxv, lxx, lxxiv–lxxv, lxxvii, 4–5, 8, 13–14, 39–40, 42, 47, 50, 61–62, 72, 75–76, 88–90, 94, 104, 106, 142–43, 188–90, 195, 197–98, 252–53, 260, 269, 280–81, 330–31, 342, 355–57, 374–75, 377–79, 397–99, 415, 429–30, 448–49, 452–54, 497–98, 501, 503–5, 508–9, 548–49

Word, li, lv, 2, 4, 7, 9–15, 17, 20, 23, 31–32, 69, 71, 88–89, 99, 123, 159, 172–77, 276–77, 318, 385, 419, 458, 460–62, 482, 518, 532, 538, 541

word of God, 172–77

work(s), 75–76, 106, 145, 148, 152, 157, 170, 238, 274–76, 278–79, 313–31, 438, 461, 476
world, 24–25, 120, 221–22, 345, 431–32, 434–35, 443–56, 457–58, 461, 463–66, 468–70, 480, 482, 492, 501, 507
World Council of Churches, 331
worship, 20, 26, 69–70, 120, 124, 193–94, 197–98, 236, 246–47, 279, 281, 398, 467, 526–27
 false, 117–18, 246
 true, 119
Writings, 11

Yamaguchi, Satoko, lxiii, lxxiv, 218, 339
Yavneh, li–lii, 79
Yee, Gale, 273
Yichrah, 24–26
Yohanon b. Beroka, 198

Zeus, 273
Ziegler, Joseph, 218
Zion, daughter of, 342, 452–53, 522
Zipporah, 111, 252–53
Zsengéller, Jozsef, 177, 180–81
Zumstein, Jean, 149, 151, 254, 366–67, 371, 402–3, 548

Author

Mary L. Coloe, PBVM, is a professor of New Testament within the University of Divinity in Melbourne, Australia. She has published books, essays, and articles on John for academics and nonprofessionals, some of which are listed at http://marycoloe.org.au/homepage/. For her revised dissertation, *God Dwells with Us: Temple Symbolism in the Fourth Gospel* (Liturgical Press, 2001), she was awarded a large Australian Research Grant, resulting in *Dwelling in the Household of God: Johannine Ecclesiology and Spirituality* (Liturgical Press, 2007). Mary was appointed for six years to an international dialogue between the Catholic Church and the Church/Disciples of Christ and has been outspoken on the need for justice in relation to women's place in the Catholic Church.

Volume Editor

Mary Ann Beavis, editor of this volume, is professor emerita of religion and culture at St. Thomas More College in Saskatoon, Canada. She is the coauthor, with HyeRan Kim-Cragg, of two volumes in this Wisdom Commentary series, *Hebrews* (2015) and *1–2 Thessalonians* (2016), and has written *What Does the Bible Say? A Critical Conversation with Popular Culture in a Biblically Illiterate World* (Eugene, OR: Cascade, 2017), and *The First Christian Slave: Onesimus in Context* (Eugene, OR: Cascade, 2021). Her current research interest is in the area of slave religiosity in early Christianity.

Series Editor

Barbara E. Reid, general editor of the Wisdom Commentary series, is a Dominican Sister of Grand Rapids, Michigan. She is the president of Catholic Theological Union and the first woman to hold the position. She has been a member of the CTU faculty since 1988 and also served as vice president and academic dean from 2009 to 2018. She holds a PhD in biblical studies from The Catholic University of America and was also president of the Catholic Biblical Association in 2014–2015. Her most recent publications are *Luke 1–9* and *Luke 10–24*, coauthored with Shelly Matthews, volumes 43A and 43B in Wisdom Commentary series, *Wisdom's Feast: An Invitation to Feminist Interpretation of the Scriptures* (Eerdmans, 2016), and *Abiding Word: Sunday Reflections on Year A, B, C* (3 vols.; Liturgical Press, 2011, 2012, 2013).